# Otto Weininger

The Chicago Series on Sexuality, History, and Society
Edited by John C. Fout

Otto Weininger, 1880–1903. (Photo courtesy of Matthes & Seitz Verlag, Munich)

# Otto Weininger

## Sex, Science, and Self in Imperial Vienna

Chandak Sengoopta

The University of

Chicago Press

*Chicago and London*

Chandak Sengoopta is a lecturer at the Wellcome
Unit for the History of Medicine, The University of Manchester.

The University of Chicago Press, Chicago 60637
The University of Chicago Press, Ltd., London
© 2000 by The University of Chicago
All rights reserved. Published 2000
Printed in the United States of America
10  09  08  07  06  05  04  03  02  01  00    5  4  3  2  1

ISBN (cloth): 0-226-74867-7

Library of Congress Cataloging-in-Publication Data

Sengoopta, Chandak.
    Otto Weininger : sex, science, and self in imperial Vienna / Chandak Sengoopta.
        p.    cm. — (The Chicago series on sexuality, history, and society)
    Includes bibliographical references and index.
    ISBN 0-226-74867-7 (alk. paper)
        1. Weininger, Otto, 1880–1903.    2. Weininger, Otto, 1880–1903. Geschlecht und
    Charakter.    3. Vienna (Austria)—Intellectual life.    I. Title.    II. Series.
    B3363.W54 S46    2000
    193—dc21                                                                                    99-088081

To Anuradha Sen Gupta

and to the memory of

Asha and Debabrata Sen Gupta

# CONTENTS

# ACKNOWLEDGMENTS

This work began quite a few years ago as a seminar paper, matured into a doctoral dissertation funded by the Johns Hopkins University's Department of the History of Science, Medicine, and Technology, and was revised into its current shape under the auspices of the Wellcome Institute for the History of Medicine. Of the many people who have nurtured the project over these years, Daniel P. Todes, my doctoral advisor, has been a model critic, mentor, and friend: his spiritual generosity, sensitivity to language and style, and commitment to intellectual history will always be exemplary. It was Vernon Lidtke's seminar for which I first attempted to write on Weininger, and it was his guidance through the complexities of Central European history that gave me the confidence to attempt a more expansive study. I am indebted to Gert Brieger, Chair of the Department of History of Science, Medicine, and Technology, for his keen interest in the project and to the Wellcome Trust for supporting me during the revisions. Ajita Chakraborty and Mark Planty, then the International Services Coordinator of the Johns Hopkins Medical Institutions, saved the project during its darkest phase: no word of thanks could ever express what I owe to them.

Going far beyond the call of duty, Mark Micale commented in detail on the first draft of the work: his perceptive suggestions and critiques did wonders for the study. Allan Janik encouraged my initial idea to work on Otto Weininger: his intellectual support, comments, and advice were invaluable. Will Provine, my first mentor in the history of science, kept me focused and intellectually alive long after he had ceased to be officially responsible for my training. My warm thanks to Steven Beller, JoAnne Brown, Sharon Kingsland, Harry Marks, and Frank Sulloway, who, on different occasions, alerted me to themes demanding further attention; to Janet Browne, Bill Bynum, Chris Lawrence, Michael Neve, Vivian Nutton, and Roy Porter for their intellectual support, collegiality, and friendship; to Lesley Hall for her interest in the project; to the Interlibrary Loan Departments of the Welch Medical Library and the Milton S. Eisenhower Library for their efficiency in obtaining obscure books and documents; to Axel Matthes and Matthes & Seitz Verlag, Munich, for permission to reprint a rare photograph, and to Michele

Minto and the Medical Photographic Library of the Wellcome Trust for supplying a reproduction of it at very short notice; and to Dolores Sawicki and Sally Bragg for extricating me from innumerable administrative tangles with patience and good humor. John Fout, the series editor, Doug Mitchell of the University of Chicago Press, and Richard Allen, the manuscript editor, have been the most understanding and supportive of editors, and the two anonymous referees of the University of Chicago Press provided many valuable suggestions for improving the work.

Punam Zutshi, who had first encouraged me to think of history of science as a career, watched over my progress (and, frequently, lack thereof) with affection, empathy, and good humor. Over the years, Ananda Chanda, Arup Chatterjee, Alasdair Clarke, Dee Finney, Natsu Hattori, Mary Lindemann, Vera Cecilia Machline, Andrea Meyer-Ludowisy, and Saumitra SenGupta have been the most stimulating of interlocutors, and, when required, the most patient of therapists! Jane Henderson, whom I came to know only during the final phase of the project, has filled my life with warmth and joy—I wish I knew of a way to infuse my prose with some of her wit and grace!

The years have brought much but they have also inflicted grievous losses. Satyajit Ray, mentor of mentors and friend beyond compare, died just after I had started working on the very first draft, and my parents, Debabrata and Asha Sen Gupta, died while I was struggling to complete it. I could continue only because of the support of my sister Anuradha Sen Gupta and of Aniruddha Deb, Kanika Mitra, Paritosh Kumar Mitra, Dipankar Mukherjee, the late, deeply missed Nirmalya Acharya, and above all, Bappaditya Deb. To each of them I shall remain forever in debt.

# Why Read Otto Weininger
# Today? and How?

Otto Weininger (1880–1903) is a notorious figure in modern European history. A young Jewish philosopher of Vienna, Weininger killed himself shortly after publishing *Geschlecht und Charakter: Eine prinzipielle Untersuchung* (Sex and Character: An Investigation of Principles, 1903), a voluminous treatise which "proved" that women and Jews did not possess a rational and moral self and, therefore, neither deserved nor needed equality with Aryan men or even simple liberty. Although hardly the first Western thinker to offer a racist and misogynist vision of the world, his work has had a remarkable impact on numerous writers, philosophers, scholars, artists, and, expectedly enough, on anti-Semites and woman-haters. Many of these readers have concentrated on interpreting, using, or condemning Weininger's sensational and offensive opinions rather than on exploring how those opinions were formed in relation to their author's historical situation and contexts. His admirers have seen him as a genius whose thoughts transcended narrow historical circumstances, and the majority of his critics, dismissing those thoughts as delusions, have not considered it terribly important to identify their historical contexts in any detail.

It has been indubitably established that Weininger's views were deeply (and, for most of us, revoltingly) prejudiced. A prejudiced work, however, is not ipso facto useless to the historian. If *Geschlecht und Charakter* was a mere compendium of one young man's private prejudices, then its historical value would, obviously, be modest at best. If, on the other hand, it was, with all its idiosyncrasies, shaped by attitudes, concerns, and fears that were widely shared at the time, then it would be well worth historical study. Without eliminating, let alone exculpating, its immaturity and virulence, I show that Weininger's treatise was a serious, comprehensive, and emotionally charged ideological critique of modernity in general and of women's emancipation in particular. More importantly, although Weininger was undoubtedly a loner and quite possibly psychotic at the end of his short life, his views were far from being the delusions they might appear to be on casual examination: they were securely rooted in his epoch. In order to appreciate this, we need to move beyond the analysis of isolated themes and address the book as a whole, teasing out its innumerable contextual links and ideological elements. And this is far from a sterile academic exercise. In its time, *Geschlecht und Charakter* was less a book than a weapon: if we see the work only as a catalogue of its author's personal prejudices, then we see it as far less noxious than it was actually meant to be.

Fin-de-siècle Vienna did not solely resound with lofty aesthetic debates: it was a battleground of far less noble ideas and ideologies—many of which were related to the nature of sexual, racial, and cultural identity. In an oft-quoted and characteristically apocalyptic phrase, Karl Kraus called Austria-Hungary the "experimental station for the end of the world."[1] One could say the same about Weininger's Vienna without much exaggeration. It is almost redundant to emphasize that many (perhaps most) of the ideas galvanizing the Viennese intelligentsia were half-baked, wrong, repellent, or downright inhumane by the criteria of today's liberal scholars. Nevertheless, some of those repugnant preoccupations were more characteristic of Weininger and his era than the comic operettas of Lehar or the lilting strains of the Blue Danube Waltz. Although by no means a mere synopsis of fin-de-siècle Viennese thought, *Geschlecht und Charakter* was so rooted in its times and molded so fundamentally by the currents of Viennese intellectual life and cultural politics that the text simply defies comprehension if examined in isolation from its epoch.

Immediately after his dramatic suicide—which occurred in the very house in which Beethoven had died and which, at least partly because of that, received wide coverage in the newspapers—Weininger was often portrayed as a tragic genius who had wrested one secret too many from Nature. To take the most famous example, August Strindberg attributed Weininger's suicide to his "rediscovery" of the fact that Man, representing human morality and civilization, was wholly opposed to Woman. While Weininger's personal friends could not deny his lack of mental balance toward the end of his life, even they portrayed him as a genius in the biographies they produced with impressive speed after his suicide.[2] No less a man than Sigmund Freud, who detested Weininger's views and disapproved of his methods, declared that Weininger's personality had possessed a spark of genius. Some of the finest intellects of the early twentieth century—Franz Kafka, Ludwig Wittgenstein, Karl Kraus, James Joyce—were struck, although not necessarily persuaded, by Weininger's arguments, while others wrote doctoral dissertations on arcane aspects of Weininger's theories, treating them with a hushed reverence that seems almost risible today. The Nazis, in their turn, gave a new twist to the Promethean theme of "Weininger the Tragic Genius," portraying him as a wise Jew who had killed himself on realizing that he could not eradicate his pernicious Jewishness. Although he had probably never read *Geschlecht und Charakter*, Adolf Hitler himself believed this to be the case.[3]

Since World War II, however, the tables have been turned on Weininger the Genius. Modern analysts of *Geschlecht und Charakter* have approached the work as a convenient handbook of fin-de-siècle racist and misogynist thought. For historian George Mosse, *Geschlecht und Charakter* was for long only a "classic of racist literature," and only very recently did Mosse begin to register the importance of other contexts such as the crisis of masculinity.[4] William Johnston, in his well-known overview of Austrian intellectual history, called Weininger "one of the most petulant of misogynists."[5] Sander Gilman has seconded the decades-old judgment of Theodor Lessing, declaring *Geschlecht und Charakter* to be "a work of intensive [*sic*], undisguised self-hatred."[6] In a 1997 article, the historian John Toews, acknowledging the interest in Weininger's work around the turn of the century, found it "difficult to imagine how such a cartoonishly hyperbolic, pretentiously philosophical, maniacally simplifying book, throbbing with uncontrolled misogynist and anti-Semitic feelings, could become the focus of intense concern for a broad and sophisticated audience of artists, writers, and scholars."[7] A recent full-length biography of Weininger by Jacques Le Rider attempted to provide psychoanalytic explanations of Weininger's "pathological" misogyny and self-hatred, a task that had been first attempted by Dr. Ferdinand Probst of Munich in his 1904 monograph on "the Weininger case" and then by the Norwegian psychiatrist David Abrahamsen in his 1946 psychobiography, *The Mind and Death of a Genius*.[8] These are only the most comprehensive examples of the genre: the literature is crowded with less comprehensive Freudian and quasi-psychoanalytic explorations of Weininger's psyche. Recently, there have been quite a few attempts to analyze the cultural matrix within which that psyche was formed and which it sought to influence, but such studies are still few in number and tend to be somewhat selective in their focus.[9]

The present study argues that although *Geschlecht und Charakter* reflected the private fears and dislikes of its author, those anxieties were integrated with and modulated by some of the most important strands of turn-of-the-century intellectual and cultural discourse. What kind of text resulted from such attempts? Exactly what did it argue and how?[10] This, then, is my first task: to analyze the internal structure of the work and to demonstrate the harmonies and contradictions of its complex argument.[11] Reading the text alone, of course, is not enough. While no text is absolutely self-sufficient, Weininger's is particularly heteronomous and explicitly, almost spectacularly, dependent upon other texts, other intellectual traditions, and a whole multiplicity of discourses.[12] To be sure, *Geschlecht und Charakter* was a unique work written by a remarkably idiosyncratic individual, but the issues it dealt with and many of the intellectual resources with which it did so were far from

unique in Weininger's time and place. This is my second major task: to establish the typicality of Weininger's concerns and the heteronomy of his text
without reducing either into representatives of some simplistically conceived
Zeitgeist.

   This latter task has been attempted only in fragmentary ways by previous
scholars, the reasons for which become obvious after a glance at the four-
hundred-odd pages of Weininger's tome. *Geschlecht und Charakter*, quite simply, is a monstrously interdisciplinary work: in order to make full sense of it,
one would need to know as much about the history of research on sex gland
function as about Kant's philosophy of self-consciousness and be as well
versed in the history of nineteenth-century European feminist movements as
in the psychological theories of Ernst Mach. Even in these days of interdisciplinary scholarship, that is a tall order—but one that is, I think, well worth
trying to fill.

   The erudition and interdisciplinarity of *Geschlecht und Charakter* follow
quite naturally from the vastness of Weininger's project: to analyze the differences between male and female from all perspectives—biological, cultural,
metaphysical—and to base a thoroughgoing critique of modern civilization
on that analysis. To read the book from beginning to end while relating its arguments to its sources and contexts is to take a roller-coaster ride through fin-
de-siècle thought and culture. Allan Janik has long been urging us to read
Weininger with "reference to the state of biological science, psychology and
humanistic social reform circa 1903," and, although my approach to Weininger differs significantly from Janik's, I fully concur with him that we must
reinsert Weininger and his text into history, reinscribing them within their
many intertwined contexts.[13] Such a reading would add greatly to our understanding of the fin de siècle itself and some of its most profound anxieties—
apart, of course, from illuminating a much discussed but often misunderstood work.

   My study commences with Weininger's biography, but instead of concentrating on his dramatic suicide, it emphasizes how his broad and eclectic education at the University of Vienna, combined with his participation in the
university's Philosophical Society, exposed Weininger to the most significant
intellectual issues of the day, ranging from Ernst Mach's dismissal of the concept of the self to the revival of Kantian philosophy within the academic
world. To approach *Geschlecht und Charakter* without sufficient familiarity
with these themes is to invite disaster. One could not then comprehend what
exactly Weininger was inveighing against, nor what he was advocating and
why. *One* of the fundamental aims of *Geschlecht und Charakter* was to disprove
Mach's contention that what people thought of as a coherent and unitary self
was a mere bundle of sensations. Repudiating Mach, Weininger espoused

Immanuel Kant's concept that every human being possessed a hyperempirical self, the existence of which could only be philosophically deduced and never demonstrated in empirical terms. Simultaneously, Weininger criticized the popularity of experimental research in psychology (a trend significantly influenced by the views of Mach), arguing in a Diltheyan vein that the proper task of psychology was not to measure sensations in the laboratory but to explore the totality of human consciousness, experience, and character. Psychology, urged Weininger, must reform itself into "characterology," and in order to do so, psychologists must first rebuild their entire science around the Kantian concept of the indivisible, hyperempirical self. Rejecting empiricism, psychology must renew its older affiliation with philosophy.

This salvage of the self, however, did not apply to all. We are dragged into the tense world of fin-de-siècle cultural politics with Weininger's assertion that only Aryan males possessed the Kantian hyperempirical self. It is common knowledge that women's emancipation was an explosive issue in turn-of-the-century Central Europe, and even moderately careful readers of Weininger's treatise should find it hard to overlook his repeated statements therein that his ultimate aim is to resolve the Woman Question.[14] Given these leads, and the substantive content of *Geschlecht und Charakter*, it is striking that this connection has not been explored by scholars in as much detail as it ought to have been. Two of Weininger's crucial responses to feminist arguments, his redefinition of hysteria and his devaluation of motherhood, have been mentioned often enough in the literature, but their specific links with contemporary debates over feminism have not, to my knowledge, been analyzed in any depth. I show in detail how contemporary feminist demands and beliefs shaped Weininger's arguments and analyze how Weininger resolved the Woman Question by proving—to his own satisfaction—that the typical woman neither desired nor deserved emancipation since she did not possess a truly autonomous, Kantian self. It is this interweaving of intellectual, cultural, and political themes in Weininger's work that I emphasize throughout this study. If one wishes to understand Weininger's project, one cannot focus exclusively on any one context, whether the intellectual, the political, or the cultural. All three are essential and, in the final analysis, inseparable.

Perhaps most crucially, the concept of Woman served, for Weininger and many others of the period, not merely as an uncomplicated symbol of femininity but as a sign whose meanings implicated much of modernity itself, that sweeping process of change which was hard to define but harder to remain neutral toward. Turn-of-the-century intellectual responses to modernity and modernism were ambivalent at best and hysterical at worst, but the nature and meanings of femininity (and indeed, of gender itself) were at the very heart of debates about the nature and future of civilization. To deal with the former *was* to deal with the latter and vice versa. As Christine Buci-Glucks-mann has pointed out, "It is as if, in crisis periods when the problem of modernity reappeared, it was impossible to approach the 'woman question' without considering the 'question of civilization' through a whole series of oppositions and myths."[15]

Similar points apply to Weininger's attitude toward Jews. Weininger's one chapter on the nature of Jewishness has often been regarded somewhat reductively as *the* core of *Geschlecht und Charakter*. Actually, Weininger's analysis of "Jewishness" was intimately related to his views on gender and thereby to larger questions of humanity, civilization, and modernity. At the most elementary level, it would be impossible to understand Weininger's critique of Jewishness without understanding his critique of femininity, a fact that scholars have recently begun to appreciate.[16] That, however, is not sufficient: Weininger's anti-Semitism needs to be placed in the context of specific trends in Viennese cultural criticism, in which Jews served as a symbol of Mammon and modernity. This symbolism was popular with commentators of all ideological persuasions, including liberals, of whom many, indeed, were themselves of Jewish origin. Unsurprisingly, however, conservative thinkers were the most consistent and emphatic in identifying "Jewishness" as the greatest threat to the supposedly spiritual culture of the German Volk. Some of these notions were, of course, based on traditional stereotypes, but they had all been revitalized in the nineteenth century by one of Weininger's heroes, the composer Richard Wagner, whose cultural-critical project was continued by his son-in-law, Houston Stewart Chamberlain, a longtime resident of Vienna. Perhaps the most celebrated exponent of this variety of cultural anti-Semitism was the Jewish journalist, poet, and satirist Karl Kraus, who championed *Geschlecht und Charakter* as a work of rare genius after Weininger's suicide. Weininger's critique of "Jewishness" was not identical with those of Wagner, Chamberlain, or Kraus, just as the latter critiques were far from identical to one another. They were all embedded, however, in the same discursive matrix, in which "Jew" and "German" were opposed categories locked in battle for the soul of (Germanic) civilization.

Such contextualizations, one must emphasize, do not exculpate Weininger or his contemporaries from the charge of being prejudiced. The aim, instead, is to show that their views were components of complex, consistent, and widely-shared systems of belief—as, in other words, far more dangerous in social terms than private prejudices. Far from being ritual tributes to what literary critic Nancy Harrowitz has called "the god of contextualization," the identification of the contextual conditions of sexual and racial prejudices are of crucial importance even for an ahistorical critique and opposition. We could never move beyond the rather simplistic business of criticizing an indi-

vidual thinker to the more complex but socially and critically more useful task
of criticizing whole systems of thought unless we situated individuals in their
historical contexts.[17]

One good way of retaining a clear sense of all these contexts is to set Weininger aside for a while and explore, instead, his discursive universe. J. G. A.
Pocock has argued that historians of intellectual discourse first need to identify whether a certain "language" or a "mode of utterance" existed as a cultural
resource for the use of a number of authors at any one point in time. Only after this initial exploration is the historian ready to investigate the unique ways
in which an individual author might have used this prevalent "language."[18]
Such a two-step approach ensures that the individual author is seen to be "in-
habiting a universe of *langues* that give meaning to the *paroles* he performs
in them."[19] To appreciate the uniqueness of any one author, the historian
aims, according to Pocock, "to render the implicit explicit, to bring to light assumptions on which the language of others has rested, to pursue and verbal-
ize implications and intimations that in the original may have remained
unspoken, to point out conventions and regularities that indicate what could
and could not be spoken in that language, and in what ways the language *qua*
paradigm encouraged, obliged, or forbade its users to speak and think."[20]
Obviously, none of this could be done with any expertise without knowing
the language-contexts in which the author worked. That is why I devote the
whole of chapter 2 to a sustained, multifocal analysis of the intellectual, social,
and cultural-political contexts of Weininger's treatise, ranging from the politics of the Woman Question to the psychological theories of Ernst Mach and
from the rise of neo-Kantianism to the eclipse of Viennese liberalism.

Only after exploring the different contexts in which Weininger worked do
I turn to Weininger's text itself. I read it closely and analyze its style, rhetoric,
and substantive as well as methodological inconsistencies. Throughout this
analysis of the text, I show how important textual themes constantly entwine
with the contextual issues covered in the earlier chapters: how, to paraphrase
Hayden White's comment on *The Education of Henry Adams*, "the context is
illuminated in its detailed operations by the moves made in" the text.[21] I examine Weininger's "biological" construction of an ideal-typical Woman and
his emphatically *non*-biological construction of an ideal-typical Man, and
demonstrate how the two were constructed in dialectical, mutually reinforc-
ing terms, within broader political, cultural, and intellectual contexts.
Woman, in Weininger's analysis, was reduced to sexuality alone, and Man
was elevated into Genius. This was one of the central themes of *Geschlecht und
Charakter*, although the dramatically negative portrayal of femininity has received far greater attention from scholars than the comprehensive discussion
of male nature and psychology. Weininger's project, despite its multidimen-

sionality, was fundamentally an attempt to construct an autonomous Aryan male subject and to deny autonomy and subjectivity to Woman and the Jew. Neither aim was more important than the other and both need to be analyzed together.

Weininger claimed that in his work, Man, Woman, Jew, or Aryan represented ideal types and not real individuals: every woman was not necessarily a complete embodiment of the ideal type Woman. A closer reading of the text shows, however, that Weininger eventually conflated ideal types with individuals by arguing that the ideal types Man, Aryan, Woman, and Jew were incarnated most frequently among individual men, Aryans, women, and Jews. The Woman and the Jew, of course, played particularly conspicuous roles in Weininger's criticism of contemporary culture. Weininger castigated fin-de-siècle European culture as feminized and Judaized, themes that were, independently of Weininger, common in Central European cultural criticism. What has been appreciated less often is that Weininger was not simply a Cassandra but also, in his own bizarre way, a utopian thinker. His denigration of his epoch represented one crucial aspect of his thought, but there was another side too, where he longed for a new Christianity and a new world where sexuality would be transcended. In that imagined world, Woman would lose her sexuality—which, according to Weininger, was her sole function—and that loss of sexuality would resolve the Woman Question forever. In that sexless utopia, human beings would respect each other as ends in themselves and not as means to sexual pleasure or progeny. Weininger's utopia would lead, of course, to the extinction of the human species, but that, he stated, was not the concern of the moralist. Without ignoring the outlandishness and sheer immaturity of this vision, I show how Weininger's utopia evolved out of his Kantian morality as well as his conviction of woman's inferiority, which, however, was explicitly *opposed* to simple Schopenhaurean or Nietzschean advocacy of the 'Asiatic' subjugation of women.

I then turn to a contextual analysis of Weininger's use of scientific and medical discourse in constructing a masculine identity and deconstructing feminine subjectivity. To examine Weininger's understanding and use of science with seriousness, however, is not to imply that Weininger was a scientific thinker in any sense of the term.[22] Nor, however, is it historically useful to dismiss Weininger's use of scientific discourse as pseudoscientific—a term much favored by Jacques Le Rider, who has declared that Weininger "arbitrarily selected from the most disparate realms in order to construct an apparatus of authoritative arguments that is entirely governed by a few fundamental obsessions. . . . Weininger's main 'scientific' talent lay in placing at the service of his *Weltanschauung* a vertiginous compilation of bits of information gleaned from different university disciplines and glued together with incontestable rhetorical force."[23] For Le Rider, who subscribes to a narrowly positivistic ethos of science and its history, Weininger's "mix-and-match" approach to scientific theories demonstrates that he was a pseudoscientist. Rather than debating whether Weininger was a scientific or pseudoscientific thinker, however, it seems to me much more fruitful to analyze Weininger's use of scientific theories as strategic deployments, sometimes for narrowly intellectual goals and more frequently for larger cultural objectives. Even Le Rider's own argument, although he does not realize it himself, points to the value of using Weininger as a source for investigating the general intellectual appropriation of specialist scientific discourse. What scientific ideas did Weininger appropriate? Why did he select certain ideas and reject others? What were their respective contexts? What larger purpose did the selected ideas serve in Weininger's project? Can his use of scientific ideas tell us something about the ways science was used in his time to address, analyze, or resolve social and cultural issues?

It is important to note that in his early days as a university student, Weininger did aim to be a scientist in the conventional sense. Residues of this early ambition lingered in the early chapters of *Geschlecht und Charakter,* and these elements were far from unimportant. Weininger's effort to ground sexuality in the cells, for instance, was a legitimate scientific hypothesis by the standards of his era.[24] I devote chapter 4 to explicating and contextualizing Weininger's biological theory of sexuality, which was an original and imaginative synthesis of Carl Wilhelm von Nägeli's influential theory of the idioplasm with the latest research on the function of the sex glands in determining the nature and the expression of sexuality. Weininger also claimed, along with many turn-of-the century physicians, that all human beings were partly male and partly female, albeit to degrees that varied from individual to individual. Late-nineteenth-century investigators of sexuality were almost unanimous in accepting this notion of universal *bisexuality* or *sexual intermediacy,* and Weininger, Sigmund Freud admitted, had been so remarkably successful in disseminating it to the laity that many came to think of him as the discoverer of the idea.[25]

Although Weininger qualified and even contradicted the hypothesis of sexual intermediacy in later sections of his treatise, it was one of the basic biological presuppositions of *Geschlecht und Charakter.*[26] I show, in chapter 4, how Weininger used the theory to illuminate the entire human life cycle from intrauterine development to mating. Analyzing the development of the human embryo, Weininger emphasized that it was neither clearly male nor clearly female in the initial weeks of gestation. Sex developed in the embryo by the gradual differentiation of rudiments common to all embryos. Before the establishment of the genetic paradigm of sex-determination, this was the accepted view of sexual development among contemporary embryologists, notwithstanding their disagreements on points of detail. Weininger used the notion of universal bisexuality to formulate a "Law of Sexual Affinity," which, he argued, could predict as well as explain successful matches on the basis of the degree of masculinity and femininity of the partners. While this "Law" was certainly speculative and although the algebraic equations seem ludicrous today, they can be dismissed as pseudoscientific only if one so dismisses the theory of universal bisexuality, which was one of the founding principles of nineteenth-century scientific discourse on sexuality.[27]

I then turn in chapter 5 to Weininger's chief illustration for his "Law": male homosexuality. Once again, he followed contemporary medical discourse closely but not slavishly. By the end of the nineteenth century, many physicians had begun to argue that homosexuality was the consequence of a developmental error rather than the sign of a progressive degeneration of the nervous system. I show that this reorientation in medical theory was intimately linked to the political campaign for the decriminalization of homosexuality led by the physician Magnus Hirschfeld. Weininger, like Hirschfeld and his associates, denied that homosexual orientation was the result of underlying disease. But unlike Hirschfeld and his allies, Weininger also rejected the notion of developmental error because of its pathological connotations, arguing instead that if all human beings were both male and female to varying degrees, then some would *naturally* be almost as much male as female. And these individuals would find their sexual complements only among other members of what appeared to be their own sex. Homosexuality, then, was congenital and biological but it did not represent any deviation from the norm. It was, in fact, *entailed* by the norm: an inevitable, expected, and entirely normal consequence of universal sexual intermediacy.

Weininger's theory of homosexuality illustrates one way in which he deployed the ideas and rhetoric of science in *Geschlecht und Charakter:* critique and restatement. Biographically, this was an approach characteristic of his earliest period of research, which he had begun to transcend even before embarking on his doctoral dissertation. Both the dissertation and *Geschlecht und Charakter* recorded the trajectory of Weininger's intellectual odyssey from the mere critique of science to its total and vehement rejection. Even after turning into what his own doctoral supervisor called a "full-blown mystic," Weininger did not, however, jettison his knowledge of positivistic science: he simply stopped following the *rules* of scientific discourse. Blending biomedical theories with Kantian ethics to formulate a metaphysical approach to psychology, social reform, and cultural politics, Weininger now displaced, reinscribed, and transformed current scientific ideas and recirculated obsolescent ones with an insouciance guided only by strategic compulsions. The strategies differed but the overriding ideological purpose—to define the nature of masculinity and femininity and to determine the links between gender and emancipation—remained constant.

In chapters 6 and 7, I illustrate these strategies with detailed analyses of Weininger's theories of hysteria and maternity, which were crucial to his deconstruction of female subjectivity and autonomy. In both cases, Weininger used scientific and medical ideas to deconstruct femininity from psychological, physiological, and metaphysical perspectives, but his approach to scientific discourse on motherhood differed radically from the ways in which he used psychological theories of hysteria. Accepting the structure and transforming the substance of Josef Breuer and Sigmund Freud's theory of hysteria, he "showed" that femininity was nothing but pure, undifferentiated sexuality. Woman's demure outward self was a simulacrum constructed in keeping with male expectations and assumed in order to win male esteem. Weininger's theory of hysteria was at the heart of his resolution of the Woman Question, and it was also one of the most fascinating of Viennese responses to early psychoanalysis.[28]

Equally crucial and equally intriguing were Weininger's views on maternity. It is well known that Central European feminists, in contradistinction to their Anglo-American contemporaries, reformulated maternity from a patriarchal into an emancipationist metaphor: the New Woman was seen as the New Mother. Weininger was virtually unique in his time in denying any moral worth to motherhood, and this denial demands to be analyzed as an intellectual response to contemporary feminist ideology and contextualized within the larger realm of fin-de-siècle antifeminist discourse. Historians of science, in particular, need to pay attention to the substance of Weininger's views on maternity. In a strategic move that was intellectually desperate but politically meaningful and rhetorically fascinating, Weininger resurrected obsolescent biomedical theories of remote impregnation and maternal impressions to argue that even the body of Woman was always impregnable and open to the exterior. Complementing his earlier psychological deconstruction of femininity, his argument regarding maternity attempted to deconstruct Woman somatically. Even physically, Woman was not autonomous and, therefore, could not possibly deserve social and political autonomy. Infinitely porous, infinitely malleable, and infinitely open to external influences, "Woman," concluded Weininger, "is Nothing."

Bizarre and pernicious as his work might be, there are many good reasons to study Weininger today. Some might read *Geschlecht und Charakter* to illuminate the dark underbelly of fin-de-siècle thought and to better understand the history of misogyny and anti-Semitism, others as a significant moment in the larger history of European modernity, and still others as the creation of a brilliant mind gone mad. For me, however, Weininger's work has always been a Baedeker through the labyrinthine and still incompletely explored terrain of fin-de-siècle European discourse on sexuality and gender. Weininger's own views are worthy of close analysis, but they are most profitably used, in my view, as the point of departure for a journey through this broader discourse. Idiosyncratic and bigoted, Weininger was also thorough—and thoroughly engaged in some of the most complex cultural and intellectual issues of his time. The inexhaustible series of allusions, references, citations, arguments, and counterarguments in his text can serve as a veritable map of the avenues and alleyways of social, medical, and scientific discourses on the nature and meanings of masculinity and femininity.

My goal, then, is to explore both Weininger's work as well as the discourses in which he participated, using each to provide means of illuminating, contextualizing, and understanding the other. To this end, I attempt to analyze the text in full, in detail, and in unrelenting reference to the many contexts shaping it and its author. Put another way, I disassemble *Geschlecht und Charakter* and reassemble it within its many contexts: biographical, intellectual, scientific, medical, cultural, and ideological. The Weininger who emerges remains idiosyncratic and prejudiced, but surprisingly mainstream in his essential concerns. Weininger, his text, and their turbulent historical times were bound together in one tense, complicated, but far from tenuous web. To understand Weininger and his contexts is to understand some of the most fundamental themes, concerns, and anxieties animating discourses on gender and identity in fin-de-siècle Central Europe.

## CHAPTER ONE

# The Education of Otto Weininger

Otto Weininger lived only for twenty-three years and published only one book, *Geschlecht und Charakter* (Sex and Character, 1903).[1] He was born on April 3, 1880 into a Jewish family in Vienna, the second child and oldest son of Adelheid Frey (1857–1912) and Leopold Weininger (1854–1922), a skilled goldsmith, whose work and artistic judgment were appreciated throughout Europe. A man of little formal education, Leopold was a self-taught polyglot, a devotee of Richard Wagner's music, and deeply ambivalent about Judaism. His daughter Rosa recalled that he was "highly anti-Semitic, but he thought as a Jew and was angry when Otto wrote against Judaism." He was a strict parent and, according to Rosa, his marriage was probably not very happy.[2] Otto's mother Adelheid, too, had a talent for languages but lived simply as a housewife. Her daughter later suggested that she would have been happier with an "average, ordinary husband," while Otto's brother Richard declared that Leopold treated his wife simply as a housekeeper and childcare provider.[3] Otto never mentioned his mother in his letters, and it is unlikely that there was any special bond between them.[4]

Otto was a brilliant student in the Gymnasium, exhibiting a special flair for the humanities and proving more than his parents' equal at languages: at eighteen, he "knew Latin and Greek, spoke French, English, and Italian well, and was fluent in Spanish and Norwegian."[5] At sixteen, he wrote an etymological essay on certain Greek adjectives found only in Homer and attempted unsuccessfully to publish it in a leading philological journal.[6] Later, he also developed a keen interest in the natural sciences and mathematics. For all his many talents, however, he was not a model schoolboy: he followed his own inclinations in his studies, rarely paying any heed to his teachers, and he could be something of a rowdy in the classroom.[7]

After graduating from high school in 1898, Otto enrolled on the Philosophical Faculty of the University of Vienna, ignoring his father's wish that he study languages.[8] The curriculum vitae appended to his dissertation shows that his intellectual interests, although diverse, tended to revolve around philosophy and psychology. He attended lectures on logic, experimental psychology, pedagogy, and the history of philosophy, the most important courses of which were taught by the renowned positivist philosopher Friedrich Jodl and his colleague Laurenz Müllner, who would later be Weininger's doctoral examiners. Taking full advantage of the flexibility of the German university system, he also attended the lectures of some well-known professors on mathematics, physics, chemistry, botany and zoology, anatomy, physiology, histology, embryology, neurology, and psychiatry. Among the lecturers were such Viennese luminaries as physiologist Sigmund Exner, sexologist and forensic psychiatrist Richard von Krafft-Ebing, and psychiatrist Julius Wagner-Jauregg.[9]

The curriculum vitae concludes with Weininger's statement that his approach to psychology was based on the "biological" method of Richard Avenarius and on the "practical philosophy" of Friedrich Nietzsche and Immanuel Kant.[10] Richard Avenarius (1843–96) had been Professor of Philosophy at Zürich and a theoretical ally of the physicist and philosopher Ernst Mach, both of whom are usually described as "critical positivists" by historians of philosophy.[11] Avenarius believed that thinking was governed by biological laws: all thought represented a response of the organism to a disturbance in its biological balance. Rejecting the dualism of mind and body, he argued that "experience" was one and homogeneous.[12] During his initial years at the university, Weininger spent long hours discussing Avenarius's major work, *Kritik der reinen Erfahrung* (Critique of Pure Experience) with his friends.[13] He also expressed immense admiration for Ernst Mach and was fascinated by the Mach-Avenarius program of eliminating all metaphysical (i.e., empirically undemonstrable) concepts from science, among which was the concept of the self or the autonomous, unified subject of consciousness.[14]

A somber and serious youth, Weininger scorned the alcoholic and lubricious pursuits of average university students, spending his free hours discussing "the most difficult philosophical subjects" with his friends.[15] His friend Hermann Swoboda later wrote: "He was quite indefatigable as he brought up question after question during our frequent small parties, which lasted late into the night or into the early morning. Abstract regions, from which others would turn away with a cold shiver, were his real home. He was, in short, a passionate thinker, the prototype of a thinker."[16] Weininger had little obvious interest in current events: Swoboda recalled that he had never even seen him read a newspaper.[17] Another friend, Emil Lucka, commented that happiness was essentially foreign to Weininger's nature, although he did occasionally enjoy the beauty of nature and the music of the great composers.[18] Throughout his university career, Weininger was an active member of the Philosophical Society of the university.[19] Established in 1888, the society's weekly colloquia featured distinguished speakers from diverse disciplines, not just academic philosophy. Physiologist Sigmund Exner, for instance, delivered a paper on "localized vision" in January 1899, Weininger's mentor Friedrich Jodl spoke on "Natural Laws and Accidents" in February, and physician and biologist Max Kassowitz lectured on "The Old and the New Vitalism" in December. At least one renowned speaker was not an academic: the Englishman Houston Stewart Chamberlain, son-in-law of the composer Richard Wagner, spoke to the society in December 1898 on "Richard Wagner's Philosophy." Later, Chamberlain's work would be an important source for Weininger's views on "Jewishness."[20]

In August 1900, Weininger and Hermann Swoboda traveled to Paris to participate in the Fourth International Congress of Psychology. In one paper at the congress, the psychologist Paul M.-J. Joire hailed the advent of new experimental techniques in psychological research. Weininger was one of the official commentators on the paper. In his remarks, the twenty-year-old student urged psychologists not to reject introspection in their infatuation with experimentation, but, rather, to enrich introspection by combining it judiciously with experimental procedures.[21] Weininger would soon adopt a far less balanced stance on the issue, denying that experimentation could ever play a role in "true" psychology.

Soon after their return from Paris, Swoboda embarked on psychoanalysis with Sigmund Freud. Although he was not internationally famous as yet, the Viennese intelligentsia knew Freud well: he had published the *Interpretation of Dreams* in 1899, and the *Studies on Hysteria*, co-authored with Josef Breuer, had been available since 1895. Both works had excited significant interest, although more among the literati than among physicians.[22] At the time of his meeting with Swoboda, Freud was busily working out the founding principles of psychoanalysis in an intense correspondence with his close friend, the Berlin otolaryngologist and biological theorist Wilhelm Fliess. This correspondence dealt with numerous issues, among which questions of sexuality were preeminent.[23] During his analysis, Freud once mentioned to Swoboda that all human beings were partly male and partly female or "bisexual." This was one of the topics that Fliess considered his own. Swoboda, apparently ignorant of this, reported Freud's observation to Weininger, who, galvanized by this idea, immediately decided to write a monograph on sexuality.[24] When Swoboda attempted to dissuade him from hasty publication, Weininger countered that speed was of the essence: his work would produce salutary social effects.[25]

Why, however, did the philosophically oriented and, on all accounts, puritanically disposed Weininger find sexuality so attractive as a subject of research? Obviously, his own sexual life may have influenced this choice. Hermann Swoboda believed that although he had never been deranged or mentally ill, Weininger had an "instinctual deviation" *(Triebstörung)* that "infected" his psyche and eventually destroyed it. Swoboda declined to say any more about the nature of the deviation, commenting that anybody with a knowledge of psychology could deduce it from Weininger's writings. This strange rhetoric immediately suggests that the deviation was sexual, but since Swoboda immediately ruled out homosexuality, it is impossible to identify it more precisely.[26] There is no evidence that Weininger ever had a sexual relationship with a woman, and Swoboda's denial notwithstanding, there is some evidence suggesting that Weininger may well have been homosexual and was deeply uncomfortable about it.[27] David Abrahamsen, a devout Freudian, speculated in his psychobiography that Weininger may have been sexually abused in childhood and possessed an unusually intense and aggressive sexual urge that repelled his own finer sensibilities.[28] Undoubtedly, Weininger's own sexuality may have played an important role in the genesis of his views and his text; the information we possess on the issue, however, is so unclear and fragmentary that we must interpret it with the greatest caution.

It is, in any case, more important to appreciate that while Weininger's personal sexual difficulties may indeed have led him toward the study of sexual questions, other factors might also have been of influence. Viennese artists and intellectuals—Arthur Schnitzler, Karl Kraus, and Egon Schiele, to name just three—were preoccupied with sexual themes. In fin-de-siècle Vienna, Edward Timms suggests, sexuality became a "symbolic territory" for debates on identity, reason, and irrationalism.[29] David Luft adds that Viennese intellectuals were distinctive in combining biological approaches to sex with a Schopenhauerian irrationalism, which stressed the internal reality of feelings.[30] Weininger's views were firmly rooted in this Viennese tradition while, at the same time, dissenting from it in substantial and significant ways.

Weininger's planned monograph was titled "Eros und Psyche: Eine biologisch-psychologische Studie" (Eros and Psyche: A Bio-Psychological Study), but, in spite of his conviction of its social utility, it was never published.[31] Instead, he sent a sixty-seven-page outline of the work to the Section of Mathematics and Natural Sciences of the Viennese Academy of Sciences in June 1901 for safekeeping.[32] (The academy commonly held manuscripts in order to validate later claims of priority, and the outline was recently discovered among its holdings by Hannelore Rodlauer.)[33] In the autumn of 1901, Weininger approached Sigmund Freud with an expanded version of the outline. It included a chapter on hysteria, the purpose of which, Freud suspected, was to flatter him into writing a letter of recommendation to a publisher.[34] Unimpressed by Weininger's manuscript, Freud refused to recommend publication, advising Weininger to spend "ten years" gathering empirical evidence for his assertions. "The world," Freud declared, "wants evidence, not thoughts."[35] Retorting that he would prefer to write ten other books in the next ten years, Weininger now submitted the unaltered work to Friedrich Jodl and Laurenz Müllner, and applied for a scholarship.[36] Jodl, the leading philosopher at the University of Vienna after the retirement of Ernst Mach, was quite impressed by the outline and expressed his willingness to supervise its expansion into a doctoral dissertation. He also promised to recommend it to a publisher if satisfied with the final product.[37]

Following his meeting with Jodl in the winter of 1901, however, Weininger sank into depression and became increasingly preoccupied with Henrik Ibsen's play *Peer Gynt* and with the play's portrayal of the human self and its development.[38] During this period, Weininger's intellectual allegiance shifted radically, and when he resumed work on the dissertation in March 1902, he announced that he had "completely jettisoned the epistemological views of Mach and Avenarius." Referring to Mach's conviction that the coherent, unified self was a fiction that could not be "salvaged," Weininger averred: "The self *is*. There is absolutely no need to 'salvage' it."[39] He added that he had also grown interested in "the Jewish question" and in ethical issues.[40] Weininger's interest in "the Jewish question," suggests Hannelore Rodlauer, may have been stimulated by the anti-Semitic writings of Houston Stewart Chamberlain, then a resident of Vienna. Chamberlain's influence, according to Rodlauer, is evident from the two works Weininger attempted in 1902: an outline entitled "Zur Theorie des Lebens" (On the Theory of Life) and an article on *Peer Gynt*. He planned the former work as a continuation of "Eros und Psyche," and, like the latter, it was deposited with the Viennese Academy of Sciences for safekeeping in April 1902. In it, Weininger sketched a "vitalistic" theory of sexual difference, criticized Mach's disparagement of the concept of the self, and upheld a Kantian notion of the ego.[41] It is doubtful whether these major shifts can all be attributed to Weininger's depressive bout or to his reading of Ibsen, although both must have contributed not a little. Too little is known about Weininger's life at this point to permit useful speculation about what exactly brought about his shifts in intellectual allegiance. The transformations, however, were genuine and determined the content and style of much of his subsequent work. At one level, the four-hundred-odd pages of *Geschlecht und Charakter* record the metamorphosis of a critical positivist into a hectoring prophet, resulting in serious inconsistencies in perspective and argument between early and later parts of the treatise.

By the end of April 1902, Weininger's dissertation—based largely on the outlines "Eros und Psyche" and "Zur Theorie des Lebens"—was virtually complete. He found it difficult to harmonize his new metaphysical perspective with the predominantly biological outlook of "Eros und Psyche." Weininger wrote to Swoboda that he had divided the work into two parts and was trying to highlight a certain parallelism between the two.[42] On Jodl's suggestion, the title had been changed to *Geschlecht und Charakter: Eine biologische und psychologische Untersuchung* (Sex and Character: A Biological and Psychological Investigation), and the completed version was received with some enthusiasm by the two examiners, Jodl and Laurenz Müllner. Jodl particularly appreciated Weininger's deft handling of a vast array of biological, psychological, and pathological data and his effort to synthesize them with his own observations of life. Whether Weininger's arguments could be verified or not, the dissertation, Jodl believed, proposed much that was novel and cast new light on familiar facts.[43] Concurring essentially with Jodl, Müllner praised Weininger's thoughtfulness, sharp observations, critical sense, and expressive ability.[44] Both examiners, however, recorded some strong reservations about the dissertation. Jodl observed that some of Weininger's conclusions, such as the denial of a self to Woman, "could not be described as anything other than fantastical."[45] He also reproved Weininger for the youthful immaturity with which he had attacked such stellar members of the intelligentsia as Ernst Mach.[46] Instead of criticizing experimental approaches in psychology, said Jodl, Weininger would have been better advised to cleanse his own work of speculative elements reminiscent of the worst of German idealistic psychology.[47] Müllner added that many of Weininger's conclusions were unfounded and metaphysical: large portions of the dissertation read more like a personal rhapsody than a scholarly work.[48] He also emphasized that the underlying intention of the work seemed to be the denigration of women.[49] Jodl and Müllner did agree, however, that a suitably revised version of Weininger's dissertation would be worthy of publication.[50]

The manuscript of the dissertation is lost, and one can only speculate on its actual content.[51] It is likely, however, that instead of toning down his polemical passages as his supervisors had recommended, Weininger actually expanded them before publication. The dissertation, for instance, probably did not have a chapter on "the Jewish question," whereas that chapter is a conspicuous part of *Geschlecht und Charakter.*[52] Much else in the work must have changed, too, in the months before the renowned firm of Wilhelm Braumüller published *Geschlecht und Charakter: Eine prinzipielle Untersuchung* in May 1903. Friedrich Jodl was stunned by the published volume. Defending his former student as best as he could in public, he confided in private that instead of becoming clearer and more objective, Weininger's arguments had assumed "monstrous" forms in the published treatise.[53] "He had come to me," Jodl remarked, "as a follower of Avenarius's 'Empiriocriticism' but . . . had transformed himself in a year or so into a full-blown mystic . . . his soul is a riddle to me."[54] There is no evidence that Weininger and Jodl ever discussed the content of *Geschlecht und Charakter* prior to publication or afterwards: Weininger's life after graduation was far too tempestuous (and brief) to permit such courtesies.

The doctorate proved to be more than an academic watershed in Weininger's life. Immediately after graduation, Weininger repudiated his Judaism and converted to Protestantism.[55] He had discussed the idea of conversion with his father two years earlier, but Leopold Weininger, although himself anti-Semitic, had counseled him against such a drastic step. Leopold had not noticed any genuine Christian leanings in his son and had assumed that Otto wished to convert for practical reasons.[56] In the Catholic Habsburg Empire, Jews could obtain higher government positions only if they converted to the state religion. Weininger's conversion to Protestantism rather than Catholicism, however, suggests other, deeper reasons for the conversion. Many Jews in the Habsburg Empire chose Protestantism as a gesture of allegiance to the Lutheran culture of northern Germany—and by implication at least, as a gesture of defiance against the Catholic culture of Austria, which many of them found empty, unfulfilling, and corrupt. Steven Beller has shown that middle-class Viennese Jews were immersed in Germanic culture and considered themselves to be Germans first, rather than Austrian.[57] Jacques Le Rider has pointed out that for Weininger, conversion symbolized the formalization of his allegiance to "the spiritual nation of Kant."[58] Practical reasons, one may safely conclude, were not the uppermost in Weininger's mind when he decided to convert.

After his conversion, Weininger left for a tour of Northern Europe. He was again quite depressed and wrote to his friend Artur Gerber that he was passing through a miserable and unproductive period, adding cryptically, "apart from the one you know, I lead two or three other lives that you do not."[59] Later, he confessed to Gerber that his trip had made him realize that he was "no philosopher. Really not." "But," he wondered, "am I anything else? I doubt very much that I am—."[60] Still depressed and pervaded by vague feelings of guilt and a growing, unexplained conviction of his own criminality, Weininger told Gerber after his return to Vienna: "I am a murderer! Therefore, I must kill myself!"[61] Nevertheless, he began to revise his dissertation for publication, and, in March 1903, Wilhelm Braumüller agreed to publish the book. Much work remained to be done. "I am awash in a sea of first, second, and third proofs," he reported. "I write no longer with blood but only with red ink!"[62]

The book was not, however, seriously delayed and went on sale in June 1903. It aroused little interest at first and few reviews of any note were published before October.[63] The author himself was far from jubilant, remarking to a close friend that "there are three possibilities for me—the gallows, suicide, or a future so brilliant that I don't dare to think of it."[64] He then left for a trip to Italy and returned even more deeply depressed. After spending five days with his parents, he rented a room in the house where Beethoven had died.[65] Moving there on October 3, he wrote to his father and to his brother Richard that he was going to kill himself and, later that night, shot himself in the chest.[66] Richard Weininger rushed to his brother's lodgings on receiving the letter in the morning's mail and found Otto almost dead. He was rushed to the hospital but died the same day at the age of twenty-three years and six months. He was buried according to Christian rites in a Protestant cemetery, under the supervision of his father, who also wrote the epitaph for the grave.[67] It was, as Peter Gay has remarked, "a melodramatic end to an (at least inwardly) melodramatic life."[68]

## CHAPTER TWO

# Weininger's Worlds: Identity, Politics, and Philosophy in Central Europe

Some of the most significant intellectual and cultural currents of the age rippled through Otto Weininger's brief life. *Geschlecht und Charakter* is incomprehensible without some appreciation of what Christine Buci-Glucksmann has called the "great crisis cultures of Musil, Weininger or Klee."[1] Conceived amid the political and cultural turmoil of Habsburg Vienna, the book dealt with an enormous variety of philosophical, scientific, and cultural themes: the nature of sex, the worth of femininity, the reality of the self, the poverty of psychological research, the meaning of "Jewishness," and the moral future of the human species. In order to appreciate why Weininger found these themes important and how they were related to his epoch, we must move away from him and immerse ourselves in the murky depths of fin-de-siècle thought, politics, and high culture.

### Dual Monarchy and Multiple Identities: Life in Kakania

Describing the Austro-Hungarian Empire as "Kakania, that misunderstood State that has since vanished," Robert Musil provided this celebrated summary of its many contradictions in his novel *The Man without Qualities:*

> On paper it called itself the Austro-Hungarian Monarchy; in speaking, however, one referred to it as Austria, that is to say, it was known by a name that it had, as a State, solemnly renounced by oath, while preserving it in all matters of sentiment. . . . By its constitution it was liberal, but its system of government was clerical. The system of government was clerical, but the general attitude to life was liberal. Before the law all citizens were equal, but not everyone, of course, was a citizen. There was a parliament, which made such vigorous use of its liberty that it was usually kept shut; but there was also an emergency powers act by means of which it was possible to manage without Parliament.[2]

At the helm of the Dual Monarchy was the Emperor Franz Joseph, who had ascended to the throne after the revolution of 1848. He was to reign for sixty-eight years, becoming a symbol of the apparent stability of the Habsburg family and of its multinational empire. In reality, however, this unwieldy empire, divided between peoples as different as Germans and Croats, Transylvanian Saxons and Italians, became increasingly torn by linguistic, national, and cultural dissensions.[3] Allan Janik and Stephen Toulmin have emphasized the complex, almost carnivalesque contests of linguistic and national identities in the Habsburg Empire:

> The effort to introduce German in place of Latin, so as to streamline Imperial administration, begat Hungarian and Czech cultural nationalism by reaction, and this in due course developed into a political nationalism. Slav nationalism in the politics and economics in turn begat German economic and political nationalism; and this in turn begat anti-Semitism, with Zionism as a natural Jewish reaction. All in all, it is enough to cause one's head to spin.[4]

The capital of this impossible empire was the city of Vienna: cosmopolitan and opulent at one level, poor, hidebound, and intolerant at others; a city that pioneered modern anti-Semitism, although some of its richest and most cultured residents were Jews. In the 1880s, Georg von Schönerer (1842–1921), the leader of the pan-German movement, regularly disrupted sessions of the Reichsrat with diatribes against Jews, Catholics, Liberals, and the Habsburgs. The Christian Socialist Karl Lueger (1844–1910), elected mayor of Vienna in 1895, was far more suave than Schönerer, but the rhetoric of anti-Semitism was integral to his political platform.[5]

Schönerer and Lueger symbolized a broader political phenomenon: the failure of liberalism in Austria. Liberal elites all over Europe were faced with innumerable predicaments in the late nineteenth century, but Austrian liberals were particularly weak and beleaguered. The liberals running Austria from 1867 to 1879 constituted a smallish group of urban middle-class Germans and German Jews. Elected by a political system in which only six per cent of the adult male population could vote, the Austrian liberals were greatly dependent on the toleration of the monarchy and the aristocracy and represented the interests of commerce, industry, and the professions rather than those of the general populace.[6] Liberal reforms in the Habsburg government, furthermore, had been induced not by some inevitable, Marxian rise of the bourgeoisie but by the failures of the traditional system, symbolized above all by the military humiliation in 1866 by Prussia. By the 1880s, the ascendancy of German-speaking liberals in Austria was as good as over. The new mass parties, representing the working classes and the lower reaches of the middle class, targeted liberals as their enemies, making the latter ever more dependent on the emperor and the aristocracy.[7]

Overcome by a feeling of doom, younger liberals, who had always been interested in the arts, grew obsessed with it.[8] The bourgeois liberal artist continued, Carl Schorske points out, to hold fast to individualism and "turned his appropriated aesthetic culture inward to the cultivation of the self, of his personal uniqueness."[9] The liberal predicament did not simply produce a horde of narcissistic artists but gave a new impetus to the study, analysis, and evaluation of society and its mores—a cluster of traditional liberal activities that Schorske has labeled the "moralistic-scientific" component of the liberal psyche.[10] The interaction of the artistic and the moralistic-scientific elements led naturally to the critique of culture, a genre in which the Viennese intelligentsia excelled. The easygoing camaraderie and baroque pomp of Viennese life could not, according to the city's avant garde, conceal its inner, spiritual emptiness. Although their ideas on the causes and consequences of this malaise differed quite dramatically, the younger intellectuals of the capital were virtually unanimous that the current cultural situation was unbearable.

Karl Kraus, hailed as "the first European satirist since Swift," was arguably the most celebrated representative of this quintessentially Viennese critical tradition.[11] The fundamental theme of Viennese existence, Kraus believed, was hypocrisy, and its greatest expressions he found in the popular press. One of his favorite examples was the leading newspaper's practice of carrying coyly phrased advertisements for prostitution on its back pages while adopting a high moral tone in its editorials. Newspapers were a personal target for Kraus, but he was not alone in the larger crusade against masquerade. Condemning the Viennese passion for ornate architecture, Kraus's friend Adolf Loos compared the city with the fake villages erected by Count Potemkin of Russia.[12] Robert Musil echoed the same theme. "In this country," he wrote, "one acted—sometimes indeed to the extreme limits of passion and its consequences—differently from the way one thought, or one thought differently from the way one acted. Uninformed observers have mistaken this for charm."[13] Others castigated Viennese culture for yet other reasons. For Otto Weininger, as we shall see, Viennese culture was pervaded by effeminacy and sexual immorality.[14] For Sigmund Freud, Vienna was intellectually stifling. When his biographer Ernest Jones exclaimed, "How fascinating it must be to live in a town so full of new ideas!," Freud retorted: "I have lived here for fifty years and have never come across a new idea here."[15] The paradox, of course, is that this allegedly dishonest, stultifying city succeeded in holding its intellectuals and, *pace* Freud, even managed to stimulate so many of them into producing some of the pivotal ideas of the twentieth century.

Quite a few of those ideas, predictably enough, were expressed as critiques. "The new culture-makers in the city of Freud," Carl Schorske has observed, "repeatedly defined themselves in terms of a kind of collective oedipal revolt. Yet the young were revolting not so much against their fathers.... What they assaulted on a broad front was the value system of classical liberalism-in-ascendancy within which they had been reared."[16] Most of their critiques revolved around the theme of identity: the identity of the self, of races, of the sexes. Their crusade, fought in different styles and with diverse weapons, was ultimately a crusade for authenticity, for the expression of the true identity of persons as well as objects.[17]

### The Dissolving Self: Physics, Psychology, and Philosophy

"Traditional liberal culture," according to Carl Schorske, "had centered upon rational man, whose scientific domination of nature and whose moral control of himself were expected to create the good society."[18] This conception of the rational, autonomous subject was in serious trouble by the end of the nineteenth century. The collapse of liberal politics, Schorske has argued, undermined liberal faith in the autonomous subject, hastening the birth of "psychological man," a being driven not only by reason but also (perhaps even predominantly) by feelings and instincts.[19] It was not just the collapse of liberalism, however, that had led to the demise of Rational Man. There were other, more specific factors, which Schorske did not mention. Among these, the critical positivism of physicist Ernst Mach (1838–1916) and the development of experimental psychology were most important.

Ernst Mach had come to the University of Vienna in 1895 from Prague, where he had been Professor of Experimental Physics for almost thirty years. In Vienna, however, he was appointed as the Professor of Philosophy.[20] In his long and versatile career, Mach made significant contributions to both fields and also to psychology and the history of science.[21] What united his diverse activities was the conviction that only sensations were real and knowable: references to what could not be consciously experienced were "metaphysical" and, therefore, of no scientific value.[22] For contemporary scientists, Mach's most sensational act was the rejection of the atomic theory as metaphysical. Among the literary intelligentsia, however, it was Mach's views on the self that caused the greatest stir.

Mach had always held strong views on some of the most contentious subjects in psychology. He conceptualized the mind as well as the body in terms of sensations: the same sensations, he asserted, could appear as "physical" or "mental," depending on the ways in which the sensations were related to one another.[23] The only fundamental difference between psychology and physiology was that psychology dealt with sensations—including, for Mach, ideas, moods, and dispositions—that could not yet be precisely measured, whereas physiology was concerned with sensations that could be measured scientifically.[24] This abstract focus on sensations soon took an incendiary form. In 1886, Mach published his *Contributions to the Analysis of Sensations*, in which he argued that there was no such thing as a coherent, unified self or "ego." What people thought of as their unique, distinct self was simply a complex of sensations that was differently configured in different individuals.[25] There was no clear gulf "between bodies and sensations . . . between what is without and what is within, between the material world and the spiritual world."[26]

"The self," Mach proclaimed, "is beyond salvage" *(Das Ich ist unrettbar).*[27] The intellectual elite of Vienna was electrified by this declaration. Essayist, critic, and always fashionable intellectual Hermann Bahr (1863–1934) reminisced that with that one provocative statement, "the last of the idols seemed to be smashed, the last refuge fallen, the highest freedom won, the work of annihilation completed. There really remained nothing else left."[28] Some intellectuals and artists, such as Arthur Schnitzler, Hugo von Hofmannstahl, or Robert Musil, were stimulated or even exhilarated by Mach's demolition of the self.[29] Others, such as Otto Weininger and Hermann Broch, felt deeply threatened.[30]

In the scientific field, Mach's rejection of the self was a crucial component of his seminal influence on psychology. Even in the late nineteenth century, psychologists were still in search of a scientific identity and had two basic orientations to choose from.[31] One was associated with the renowned psychologist and philosopher Wilhelm Wundt (1832–1920). This approach, according to Kurt Danziger, "had at most one foot in the camp of the natural sciences. . . . Even Wundt's physiological psychology belongs only 'half' to the natural sciences, for its task is to mediate between the latter and the *Geisteswissenschaften.*"[32] The other orientation in psychology, associated with Oswald Külpe (1862–1915) and Hermann Ebbinghaus (1850–1909), was much closer to the natural sciences. Külpe, who had been Wundt's student and assistant, believed that psychical events could be explained only with reference to the physiological processes of the "corporeal individual."[33] Külpe and his followers rejected mind-body dualism and all "mentalistic" explanations in psychology, swearing allegiance to Mach and Richard Avenarius.[34] Külpe declared that "in principle there is no topic of psychological inquiry which cannot be approached by the experimental method. And experimental psychology is therefore fully within its rights when it claims to be the general psychology of which we propose to treat."[35] Older, philosophical methods such as introspection were, therefore, unnecessary as well as useless.

Wundt, himself an experimentalist, opposed this new, hard-edged experimentalism as extreme and dogmatic. So, from a different perspective, did the philosopher and historian Wilhelm Dilthey (1833–1911). While conceding that experimental investigations could explain some simple mental processes, both argued that the human psyche was too complex to yield all its secrets to mere laboratory experiments.[36] Dilthey, who famously stressed that the natural sciences strove to "explain" while the so-called human sciences (the Geisteswissenschaften) tried to "understand," called for descriptive psychological studies of the total "lived world" of human beings. Psychological research had to begin with and remain rooted in conscious, complex, lived experience: psychologists were doomed if they imitated natural scientists and broke up the object of their study into small fragments.[37]

Much of this debate centered on the status of introspection as a method of psychological research. The exploration of one's own self through focused thought has, of course, been a prominent theme in Western cultures for centuries, going back at least to the *Confessions* of St. Augustine. If, however, we define introspection narrowly as a research methodology depending on deliberate and systematic investigation of inner experience, then it does not significantly antedate the nineteenth century.[38] In Central European thought, the status of introspection had been influenced significantly by the views of Immanuel Kant. Kant accepted the existence of an inner world that could be studied by an "inner sense" just as the outer world could be studied by the conventional senses. He added, however, that the study of the inner world could never be a science since the knowledge acquired by such study could not be synthesized and expressed in mathematical terms. Mental life, he argued, was organized in fundamental categories that were not to be found in the empirical world. They could not, therefore, be demonstrated, but only deduced. In his terminology, they were part of the *intelligible* rather than the empirical world.[39] The science of psychology, according to Kant, could only attain the knowledge of appearances, of *phenomena*. The deepest reaches of the mind were not part of the phenomenal world and therefore were inaccessible to introspection or to any empirical method.

Powerful as it was in Central Europe, the Kantian diktat did not stop investigators from trying to refine introspection into a research tool.[40] Psychologists like Wilhelm Wundt attempted to make introspection genuinely "scientific" by the experimental manipulation of the conditions of internal perception and by ensuring the replicability of observations.[41] Otto Weininger, in sharp contradistinction, rejected the very legitimacy of attempts to make psychology scientific. His aim was to reform psychology into the study of character, and he exalted introspection as the only method that could attain that goal. This may seem contradictory since he agreed with Kant that the deepest realms of the psyche were inaccessible to empirical investigation of *any* kind, whether introspection or experimentation. The contradiction, however, is only apparent. Weininger admitted that his fundamental metaphysical principle, the existence of the intelligible self, was an assumption rather than a fact discovered by introspection. The empirical study of character by introspection was not the study of the self: restricted to the outermost aspects of the mind, it analyzed patterns of behavior and thought rather than the ultimate source of all thought, the Kantian intelligible self, which was beyond the reach of the empirical scientist and could be explored by the deductive philosopher alone.

## Back to Kant!

The importance of Kantian ideas in *Geschlecht und Charakter* was so great and so repeatedly acknowledged by Weininger that one might overlook the oddity of this indebtedness. In the earlier years of the nineteenth century, the German universities had tended to neglect Kant in favor of Hegel, but the Hegelian *Geist* had become passé by the end of the century. A resurgence in Kantian thought ensued but only in Germany. In Austria, university philosophy proceeded differently: Weininger's almost worshipful invocations of Kant, which would have seemed normal in Germany, were atypical in Vienna. On this issue, as with regard to Protestantism, Weininger was much more German than Austrian.

In 1865, the German philosopher Otto Liebmann published a polemical work entitled *Kant und die Epigonen* (Kant and the Epigones). Every chapter of this work ended with the sentence "Also muß auf Kant zurückgegangen werden" (We must, therefore, return to Kant).[42] German university philosophy had been preoccupied during the mid-nineteenth century with the collapse of Hegelian Idealism and the endless internecine battles between Hegel's followers. Simultaneously, advances in the natural sciences had made all idealistic systems seem anachronistically speculative, leading to a short-lived interest in the reductionist materialism associated with Karl Vogt, Jacob Moleschott, and Ludwig Büchner. Finally, the Hegelian march of Reason through History appeared to have been definitively disproved by the failure of the revolutions of 1848.[43]

After the collapse of Hegelianism, Kant returned to the forefront of academic philosophy. The neo-Kantian movement gained further momentum with Friedrich Albert Lange, socialist activist and author of the renowned *Geschichte der Materialismus* (History of Materialism, 1866), who declared Kantian philosophy to be more compatible with modern science than any other.[44] By the turn of the century, neo-Kantianism had become a heterogeneous movement "whose common denominator," according to a recent historian, "was at most an alleged recourse to Kant but which never represented an individual, definable philosophical tendency."[45]

Two streams of neo-Kantian thought attained particular prominence: the Marburg School led by Hermann Cohen and Paul Natorp and the Heidelberg (or Baden or South-West German School) of Wilhelm Windelband and Heinrich Rickert. Both schools asserted that the proper object of epistemological investigation was the logical structure of science itself. The work of the Marburg School was aimed at identifying the transcendental principles of logic and mathematics, whereas the Heidelbergians proceeded similarly with regard to the so-called cultural sciences, which studied humanity and its history. Both the Marburg and Heidelberg versions of neo-Kantianism were vehemently opposed to all kinds of empiricism, biologism, historicism, and psychologism. For them, the rational Geist was beyond all external influence.[46]

While all this was happening in Germany, Austria followed a different path.[47] Austrian philosophers, influenced strongly by Johann Friedrich Herbart (1776–1841), Bernard Bolzano (1781–1848), and Friedrich Heinrich Jacobi (1743–1819), were strongly drawn to empiricism, realism, and the philosophy of science. Perhaps most significant was the Austrian interest in the criticism of language *(Sprachkritik)*.[48] Leibniz, Locke, and Hume were more important to Austrian philosophers than Kant or Hegel. Kant's "Copernican Revolution," which had grounded knowledge in transcendental laws of human understanding, had not, according to Rudolf Haller, affected Austrian philosophy.[49] In the late nineteenth century, "John Stuart Mill seemed to be exercising a greater influence on Viennese modernity than Kant."[50] Rejecting Kant's distinction between empirical and transcendental methods of philosophical investigation, the charismatic Catholic priest and philosopher Franz Brentano (1853–1917) taught an exclusively empirical, "scientific" philosophy at the University of Vienna, emphasizing "the application of critical and analytical methods to language as a means of discovering and removing fictions and pseudo-problems from philosophy."[51] In opposition to the neo-Kantian separation of the natural sciences from the cultural sciences, Brentano insisted on the unity of all knowledge.[52] In spite of technical differences in outlook, Brentano's influence was reinforced by his successor as Professor of Philosophy at the University of Vienna, Ernst Mach.[53]

After overcoming his early intellectual allegiance to Mach and Richard Avenarius, Otto Weininger affiliated himself completely with neo-Kantianism.[54] His approach to philosophy and psychology was transcendental in the Kantian sense, owing little to Austrian empiricism. Nor did the Austrian tradition of Sprachkritik have much appeal for him: from the days of Francis Bacon, he remarked, "all flatheads have been critics of language" (176). But how could a student in the Philosophical Faculty of the University of Vienna, whose doctoral advisor was the positivist Friedrich Jodl, be drawn so powerfully to the German neo-Kantian tradition? Hannelore Rodlauer speculates that Weininger may have been influenced by Robert Reininger (1869–1955), one of the rare Kantians on the Austrian academic scene, whose habilitation as a Privatdozent had been sponsored by the remarkably broadminded Jodl, and who later became Professor of Philosophy at the University of Vienna.[55] More importantly, Rodlauer has discovered that Alois Höfler, the chairman of the university's Philosophical Society, had been entrusted in 1901 by the Berlin Academy of Sciences with the task of editing Kant's *Metaphysical Foundations of Natural Sciences* for their complete edition of the philosopher's works. Höfler had recruited three assistants to read and compare different versions of the text: Otto Weininger was one of them. Rodlauer suggests that even if this exposure to Kant did not by itself *cause* Weininger's flight from contemporary "scientific" psychology, it was significant in influencing its direction.[56] While these are obviously important points, one must not overlook that Weininger's espousal of Kantianism was also guided by his own chosen identity as an intellectual representative of a Greater Germany— and therefore that it was at least indirectly a gesture of defiance toward Austrian academic orthodoxy, just as his later adoption of Protestantism symbolized a defiance of Judaism as well as the Catholic culture of Vienna.

### The Woman Question: Feminism as Apocalypse

Weininger's Kantian salvage of the self was a political as well as an intellectual act.[57] He did not simply claim that the self existed but argued that the Kantian intelligible self, the source of human autonomy and subjectivity, existed only in the male Aryan. Females and Jews, he happily conceded, were not autonomous subjects but mere Machian bundles of sensations.

The emergence of feminist movements in the late nineteenth century generated theoretically complex analyses of "the nature of woman" and new justifications for traditional ideas on gender roles. Although few of the feminist demands for equal intellectual, moral, and political rights were fulfilled during the period, the cultural and intellectual impact of early feminism far outstripped its numerical strength or political successes. The very fact that women were demanding equality was seen as apocalyptic. Most male European intellectuals of the late nineteenth century subscribed to norms of gender that were firmly established only at the end of the eighteenth century but that seemed, nevertheless, to be eternal, natural, and obvious.[58] Even the slightest suggestion for a revision of those apparently immutable codes was taken as a portent of doom, not simply for men but for civilization itself.

We cannot do better than to begin with Immanuel Kant, Otto Weininger's intellectual ideal and the prototypical German thinker of the Enlightenment, who believed that women and men had different "characters" and that this difference was ordained by a higher power. Women, according to Kant, acted on inclination and needed to be governed by men, who acted according to reason. Morally, women could not be their own masters and, therefore, could not be full and active citizens.[59] Kant's fundamental conviction of women's lower intellectual and moral position was widely shared.[60] From the

end of the eighteenth century, however, it was expressed increasingly in biological and psychological terms. The body and mind of woman were now
thought to be designed primarily to serve the reproductive needs of the
species. The male, on the other hand, was biologically and psychologically
designed for intellectual and cultural activity. The social inequality of the
sexes, then, had been decreed by nature, and this made it acceptable to liberal
political philosophy.[61]

Two major thinkers of the nineteenth century, Arthur Schopenhauer and
Friedrich Nietzsche, evolved a rhetoric of misogyny that, in many ways, foreshadowed Weininger's. Schopenhauer considered women to be childish,
frivolous, cunning, and deceitful creatures lacking physical and mental
strength, genuine intelligence, memory, and an aesthetic sense. Existing
solely to reproduce the species, they were inferior to men in every respect.
Ridiculing the European reverence for women as the "highest product of
Teutonico-Christian stupidity," Schopenhauer advocated an "Asian" subordination of women in society.[62] Nietzsche once observed that Schopenhauer
taught one how to live *against* the values of one's age: with regard to women,
however, neither philosopher proved particularly iconoclastic.[63] Although
original in his rejection of the conventional wisdom that women were less
sexual than men, Nietzsche was entirely conventional in interpreting female
sexuality as no more than the biological urge for pregnancy.[64] Believing intellectuality to be wholly incompatible with motherhood, Nietzsche argued
that emancipation would lead to the degeneration of women, making them
incapable of their "first and last profession—to give birth to strong children."[65] Women, he believed, should be treated as property, and following his
master Schopenhauer, he lauded the "Oriental" subjugation of women.[66]

Nineteenth-century feminists did not have to do much, then, to acquire an
apocalyptic significance in the eyes of many male intellectuals. The simple
expression of the conviction that women were not "naturally" inferior to men
and deserved equal social, political, and intellectual rights was enough to
cause a full-blown cultural crisis. "By the late nineteenth century," Theodore
Roszak observes, "this supposedly marginal curiosity called the 'woman
problem' had become one of the most earth-shaking debates in the Western
world. . . . One would be hard pressed to find many major figures of the period in any cultural field who did not address themselves passionately to the
rights of women."[67]

The voice of science was heard with great respect in this scientist epoch;
biologists and physicians were vociferous in their opposition to the "unnat-
ural" and potentially dangerous imposition of sexual equality.[68] The most
memorably titled work in this genre was the German psychiatrist Paul Julius
Möbius's *Über den physiologischen Schwachsinn des Weibes* (On the Physiolog-

ical Feeble-Mindedness of Woman, 1900), which claimed that women were *naturally* weak-minded: creative intelligence in a woman was not a sign of superiority but of degeneration.[69] The Italian psychiatrist, anthropologist, and criminologist Cesare Lombroso's theories on femininity were even more influential.[70] Lombroso believed that women's perceptual abilities were duller than men's, that women were liars by nature, and that prostitutes had no maternal feelings.[71] Numerous cultural critics, artists, philosophers, social thinkers, and politicians of the time agreed fundamentally with Lombroso and Möbius and expressed their agreement in volume after antifeminist volume.[72] Much of this interest in woman's nature, including a lot in Otto Weininger's *Geschlecht und Charakter,* was a direct response to feminist demands for equality and emancipation.

### Woman Power: Feminist Activism in Central Europe

In nineteenth-century Germany, according to Richard Evans, "the family, the school, the State and the nation . . . were analogous institutions. . . . In each case the role of each sex was clearly defined; men were to rule, women were to obey; men were to think, to create, to develop their own personality, women were to lead a life of emotion and feeling, to sacrifice their individuality and potential to the interest of the larger social unit to which they belonged."[73] By 1900, this cultural imperative was being questioned, and Germany by then had no less than 850 organizations with close to a million members campaigning for women's rights.[74] Austria, too, had active women's organizations, albeit fewer in number.[75]

Inspired initially by a liberal individualist ideology, these organizations represented what some historians have described as "bourgeois feminism," a term that also serves to separate them from the rival tradition of "socialist feminism." Germany's Social Democratic Party was committed to women's equality, and the socialist leader August Bebel's 1879 treatise, *Women and Socialism,* was an extremely popular work.[76] In this book, Bebel provided a historical study of the subjugation of women as well as a visionary account of women's emancipation under universal socialism. For several generations of German socialists, it was a "veritable Bible."[77] The essential difference between the "bourgeois" and "socialist" feminists was that the latter believed that women could never be emancipated before capitalism had been overthrown.[78] Women's suffrage was a key demand for Central European feminists, but it had a somewhat lower priority than in the USA and Britain.[79]

The character of the German feminist movements was far from static. Even at the most superficial level of analysis, one must divide their history into two fairly distinct phases. According to Richard Evans, the women's movements took on a radical character between 1894 and 1908, which, in fact, was an active and radical period for most liberal causes in Germany. After 1908, when the liberal traditions turned more conservative, German feminism, too, became less radical.[80] The earlier, more radical period is crucial for our purposes, since it generated an extreme degree of anxiety among fin-de-siècle intellectuals.

Before 1900, the states of the German Empire had many different civil law codes. In the most powerful state, Prussia, the married woman was not a "legal person": the husband was the legal guardian of his wife. All her property passed to him on marriage, as did her subsequent earnings. She needed his permission to take a job or sign a contract. Except for surprisingly progressive provisions for divorce, the Prussian law gave women fewer rights than did the contemporary statutes of major Western nations.[81] German women were forbidden to participate in politics. Nor were they admitted as full-time students in the German universities until 1901, well after universities in England (1878), France (1861), and the United States (1853) had been opened to women.[82] Even Habsburg Austria, conservative in so many ways, was ahead of Germany on this: the University of Vienna had first allowed women to study for an arts degree in 1897, and, after a protracted controversy, it opened the medical faculty to women in 1900. Moreover, Austrian women could seek employment without the husband's permission, vote in some local elections, and own some property.[83]

In spite of the official prohibition on women's participation in politics, the first German feminist organization, the General German Women's Association (Allgemeiner Deutscher Frauenverein), was founded in 1865, and the first feminist organization in Austria, the Viennese Women's Employment Association, was established in 1866.[84] Both organizations were politically undemanding and concentrated on vocational and educational issues.[85] Soon, however, German feminists began to address more controversial matters, and these concerns were frequently rather different from those of other Western feminist traditions.

One distinctive trait of German feminism was its stress on the social, cultural, political, and metaphorical importance of motherhood. Women, the German feminists believed, were not just biological mothers but spiritual mothers.[86] Consequently, early German feminists were especially active in welfare-work and charities. Richard Evans interpreted this as part of a general rightward shift within the liberal feminist tradition.[87] Evans's view has been strongly contested by Ann Taylor Allen, who persuasively links the successes of German feminists to this strategic deployment of motherhood, a womanly role and function honored even by conservatives.[88] In Vienna, maternalist feminism was given a radical twist by Grete Meisel-Hess, who claimed that the liberated woman made the best mother and that there was no better way to undermine the patriarchy than by exerting the ancient "mother-right" against fathers.[89] The feminist challenge to patriarchy was one of the driving anxieties of Weininger's treatise, even though he died before he could have read Meisel-Hess.

During the 1890s, German feminists grew increasingly vocal in demanding the vote and the elimination of prostitution.[90] Viennese feminists were deeply perturbed by prostitution, and this is particularly important for contextualizing Weininger's work.[91] Many of the more radical feminists initially attributed prostitution largely to male sexual indiscipline. With time, however, they came to adopt a more libertarian credo, arguing that prostitution could be abolished only if society grew more liberal on sexual matters in general. Helene Stöcker (1869–1943), a romantic individualist greatly influenced by the views of Nietzsche, claimed that prostitution existed because of destitution consequent upon unmarried motherhood. In order to root prostitution out, therefore, it was necessary to prevent unwanted pregnancies by distributing contraceptives.[92] In Vienna, brothels were not officially permitted, even though prostitutes circulated freely within the city.[93] In 1892, the city government planned to introduce legal brothels, and, in protest, the General Austrian Women's Association sent a petition to parliament. The petition, probably written by Rosa Mayreder, argued that prostitution was caused not just by the economic needs of the prostitutes but by social and moral restrictions on premarital sex. Since men earned enough money to marry only long after reaching puberty, they turned to prostitutes for sex. The petition implied that men and women should be permitted to cohabit freely before marriage.[94]

Helene Stöcker later became involved with the League for the Protection of Mothers and Sexual Reform, which called for the "restoration of a matriarchate," the end of capitalism, and the eugenic "breeding" of healthy children for the improvement of the nation. Eventually, the league eliminated the more Social Darwinist items on its agenda and concentrated on maternal welfare and the provision of homes for unmarried mothers in the major cities. Stöcker, however, always remained a fervent believer in sexual freedom, arguing that the conventional patriarchal marriage was actually inimical to sexual passion and destroyed the individuality of women. Only the end of patriarchy would make marriage a passionate, equal, and fulfilling bond.[95] The league found many male members, most of them of a left-liberal orientation.[96] Some were Social Democrats, and the league was the only "bourgeois feminist" organization that many socialist women felt close to.[97] In the final analysis, however, the practical success of the league was small, and its public image one of depravity. The support of socialists and Jews certainly did not enhance its respectability among middle-class Germans, and its reputation was fatally tarnished by its emphasis on sexual freedom.

The members of the league were not the only feminists opposing the bourgeois sexual code.[98] One could even argue that August Bebel had himself encouraged promiscuity. Acknowledging the power of the sex drive and following contemporary medical opinion that sexual abstinence was harmful to health, Bebel had advocated "unconstrained intercourse between the sexes."[99] While most Social Democrats were actually quite conservative in matters of sex, contemporaries attacked the Social Democratic Party for encouraging immorality and "female egotism" and thereby weakening women's desire for motherhood.[100]

Toward the end of the first decade of the new century, explicitly antifeminist organizations also came into being in Central Europe. In 1912, the League for the Prevention of Women's Emancipation (Bund zur Bekämpfung der Frauenemanzipation) was founded by a number of little-known academics, military men, and pan-German racialists.[101] They claimed that the women's movement was dividing and weakening the German Empire by destroying its greatest source of inner strength: the family. Some antifeminists were convinced that feminist activism had been launched by an international Jewish conspiracy to destroy Germany and the very concept of the nation state. Comparing feminism with social democracy, they dismissed both as Jewish and therefore evil. Even feminists from Christian families were accused of concealing their real Jewish identities.[102]

Antifeminists often described feminist activists as "men-women."[103] This metaphor and its variants were popular even among the higher reaches of the intelligentsia. The dramatist August Strindberg, for instance, referred to feminist agitators as "hermaphrodites" and "half-women."[104] Among the scientific elite, the preeminent Viennese psychiatrist Richard von Krafft-Ebing pointed out that "the masculine soul, heaving in the female bosom" of lesbians led them to idealize "certain female characters who in the past or the present have excelled by virtue of genius and brave and noble deeds."[105] German sexologist Iwan Bloch stated more directly that homosexual (and therefore masculine) women were prominent in the feminist movement; such women, said Bloch, craved spiritual contact with men and desired to change the current social order much more intensely than the average, truly feminine woman.[106]

Perhaps surprisingly, some radical feminists accepted this analysis but gave it an intriguing political spin. In a 1904 lecture at a gathering of homosexual emancipationists, Anna Rüling, herself homosexual, declared that the lesbian was biologically closer to the average male than to the average female: she was more objective, more energetic, and more focused. The lesbian did not imitate males: she *was* partly male.[107] Consequently, the lesbian was biologically unsuited for marriage and motherhood but—and this was the crux of the argument—equipped by Nature to be a professional or a university professor, and should not be obstructed because of her apparent sex.[108] Many prominent feminist leaders, Rüling declared, were indeed lesbians and could easily be recognized as such by anybody with the slightest understanding of lesbian traits.[109]

*Feminism and the Crisis of Masculine Identity: A Viennese Dialectic?*

The strong opposition of a Karl Kraus or an Otto Weininger did not prevent a significant number of Viennese male intellectuals from supporting feminist causes. Rosa Mayreder once remarked that she could not "see 'men' as the enemies of women's concerns" and believed that male support was even wider than feminists usually believed.[110] Ernst Mach was unequivocal in his support for women's higher education and entry into the professions. Anatomist Emil Zuckerkandl, classicist Theodor Gomperz, and physicist Ludwig Boltzmann were associated with feminist organizations demanding educational opportunities for women. Left-wing politicians such as Engelbert Pernerstorfer submitted women's petitions to the parliament since women were excluded from membership or attendance.[111]

Jacques Le Rider, dismissing the Viennese feminist movement as "one of the least powerful in Europe," has discounted any feminist impact on the work of Weininger and other Viennese modernists. Instead, Le Rider attributed their antifeminist views to a psychoanalytically conceived crisis of masculine identity preceding any feminist impact.[112] It was feminine nonbeing that came naturally to Viennese modernists; masculinity was "always . . . to be conquered, on penalty of regression into the femininity which is always eager to reoccupy lost ground."[113] Apart from the feminization of the individual male, another common concern of Viennese artists and critics was the feminization of culture itself. "Nervous sensibility," the literary critic Rudolf Lothar wrote in 1891, "is the characteristic of the last years of our century. I am inclined to call this trend 'feminism,' for everything goes to show that women's will to power, their desire to compete with men, has meant that the female hypersensitivity of gaze, of pleasure, of thought and of feeling, has been communicated to men and is taking them over."[114] Sexologist Iwan Bloch noted that the urge to affirm a "masculine culture" was leading even some heterosexual men to renounce women in horror. Such people, according to Bloch, almost belonged to a "fourth sex." He saw the philosophy of Schopenhauer as the intellectual fountainhead of this pathological fear of the feminine, and the work of August Strindberg and Otto Weininger as its most full-blown expressions.[115]

Rosa Mayreder once argued that the feminist movement did not aim to conquer the male world. The males, she claimed, had already surrendered.

Modernity had undermined old male "warrior values": men had become passive and feminized, although they still chose to subscribe to archaic myths of virility.[116] Mayreder quoted the mid-nineteenth-century literary critic Otto Ludwig's question: "Since men have turned into women . . . do women have any choice but to occupy the ground men have abandoned?"[117] Le Rider offered this as the crowning piece of evidence for his thesis that a masculine identity crisis, rather than the impact of feminist movements, produced the Viennese preoccupation with issues of gender. I would argue, however, that instead of reducing Mayreder's fascinating piece of political rhetoric into a report, we should take it as a tactical argument, in which Mayreder depicted a fait accompli so as to imply that antagonism to feminist movements was futile.

The historical evidence does not, of course, rule out a crisis of masculinity completely. All the evidence suggests, however, that neither feminism nor the crisis of male identity was *alone* responsible for the widespread concern over gender issues in turn-of-the-century Vienna and in European cultures in general. Even a superficial glance at the writings of Karl Kraus, Weininger, and comparable figures shows that *both* the crisis of masculine identity *and* the feminist movement simultaneously affected the consciousness of male intellectuals. Kraus, for example, fulminated against the "vaginal age" as well as against suffragettes; Weininger lamented the effeminacy of the times but also condemned feminist activism.[118] The fin-de-siècle crisis, in short, was one of gender as a cultural category rather than a crisis of masculinity alone or a crisis related solely to the Woman Question. Feminism, by challenging already weakening conceptions of masculine as well as feminine identity, triggered a dialectical process leading to modifications in both. The New Woman did not simply threaten patriarchy but, directly as well as indirectly, engendered what James Joyce, in a different context (but inspired by Weininger), called the "New Womanly Man."

*Enemies of the* Volk? *German Thinkers and the Question of "Jewishness"*
The turn-of-the-century crisis of gender was closely related to a crisis of Jewish identity. The late nineteenth century saw an upsurge in political and cultural anti-Semitism in Central Europe, and Vienna was at the center of this dubious renaissance.[119] Viennese anti-Semitism was heterogeneous but omnipresent. Otto Weininger, even if he had not had an anti-Semitic father, would have encountered anti-Semitism among his father's fellow artisans or among his professors and fellow students at the university.

One theme that unites all anti-Semitic discourse across time and space is the conviction that Jews never identify with the nation they live in: considering themselves the "chosen people," they set themselves off from others and constitute a "nation within a nation." This theme recurred in nineteenth-century Central Europe with a vengeance, but German anti-Semitic traditions did not rest content with that one charge. Jews were not simply ethnically distinct; they also lacked such basic human traits as morality, love, and the desire for freedom. The so-called Jewish "national character" was defined in psychological, religious, and cultural (as opposed to biological) terms, and references to it were not unique to anti-Semites. Even some of the strongest supporters of Jewish emancipation stressed that Jews had to transcend their "Jewishness" in order to become worthy of freedom.[120]

In nineteenth-century Central Europe, anti-Semitism followed no clear political lines, spanning, as Paul Rose has emphasized, the Left and the Right.[121] A hatred for Jews and "Jewishness" was integral to "German revolutionism," a loosely defined political project for the renewal of German life on new moral, philosophical, and cultural principles, to which thinkers such as Immanuel Kant, Johann Gottlieb Fichte, Johann Gottfried von Herder, and later, Arthur Schopenhauer and Richard Wagner all subscribed in their own ways.[122] All more or less anti-Semitic, they considered the Jewish and the German national characters to be ancient, distinct, and in most respects, mutually opposed. Jews themselves often agreed: poet Heinrich Heine and journalist Ludwig Börne refurbished an old stereotype, portraying the modern Jew as a heartless capitalist, an image recirculated by Karl Marx and Friedrich Engels as well as by countless others of diverse political creeds.[123]

Among philosophers, Kant's faith in the Enlightenment ideal of universal brotherhood co-existed quite comfortably with a clear antipathy toward Judaism and the Jewish "character." (Just as it did with his belief that women lacked reason and needed to be governed by men.) The Jews, Kant thought, were invincibly alien: they were "the Palestinians who live among us." Judaism was not a true religion: Jews obeyed an externally imposed law rather than the imperatives of inner, autonomous morality. Judaism, therefore, followed ethical principles that were diametrically opposed to the Kantian concept of moral autonomy. Kant did not, however, consider "Jewishness" to be immutable. Even without mass conversions, Jews could move closer to Germans if "purified religious conceptions awaken among them and they discard the old ones."[124] Kant's vision of the German future included Jews but only on condition of what Rose calls their voluntary "euthanasia of Judaism."[125] Other philosophers were even harsher. Johann Gottfried von Herder, who has often been seen as philo-Semitic, described Jews as "the parasitic plant that has attached itself to almost all the European nations."[126] This metaphor of the parasite recurs repeatedly in modern European history: one finds it in the work of Arthur Schopenhauer, in Nazi rhetoric, and in the notebooks of Ludwig Wittgenstein.[127] Schopenhauer saw the Jews as a "foreign, oriental people" who lived parasitically on others: Jews belonged everywhere and nowhere.[128] Jewish solidarity represented patriotism without a fatherland: *Patriotismus sine patria.*[129]

Richard Wagner, arguably the most celebrated artistic figure of nineteenth-century Central Europe and certainly the artist Otto Weininger most admired, was a great devotee of Schopenhauer and far exceeded him in anti-Semitism.[130] For many, Wagner's musical dramas—conceived as "total works of art" rather than mere operas—embodied a distinctively German philosophy of life. From 1848, when he had been an associate of Mikhail Bakunin, Wagner had aimed to revolutionize German society through his art. The greatest obstacle to that revolution, Wagner believed, was materialism: the "demonic idea of Money," egoism, heartlessness, and greed.[131] The Jews symbolized materialism while the spirit of the German Volk represented all that was pure and holy: the true German, consequently, was "instinctively repelled by any actual, operative contact" with Jews. In the arts in particular, the Jewish presence had been calamitous: "What the heroes of the arts . . . have wrested from . . . two millennia of misery, today the Jew converts into an art-bazaar (*Kunstwaarenwechsel*)."[132]

Later, in the 1870s, Wagner's cultural anti-Semitism hardened further. He even denied the Jewishness of Jesus and came under the sway of his fervent admirer, Count Arthur Gobineau, whose racial theories Wagner and his devotees helped disseminate in Germany.[133] Unlike Gobineau, however, Wagner did not believe that the Teutonic races were in irreversible decline: the leitmotiv of Wagner's later writings was "regeneration."[134] His last music-drama *Parsifal* can be seen as depicting the redemption of the debilitated race by the chaste, naive, Aryan boy Parsifal.[135] Simultaneously, Wagner lashed out against the intermarriage of Jews and Gentiles, describing it as "the degenerative mixing of the heroic blood of the noblest races with that of the former eaters of humans, now trained to be the business-agents of society."[136]

Wagner spent his last years in Bayreuth, a small Bavarian city where he erected a Festival Theatre. Wagnerian societies and journals proliferated all over Europe, and, after the master's death in 1883, Wagnerism was transformed almost into a religion by his widow Cosima. At its peak, Wagner and Cosima "were regarded as semi-divine," while the leaders of the cult saw themselves as "Grail knights, guardians of the sacred cup."[137] One leading member of this innermost "magic circle" was the emigré Englishman Houston Stewart Chamberlain (1855–1927). Chamberlain's peripatetic childhood had been spent in various parts of continental Europe. In his early youth, he had married a German, and his spiritual love for German culture gradually deepened almost into worship. Once fairly cosmopolitan, he developed into a staunch German nationalist, a transformation catalyzed by the music of Wagner. In 1889, Chamberlain moved to Vienna, second only to Bayreuth as a center of Wagnerism, and quickly made a name for himself among the intelligentsia, finding political friends in the pan-German circles. Predictably, Chamberlain wrote copiously on Wagner's music, but was also prolific on subjects ranging from the life of Kant to the science of race.

Chamberlain's biographer Geoffrey Field has described him as "one of the most successful exemplars of a new literary type: the popular synthesizer who, in an age of specialization, dispensed with academic caution and strove to impose an order on the chaos of experience by drawing together all his knowledge in an easily grasped unified vision."[138] This vision was expressed most comprehensively in Chamberlain's magnum opus, *The Foundations of the Nineteenth Century*.[139] Published in two volumes in 1900, it soon became an essential text of German racial theory. Marshalling a wide array of arcane and unrelated lore, Chamberlain argued that the history of humanity was the history of struggle between different races.[140] After the Roman Empire had collapsed in "racial chaos" induced by miscegenation, there arose two pure races: the Jews and the Teutons. From the sixth century onward, European history had been little more than the story of Teutons fighting Jews.[141] The Jewish race, according to Chamberlain, aimed to "be Lord and possessor of the whole earth." By encouraging their daughters to marry outside the race and by preventing their sons from doing so, they infected "Indo-Europeans with Jewish blood," while ensuring the racial purity of their principal male line. If this continued unabated, Europe would soon be left with only one pure race: the Jews. "All the rest would be a herd of pseudo-Hebraic mestizos, a people beyond all doubt degenerate physically, mentally, and morally."[142] The rootless urban Jew was the destroyer of European civilization, while the idealistic, chaste, and profound Teuton was its redeemer. Rejecting the "Judaized" Christianity of the Roman Catholic Church, Chamberlain resurrected Wagner's Aryan Jesus: Christ's character traits, he argued, were predominantly Aryan and Teutonic.[143]

Although he spoke of race rather than of religion, Chamberlain was far from unequivocal on the immutability of Jewishness. He wrote in the *Foundations* that "it is pointless to call the purest bred Israelite a Jew, if he has succeeded in throwing off the shackles of Ezra and Nehemiah and no longer acknowledges the law of Moses in his mind or despises others in his heart." Elsewhere, however, he almost contradicted himself by using quasi-biological arguments. This same equivocation was characteristic of the Bayreuth circle as a whole.[144] But despite their internal contradictions, Wagner and Chamberlain provided new intellectual and cultural credentials for anti-Semitism. The Nazis would honor them as visionaries, but their impact long predated the Third Reich and was not even restricted to gentiles. In Vienna itself, the Jewish-born Karl Kraus published Chamberlain's articles in his journal and shared his conviction that Jews were the forces of Mammon.[145] The Wagnerian brand of anti-Semitism caught the mood of the century as unerringly as the Wagnerian brand of opera, and nowhere was this more apparent than in Vienna.

*Jews and Viennese Culture: Assimilation, Uniqueness, "Self-Hatred"*
On arriving in Vienna in 1889, Houston Stewart Chamberlain wrote a joyous letter to a friend. After praising the beauties of the city and "the pretty women of easy morals," he added that the one drawback of Vienna was the "enormous quantity of Jews."[146] The Jewish population of Vienna had indeed been rising since 1848, when the government had revoked older laws barring Jews from residing in the city. Jews from the eastern regions of the Habsburg Empire had then begun to emigrate to Vienna in large numbers, and, until the 1890s, the Jewish population of the capital grew faster than the general population, rising from around 4,000 in 1848 to about 150,000 by the end of the century, which amounted to some nine per cent of the city's total population.[147]

Recent emigres from the East apart, many Viennese Jewish families came to be characterized by their assimilation to and admiration for German culture. More than thirty percent of students in the classical Gymnasia, for example, were Jewish. Since the primary aim of the Gymnasia was to train students for higher education and the professions, it was hardly surprising that forty-eight percent of students in the medical faculty of the University of Vienna were Jewish. The law and philosophy faculties had fewer Jewish students, but their numbers were not insignificant. Among professors, the medical faculty, once again, led the rest with more than fifty percent Jews. The Viennese press was preponderantly Jewish, a fact that Karl Kraus repeatedly emphasized.[148]

Historian Norman Stone has argued that "most of the twentieth-century intellectual world was invented" in Vienna. This was as sudden in historical terms as it was unexpected. While turn-of-the-century Austria produced leaders in practically every field ranging from music to nuclear physics, the empire had never previously been the leader in any field other than music. Vienna, especially, had been "rather a backward place" by European standards. Stone argued that the rapid intellectual flowering of Vienna in the early twentieth century can be explained only by the preponderance of secularized Jews.[149] His doctoral student Steven Beller developed this suggestion in a comprehensive cultural history of Jewish Vienna, arguing that most cultural innovators in Vienna were of Jewish descent: Sigmund Freud, Ludwig Wittgenstein, Gustav Mahler, Arnold Schoenberg, Karl Popper, Hans

Kelsen, Arthur Schnitzler.[150] "Not only were the cultural producers Jewish," concluded Beller, "but also the consumers, the audience."[151]

Even the scions of thoroughly assimilated families—such as Wittgenstein or Hugo von Hofmannsthal, both raised as Christians and steeped in classical German culture from childhood—were always conscious of their Jewish identity, which did *not* imply any interest in Judaism. Much of this identity, one must emphasize, was imposed from without: it was more a product of being perceived as a Jew by others than due to any spontaneous feeling of belonging to the community.[152] Rejecting the racial and essentialist notion of a "Jewish mind," Beller argued that the work of Jewish intellectuals and artists were characterized by two traditionally Jewish themes: the study of the Word and the exploration of issues relating to ethics and personal identity. The Jewish stress on religious learning fused easily with the German interest in self-cultivation *(Bildung)* through wide learning.[153] The preoccupation with ethics and individual identity, again, was Jewish but eminently compatible with German Protestant culture. Protestantism was a minority faith in Habsburg Vienna, but many Jewish intellectuals, when they converted to Christianity, chose Protestantism rather than the state religion of Catholicism.[154] This liberal-Jewish-Protestant individualism encouraged a preoccupation with inner truth and a Kantian conviction of moral autonomy. It was this ethical perspective that, according to Beller, generated the belief that aesthetics was secondary to ethics and derived from the latter.[155] This belief was expressed in its most famous form by Ludwig Wittgenstein: "Ethics and aesthetics are one."[156] An identical conviction, however, was shared by Karl Kraus, Otto Weininger, and Arnold Schoenberg.[157]

Politically, assimilated Jews were overwhelmingly liberal, although later generations often turned away from liberalism in reaction to the many failures of Viennese liberal politics in the late nineteenth century. The Jewish brand of liberalism, however, entailed an obligation to purge oneself of Jewishness and to become a complete human being, a full citizen, and a German. Emancipation from the ghetto, many Jewish liberal intellectuals argued, had to be followed by emancipation from Judaism.[158] One popular path toward that second emancipation was immersion in German literature, philosophy, and science. Jews, by and large, ignored the ostentatious Catholic culture unique to Austria: Rome was seen as the enemy of German *Bildung,* and Protestant Germany as the promised land of Kant and Goethe. The Habsburg monarchy received grudging Jewish support only because the Habsburgs were a German family.[159]

By the end of the century it was clear, however, that this assimilationist project had failed. The rapid rise in anti-Semitism and the simultaneous collapse of liberalism evoked diverse responses from Jewish intellectuals: the erstwhile assimilationist Theodor Herzl's move to Zionist separatism was only the most dramatic.[160] Most assimilated Jewish intellectuals, however, could not repudiate their affiliation with German culture, and the Zionist project was criticized by many of them, notably by Karl Kraus, as being opposed to the historical evolution of Jewish cosmopolitanism.[161] Even the most cosmopolitan Jews of the time, however, felt their world constrict and their identity villainized.[162] Increasingly, many retreated into the self, even if Ernst Mach had argued that the self was a fiction, and even if life had shown there was no free will. The Kantian autonomous self—the locus of moral freedom inaccessible to the world—was a myth one needed in order to live. For Arthur Schnitzler, it was artistic creativity that led inward; for Sigmund Freud, it was the elaboration of psychological theory; and for Otto Weininger, it was the philosophical validation (and cultural utilization) of Kant's concept of the intelligible self.

More than just the self, it was identity itself—and its breakdown—that preoccupied Jewish intellectuals. John Toews's observation on the Jewish characters of Schnitzler's novel, *Der Weg ins Freie* (The Road into the Open), is applicable to Viennese Jewish intellectuals at large: "The Jewish crisis is both exemplary of a general cultural crisis and an extreme form of that crisis. . . . The particular experience of the dilemmas of Jewish emancipation and cultural identification forces an articulation and thinking through of a general cultural crisis of subjective autonomy and communal identity. . . . It is the Jews who theorize, politically and philosophically . . . the ambivalence of 'freedom' in a world without anchors where all are strangers within their own homeland. . . . As outsiders within, as foreigners in their own country, as experiments in self-construction whose emancipation has left them bereft of all natural identities, the Jews articulate the fate of the human."[163]

For some, concerns with identity crystallized into a repugnance for their Jewish identity, a phenomenon described as "self-hatred" by Theodor Lessing in 1930.[164] Weininger occupied a prominent position in Lessing's analysis, and he has continued to do so in virtually every other study of the subject since then.[165] This labeling has been challenged by Allan Janik. Lessing, argued Janik, accused Weininger of self-hatred out of a racism that was much more pathological than Weininger's. Lessing saw Jewish identity as a matter of blood and condemned Weininger for denying that immutable, quasi-biological identity.[166] Now, a biological racist was one thing that Weininger indubitably was not.[167] In the absence of an immutable concept of race in his work, and given the lack of biographical data on Weininger's personal views on Jewishness, one cannot even say that Weininger, although born in a Jewish family, *"had a Jewish identity in the first place."*[168] If Weininger did not identify himself as Jewish to himself, then, contends Janik, one cannot reproach him with self-hatred at all. While I agree with Janik that concepts of self-hatred are often founded in quasi-biological conceptions of identity such as Lessing's, his argument that Weininger might not have identified himself as Jewish is problematic if only because Weininger declared that he was "of Jewish descent" in a footnote early in his chapter on Judaism (406) and that chapter, quite indubitably, identifies "Jewishness" as a cultural disease.

Nevertheless, it is also beyond dispute that the biologically well-informed Weininger was most emphatically not a biological racist. His concept of "Jewishness" and his opinions on it are surely revolting today, but it would be hard to portray Weininger as anything other than a cultural anti-Semite. Nor was this an eccentric position in his time and place. Apart from Richard Wagner and Houston Stewart Chamberlain, Karl Kraus depicted the Jew as greedy, dishonest, and sycophantic. In 1913, Kraus declared that he was "entirely free of all those characteristics of the Jews, which in the present state of affairs we may by common consent identify."[169] The crucial phrase here is "in the present state of affairs." Sigurd Paul Scheichl has shown how even Jewish socialists such as Victor Adler used anti-Semitic language against Jewish capitalists and the bourgeois press. Adler and his associates supported Dreyfus and Emile Zola, for instance, while denouncing Dreyfus's supporters among Jewish financiers and newspapermen.[170] Scheichl warns that unless we pay close attention to the context and nuances of anti-Semitic language, we run the risk of identifying Georg von Schönerer with Karl Kraus.[171] Prejudice, in short, came in different shapes in fin-de-siècle Vienna and caused different consequences: as late-twentieth-century liberals, we might condemn them all, but as historians, we are obliged to first determine their differences of origin, intention, and effect.

To sum up, any critic of modernity in fin-de-siècle Vienna might use anti-Semitic rhetoric because of the widespread identification of Jews with capitalism and other aspects of modernity. Rhetorical convergence with anti-Semitic politicians or street thugs did not *necessarily* indicate a convergence in goals. Kraus and Weininger, Scheichl has argued, acknowledged their own Jewish origins, were against the persecution of Jews, did not espouse biological theories of race, had Jewish friends, and frequently emphasized the nonpolitical nature of their critiques. Their projects, in the contexts of their time, were critical and, incredible as it may sound today, reformist. It is not a question of separating the good racists from the bad (if such a distinction were even possible) but rather of identifying the different intentions that underlay the anti-Semitism of different people in fin-de-siècle Vienna.

Weininger's racial context, in short, was that of a profound but diverse anti-Semitism. Much of this anti-Semitism was essentially cultural, and it followed the Wagner-Chamberlain line on Jews as the enemies of Germanic culture. This fundamental conviction, however, was expressed with different aims by different people. Socialist Victor Adler, Pan-German leader Georg von Schönerer, conservative satirist Karl Kraus, and philosopher Otto Weininger all used similar rhetoric but in different contexts and for different purposes. To say this is not to "disinfect" Kraus or Weininger but to identify their historical personae with greater specificity than would be possible with undifferentiated conceptions of anti-Semitism or self-hatred.

## CHAPTER THREE

# Man, Woman, Text: The Structure
## and Substance of *Geschlecht und Charakter*

The fundamental aim of *Geschlecht und Charakter*, simply stated, was to ana-lyze the biological, psychological, cultural, and ontological meanings of mas-culinity and femininity. The vastness and complexity of such a project, together with the acerbic personality of the author, were reflected only too clearly in the dense prose and convoluted arguments. The reader is further impeded by the many inconsistencies—of argument as well as presentation— between different sections of the book and the consignment of many sub-stantive points to the critical apparatus. The treatise would remain inexplica-ble if one approached it without an adequate understanding of its structure and style.

*Weininger's Woman: The Biology of Femininity*
Allan Janik has pointed out that the arguments of *Geschlecht und Charakter* in-corporate four reciprocally interactive "analytic moments": the biology of sexuality, an idiosyncratic version of neo-Kantian ethics, Nietzschean cul-tural criticism, and a Diltheyan psychology of "lived experience."[1]

The first "moment" is of far greater importance in *Geschlecht und Charakter* than scholars have usually appreciated: a very significant part of Weininger's quest for the meaning of sex was concerned with such issues as the biology of protozoa, the nature of cells, and psychiatric theories of hysteria. From the mid-nineteenth century, sexuality and gender had become medical concerns, and no serious researcher at the turn of the century could possibly ignore the enormous biomedical literature on the subject. Weininger went far beyond this minimal requirement, engaging at great depth with scientific theories of sex. His knowledge of the discourse of contemporary biomedical science was impressive, and his own text and theories were profoundly influenced by it. We should recall, moreover, that in his earliest days as a university student, Weininger approached the study of philosophy in a broadly positivistic way and enrolled in many scientific and medical courses. His initial aim in writing what became *Geschlecht und Charakter* was to help in reforming society by dis-seminating the scientific truth about sexuality and gender. Having begun the work with this aim, however, he abruptly lost faith in science and retreated into speculative philosophy. The later chapters of his work were sharply antipositivistic and so floridly speculative as to have seemed like a personal rhapsody to one of his doctoral examiners. What would probably always have seemed to be a difficult book thus became not merely complex but also disjointed and chaotic. Weininger himself appreciated the importance of this issue and, as we shall see, tried (largely in vain) to explain it logically.

Geschlecht und Charakter was divided into two parts. The first, "preparatory" section entitled "Sexual Diversity" had six short chapters amounting to less than one hundred pages. The second, "main" section called "The Sexual Types" comprised fourteen longer chapters sprawling over some four hundred pages.[2] While neither section was wholly devoted to any of Janik's specific "moments," the first section was predominantly concerned with biological aspects of sexuality and the second with its metaphysical analysis. In his preface, Weininger acknowledged the disjunction. Describing the two parts as, respectively, "biological-psychological" and "psychological-philosophical," he conceded it might have been more appropriate to have published them as two separate works: one purely scientific and the other metaphysical (ix). He argued, however, that he had to "free" himself of biology before he could become a pure psychologist (ix–x). The first part, where he had paid due homage to biology, should, he hoped, establish his scientific credentials with readers appalled by the speculative second part, in which he had shown how to liberate psychology from the clutches of biology (x). I demonstrate in subsequent chapters that Weininger used the discourse of science and medicine throughout his book and not just in the first part.[3] His own distinction between a "scientific" first part and a "metaphysical" second part does not apply to the content but rather to his rhetoric and style.

The first part of Geschlecht und Charakter consisted of short, temperately phrased chapters that began with facts or theories accepted by contemporary scientists. Original hypotheses were presented in relation to orthodox theories as suggestions, revisions, or potentially fruitful analogies. Each assertion in the text was backed by numerous references and copious endnotes. Wherever he disagreed with current scientific beliefs, Weininger tried to explain his reasons and cited others with similar views. Stylistically, most of the first part of Geschlecht und Charakter read no differently from monographs on sexual subjects by contemporary scientists and physicians, and the tone was respectful enough for a dissertation.

The first part dealt mainly with the biology of sex. Weininger conceived of Male and Female as mutually opposed ideal types that could never really exist. Physicists, he pointed out, spoke of completely elastic or inelastic bodies, although no empirical entity was ever completely elastic or completely lacking in elasticity. Such ideal types were fictions indispensable for the ordering of empirical reality. Individual men and women, for instance, could not be accurately ordered as "more" or "less" male or female unless compared with an ideal complete Man or Woman (10). But why should there be the need to categorize people as more male or more female? Is not every individual man male and each individual woman female? No, said Weininger, individual humans never belonged exclusively and totally to one sex but possessed elements of both sexes.

Virtually every nineteenth-century biologist would have agreed with him. By 1900, the biological boundaries between the sexes had been shown to be shifting, indistinct, and fluid. There were no fundamental biological differences that separated *all* men from *all* women (6). Anatomically, innumerable men possessed such "feminine" traits as a wide pelvis or full breasts; "masculine" women with facial hair or a narrow pelvis were equally common. Moreover, as embryologists knew, all human embryos developed into males or females from an initial, sexually undifferentiated condition (7). Every individual, then, was both male and female, albeit to varying degrees. There was no absolute male or absolute female in nature: all organisms were situated on a spectrum extending between these two imaginary poles. Some were closer to one pole and some to the other, but all were intermediate between the two. This "principle of sexual intermediacy" or "bisexuality" was well known to contemporary physicians and scientists, who used it to explain phenomena ranging from hermaphroditism to homosexuality.

What was, however, original to Weininger was his speculative notion that the organism was constructed of two basic components: a male plasma and a female one. Each *cell*, according to Weininger, was part male and part female, with the *degree* of masculinity or femininity differing among cells and cell-groups. Thus, an otherwise virile man could have a scant growth of beard because the cells of his facial region were more feminine than those of the rest of his body. Sexual intermediacy was not just an overall feature of the individual: it was inherent in the building blocks of the organism. Returning then to the organismal level, Weininger explained mating by a mathematical law that depended on the degrees of masculinity and femininity of the partners. He illustrated his "Law" with male homosexuality. According to many prominent physicians and activists of the era, a homosexual orientation was neither a disease nor a vice but a prime example of sexual intermediacy. A homosexual male was simply more female than the average male—hence he could mate successfully only with another, more masculine male. Weininger accepted and refined this idea, while rejecting its pathological undertones.

He then turned to the possibility of applying the principle of sexual intermediacy to the study of human character. Physical sexual intermediacy, he argued, was reflected in the psycho-behavioral realm: morphology and psychology should ideally be twin sciences (71). It was not enough, he warned, to classify somebody as more feminine or more masculine; one must also assess the exact degree of masculinity and femininity in an individual and, finally, determine whether each specific deed or thought stemmed from the male or the female element of that individual. Such an approach, Weininger argued, would "individualize" each human being, providing a basis for the study of individual psychological differences or "differential psychology" (62–63, 499).[4] Pedagogy would be transformed in the light of differential psychology: to educate all boys in one uniform way and all girls in another was senseless because all boys were not equally masculine, nor all girls equally feminine. The rigidity of pedagogical assumptions could be eliminated only by acknowledging the differential psychology of individual students and by catering to their particular abilities and inclinations (69–70).[5] Weininger then added that the male and female elements of a person's character were not necessarily active at the same time. It was more likely, he asserted, that human beings oscillated between the male and female poles of their personality. The degree of this oscillation differed between individuals and might be regular or irregular: a man, for example, might feel "more male" every evening, which would indicate a small regular oscillation. It followed, therefore, that the inherent sexual duality of humans might be evident only in chronological succession, rather than simultaneously. The changes might be regular or irregular and the amplitude of oscillation toward one sex greater than the amplitude of oscillation toward the other (64–65). Weininger thus transformed sexual intermediacy from a static, morphological phenomenon into a potentially periodic event.[6] Surprisingly, however, he did not return to this concept in later sections of his book.

In the final chapter of the first part, Weininger turned to the raison d'etre of his book: the Woman Question. While Weininger's views on the subject eventually turned out to be quite exceptionally dramatic, this particular chapter differed little from the standard response of contemporary intellectuals and scientists to feminist demands for equal rights.[7] Weininger himself remarked that his analysis, although completely independent, was very similar to that of a pseudonymous contributor to a well-known medical publication concerned with homosexual emancipation and other aspects of sexual politics.[8]

Weininger defined emancipation as equality of spiritual and moral freedom between men and women (80). A woman's desire for such freedom and her capacity to handle it responsibly were grounded, he declared, in her masculine element. The feminine element had neither the need for this inner freedom nor the ability to use it. All contemporary feminists as well as all truly talented women across the ages displayed numerous traits that were either anatomically masculine or features of psychological masculinity, i.e. homosexual orientation: Sappho, Catherine II of Russia, Queen Christina of Sweden, and George Sand (80–82). What, however, of heterosexual women who desired emancipation? Here, too, there was unmistakable, albeit more subtle, evidence that Weininger's equation of masculinity and talent was "no caprice, no egotistical wish of a man to associate all the higher manifestations of intelligence with the male sex" (82). Heterosexual women of talent were drawn invariably, Weininger declared, to effeminate men. Mme. de Staël, author of "perhaps the most significant book ever written by a woman," was probably involved with the homosexual August Wilhelm Schlegel; Clara Schumann married Robert, whose music was effeminate and who, at certain periods of his life, looked more like a woman than a man; and George Eliot had "a broad, massive forehead" and her movements "lacked all womanly grace" (82–83). All historical evidence, in short, supported the popular belief that the longer the hair, the smaller the intellect ( *Je länger das Haar, desto kürzer der Verstand,* 84).

Weininger's proposed solution to the Woman Question was simple. Women whose genuine psychic and biological needs, frequently reflected in their physical attributes, drove them toward masculine occupations should not be prevented from pursuing their goals (87). Full equality with men, however, was impossible: even the most gifted woman, he explained, was only a little more than fifty percent masculine and owed her achievements to this small excess over other women. Neglecting to disclose how he calculated this figure, he asserted that this modest additional amount of masculinity could not ensure the full equality of a talented woman with even the average man, who, despite being sexually intermediate, possessed a much stronger masculine element (88). Not one woman in history, he announced, could equal even a fifth-rate male genius (85).

Woman's lack of creativity, Weininger emphasized, could not be blamed on any lack of social autonomy. Emancipated women had appeared in all ages, albeit not in equal numbers.[9] Demands for women's emancipation had been prominent during the tenth, fifteenth, sixteenth, nineteenth, and twentieth centuries (90). This was not just Weininger's own conviction: he quoted an expert on genealogy who had pointed out in 1898 that feminism did not flourish in ages that regarded masculine women as unattractive.[10] Weininger expanded this suggestion into the argument that movements for women's emancipation were brought about by the birth of excessively masculine females or effeminate males during particular periods (90).[11] He found scientific evidence for such sexual variations in Charles Darwin's observation that older or sick female birds were masculinized more frequently during certain years than during others (504).[12] His own era, Weininger claimed, was one of virilized women and feminized men. Denouncing the "Secessionist" taste for tall, slender women with flat breasts and narrow hips, he expostulated about the "monstrous increase" of fops *(Stutzertum)* and homosexuals in recent years. All this established the "greater femininity" *(grösseren Weiblichkeit)* of the epoch (91). Challenging the conventional belief that evolutionary progress led to the greater differentiation of sexes, Weininger quoted biologist August Weismann's observation that sexual differentiation was greatest in lower species of animals rather than among humans.[13] There was, then, no reason to believe that the human sexes were programmed to move further apart with time. Periods of lesser differentiation between males and females might well alternate with periods of greater sexual differentiation, when men were biologically more masculine and women more feminine. With the coming of those latter times, feminism would be negated and true femininity, antithetical to the idea of emancipation, would assume its proper, servile position (93). Some of these beliefs were somewhat novel at the time, but they were not at all extreme or unbalanced in comparison to contemporary discourse on the Woman Question.

Within a few pages following this chapter, however, the tenor of the argument changed quite radically. The second part of *Geschlecht und Charakter,* entitled "The Sexual Types," commenced with a "restriction" of the biological principle of sexual intermediacy. In spite of biological intermediacy, Weininger now announced, every human being, *psychologically,* was either male or female, at least at one and the same time (97–98). After arguing in the first part that no individual was ever exclusively masculine or feminine, and that morphology and psychology were interrelated sciences, Weininger seemed to contradict himself with this unqualified assumption of psychological monosexuality, which would be fundamental to the second part of *Geschlecht und Charakter.* This would, in fact, have been the logical place to emphasize his earlier notion that sexually intermediate forms need not be male and female at the same time; they could periodically oscillate between the two. Weininger did not, however, do so, and the transition between the two parts of his book remained its logically weakest—and culturally most revealing—point.

Conventionally, said Weininger, all apparent mental and behavioral differences between the two sexes were attributed to the greater intensity of the male sexual drive. Questioning whether mental attributes depended upon the strength of the sex drive, he challenged the view that women had a weaker sex drive than men.[14] The crucial difference between men and women resided, in his view, in the relationship between the component instincts of their sexual urges (109). The sexologist Albert Moll had suggested that the sex drive was divisible into two component impulses: the primary component

was the urge to "cause a physical change in the genitals"—in the male, to ejaculate. Although human females did not ejaculate, Moll had stressed that they,
too, experienced the need to "relieve the tension of the sexual organs." Moll
had named this the impulse of detumescence *(Detumescenztrieb)*. The second
major component of the sex drive was the impulse to "approach, touch, and
kiss" another person, which Moll had termed the impulse of contrectation
*(Kontrektationstrieb)*.[15]

Weininger accepted this scheme, asserting that Man possessed both drives,
while Woman lacked the detumescence drive (109). He cited Moll and the
gynecologists Rudolf Chrobak and A. von Rosthorn to this effect, ignoring
that Moll had expressed the opposite view on the very page he cited (508).[16]
In Weininger's scheme, then, Woman possessed only the contrectation drive,
and that in a very passive form: she only desired to be touched.[17] In Man,
however, the contrectation drive was active and more visible, reflected in the
motile spermatozoa's journey to the passive and stationary ovum. Woman's
contrectation drive, although less visible because of its passivity, was, however, tremendously intense (110–11). Women, for instance, did not mastur-
bate to satisfy the impulse of detumescence but to induce, intensify, and
prolong the state of sexual stimulation *(Erregtheit)*, which represented the
highest point of female existence. Woman was completely sexual—this
would be the central theme and fundamental contention of the second part of
*Geschlecht und Charakter*—whereas Man was sexual as well as asexual, interested in a diverse range of activities including war and play, scholarship and
discussion, politics, religion, and art (112).[18] This difference was mirrored by
morphology. Men had fewer and more sharply localized sexually sensitive
zones, whereas women's bodies were diffusely erogenous (114–15). Charles
Darwin had observed that female animals "seldom offer remarkable secondary sexual characters" (508).[19] In an astonishing conceptual leap, Weininger inferred from Darwin's statement that females must, therefore, be
sexual throughout! Extrapolating to the human female, Weininger closed
this section with one of his most frequently quoted aphorisms: "Man possesses the penis, but the vagina possesses the Woman" *(Der Mann hat den Penis, aber die Vagina hat die Frau*, 116).

*From Woman to Man: The Dialectic of Masculinity and Femininity*
The next seven chapters of *Geschlecht und Charakter* addressed lofty themes of
no obvious relevance to gender: logic, ethics, genius, and the self. This cluster
of chapters, however, played an important role in the overall scheme of the
treatise. Since so much of the text concentrated on defining and evaluating
femininity, it would be easy to overlook that it did not neglect the complementary task: the construction of the ideal Man. It was in these seven arcane

chapters that Weininger unveiled his conception of masculinity, while relating it constantly and dialectically to his theory of femininity. Weininger's
Woman was constructed largely in biomedical terms, whereas his ideal-
typical Man was a psychological and philosophical construct. In his analysis
of masculinity, Weininger moved sharply away from biomedical discourse,
turning instead to the philosophy of Kant, and he framed his Kantian image
of Man within a biting critique of contemporary "soul-less" psychology. As
Christine Buci-Glucksmann has remarked, "Weininger called for a 'return to
Kant,' via the neo-Kantianism of his times and various Platonist meditations—a return to the theoretically and existentially neuralgic point of the
ego, of self-identity. Weininger, then, sought to reconstruct a logic and ethic
of identity, a new variant of a metaphysics of the ego centered on a veritable
ontology of the masculine. Between Being and Nothingness lay an ontologically grounded inequality of the sexes."[20]

Woman, Weininger claimed, was capable only of feeling and could not differentiate between feeling and thought.[21] Females had vague and unformed
thoughts, which Weininger called "henids."[22] Acknowledging that every
thought, whether in males or in females, began in "a kind of half-thought, a
condition in which vague geometrical figures, visual phantasms, nebulous
images hover in the mind," Weininger emphasized that in Man such "proto-
thoughts" underwent clarification and refinement but that they remained
eternally nebulous in Woman (122).[23] Males and females possessed the same
psychic material, but in Woman thought remained indistinguishable from
feeling.[24] The male's clear thought was a sexual attribute: most women
wished to marry men who were cleverer *(gescheiter)* than they and were sexually repelled by men who thought and expressed themselves formlessly (129).

Without deigning to disclose the facts justifying such conceptions of
female sexual choice, Weininger proceeded to a meandering discussion of genius. Arguably the most abstruse section of *Geschlecht und Charakter*, it was
nonetheless indispensable to the text's project of constructing the ideal-
typical absolute male. The principles of logic, the nature of genius, and Kantian ethics were all integral to Weininger's model of Man. For Weininger, the
man of genius had "incomparably greater understanding of other beings than
the average man."[25] Neither the "man of deeds" nor the great scientist but
only the great artist or philosopher could be called a genius.[26] Men of action
created nothing that survived for eternity, and even the modern scientist, unless he was also a philosopher, was not a universal thinker. "The ideal of an
artistic genius is to live in all men, to lose himself in all men, to reveal himself
in multitudes; and so also the aim of the philosopher is to discover all others
in himself, to fuse them into a unit which is his own unit" (178–79).[27]

The supreme exemplar of such a genius was, of course, Goethe, who,

Weininger remarked, even understood the mind of criminals and the nature and motivations of every form of crime (135). Genius consisted, first and foremost, in the union of innumerable contrasts and types within one individual: the genius was supremely conscious and infinitely sensible. His thought, then, was at the farthest remove from henids. Since henids were typically feminine, genius was perfected masculinity *(eine ideale, potenzierte Männlichkeit)*. Femininity and genius, therefore, were antithetical: females could never aspire to the transcendent clarity and totally conscious existence of the genius (141, 144). Switching to his cultural-critical mode, Weininger lamented:

> It is only too obvious that an era that sees its essence expressed best in vague and dubious words, an era whose philosophy, in more than one sense, has become the Unconscious, cannot have a single truly great man. For Greatness consists of Consciousness, which disperses the Unconscious as the sun dissolves a mist. (150)[28]

The elevated consciousness of the genius, said Weininger, implied perfect memory. The genius could remember "his entire past, everything that he has ever thought or heard, seen or done, perceived or felt."[29] "Universal remembrance" did not imply the recollection of all that the person had learned in life; it applied only to what he had actually experienced (145-46).[30] These memories were not stored discretely in the psyche: all of them were "in some mysterious way one great whole" (157). Such continuity was rare in most people, but Woman lacked it completely: when she looked back on her life, a woman recollected only a few isolated moments related to her sexual experiences—memories of paramours, of her wedding night, of poems written to her by men (158).[31]

Not even the most complete male, of course, could possibly remember all his experiences; nor could he forget them all. There were, then, different degrees of genius and "no male is quite without a trace of genius" (147). To recapitulate Weininger's argument, females thought in henids and therefore did not really have memories; all males had clearer consciousness and better memory than any female; memory was the sine qua non of genius; hence, all males possessed some genius. Whatever might be the logician's verdict on this argument, there is no denying its importance in Weininger's model of masculinity.

Having argued that memory was intimately related to genius, Weininger claimed that memory was also the basis of logical and ethical thought. He rejected a theory of memory going back to the eighteenth-century scientist Charles Bonnet (1720–93), which had been revived in the late nineteenth century by Ernst Mach and physiologist Ewald Hering. It argued that human memory was a special instance of the universal quality of all organized matter, whereby reactions to new stimuli occurred more slowly than reactions to familiar stimuli.[32] But human memory, Weininger protested, was not comparable to a reflex; in it, the past was actually reproduced with all its individual qualities. Nor was Weininger satisfied with the associationist theory that explained memory by the formation of "mechanical" links between ideas and representations *(Vorstellungsverknüpfungen)*. Such a view, Weininger argued, overlooked the fact that memory was fundamentally a function of the will: "I can remember something when I actually wish to" (184–85). It was the will that activated chains of associations: the process was in no way mechanical.[33]

Memory, then, was a higher, specifically human function, related closely to "mankind's most peculiar qualities": logic and ethics. Liars had proverbially bad memories—male liars, Weininger averred, were uncommon while females were legendary for their mendacity. "It is evident that a being whose memory is very slight, and who can recall only in the most imperfect fashion what it has said or done, or suffered, must lie easily if it has the gift of speech" (187). Because of her inadequate memory, the absolute female possessed no sense of her identity at different stages of life. She could not, strictly speaking, remember the entity A for long enough to appreciate that it was still A after the passage of a moment. She could not, therefore, decide on the truth or falsity of the proposition $A = A$, thus failing to satisfy the fundamental requirement of logical thought: ability to discern identity and its contradiction (191). Logic was, at best, a means for Woman, rather than the criterion of all thought. Woman, Weininger declared, suffered from "logical insanity" (192). Man's life, on the other hand, was sequential, logical, and ordered in accordance with the laws of cause and effect (188–89).

Moving on to ethics, Weininger asserted that "the source of all error in life is failure of memory." Memory was indissolubly linked with morality because repentance was impossible without memory. A being without memory lied of necessity. This mendacity was not immoral, since there could be no immorality in the absence of a standard of truth. Woman lied because she lacked memory: she was, therefore, not immoral but simply amoral (193–94).[34] Yet, the continuous memory that enables Man to be truthful and logical did not directly engender the desire and need for truth. The latter came from a deeper source that was absolutely unchangeable and independent of time (194–95).

Kant had declared that human morality originated in the intelligible self, the existence of which could be philosophically deduced but never empirically verified.[35] Weininger agreed with his master that this intelligible self was independent of space, time, and ordinary causal laws. It could not be investigated by scientific methods (195). The Kantian concept of the intelligible self was pivotal to Weininger's analysis of masculinity and femininity. His exposition of Kant's concept, however, was not simply a philosophical translation of his views on gender but also provided a foundation for his deeply-felt critique of empirical psychology, in particular of newer psychological opinions on the nature of the self.

David Hume had argued that the human self was not unitary but a mere "bundle" of constantly shifting sensations and perceptions (197).[36] More recently, Ernst Mach had proffered the same theory, claiming that the ego or the self was a fiction beyond salvage.[37] It was astonishing, Weininger exclaimed, that a man of Mach's erudition and intelligence could overlook the fact that every organic being was an indivisible monad, different from other monads. The primary difference between the living and the nonliving, in fact, was that living beings were individuals distinct from one another. The human ego, Weininger asserted, was not "simply a waiting-hall for perceptions" (*blosse Wartesaal für Empfindungen*, 198–99). Human individuality was determined by the "intelligible character" of humans, which could not be demonstrated but only deduced philosophically. The intelligible self was noumenal in Kantian terms: it was a "thing in itself," as opposed to the empirical self, which was phenomenal and scientifically demonstrable. The reasons for believing in such an undemonstrable entity as the intelligible self were logical and ethical (199). In logic, the proposition $A = A$ was self-evident and axiomatic, and that simple axiom was the basis of all distinctions between truth and error. To say $A = A$, however, was to posit something that remained constant against a shifting backdrop of changing and swirling perceptions. This permanence of the concept could be asserted only by "something" that was equally constant. To say $A = A$, therefore, was to say "I am" (204). "Were I part of the stream of change," Weininger argued, "I could not recognize that A had remained unchanged." This permanent "something," immune to change and experience and temporality, was Kant's noumenal, intelligible self (205).[38] It followed, therefore, that human beings were fully human only when they were completely logical (205).

The intelligible self was equally essential to ethics. All errors were sins. It was the duty of human beings to seek truth: logic and ethics, therefore, were among the duties of the empirical ego toward the intelligible self (205–206). Logic and ethics, in fact, were fundamentally one and the same: "All of ethics is conceivable only along logical lines, and all of logic constitutes an ethical law. Not only virtue, but also insight, not only sanctity but also wisdom, are the duties and tasks of human beings: through the union of the two alone comes perfection" (207).

Weininger then returned to the relationship of the intelligible self to genius. All great men, Weininger stated, had been convinced of possessing "an ego in the higher sense" (*ein Ich im höheren Sinne*, 214). What, however, was the nature of the genius's ego? The "absolute genius," if he could exist in reality, would be related in vivid, intimate, and immediate terms with every entity in the universe. Universal comprehension required that the comprehender possess similar qualities in himself. The absolute genius, therefore, would be nothing less than the "living microcosm" (*der lebendige Mikrokosmus*), with his own ego at the center of that microcosm (219–20).[39] This microcosmic psyche, Weininger warned, was not analogous to a mosaic or to a chemical compound. The genius formed connections intuitively: his psyche was not constructed from isolated fragments (220). While the scientist or the scholar added pieces of knowledge to other pieces without ever forming them into a whole, the genius held "chaos and cosmos, details and totality, all plurality and all singularity in his own inner self," representing "the divine element in man" (222).

Later, Weininger transcribed a long passage from the Renaissance humanist Giovanni Pico della Mirandola's *Oration on the Dignity of Man* (237–38).[40] Pico (1463–94) had emphasized that "man is the only creature whose life is determined not by nature but by his own free choice; and thus man no longer occupies a fixed though distinguished place in the hierarchy of being but exists outside this hierarchy as a kind of separate world."[41] In the passage quoted in its entirety by Weininger, Pico says:

> On man when he came into life the Father conferred the seeds of all kinds and the germs of every way of life. Whatever seeds each man cultivates will grow to maturity and bear in him their own fruit. If they be vegetative, he will be like a plant. If sensitive, he will become brutish. If rational, he will grow into a heavenly being. If intellectual, he will be an angel and son of God. And if, happy in the lot of no created thing, he withdraws into the center of his own unity, his spirit, made one with God, . . . shall surpass them all.[42]

Weininger used spaced type (*Sperrdruck*) to highlight the last sentence of the quotation, indicating the similarity between Pico's unified man and his own "absolute genius." But, Weininger added, it was not only the fictitious absolute genius who could aspire to universality. Even the ordinary man could attain some genius by cultivating his inner self since all human beings had the potential to embrace the universe in their souls. Lamenting contemporary neglect of the Renaissance notion of the microcosmic soul, Weininger asserted that "all humans have genius, and no human is a genius. . . . The genius is completely human; the humanity that is latent in all is fully developed in the genius" (223–24). Not only was it possible for an ordinary man to attain genius, "it is every one's duty" to attain it (236).

To attain genius, therefore, was an ethical duty. What, however, of the morality of the genius? Ideas that great men are naturally evil, Weininger claimed, were false (235–36). Since the genius was the true universal spirit, he was always interested in his fellows, suffered with them, and already had them, as it were, in his own microcosmic self (229–32). The genius could not kill—neither himself nor anybody else—since he knew that to kill himself was to kill the universe—an intriguing statement in the light of Weininger's own suicide—and to kill another was to kill himself in the victim (233). Nor could the genius ever commit the Kantian crime of using other people as means to a goal. The genius respected individuality, considered others as ends in themselves (230), and regarded I and Thou as indissolubly linked entities (233).

Now, since all logical thought and ethical behavior originated in the intelligible ego, Weininger continued, it followed that a consistently unethical or illogical being did not possess an intelligible self. Since Woman was such an amoral and alogical being, he triumphantly concluded that she did not possess an intelligible self (239–40).[43] What, however, of individual women? The sexually intermediate nature of individuals notwithstanding, most individual women, Weininger asserted, resembled the absolute female very closely (241).[44] Men, on the contrary, were distinct individuals and did not necessarily embody every attribute of the absolute male. The absolute male possessed everything, including the potential for femininity: the individual man chose to develop one or more of these qualities. If he chose the lowest traits, the individual male could easily reach the nadir of humanity, which, according to Weininger, explained the existence of feminine men. While the male type could acquire the attributes of the female type, the reverse possibility did not exist. "The woman," Weininger asserted, "could never become a man" (*Aber die Frau kann nie zum Manne werden*, 241).

The impossibility of woman becoming man represented the most important qualification of the notion of universal sexual intermediacy. Weininger's anecdotal, confusing argument for this conviction deserves to be quoted in full:

> I know a large number of men who are psychologically almost completely female. . . . I even know many women with masculine traits but not one woman who is not fundamentally female, even when this femininity is hidden by various means not just from others but also from the person herself. One is either man or woman, however many features of both sexes one might possess, and this "Being" *(Sein)* . . . is determined by one's relationship with ethics and logic. While there are individuals who are anatomically men but psychologically women, there is no individual who is physically a woman but psychologically a man, regardless of external masculine traits. (242)

Now armed with complete ideal types of the sexes, Weininger returned to his critique of psychology. The psychology of Woman, he stated, could be represented in purely empirical terms but not that of Man (269). "Scientific psychology" was deterministic, with no room for free will and free thought

(271). Hume and Mach had banned the psyche from psychology, leaving only "impressions," and modern psychology proudly described itself as "psychology without a soul" (269).[45] In Weininger's terms, therefore, it was "an eminently feminine [eminent weibliche] psychology" (270). It was good enough, no doubt, for studying the female mind, which was fragmented, incoherent, and intimately linked with the body.[46] The psychology of Man, however, was utterly impregnable to the new psychology. Man was the free, intelligible subject: his psyche was unanalyzable, irreducible, and independent of his body (278).

Experimental psychology, Weininger declared, had failed to discover anything conclusive about the deeper levels of masculine thought. Its greatest failure, however, was methodological: it attempted to reach the depths of the psyche by examining superficial attributes and responses (270). But each of those empirical phenomena depended upon such empirically unverifiable attributes as the will and judgment (271–72). If one did not proceed beyond the facts of experience, one was left either with the atomism of sensations and the laws of association or one had to convert psychology into "an annex of physiology and biology" (272). Both of these approaches to psychology negated the psyche by trying to derive it from its parts. But, Weininger concluded with a flourish, the concept of the psyche as a unitary whole negated, in turn, modern psychology itself (273).

### Love, Gender, and Morality

Given the unbridgeable intellectual and moral gulf between the two sexes, how could men love women? Weininger used a whole chapter to answer this question, arguing, essentially, that erotic relations between human beings were radically different from the pure sexual attraction one saw among animals: human eroticism was fundamentally and qualitatively different from sexual attraction.[47] In abstract terms, love was, in fact, antithetical to the desire for coitus, although in real life no love was ever entirely free of sexual desire. That did not, however, mean that the two were identical. Hope and fear, too, occurred simultaneously and were often intertwined, but they were not for that reason considered to be the same (315–17). Sexual attraction increased with physical proximity, whereas love was "strongest in the absence of the beloved." Also, the woman merely desired by a man (particularly a great man) was often completely different physically and mentally from the woman he loved (317–18). Professors of psychiatry, Weininger allowed, might scoff at the idea of "platonic love" but, for him, that was the only love there was. Sexual desire was symbolized by the Whore of Babylon, whereas true love was the worship of the Madonna, symbolized by Dante's love for Beatrice.

But could soulless Woman ever be the true object of this metaphysical love? How was such a low creature converted in the mind of the smitten man into the pure and beautiful Madonna? (318). Addressing physical beauty first, Weininger asserted that the naked female body was far from beautiful: it looked "unfinished" *(Unfertigem),* and this was incompatible with beauty (319). The female genitals, he added, were particularly ugly (320). The female body seemed beautiful only when love was projected on to it, just as all hatefulness in an object was a projection of hate from the subject. Feminine beauty, then, was a creation of male love: the two, in essence, were identical (321). This process of projection did not create beauty alone but also morality. The moral qualities a man saw in his beloved emanated, in fact, from the man himself. "In all love Man loves only himself": not the weak and limited being he actually is, but the man he "wants to be and ought to be, his truest, deepest intelligible essence, free from all fetters of necessity, and from all taints of earth" (322). In love, man found his higher self; many men realized they possessed a soul only when they experienced love (323). Like art, love created form out of chaos (324–25).

Being a projective phenomenon, love could never be a relationship of equals. Obviously, too, it was an exclusively masculine emotion (325). The absolute female was incapable of love; she experienced sexual attraction alone (336–37).[48] Later, Weininger devoted an entire chapter to the thesis that there were only two fundamental types of woman: the Mother and the Prostitute. Both were completely sexual, the Mother in the reproductive domain and the Prostitute in the purely physical arena. Love for either type of woman was a masculine illusion: "It is a supremely heroic effort to find worth and value where there is none." A man's love for a woman was nothing but self-projection and necessarily doomed to failure (327).

Although fundamentally different, love as well as pure concupiscence entailed using women as means to an end. The sexual use of women, of course, was too well known to need much explanation. But how could the purest, most devoted love be seen as equally exploitative? Lovers, argued Weininger, used women to create "value" *(Wert),* and the artist used them to produce "children of the soul" (330). As soon as a man fell in love with a woman, he ceased to understand her. Since understanding was the sole moral basis for associating with another individual, falling in love with a woman was fundamentally as immoral as using her to gratify one's lust or as a means to produce children of the flesh (330, 332). In Weininger's Kantian universe, it was always wrong to use individuals as means, no matter how noble the end: "The sexual impulse negates the body, and the erotic impulse the mind of the female" (332). Love, apart from being unethical, was illogical since it could arise only on the basis of a denial of the objective nature of the woman (333). Madonna worship could be beautiful, as with Dante, but never logical or moral (334).

*The Ontological (In)Significance of Woman*

"The deeper we have delved in our foregoing analysis of Woman's claim to esteem," Weininger declared, "the more we have had to deny her of what is lofty
and noble, great and beautiful" (342). Nevertheless, he emphasized, he did
not wish to advocate an "Asiatic" oppression of women. He supported the *legal* equality of men and women, but could not countenance any demand for
intellectual and moral parity. The latter was impossible because the most de-
graded man still had something ineffable in him that raised him morally and
intellectually above the noblest woman (342). Medical writers on the
Woman Question such as Paul Julius Möbius had been wrong, Weininger asserted, to consider the average woman as "physiologically weak-minded" and
the extraordinary woman as degenerate. Women with talent should be regarded as the reverse of degenerate: they were at least partly masculine, and
therefore, had taken at least one step beyond lowly, amoral femininity. As for
"physiological weak-mindedness," Woman was neither strong-minded nor
weak-minded: she was simply mindless *(un-sinnig)*, although she could be
far more cunning and calculating than Man (343–44). What, then, was the
real nature of Woman and her ontological significance?

Identifying "match-making," of all things, as an invariable propensity
among women, Weininger argued that this indicated Woman's constant preoccupation with sexuality—not simply with her own sexual urges but with
sexuality in general, and in the most physical sense. "The transcendental
function of Woman" was to bring about the physical union of male and female
(351). How, then, had women veiled their true nature, acquiring such a pure
and saintly image across history? Woman had been able to hide her true nature because she was so completely passive and so impressionable: she acquired and acted out male ideas of female purity. Emphasizing that this
camouflage was unconscious, Weininger embarked upon a fascinating analysis of hysteria (352–54). Basically a radical reinterpretation of Sigmund
Freud and Josef Breuer's theory of hysteria, Weininger's analysis was of fundamental importance to his argument on woman's status. Hysteria, according
to Weininger, demonstrated that Woman comprised an inner, completely
sexual self, and an outer "false self" constructed in unconscious response to
male expectations. The "real self" of Woman was nothing more than pure,
undifferentiated sexuality. It could not have any ontological weight since this
sexuality was not linked with individual men: female sexuality was a simple,
supraindividual craving for coitus, not a desire for union with a specific man.
Woman could not comprehend the individuality of a man; she could only
comprehend masculinity (397).

Ontologically, the relationship between Man and Woman was the Aristotelian one of form and matter. Woman was pure, unindividualized matter,

on which Man conferred form. The sole reason why it was proper to ac-knowledge women as human beings (as opposed to animals or plants) was because they complemented men (390). To be formed by Man was Woman's sole destiny and greatest fulfillment (391–96). Man, built in the image of God, represented Being, whereas Woman—including the feminine element in a male—was the symbol of Nothing (*das Symbol des Nichts*, 398). The fear of Woman was the deepest fear in Man: she represented nullity and total ab-sence of significance (*Sinnlosigkeit*, 399).

This absolute lack of significance, according to Weininger, was the cosmic significance of Woman. She represented the polar opposite of Godhood *(den Gegenpol der Gottheit)* while Godhood was the proper goal for Man. Conse-quently, there was nothing so contemptible as the feminized man (398). Woman existed due to Man's immoral affirmation of his own sexuality and his denial of the Absolute in him. It was male sexuality that created and gave meaning to Woman: "Woman is the sin of man" (401). In order to ensure her existence and significance, therefore, Woman encouraged Man to be sexual. Woman, in a very real sense, *was* sexuality: if sexuality could be transcended, femininity itself would disappear.

### Gender and Jewish Identity

Having finished with love, Weininger turned abruptly to an examination of Judaism. His anti-Semitism has sometimes been seen, in his time as well as in ours, as the predominant or even the fundamental theme of *Geschlecht und Charakter*. Actually, however, Weininger's discussion of Jewishness was sub-sidiary to and closely entwined with his analysis of femininity, a relationship that was far from uncommon at the time. Jacques Le Rider, for instance, pointed out that Rabbi Adolf Jellinek provided a "feminized" description of Jewish traits, and that a dual antipathy toward Jews and women marked the work of Arthur Schopenhauer and D. H. Lawrence. The connection, how-ever, was drawn most forcefully in *Geschlecht und Charakter*.[49]

Weininger's discussion of "Jewishness" commenced with a problem related to gender: why did certain races approach the transcendent qualities of his ideal male type only very rarely? It was unlikely, after all, that all males be-longing to those races were biologically closer to the absolute female (404). The "psychical peculiarity of the Jewish race" posed a particularly intriguing problem (405). He was not concerned, Weininger clarified, with the racial origins or the physical anthropology of Jews, adding in a footnote that he himself was of Jewish descent. He defined Jewishness "only as a psychical ten-dency or constitution, which is a possibility for *all* humans but had reached its fullest expression among the Jewish people" (406). Many racial Aryans, he ar-gued, were psychologically more Jewish than many ethnic Jews, and many of the latter were mentally more Aryan than some of the former (407). His concern, he explained, was with all humans who, regardless of their racial origin, expressed in themselves "the platonic idea of Jewishness" (409).[50]

Later, after several vitriolic pages on this "platonic idea," Weininger emphasized that in spite of his low opinion on Jewishness, he was wholly opposed to "any practical or theoretical persecution of Jews" (417–18), an attitude that complemented his stance on women. It was, in fact, anti-Semitism that, he contended, proved that Jewishness was not confined to the Jewish race. The true Aryan was seldom an anti-Semite, even though he might be repelled by aspects of Jewish culture. Those Aryans who often wrote philo-Semitic tracts were nevertheless the very people who understood Jews the least. The aggressive anti-Semites, on the other hand, frequently possessed Jewish traits themselves. Emile Zola, says Weininger, was a typical philo-Semite. All geniuses in history, however, had been anti-Semites, because, being microcosmic, they possessed all traits, including Jewish ones.[51] People hated in others what they hated in themselves: "Whoever detests the Jewish disposition detests it first of all in himself" (406–407).

What, however, was the Jewish disposition? Here is Weininger's own definition: "The Jewish race *[Judentum]* is pervasively feminine. This femininity comprises those qualities that I have shown to be in total opposition to masculinity. The Jews are much more feminine than Aryans . . . and the manliest Jew may be taken for a female" (409). Although Weininger was unwilling to argue for the complete identification of the Jew with Woman, he argued that the two ideal types shared many attributes. Neither, for instance, understood the notion of personal property and both showed a marked preference for communism—not, however, for socialism, which Weininger identified as Aryan! (410).[52] Zionism, Weininger conceded somewhat unpredictably, had expressed some of the noblest qualities of Jews but it was an impossible dream. Jewishness necessarily implied the dispersion of Jews all over the world. The Jew could not grasp the idea of the state: as deficient in personality as females, Jews could not associate as free and equal individuals within a larger whole. "Citizenship is an un-Jewish thing," and Zionism, therefore, was a negation of Jewishness itself (411). "To be capable of Zionism," Weininger declared, "Jews must first overcome Jewishness." Each Jew must fight relentlessly against his own Jewishness, and, once that inner battle had been won, he earned the right to be considered by Aryans as an individual and not as the member of a certain race (418–19). Jesus, according to Weininger, evolved Christianity—which was the complete negation of Judaism—by overcoming the Jew within himself (439). Christ was "the greatest man because he conquered the greatest enemy" (440).

Weininger surrounded these lofty statements with a banal set of anti-

Semitic clichés. Examples: Jewish men were avid match-makers, and this was "the strongest similarity between femininity and Jewishness"; the Jew was "always more absorbed by sexual matters than the Aryan, although he is notably less potent sexually" (417); Jewish acquisitiveness was not the consequence of centuries of oppression but an inborn tendency (413); and finally, Jews were seldom actively immoral: they were feminine in their amorality. "Greatness," Weininger pronounced, "is absent from the nature of the Woman and the Jew, the greatness of morality, or the greatness of evil" (414–15). Admitting that analogies between femininity and Jewishness could not wholly fathom the inner mystery of Jewish identity, Weininger turned to an examination of Jewish religious and moral codes. The Jew, he asserted, was a slave, following a moral code promulgated by an external authority: Yahweh.[53] The Jewish God was abstract and external to the individual; the Jew knew nothing of the divine in every man: "For the God in man is the human soul and the absolute Jew is devoid of a soul" (420).

Weininger had to accept, however, that those "slaves of Yahweh" became materialists or freethinkers with the greatest ease. "It is merely," he hastily remarked, "the obverse of slavery," and he moved on to identifying Jewish arrogance as one of the driving forces of modern, materialistic science. Jewish science was hostile to all transcendentalism because the Jew had no respect or fear for the mysteries of life; he reduced the world to banality (421). The Jew was the fieriest follower of Darwin's "ridiculous theory of the descent of man from apes" and also the staunchest upholder of materialist, economic, or social interpretations of history. Lacking an intelligible self, the Jew understood only matter and he attempted to drag all of humanity down to his level (422).

### "Ours is Not Only the Most Jewish, but also the Most Feminine of Ages": Weininger as Cultural Pathologist

Weininger's argument now turned overtly toward the criticism of contemporary mores. Femininity and Jewishness were the two qualities by which he judged a culture, and he found plenty of each in the Viennese milieu. From the last pages of the chapter on Jewishness until the end of *Geschlecht und Charakter*, Weininger spoke as a diagnostician of cultural malaise and its therapist. His criticism of modern culture, rooted in his ideas on femininity and Jewishness, was abrasive, anti-Semitic, and misogynistic. Nevertheless, venom was not all that he spewed. He also attempted to construct a future utopia, in which, he hoped, even women would become fully human.

Not since Herod's time, Weininger announced, had Jews attained such power and influence as in contemporary times. "The spirit of modernity," he declared, "is Jewish." Sexuality pervaded society, and contemporary ethics affirmed the glories of coitus. This sexualization of life reflected the influence of the Jew and the Woman, both obsessed with sex and determined to drag humanity down into the mire of sensuousness. "Ours is not only the most Jewish," Weininger expostulated, "but also the most feminine of ages" (440–41). The purely physical side of sexuality was being celebrated with a brazenness unequalled in history, and, in the name of freedom, women were revolting *against* motherhood and *for* prostitution. Contemporary men, influenced by Judaism, had accepted the new order. Male chastity was ridiculed and Woman was no longer regarded as the embodied sin of man. Sexual excess had become a symbol of status. Only the Woman without a lover was a figure of shame. Revolted by this "modern coitus-culture," Weininger lamented: "But this means there are no men left" (443–44).

The Jewishness and femininity of the epoch had led to pervasive cultural degradation. Art had degenerated into "daubs," and, in literature, the cult of the Madonna had been replaced by the cult of the whore. Anarchy was rampant in political and social life, and nobody believed any longer in the state or in the rule of law. Beguiled by historical materialism, that most foolish of concepts, historians believed they could explain the evolution of science, scholarship, and culture with reference to changes in political economy. Psychiatrists saw genius as a form of insanity, and the age had not produced a single great artist or philosopher (441).

A "New Christianity," Weininger hoped, might still emerge from this "New Judaism." Humankind, however, had to choose, as in A.D. 1, between Judaism and Christianity, between female and male, between business and culture, between earthly and heavenly life. There was no third way (441). Cultural regeneration would require chastity, which, contrary to conventional opinion, was a male attribute. Women valued virginity only because men seemed to prize it. Woman did not even understand the pure, projective, Platonic love of man, although she felt flattered by it: she understood sensuality alone.[54] "In coitus lies woman's greatest humiliation," Weininger elaborated, "in love her supreme exaltation. Since woman desires coitus and not love, she proves that she wishes to be humiliated and not worshipped. The ultimate opponent of the emancipation of women is Woman" (447).

Pleasure, for Weininger, was neither moral nor immoral in itself. Coitus was immoral not because it was pleasurable but because it induced men to use women as means to pleasure or to children. True, added Weininger, it was Woman who *wished* to be used in this way, but the use of a person as a means remained immoral regardless of who instigated such use (448). If men wished to treat women as they desired to be treated, then there was no way out of the immoral predicament: "He must have intercourse with her, for she wishes it; he must beat her, because she wants to be beaten; hypnotize her, because she desires it" (449).

Kantian morality demanded that Man must see Woman as a human being and respect her individuality. The emancipation of women was analogous to the emancipation of Jews and Blacks. "Undoubtedly," said Weininger, "the principal reason why these people have been treated as slaves and inferiors is to be found in their servile dispositions; their desire for freedom is not so strong as that of the Indo-Germans." But, in spite of the low moral worth of these groups, Weininger insisted that right was "on the side of the emancipators" (449). No matter how worthless, Jews, Blacks, and women were human and one must respect their humanity, treating them as ends in themselves (450). Moreover, since there was no absolute Woman, all individual women possessed at least faint traces of an intelligible self, and one must respect that vestige of true humanity, even if one detested femininity. Weininger condemned Friedrich Nietzsche's assertion that the "Asiatic" oppression of women was the most civilized and ethical approach to man-woman relations (454).[55] "Woman and man," Weininger declared, "have the same rights." He immediately added, however, that women could not be allowed to share political power: they must be excluded for the same reasons that children, the mentally handicapped, and criminals were excluded. Female influence could only be harmful to public welfare (450).

He emphasized, nevertheless, that women had the right to justice and the right to be regarded as free individuals, even if they "never prove worthy of such a lofty view." Moral relations with women entailed the avoidance of all sexual relations and even of love, since both used women as means to an end. Man must only attempt to understand woman. "Most men theoretically respect woman, but practically despise women; this should be reversed." His book, he explained, might denigrate femininity, but at a more profound level it represented the greatest tribute that had ever been paid to women (451). Every woman must be encouraged to develop whatever "germ of good" she possessed. Since femininity was amoral and all morality was masculine, "Woman must cease to be Woman and become Man" (452). This did not, he stressed, mean that women should try to *appear* masculine; rather, they must masculinize their inner selves, denying and transcending their femininity, which, in Weiningerian terms, meant transcending sexuality itself (453). "Woman, as Woman, must disappear." Without the total and unequivocal negation of femininity, there could be "no kingdom of God on earth." Pythagoras, Plato, Christianity, Tertullian, Swift, Wagner, and Ibsen had all called for the emancipation of Woman—not from men but from the shackles of femininity itself (455).[56]

This liberation of women from Woman was unlikely, of course, to be achievable through female effort alone: "The spark in her," Weininger explained, "is so flickering that it always needs the fire of man to relight it; she must have an example to go by." Woman, in fact, was comparable to the sensuous and amoral Kundry in Wagner's drama *Parsifal* ("the greatest work in world literature"), who was released from her curse only through the help of Parsifal, a sinless and immaculate man (456).[57] The Woman Question could not be resolved unless Man became as chaste as Parsifal. Only chastity could negate the very purpose of woman's existence—sexuality—and remove the greatest obstacle to women's emancipation. Woman would then be destroyed as a sexual being but "rise rejuvenated from the ashes as a genuine human being" (457).

In such an ethical utopia, there would, of course, be no reproduction, and the human species would soon be extinct. This objection, according to Weininger, stemmed from a cowardly and irreligious lack of belief in individual immortality: "The rejection of sexuality leads merely to the physical death of humanity and gives full play to the spiritual element of life. . . . It follows, therefore, that it is not an ethical duty to ensure the continuation of the species." Did anyone ever have coitus out of concern for the future of the species? All fecundity was "loathsome" and involved treating other human beings as means (458).[58]

Only in these final pages of his long work did Weininger consider possible social reasons for women's inferior status. The education the average woman received did not, he agreed, equip her to rise above "her real bondage." Women's education was geared toward making them marriageable: if they failed to behave in certain ways, they were warned that they would never find a man. Such training, Weininger argued, "would have little effect on Man, but it serves to accentuate Woman's dependent and unfree status." The only solution was to entrust the education of women to men. "The education of all humankind," in fact, "must be taken out of the hands of the mother" (460).[59]

To sum up, then, *Geschlecht und Charakter* began by stating that all individual humans were both male and female, albeit to varying proportions, and this conviction of universal sexual intermediacy was established with reference to current biological and medical theories. Sexual intermediacy crucially affected human mating, a hypothesis expressed by Weininger through algebraic formulae explaining choice of mates as the function of the masculine and feminine elements of both partners. This relationship was studied in greater detail through an examination of male homosexual mating, where a feminine man always (purportedly) chose a more masculine partner. The book then proposed that human character, being as sexually mixed as the human body, should also be analyzed into male and female traits. Although all individuals were both male and female, this duality need not, however, be present at one and the same time. In other words, a sexually intermediate organism could be *sequentially* male and female and, at any one time, possess *either* a male *or* a female "character." Turning then to the Woman Question, the treatise argued that the inferior position of women in contemporary society could not simply be attributed to social and economic oppression; it had deeper "characterological" reasons. True femininity was antithetical to intellectuality and independence: emancipationist females sought liberty and autonomy because they, unlike their "normal" sisters, were masculinized.

So far, so consistent. Confusion began, however, with the premise of the second part of the work that despite morphological bisexuality, an individual was psychologically *either* a man *or* a woman. Since this assertion was not linked to the notion of sequential sexual intermediacy, it seemed to contradict the earlier argument of universal sexual intermediacy and significantly so, because the rest of the long book was based on the premise of psychological sexual polarity: one was mentally either Man or Woman *and* these two types were wholly opposed to each other.[60]

Woman was wholly passive, did not possess an intelligible self, and had no conception of logic and ethics. All the qualities lacking in Woman were found in Man, the active, autonomous being created in the image of God. The essence of femininity was sexuality alone. But since this sexuality was universal and indiscriminate, the female could never be an autonomous subject: "Woman is Nothing." Man, on the other hand, was the complete, autonomous subject, the male psyche possessing a microcosmic quality akin to genius: part of it could even be female! The female, however, could never be psychologically male, although some women may well possess masculine traits. This ideal type of Woman had much in common with Weininger's ideal type of Jew, and, without completely equating the two, their correspondences were emphasized in the treatise.

At its end, *Geschlecht und Charakter* returned to the Woman Question. Although he underscored Woman's delight in servility and her lack of moral personhood, Weininger now urged the moral treatment of women as persons. Since, however, Woman was exclusively a passive sexual object, she could be elevated to subjecthood and full humanity only by the negation of sexuality itself. Man and Woman must, therefore, transcend their sexuality and live in total chastity. Only then could women be emancipated from their sexual bondage to men and be treated as free and equal individuals. Although it would mean the end of the human species, it was far more important to follow the Kantian injunction to treat persons as ends in themselves than to obey the biological imperative to reproduce the species.

### Text, Argument, and Meaning
*Geschlecht und Charakter* is clearly a heterogeneous, even bewildering text. Weininger's goal was ostensibly simple and unitary: to resolve the Woman

Question. And that was precisely why the text became so complicated. It did not focus on a single aspect of the Woman Question but instead addressed the fundamental ontological questions of gender itself: What was male? What was female? What were their differences? Were those differences eternal and essential? Nothing if not thorough, and unhampered by any particular professional specialization, Weininger trudged through virtually every field of thought that had ever addressed these issues. Since those fields were as different as zoology, epistemology, psychology, moral philosophy, and psychiatry, the work acquired a thematic and substantive diversity one rarely encounters in contemporaneous texts on the Woman Question.

But Weininger's project was far from exclusively ontological. His metaphysical lucubrations had an explicit political aim: the resolution of the Woman Question. Virtually every section of *Geschlecht und Charakter* carried that powerful political charge, giving its rhetoric a decidedly nonacademic edge. To make matters more complicated, Weininger's virulent misogyny and his only slightly less intense anti-Semitism did not merely serve negative ends alone: they led ultimately to his bizarre vision of a Kantian utopia, in which men and women, having transcended sexuality, had attained true humanity and moral freedom.

The book, obviously, was the work of a deeply anxious (and very young) man. Weininger's anxieties came partly from the circumstances of his own life—on which we do not have too much concrete information—and partly from his cultural and discursive universe. A learned, sensitive youth living in turn-of-the-century Vienna could not possibly avoid confronting questions of racial, sexual, and national identity. Could a Jew be German? Did the social disparities between the sexes reflect underlying constitutional, intellectual, and moral differences between men and women? Were men—all men—becoming decadent and feminized in modern times? Such questions were by no means unique to Weininger. Nor, as we shall see, were all of his answers. What was unique, however, was the book's combination of lofty Kantian speculation and dauntingly profound scholarship with schoolboyish misogyny, logical howlers, ludicrous circular arguments, and rather banal outbursts of anti-Semitism. And this daunting mixture was served up to the reader in prose that was always convoluted and frequently ungainly. The challenge of reading *Geschlecht und Charakter* is to give equal weight to all of these factors, which affect its style as well as its substance, and at the same time, to relate its diverse content to the many contexts that shaped the treatise and its author.

## CHAPTER FOUR

# The Biology of Sex and the Deconstruction of Gender

Scientific discourse is almost omnipresent in *Geschlecht und Charakter,* but it is used in diverse, heterogeneous ways. Weininger rarely used scientific notions without in some way revising, extending, or modifying the original arguments. Sometimes, for strategic reasons, he transformed them entirely. More frequently, he simply extracted an isolated point from a scientific work while ignoring the larger context in which that point had been made. Any scientific notion that might illuminate—or could be *claimed* to illuminate—the nature of masculinity and femininity was grist for his mill. Consequently, one must determine exactly which scientific notions he used, where he used them, what kind of arguments he integrated them with, how his larger project was shaped by these appropriations, and how the nature and extent of the appropriations were determined by the larger goal of the project: the resolution of the Woman Question.

In this chapter, I shall explore the biological conceptions of sexuality fundamental to the first part of *Geschlecht und Charakter.* Allan Janik has pointed out that Weininger's understanding of sexual biology was inspired by Carl von Nägeli's theory of the idioplasm, which passed out of vogue shortly after the publication of *Geschlecht und Charakter.*[1] Janik does not, however, mention Weininger's valiant effort to "graft" the theory of idioplasmic sexuality onto newly emerging theories of sexual endocrinology. My discussion, therefore, will range from morphology to physiology, from the idioplasm to the internal secretions, both of which were crucial to Weininger's conceptualization of sexuality, which, in turn, provided the foundation for Weininger's larger argument that all existing individuals were always partly male as well as partly female—"bisexual" or "sexually intermediate." While Weininger would curtail and ignore this very concept in later sections of his treatise, the idea of universal bisexuality is crucial for the overall argument of *Geschlecht und Charakter.* To fully appreciate the nature and depth of the well-known disjunction between the two sections of the text, one must understand this hypothesis at some depth and have a clear idea of its place in Weininger's argument.

*The Sexual Characters: Primary, Secondary, Tertiary*

Biologists have long recognized that few of the anatomical differences between males and females play any direct role in reproduction. From the eighteenth century, differences between the reproductive systems of males and females have been termed the "primary sexual characters," whereas other morphological differences between the sexes have been labelled "secondary," a distinction first suggested by the British surgeon and anatomist John Hunter (1728–93), then popularized by Charles Darwin in the nineteenth century, and expanded subsequently by the British sexologist Havelock Ellis. Weininger began his exploration of sexual biology by outlining and modifying their views.

In 1780, John Hunter reported to the Royal Society of London on an "extraordinary [female] pheasant" that had, in old age, developed masculine features. Hunter noted that in sexually differentiated species, the anatomical differences in the genitalia were not the only differences between the sexes. "The varieties which are found in the parts of generation themselves I shall call the first or principal marks," Hunter stated, adding that "all others depending upon these I shall call secondary, as not taking place till the first are becoming of use."[2] In other words, the primary sexual characters—the reproductive organs alone—existed from birth but became active at puberty, which was also when the secondary characters—every macroscopic sexual difference except for the reproductive organs—began to develop. Darwin, Weininger pointed out, used Hunter's distinction in order to exemplify his rule that "a part developed in any species in an extraordinary degree or manner, in comparison with the same part in allied species, tends to be highly variable."[3] Darwin, however, had his doubts whether the distinction between primary and secondary was absolute. In *The Descent of Man*, he had acknowledged that the secondary sexual characters often "graduate into, and in some cases can hardly be distinguished from, those which are commonly ranked as primary, such as the complex appendages at the apex of the abdomen in male insects."[4] Havelock Ellis, approaching the issue from the perspective of the clinical sexologist, also had his problems with the primary/secondary distinction. Instead of discarding it, however, he had attempted to refine the classification by adding a third category to the scheme: the "tertiary" sexual characters. According to Ellis, the primary sexual characters comprised the sex glands and "the organs for emission and reception in immediate connection with these glands."[5] The secondary characters remained a heterogeneous group: Ellis defined a secondary sexual character simply as "one which, by more highly differentiating the sexes, helps to make them more attractive to each other, and so to promote the union of the sperm-cell with the ovum-cell."[6] Even such a broad definition of the secondary characters left numerous less striking differences unaccounted for. These features were sometimes perceptible not in individuals but only in large groups, such as the shallowness of the female skull or the smaller proportion of red corpuscles in female blood. "These differences," remarked Ellis, "are not of great importance from the zoological point of view, but they are of considerable interest from the anthropological point of view, very often of interest from the pathological point of view, and occasionally of great interest from the social point of view." These he labelled the tertiary sexual characters.[7]

While accepting the rationale of Hunter's original primary/secondary distinction, Weininger pointed out that it was unsatisfactory to classify the gonads (testicles or ovaries) as well as their adnexae (such as the seminal vesicles, uterus, and the external genitals) as "primary," since there were many reports in the medical literature of cases of hermaphroditism where the external genitals resembled those of one sex while the gonads seemed to be those of the other.[8] Weininger, therefore, proposed that Hunter's "primary" category be subdivided into "primordial sexual characters," comprising the gonads alone, and "primary sexual characters," comprising the external genitals and the adnexae of the gonads (18, 474). Leaving the category of the secondary sexual characters largely unmodified, Weininger went on to elaborate his own notion of tertiary characters, which, unlike Ellis, he reserved for what he considered to be *inborn* psychological differences between the sexes, such as a greater spirit of independence *(Eigenwilligkeit)* in males. Yet another category, Weininger argued, was needed for those sexual differences (such as the male predilection for smoking and drinking) that were purely social. This new group he called the "quaternary sexual characters" (18, 478). The first part of *Geschlecht und Charakter* dealt with the primordial, primary, and secondary sexual characters. The second, metaphysical section of the work was almost entirely devoted to establishing the existence of inborn psychological and ontological differences between the sexes, which Weininger considered tertiary. Interestingly, Weininger's most original category—that of the purely social "quaternary" sexual characters—was never addressed in any detail in *Geschlecht und Charakter*.

By the end of the nineteenth century, European biologists and physicians had produced a voluminous literature detailing ostensible anatomical and physiological differences between the sexes. These differences largely concerned the secondary sexual characters, and were often used to determine and prescribe gender-appropriate functions and behavior. Although well-acquainted with this literature, Weininger attempted to move beyond the listing of significant differences in the brain, skull, pelvis, and blood cells and to establish that sexual differences were to be found in *every* part of an organism, not simply in some organs or functions.[9] His argument drew upon nu-

merous biomedical sources, of which the most important were the writings of
the Danish zoologist Johannes Japetus Smith Steenstrup (1813–97) and of
the celebrated Munich botanist Carl Wilhelm von Nägeli (1817–91).

## The Sex of Cells

Japetus Steenstrup had argued in the mid-nineteenth century that the sex of
an organism was not localized in any particular anatomical zone: each and
every part of the organism was endowed with sex. Steenstrup's remark was
made in the context of his investigation into the widespread belief that many
"lower" organisms were naturally hermaphroditic.[10] Steenstrup not only rejected this belief on the basis of his own empirical research but denied that
hermaphroditism was possible at all, whether in lower animals or in humans.[11] If an animal's sex was located only in its genitals, then, Steenstrup argued, two opposed sets of genitals could conceivably coexist in the same
individual. But it was his explicitly a priori conviction that sex was not, in fact,
so localized: it was an attribute of the entire organism and expressed in each of
its constituent parts. Genuine hermaphroditism would, therefore, entail the
simultaneous presence of masculinity and femininity in each part of the organism, which would lead to a negation of one by the other, culminating in
the extinction of sexuality itself.[12] Steenstrup's ontological presupposition
was based upon a completely polarized notion of the sexes and could be used
to support historian Thomas Laqueur's hypothesis that in modern times the
two sexes have been perceived as wholly separate and opposed.[13] Contra
Laqueur, however, such a conception was not universally shared. The embry-
ologist Rudolf Leuckart, for instance, criticized Steenstrup's polarized model
as redolent of the quasi-mystical theories of the *Naturphilosophen* about the
fundamental polarity of nature.[14] Steenstrup's denial of the possibility of hermaphroditism, argued Leuckart, had followed logically from his mistaken
premise that masculinity and femininity were equal and opposed forces that
could not co-exist without "neutralizing" one another. Equating sexuality
with genitality, Leuckart pointed out that sexuality was not a force but a simple attribute of male and female genitals. Genital differences were complementary and could not oppose, let alone neutralize, each other.

Rejecting the genital-centered approach of Leuckart, Weininger accepted
Steenstrup's idea that sex was an attribute of every part of the organism.
Steenstrup's conclusion that this diffuse sexuality ruled out the possibility of
hermaphroditism, however, Weininger blithely ignored. Weininger's biological scenario, in fact, was founded in the diametrically opposed belief that all
organisms were masculine as well as feminine in differing proportions, a notion fundamentally incompatible with Steenstrup's conception of sexuality.
This, in fact, was entirely characteristic of Weininger's selective use of scien-

tific discourse: he took exactly what he needed—or what he *thought* he needed—and rarely explained why he rejected the rest. Even in the most overtly "scientific" sections of his text, Weininger was not quite the standard scientist of his time—his use of science was determined by his larger, nonscientific objectives, not by the accepted conventions of scientific discourse.

Having appropriated Steenstrup's conviction that sex was located everywhere in the organism, Weininger anchored it in Carl Wilhelm von Nägeli's late-nineteenth-century theory of the idioplasm. One of the foremost botanists of the nineteenth century, Nägeli also made significant contributions to anatomy, cytology, morphology, and systematics.[15] In the last decade of his life, he had published the voluminous work, *Mechanisch-physiologische Theorie der Abstammungslehre* (1884), in which he had attempted to explain phylogeny and the basis of heredity.[16] Struck by the fact that an embryo, in spite of developing from the fusion of the spermatozoon with the much larger ovum, possessed approximately equal proportions of maternal and paternal traits, he had concluded that much of the protoplasm of the ovum must therefore be unrelated to inheritance, while almost all of the protoplasm of the sperm cell carried hereditary material.[17] Coining the term "idioplasm" for the portion of the protoplasm carrying the hereditary material, Nägeli attributed hereditary differences between individuals and species to molecular differences in their idioplasm. The idioplasm, he stressed, was present not only in the germ cells: the original idioplasms of the ovum and the spermatozoon were divided and redistributed within *each* cell of the embryo. Since the idioplasm bore *all* traits of the species to which the individual belonged, each cell of every organism, too, contained the rudiments of every trait of its species. "In propagation," wrote Nägeli, "the organism hands down the sum total of its characters as idioplasm . . . the idioplasm of the germ would therefore be the microcosmic image of the macrocosmic full-grown individual." That did not, however, imply that all the traits transmitted by the idioplasm would undergo full development or any development at all. Nor did Nägeli believe that the molecular structure of the idioplasm was a replica of the cellular structure of the individual organism.[18]

Despite his early work in cytology, Nägeli did not present his theory of the idioplasm in a rigorously cytological framework. While applauding Nägeli's effort to explain heredity on a strictly physical basis, cytologist E. B. Wilson was to regret that "Nägeli made no attempt to locate the idioplasm precisely or to identify it with any of the known morphological constituents of the cell. It was somewhat vaguely conceived as a network extending through both nucleus and cytoplasm, and from cell to cell throughout the entire organism."[19] Its cytological deficiencies notwithstanding, Nägeli's theory did not fall on barren ground. Wilson himself recalled that the notion that the idioplasm was "the physical basis of inheritance" greatly influenced the research of leading biologists of the time. Oscar Hertwig, Edward Strasburger, and Albert von Kölliker all found Nägeli's idea of heuristic use; so did August Weismann, although he expressed very strong reservations about it. Their independent research led eventually to the consensus that "the nucleus contains the physical basis of inheritance, and that chromatin, its essential constituent, is the idioplasm postulated in Nägeli's theory."[20]

Weininger appropriated three notions from Nägeli's theory of the idioplasm: first, all biological differences between individuals were due to idioplasmic differences; second, each and every cell of the organism possessed a certain amount of idioplasm; and third, each cell, therefore, had the potential to form a new individual, but the realization of that potential depended not on the idioplasm but on the properties of the surrounding nutritive plasm. In lower plants, for instance, every cell possessed the ability to form an entire plant. Many cell groups in the higher plants, however, had lost this ability and in animals, only the germ cells could form a new individual.[21] This issue had been highlighted in Oscar Hertwig's textbook of microscopic anatomy, *Die Zelle und die Gewebe,* one of Weininger's favorite sources of biological information.[22] Hertwig, who had attempted to provide a cytological foundation for Nägeli's theory by localizing the idioplasm in the nucleus, had enumerated various ways in which plants and lower animals could "regenerate" from fragments, concluding that all species characters were present in these fragments. The idioplasm, he had added, also contained *latent* characters that were expressed only in unusual or abnormal conditions of regeneration.[23]

Hertwig's hypotheses carried profound implications for that great question of nineteenth-century biology: could acquired characters be inherited? While many biologists agreed with Hertwig that all attributes of a species were present in the idioplasm of each individual cell, they had a powerful opponent in August Weismann, whom Weininger described as "the greatest opponent of the theory of the idioplasm" (480). Actually, Weismann did not completely reject the concept of the idioplasm but simply—and famously—denied that each cell of an organism could regenerate into a complete individual. Such regeneration would imply that somatic cells could give rise to somatic as well as germ cells, a possibility ruled out by Weismann's conviction that the germ cells and the somatic cells were absolutely and permanently separate.[24] "Before it has been proved that 'somatic' idioplasm can ever be changed into germ plasm," Weismann declared, "we have no right to trace the development of germ cells from the former."[25]

Although not a particularly passionate believer in the inheritance of acquired characters, Weininger was no Weismannian ultra-Darwinian either; in any case, he needed Nägeli's original concept of idioplasm in order to establish that every cell of the body was endowed with sex. Although Weininger did try to take issue with Weismann, proffering some unimpressive evidence suggesting linkages between the soma and the germ plasm from the biological literature, he quickly dismissed the whole theme and moved on to an original, elegant, but entirely speculative formulation relating sex and sexual intermediacy to idioplasmic differences between individuals.[26]

He postulated that the idioplasm could theoretically occur in two idealtypical forms: male (arrhenoplasm) and female (thelyplasm). But as with organisms, so it was with cells and plasmas: absolute masculinity or femininity was unattainable in reality, and the idioplasm of each cell was partly arrhenoplasmic and partly thelyplasmic. The proportions of masculinity and femininity, Weininger emphasized, were not necessarily identical in all cells in one individual: each individual was a mosaic of cells, all of them endowed with varying degrees of sexuality (20–21). In other words, cells, like individual organisms, were located at different points on the spectrum stretching from absolute masculinity (arrhenoplasm) to absolute femininity (thelyplasm). "Each cell, each cell-complex, each organ has a certain index, which indicates its position between arrhenoplasm and thelyplasm" (28). This explained why, for instance, a very masculine man might have a sparse beard or weak musculature, why an effeminate man might still have a full beard, and why a man might have a feminine upper body and a masculine lower body (21–22). Such localized sexual asymmetries could only be due to local variations. Weininger emphasized that these variations were primarily idioplasmic and not, as some scientists were beginning to suggest, primarily determined by the secretions of the sex glands. Without rejecting contemporary research on the internal secretions, Weininger refused to recognize them as the *primary* determinants of sex.

*Sexual Chemistry*

Weininger's moderate skepticism on this issue was not at all unusual even among contemporary scientists and physicians, many of whom believed that the internal secretions of the sex glands could act only on a congenitally determined sexual soma. The role of the sex glands, they argued, was important but secondary. As late as 1910, physiologist Artur Biedl devoted many paragraphs to a careful discussion of this very question in his classic textbook of endocrinology, concluding that the only way to decide upon the question was to study the development of an organism after extirpating the earliest foetal rudiment of the sex gland. Such an *experimentum crucis,* however, was still technically impossible.[27] In spite of great scientific interest in the function of the sex glands, no consensus on the extent, significance, and mechanism of their influence was reached until long after Weininger's death and the whole field was rife with debate at the turn of the century.[28] Weininger summarized, documented, and annotated some of the major issues in this debate quite competently, adding his own hypothesis and some sensible suggestions for future research.

The ductless or internal secretory glands—glands that issued secretions directly into the bloodstream, of which the most well known were the thyroid, the adrenals, the testicles, and the ovaries—were at the forefront of medical interest at the turn of the century. Nineteenth-century researchers had found these diminutive organs to control many vital functions, and the gonads, in particular, came to be seen as organs holding the keys not simply to reproduction but to life itself. The most dramatic illustration of this new perspective was the renowned physiologist Charles-Edouard Brown-Séquard's announcement to the Paris Society of Biology in 1889 that he had "rejuvenated" himself by subcutaneous injections of canine testicular extracts.[29] Brown-Séquard, ironically, died only five years after his "rejuvenation," but his report stimulated some very serious research on glandular physiology. It also inaugurated "organotherapy," the fin-de-siècle trend of treating vague or intractable conditions with the extracts of glands and other tissues.[30]

Despite the popularity and the putative successes of organotherapy and despite the progress of research on glandular functions, many authorities continued to doubt that the sexual characters originated in and were maintained entirely by the chemical, blood-borne secretions of the gonads. After listing the many ways in which the secondary sexual characters were affected by castration in males or during old age in female animals, Oscar Hertwig asked in 1893: "Is this correlation between organs that have no direct functional relationship with one another mediated through the nervous system? Or do certain substances secreted by the testes or the ovaries into the blood bring about this correlative development of widely separated parts of the body?"[31]

He stressed that there was as yet no experimental basis for deciding between the two alternative explanations. Hertwig was not alone in his doubts. In his 1898 textbook of pathology, Ernst Ziegler, Professor of Pathology and Pathological Anatomy at the University of Freiburg, merely conceded that the secretions of the sex glands probably exerted "a certain influence" on the functions, development, and growth of the body. The extent of this influence he left to be determined by future research.[32]

Citing both these authors, Weininger took an informed, unequivocal stand on the issue. Hertwig and Ziegler, he remarked, had little reason to be so uncertain, given the evidence of the 1874 report of Friedrich Goltz (1834–1902) that a bitch with her spinal cord transected at the level of the first cervical vertebra had gone into estrus, mated (with a male toward whom she had previously been antagonistic), and became pregnant with triplets.[33] It had long been known that estrus did not occur in the absence of the sex glands, but Goltz's experiment began to indicate how the sex glands might affect the brain to produce the mating urge characterizing estrus. In an intact animal, Goltz argued, one could assume that centripetal nerve fibers from the sex glands stimulated the brain to produce estrus, but that hypothesis was obviously inapplicable to an animal whose spinal cord had been completely separated from the brain. Goltz, therefore, concluded that the sex glands exerted their effect on the brain by releasing specific chemical substances into the blood during estrus.[34]

Even stronger evidence in favor of the chemical hypothesis, argued Weininger, could be found in recent reports of experimental transplantation of ovaries by Emil Knauer and Josef Halban. The testes, according to a historian of endocrinology, have been "the oldest key to the endocrine treasure trove."[35] While this is generally true, clinical interest in the ovary was the more important stimulus to glandular research in Weininger's Vienna. The removal of ovaries from women suffering from various organic as well as vague neuropsychiatric disorders—the same disorders for which, confusingly, ovarian extracts were being prescribed by many physicians—was fairly common during the late nineteenth century.[36] At the Vienna Medical School, the gynecologist Rudolf Chrobak (1843–1910) had noticed similarities between symptoms following oophorectomy and those following thyroidectomy. He reasoned that since the latter could be alleviated with thyroid extract, the former might respond to organotherapy with ovarian preparations.[37] Chrobak, a former student of physiologist Ernst von Brücke (1819–1892), did not rest content with organotherapy. He asked his assistant Emil Knauer (1867–1935) to conduct experiments on rabbits to test whether ovarian transplantations were feasible or useful.

Knauer removed ovaries and then transplanted them elsewhere within the abdominal cavity of the same animal.[38] The grafts usually survived, the ovaries continued to develop ova, and the uterus did not atrophy.[39] Once, Knauer even succeeded in inducing a pregnancy terminating in a normal birth. Another young Viennese gynecologist, Josef Halban (1870–1937), who worked at the clinic of the celebrated surgeon Friedrich Schauta (1849–1919), focused on the developmental influence of the ovaries. The uterus, it was widely known, did not grow in females whose ovaries had been removed during infancy. Halban demonstrated that the uterus developed quite normally if infant, oophorectomized animals were grafted with ovaries anywhere in the body.[40] Since the sexual characters were unaffected when the ovaries were moved from one location to another, it was highly probable that their influence was mediated by chemicals rather than by nerves, which would have been resected during removal.[41]

Weininger now tried to harmonize such chemical theories of sex with his idioplasmic hypothesis by analyzing the consequences of castration. Castration was one of the preeminent experimental procedures in early research on glandular physiology: the functions of the sex glands were deduced from the results of their removal, an epistemologically venerable procedure going back at least, as Weininger pointed out, to Aristotle, who had noted that after castration, male animals "really change over into the female state."[42] The same point had also been made by a number of more recent biologists. The British naturalist William Yarrell (1784–1856), for instance, had provided a classic description of the changes in the castrated cock:

> The capon ceases to crow; the comb and gills do not attain the size of those parts in the perfect male; the spurs appear, but remain short and blunt; and the hackle feathers of the neck and saddle, instead of being long and narrow, are short and broadly webbed. The capon will take to a clutch of chickens, attend them in their search for food, and brood them under his wings when they are tired.[43]

Charles Darwin, citing Yarrell, had asserted that the capon takes on "characters properly confined to the female" and "takes to sitting on eggs, and will bring up chickens."[44] Darwin believed that this phenomenon supported his belief that "the secondary characters of each sex lie dormant or latent in the opposite sex, ready to be evolved under peculiar circumstances."[45] August Weismann accepted Darwin's hypothesis, adding that "men who have been castrated in their youth retain a high voice like that of the other sex, and the beard does not become developed."[46]

Weininger recognized that these views threatened his hypothesis of idioplasmic sexuality: if the removal of the sex glands could radically modify the sexual characters of the organism, then sex could not be an innate attribute of each cell of the body (23). Thus, it was with almost palpable relief that he reported that recent research by Hugo Sellheim, Konrad Rieger, and Arthur Foges demonstrated that Aristotle, Darwin, and Weismann had all overestimated the degree of feminization caused by castration. Of the reports mentioned by Weininger, Sellheim's 1898 study of two castrated cocks was probably the most significant.[47] The animals operated upon, Sellheim declared, did show changes, but few of the changes were similar to those reported by earlier biologists. The cocks could still crow, although they did not usually do so. Far from being timid, they fought constantly among themselves and also with normal cocks and hens. Their combs differed from those of normal cocks but also from those of hens. Sellheim had concluded that castrated cocks did come to differ from intact males but did *not* become feminized.[48] Konrad Rieger, a staunch critic of what he regarded as the "overvaluation of the testicles," argued that while a male castrated long enough before puberty did not develop masculine secondary sexual characters, there was no strong evidence to assume that he developed *female* secondary sexual characters.[49] Viennese physiologist Arthur Foges, too, showed, in a series of experiments on cocks, that while the sexual characters of the capon differed from those of the uncastrated cock, they were not similar to those of the hen.[50] These findings were soon accepted by most scientists, and in 1910, Artur Biedl declared:

> The secondary male characteristics do not as a rule attain complete development where castration is performed before the age of puberty. Observation of man and of animals of widely different species shows, beyond any manner of doubt, that castration does not impart characteristics peculiar to the opposite sex, and that transformation into the heterosexual type [i.e., feminization in males or masculinization in females] is never observed.[51]

Another longstanding, parallel belief was that females became masculinized after menopause. Once again, Weininger provided a long list of authoritative sources for this view from Aristotle to Oscar Hertwig (23, 482–83). In his account of the "extraordinary pheasant," John Hunter had suggested that the masculinization of female birds was a consequence of senility. Referring to Hunter's report, William Yarrell had argued in 1827 that age, in itself, was unimportant with regard to masculinization, which could occur at any age after "the destruction of the sexual organs," whether by disease or by surgical means.[52] Yarrell suspected that "a law of nature" changed the secondary sexual characters into forms "intermediate between the perfect male and female" whenever the sex glands were deactivated.[53] Charles Darwin as well as Oscar Hertwig agreed with Yarrell.[54]

Rejecting the link between masculinization and menopause or surgery, Weininger argued that the former could occur even without menopause or surgery. Dramatic instances of spontaneous sexual "transformations" had been reported in humans by sexologist Richard von Krafft-Ebing, who in his *Psychopathia Sexualis* had narrated the history of a male physician who had gradually felt himself change into a female. "I feel like a woman in a man's form," the patient had reported. "Thus, for example, I feel the penis as clitoris . . . the skin all over my body feels feminine."[55] Krafft-Ebing had also recorded a female counterpart to this case: a married woman with six children, who, when bedridden after a severe stroke, developed an acute antipathy to "feminine" activities. "Her hitherto soft and decidedly feminine features," stated Krafft-Ebing, "assumed a strongly masculine character. . . . She was horrified to notice her breasts disappearing, that her pelvis grew smaller and narrower, the bones became more massive, and her skin rougher and harder. . . . Her voice also grew deeper, rougher, and quite masculine."[56] Obviously, reasoned Weininger, there was no evidence to attribute these spontaneous transformations to changes in the sex glands. Feminization and masculinization, therefore, were not the exclusive and *necessary* sequelae of castration or its functional equivalents (482). If, then, feminization or masculinization of the sexual characters could occur without any interference with the gonads, it followed that the cells of the body must be endowed with an innate sexuality controlled by unknown forces that had nothing to do with the gonads (484).[57]

Weininger emphasized that he was not denying that the internal secretions of the sex glands influenced sexuality. He simply rejected the extreme contention that sexual characters were generated and maintained *exclusively* under glandular influence. It was his conviction that the sexual action of the glandular secretions consisted in enhancing the innate, idioplasmic sexuality of the cells. Each cell possessed a quantum of idioplasmic sexuality, to which the internal secretions contributed an additional degree, leading to the attainment of a degree of masculinity or femininity, which, although it could never be maximal in sexually intermediate species, was more pronounced than it would be without any help from the glands (19).

Continental physiologists apparently ignored Weininger's synthesis of Nägeli's hypothesis of the idioplasm with the burgeoning hypotheses on internal secretions.[58] A leading British physiologist, however, did not. In his pioneering treatise on reproductive physiology, Francis H. A. Marshall summarized Weininger's ideas on the arrhenoplasm and the thelyplasm, remarking: "Weininger made no suggestion as to what it is that determines the differentiation of the original protoplasm into arrhenoplasm and thelyplasm, but his idea, though somewhat too morphologically conceived, is useful if only because it emphasizes the fact that male and female characters coexist (though they are very unequally represented) in most if not in all dioecious individuals."[59] Another British biologist, Edward A. Minchin, remarked that Weininger's hypothesis that "sex is a fundamental attribute of living things, and that the living substance, protoplasm, consists of arrhenoplasm and thelyplasm united in varying proportions" had been supported by "certain observations of F. Schaudinn. . . . In *Trypanosoma noctuae*, for example, Schaudinn found that the process of reduction in one gamete took an opposite course to that which it took in the other gamete."[60]

The importance of Weininger's biological understanding of sexuality, however, lies less in any scientific approval it may have found but rather in the role it played in his analysis of masculinity and femininity. The fundamental aim of the first part of *Geschlecht und Charakter* is to deconstruct the traditional notion of sexual difference, the idea that men and women could be easily distinguished on the basis of a few macroscopic features. Weininger believed that even macroscopically, males and females were far more "mixed" or "intermediate" than most people believed; and he supported that conviction with the scientistic claim that, even at the microscopic level, each individual organism was male *and* female. There was, then, no simple, exact way to label an individual as a "man" or as a "woman" (29).

### The Biology and Mathematics of Mating

Sexual intermediacy, Weininger clarified, was not only a characteristic of the solitary adult individual but governed the entire life cycle. It manifested itself at the advent of life and regulated the perpetuation of life: the embryo, in its earliest stages, was neither male nor female, and successful mating required precise matching of the two partners according to their degree of sexual intermediacy. Far from being a haphazard affair, mating depended on biological complementarity, and that complementarity, Weininger claimed, could be expressed with mathematical exactitude.

Conventional wisdom, of course, had always acknowledged that every individual was sexually drawn only to a certain kind of individual and, conversely, repelled by certain other types (31–33). But what determined the complementarity of certain types? Why did one's preference for certain types persist unchanged for life? Could one identify the qualities of a man's ideal mate from the attributes of the man himself? Could sexual affinity be predicted?[61]

Charles Darwin had argued in his theory of sexual selection that since males outnumbered females in most species, mating females always had a pool of available males to choose from. Males had evolved greater aggressiveness and strength because of the consequent necessity to compete with other males for females, and, in many species, they had also developed elaborate physical ornamentations because the females of those species preferred conspicuously ornamented mates.[62] "Does every male," Darwin had wondered, "equally excite and attract the female? Or does she exert a choice, and prefer certain males? This question can be answered in the affirmative by much direct and indirect evidence."[63] Without offering any empirical counterevidence, Weininger criticized Darwin's exclusive focus on female sexual choice, arguing that the choice or rejection of females by males was at least as important a factor in sexual selection (489).[64]

Armed with little more than anecdotes and the unshakable conviction that mating is governed by natural laws, Weininger claimed that the ideal couple comprised one complete male and one complete female. Universal bisexuality, however, ruled out the existence of completely male or female individuals: any male was partly feminine and any female partly masculine. How, then, could Nature's decree be fulfilled? Resolving this dilemma with remarkable ingenuity, Weininger suggested that in an ideal sexual relationship, the *total* masculinity and femininity of the two partners must amount to 1 in algebraic terms. A male who was three-quarters masculine and one-quarter feminine would be ideally complemented by a woman who was one-quarter masculine and three-quarters feminine.[65] This biological complementarity was the indispensable foundation of a successful sexual relationship: aesthetic factors were at best secondary (34–37).[66] This "law of nature," Weininger proclaimed, was unknown prior to his work, except for the intuitive comments of Arthur Schopenhauer and a somewhat similar remark by sexologist Albert Moll (32, 488). Although he claimed that both sources were unknown to him when he "discovered" the Law in early 1901, he acknowledged Schopenhauer's partial priority and quoted him at length (489).[67]

Conceding that other laws of sexual attraction probably remained to be discovered and that his Law was as yet inexact and somewhat dogmatic, Weininger sought to strengthen it by citing a series of analogies from botany and zoology. His first supporting analogy was the botanical phenomenon of heterostyly—the existence of two or more different arrangements of reproductive organs in hermaphroditic flowers of the same species. In one typical form of a heterostylous flower, the style—the connecting stalk between the ovary and the pistil—was long, while the stamens—the male reproductive organs comprising anthers and filaments—had short filaments. In another form, the style was short and the stamens long. This phenomenon had been known from the sixteenth century but had usually been dismissed as an example of mere variability. Charles Darwin, however, had been convinced of its deeper biological significance after observing that pollen from a long-styled flower was fertile when it landed on the stigma of a short-styled flower but almost sterile when placed on the stigma of another long-styled flower. This suggested that heterostyly was a device to favor cross-fertilization.[68] Weininger's account of heterostyly was based on Darwin's treatise, *Different Forms of Flowers on Plants of the Same Species* (1877), and on the Darwinian account given in Julius Sachs's lectures on plant physiology.[69] Flowers with tall styles and short stamens, according to Weininger, were more feminine than those with shorter styles and longer stamens (38–39). Darwin had suggested a similar interpretation, which was part of his larger hypothesis that hermaphroditic heterostylous plants were in the process of evolving into sexually differentiated forms.[70] Weininger disagreed. Heterostylous flowers, he argued, were not evolving toward anything: they merely exemplified the continuously variable sexual intermediacy of all forms of life (38–39). Fertilization, he pointed out, was most successful when pollen from a "masculine" flower fertilized a "feminine" flower and failed when the forms were not sexually complementary (40–41). Weininger proposed, therefore, that an elective process was at work in the stigmas and that this was a fundamental property of the flower itself. The process was similar to the human mating process illustrated by his Law, and the analogy was supported by the fact that the pollen grains in the plants with longer stamens were larger (and, thus, more "male") than in those with shorter stamens (42).[71]

Returning to his Law of Sexual Relations, Weininger refined it to include the *strength* of attraction between the partners. Imagining two hypothetical entities $X$ and $Y$, whose masculinity was indicated by $M$ and femininity by $W$, Weininger assumed that $X$ possessed $\alpha M$ and $\alpha' W$, whereas $Y$ had $\beta W$ and $\beta' M$. Now, if $A$ was the strength of attraction between the two, then

$$A = (k/\alpha - \beta) \cdot f(t)$$

where $k$ was a factor covering all known and unknown laws of sexual affinity, including those related to race, species, and deformity, and $f(t)$ was a temporal function, indicating the period during which the two entities were in proximity to each other. When $\alpha = \beta$, $A$ was infinite. This was the strongest and most elemental form of attraction.[72] The factor "t" was analogous to the "reaction time" of chemistry: the time of interaction between partners was so obviously important in generating or maintaining sexual attraction that Weininger speculated that $A$, the strength of the sexual attraction itself, could perhaps depend mathematically on $t$ (49).[73] Sexual attraction, according to Weininger, was akin to what botanist Wilhelm Friedrich Pfeffer (1845–1920) had named "chemotaxis."[74] Chemotaxis, Weininger argued, need not be unique to plants since all sexual attraction was fundamentally—and literally—chemical.

In a characteristic discursive switch, Weininger then moved quickly from the world of positivistic science to that of imaginative literature. Quoting Goethe's portrayal of adultery in *Elective Affinities*, he argued that the formation and dissolution of erotic bonds followed the same principles as chemical bonds.[75] When $FeSO_4$ (ferrous sulphate) reacted with KOH (potassium hydroxide), the sulphate ion ($SO_4$) left the ferrous ion (Fe) to combine with the potassium ion (K). This was exactly analogous to adultery. A marriage might be contracted for diverse reasons, but it was doomed from the moment one of the partners encountered a more complementary sexual partner than the present spouse. Moral injunctions were impotent against such an elemental natural phenomenon (47–48). Marriage, therefore, should be based on the degree of sexual attraction, not on other (such as monetary) considerations—the Jews, remarked Weininger, had degenerated physically because their marriages were arranged by parents for pragmatic reasons having nothing to do with the elemental logic of sexual affinity (50–51).

### Inheriting Sex

Instead of following up with a more comprehensive analysis of what was good breeding practice, Weininger, in his grasshopperish manner, turned then to questions of inheritance and ontogeny. Although Gregor Mendel's work had been "rediscovered" in 1900, and what we now call the sex chromosome had been identified in 1902, biologists had not reached a consensus on the origin or inheritance of sex before the second decade of the century.[76] Jane Maienschein has shown that various approaches to the issue competed with one another until 1910, when a new synthesis, limited strictly to inheritance, began to emerge.[77] Even this limited consensus was lacking around the time when *Geschlecht und Charakter* was written, and the inheritance of sex was the subject of numerous speculative theories that did not clearly differentiate the subject from the ontogeny of sex. Among these theories, those of Charles Darwin and August Weismann were undoubtedly the most important, and Weininger put them at the forefront of his discussion.

Darwin had taught that every female and every male possessed the secondary sexual characters of the other sex in latent forms, which could manifest themselves in special conditions.[78] The fertilized germ, he had written in a famous passage, was "crowded with invisible characters, proper to both sexes . . . and these characters, like those written on paper with invisible ink, lie ready to be evolved whenever the organisation is disturbed by certain known or unknown conditions."[79] Although just as unable as Darwin to explain the precise mechanics of the process, August Weismann, too, argued in identical terms.[80]

Embryologists of the period were concerned with similar issues. The potential hermaphroditism of the embryo and the latent presence of the characteristics of the other sex were two recurrent motifs in most discussions of the ontogeny of sex. Weininger relied heavily on embryology to validate his thesis of universal bisexuality. By the end of the nineteenth century, numerous scientists had investigated how exactly an embryo became male or female, but an empirically irrefutable answer to the question remained elusive.[81] Even today, the embryology of the vertebrate urogenital system is recognized to be an unusually complicated area of research. The internal and external genitals develop differently, and the crucial structures, such as the Wolffian or Müllerian ducts, are minute and ambiguous. Before the advent of advanced microscopic techniques, embryologists differed greatly in their interpretations of the sequence of development and of its broader biological significance. Weininger summarized the history of theories of embryonic sexual development (466), citing embryologists Friedrich Tiedemann (1781–1861), Martin Heinrich Rathke (1793–1860), Johannes Müller (1801–58), Gabriel Gustav Valentin (1810–83), and Wilhelm Waldeyer (1836–1921).[82] He also reprinted a detailed table from the latest edition of Oscar Hertwig's textbook of embryology depicting the current understanding of the sequence of development of sex in embryos and of the origins and homologous parts of male and female genitals (466–67).[83]

Friedrich Tiedemann, Professor of Anatomy at the University of Heidelberg, had achieved great renown for his research on fetal neurology, the physiology of digestion, and physical anthropology. In 1813, he had published a treatise on malformed and aborted human fetuses. Examining nineteen embryos aborted between five and twenty weeks of gestation (that is, long before full development), Tiedemann had noticed that all of these embryos had female external genitals. He had concluded from this observation that *all* embryos passed through an initial female state, and only some subsequently developed male genitals. Until the fifth week of gestation, said Tiedemann, the human embryo had no external genitals at all. By the seventh or eighth week, the embryo developed a small, clitoris-like organ, which grew further by the end of the ninth week. The labia majora also began to develop at this point. Only at the end of the fifteenth or sixteenth week were the labia majora converted in some embryos into the scrotum and the clitoris-like organ into the penis. In females, the genitals grew merely in size after the ninth week: there was no significant change in their form.[84]

In the mid-nineteenth century, a new generation of German biologists, led by Karl Ernst von Baer (1792–1876), radically revised the aims, scope, and methods of embryological research. Martin Heinrich Rathke and Johannes Müller were two of the most celebrated members of this group.[85] Rathke, educated at Göttingen and Berlin, was chief physician at the city hospital in Danzig (now Gdansk) when he conducted the important embryological investigations cited by Weininger. Embryos at their earliest stages, said Rathke, were sexually so undifferentiated that Tiedemann's theory of universal primordial femininity was meaningless. One could, if one wished, make an equally strong case for a primordial condition of universal masculinity. The actual condition in the earliest stages of embryonic life, Rathke argued, was one of complete sexual neutrality.[86] This interpretation was accepted and experimentally confirmed by Johannes Müller and Gabriel Valentin, both of whom Weininger quoted. Wilhelm Waldeyer (1836–1921), Director of the Institute of Anatomy at the University of Berlin, added a new twist to the issue in 1870 by arguing that the embryo, in its earliest stages, was not sexually neutral but rather hermaphroditic, since it possessed precursors of both testes and ovaries, not simply a "neutral" rudiment that could develop into either. This dual sexual potential was resolved with the development of the testes or the ovaries. Each individual, therefore, was "a true hermaphrodite at a certain stage of development."[87] This notion that the internal genitals were initially hermaphroditic was widely accepted by the turn of the century.[88] Most importantly for our purposes, Waldeyer's conception was adopted by Oscar Hertwig, whose textbook of embryology was Weininger's main source for current information on the subject.[89]

Nineteenth-century embryological literature on sexual development was far from ideologically neutral. Tiedemann believed, for example, that female genitals represented a failure of development, whereas male genitals signified full development.[90] Masculinity was not a simple developmental alternative but a higher stage in a genital hierarchy that could be reached only by some. Rathke spoke eloquently against Tiedemann's conception that all embryos were initially female but did not essentially disagree on the developmental status of femininity. Males, he declared, were equipped with sexual apparatus that went beyond the requirements of procreation. Even where the organs were similar in the two sexes, the male versions were always more complexly structured and, therefore, better developed.[91] Oscar Hertwig, Weininger's source for current knowledge, expressed himself with greater sobriety. A careful examination of his dry prose reveals, however, that he, too, regarded genital development as reflecting a hierarchy of nature. Until the fourth month of intrauterine life, the male and female external genitals, wrote Hertwig, were indistinguishable from each other. With genital differentiation, however, changes in females were "only of a trivial kind" *(nur geringfügiger Art)*. The development of the clitoris was "slow" *(nur noch langsam)* while that of the penis involved an "extraordinarily marked growth in length" of the common precursor *(ein ausserordentlich starkes Längenwachsthum)*. The words Hertwig chose to describe the processes of differentiation indicate his underlying convictions: *Umbildung* (reorganization) for females, and *Umwandlung* (transformation) for males.[92] Tiedemann, Rathke, and Hertwig were among the leading scientists of their generations, but their concepts of gender, even if not identical to those of the philosopher Weininger, were eminently compatible with the latter.

Weininger's discussion of ontogeny and sexual affinity served his project in two fundamental ways. First, they established that universal bisexuality was more than an ancient poetic metaphor: it was a crucial biological fact. The concept explained why individuals mated most successfully only with particular individuals, and it suggested that one could use the degree of sexual intermediacy to predict one's actual choice of mate. Weininger's Law of Sexual Affinity, which might be dismissed today as a piece of baroque pseudomathematics, was in fact firmly grounded in the idea of universal bisexuality, which was, in his time, impeccably scientific. Second, the sections on ontogeny helped extend the focus of Weininger's analysis from the morphology of the adult individual to the dynamic realms of development and behavior. A focused ideological analysis of his scientific sources suggests, furthermore, that at least the kernels of some of Weininger's notorious ideas on femininity were also to be found in them.

## CHAPTER FIVE

# Normalizing the Homosexual

After establishing that all individuals were morphologically androgynous and that this sexual intermediacy governed the entire life cycle, Weininger turned from the individual to the species. Since humans were androgynous to different degrees, it was statistically probable that there would be a group of humans who possess almost equal amounts of masculinity and femininity. Homosexuals, Weininger claimed, constituted that middle group (53–62). Although his argument on homosexuality was anchored in medical discourse, he rejected both the traditional medical opinion that homosexuality was a disease as well as the conviction of a younger generation of physicians that it was the result of a developmental anomaly. Instead, Weininger adopted a populational perspective, arguing that homosexuality represented the inevitable consequence of human sexual intermediacy, and that homosexual mating demonstrated the truth of his own Law of Sexual Relations.

Homosexuality was an important cultural issue in fin-de-siècle Europe.[1] In the German-speaking areas, a homosexual emancipation movement had gathered strength around the turn of the century, and, although not by any means as prominent as the feminist movement, it was a prominent feature of contemporary cultural politics.[2] Physicians and medical discourse played a major role in this movement; the political program of the emancipationists in turn influenced the medical discourse on homosexuality.[3] Weininger's views on homosexuality, when analyzed in the light of their medical and political contexts, illuminate much of this complex history.

Weininger's sources on homosexuality were almost exclusively biomedical and almost entirely devoted to male homosexuality. Although the existence of female homosexuality was universally recognized by the physicians of the era, male homosexuality received much greater attention in medical discourse.[4] Following this convention, Weininger sought to prove that male homosexuality was neither a vice nor a disease but a natural consequence of the bisexuality of the human species. According to his Law of Sexual Relations, the partners in a fully compatible couple must together amount to one ideal male and one ideal female. The perfect partner for a man with 48 percent of masculinity would, therefore, need to be 52 percent male. Such a mate could be found most easily only among men (55–61). A homosexual, then, was a markedly feminine male but not qualitatively different from the average human being, who, too, was neither completely male nor completely female. The homosexual was situated in the middle of the spectrum of sexually intermediate forms extending between the two imaginary poles of absolute masculinity and femininity. Since all human beings were androgynous to different degrees, everybody was both homosexual and heterosexual in different proportions. Those near the middle of the spectrum of intermediacy were predominantly (but not necessarily exclusively) homosexual, while those near either end of the spectrum were predominantly (but again, not exclusively) heterosexual (57). The homosexual, therefore, was simply a natural variant.

In order to make this claim, Weininger had to take a stand on two of the most contentious issues in the history of medical theories of homosexuality. First, he had to establish that homosexuality was always innate, because if it could be acquired in response to environmental conditions, then one could not claim that homosexuality was an expression of biological sexual intermediacy. Second, Weininger needed to establish that although inborn, homosexuality was not a pathological phenomenon. Both of these topics had fuelled years of medical debate, and an examination of the related discourse reveals a highly complex history.

### Innate or Acquired?

It was absurd, said Weininger, to argue that homosexuality could be acquired through seduction or heterosexual abstinence. There was, of course, always an occasion that first "released" homosexuality, but such occasions were concerned only with the *expression* of an inborn trait. It was, after all, no different with heterosexuals. There was always one particular occasion when a heterosexual first experienced attraction toward a member of the other sex without anybody ever doubting that the person had been heterosexually inclined before that event (53–55). Like all late-nineteenth-century theorists, Weininger presented the issue of innate/acquired as an either/or question, ignoring, as they did, the many ambiguities involved, and he named Albert von Schrenck-Notzing (1862–1929), Emil Kraepelin (1856–1926), and, mistakenly, Charles Féré (1852–1907) as prominent physicians who wrongly believed that homosexuality was an acquired preference.[5] A closer examination of the professional discourse on the subject reveals that the question was far more complex than Weininger or his sources admitted.[6]

Albert von Schrenck-Notzing, a Munich physician, claimed that since hypnotic suggestion could change a homosexual into a heterosexual, it was logical to assume that the cause of homosexuality was environmental rather than innate. He acknowledged, however, that homosexual associations were formed only in the presence of an inherited weakness of the nervous system, which reduced the individual's ability to resist "perverted" ideas triggered by accidental circumstances.[7] The renowned psychiatrist Emil Kraepelin thought no differently.[8] Although Schrenck-Notzing and Kraepelin could not completely exclude congenital components from their theory of homosexuality, they became known as upholders of the "acquired" hypothesis because they emphasized that the inherited nervous weakness could not *lead* to homosexual behavior in the absence of conducive environmental factors, a euphemistic phrase that usually meant seduction.

Other physicians of the time claimed that homosexuality was entirely innate, without denying that homosexual behavior could be learned or resorted to in exceptional circumstances. "Acts," however, did not constitute a "perversion."[9] For the Berlin sexologist Iwan Bloch (1872–1922), isolated homosexual acts (such as sexual relations among male prisoners with no access to women) signified "pseudohomosexuality," whereas "real" homosexuality was inborn, lasting, and integral to the personality, a distinction accepted by the physician and leading homosexual emancipationist Magnus Hirschfeld (1868–1935).[10]

Another way to exclude some homosexual acts from true homosexuality was to acknowledge the "normality" of such behavior at a certain developmental stage. The psychologist Max Dessoir (1867–1947) and, later, sexologists Havelock Ellis and Albert Moll postulated that prepubertal sexual desire was directed merely toward "a warm human body" rather than toward members of a specific sex.[11] Homosexual behavior during this stage did not interfere with the development of an adult heterosexual identity.[12] For most people, the sexual urge "differentiated" around puberty, coming to be focused on the other sex. In some, however, the "undifferentiated" state persisted, leading to bisexual behavior. Weininger endorsed the idea of "normal" prepubertal homosexual behavior (57).[13] Perhaps the most powerful way to dismiss the notion that adults could acquire a homosexual orientation was, however, with the theory of "latent" or "tardive" homosexuality, according to which homosexual behavior occurring late in the life of a heterosexual was due to the release of a congenital but hitherto dormant homosexual disposition. Havelock Ellis accepted this concept, realizing that if homosexuality was innate but could lie dormant for years, expressing itself long after puberty, then it was impossible to establish any particular instance of homosexual behavior as acquired.[14]

The "innate/acquired" debate was conducted most often within a larger debate on the nature and pathological status of homosexuality. To portray it as an acquired condition often implied that it was a vice deserving social censure and medical "correction." If it was innate, however, then censure was useless and treatment difficult if not impossible. To make matters more complicated, an innate condition could be a disease, an anomaly, or a mere anthropological variation like colored skin. To appreciate Weininger's originality in claiming homosexuality to be a natural human variation, we need to examine the medical debate over the status of homosexuality—and its political context—around the turn of the century.

### Homosexuality: Disease, Anomaly, or Variation?

Summing up a generation of debate in one sentence, Weininger declared that few physicians believed any longer that homosexuality was a manifestation of neuro-psychopathic degeneration (55). When Weininger was born in 1880, degeneration was the great explanatory paradigm in medicine, and homosexual orientation was regarded as a characteristic manifestation of degeneration. By the time *Geschlecht und Charakter* was published in 1903, the situation had changed quite radically.

The concept of degeneration was originally a quasi-theological explanation of disease and abnormality proposed by the French psychiatrist Benedict-Augustin Morel (1809–73) in 1857. Morel explained numerous pathological conditions and deviant phenomena as variations from an Adamic "type primitif." Degeneration was always a vague concept and useful precisely because of its vagueness. It allowed physicians to comprehend diverse physical and behavioral phenomena as expressions of one underlying pathological condition. Alcoholism, tuberculosis, and homosexuality, for example, were all signs of underlying degeneration. So were cleft-lips, misshapen ears, and unretractable foreskins. These deviations from the norm, moreover, were hereditary and worsened progressively over generations until the last member of the tainted line was killed off by the sheer weight of accumulated pathology. The mentally ill and the sexual "perverts" were degenerates par excellence.[15] Degeneration, clearly, was not simply a medical concept. Within and outside the ranks of professional physicians, the idea was charged with great cultural anxiety and frequently used to exclude alcoholics, Jews, homosexuals, and the "dangerous" elements of the working classes from an ostensibly healthy core population.[16]

In one of the earliest and most influential medical attempts to explain homosexuality, Carl Friedrich Otto Westphal (1833–90), professor of psychiatry at Berlin, defined it as the symptom of an inherited pathological state of the nervous or the psychic sphere, without actually using the term "degeneration."[17] That short step was taken in 1877 by Richard von Krafft-Ebing. The future author of the *Psychopathia Sexualis* identified Westphal's "inherited pathological state" as the degeneration of the central nervous system. Homosexuality and other "perversions," he argued, were "functional signs of degeneration."[18] Krafft-Ebing emphasized the importance of degeneration with increasing conviction in successive editions of his widely influential treatise *Psychopathia Sexualis,* which was first published in 1886, in which he used the idea to explain the etiology of all the "perversions" he catalogued so painstakingly therein. At the very end of his life, however, Krafft-Ebing came to downplay the importance of degeneration in homosexuality, which Weininger referred to as a silent rejection of degenerationism (55). It is questionable whether it was anything of the kind. Krafft-Ebing had grown interested in newer explanations of homosexuality in the 1890s, but although he discussed them in detail and with considerable approval, there is no evidence that he ever completely repudiated the concept of degeneration.[19]

The degenerationist conception of homosexuality was sustained by unitary notions of normality and etiology. Each sex had one specific psychosexual personality corresponding to its anatomy. The possession of male genitalia entailed the desire for intercourse with females: any aberration from this norm was pathological and could be explained, regardless of nature or degree of manifestation, by one pathological mechanism.[20] By the end of the nineteenth century, however, many physicians had begun to argue that while heterosexuality was indeed the normal orientation, the possession of one set of genitals did not *necessarily* entail the possession of any particular sexual orientation. They explained heterosexuality as the outcome of a developmental process, analogous to but not inflexibly linked with the development of the genitalia in the embryo.

As we have seen, the human embryo, by this time, was considered to be initially hermaphroditic, a notion that was eminently compatible with the nineteenth-century conviction that each embryo recapitulated the evolutionary history of its species. Human phylogeny (as Charles Darwin had suggested) had progressed from primitive hermaphroditism to monosexuality, just as the hermaphroditic human embryo developed into a male or a female. Like all processes, however, that of human sexual development broke down at times, resulting in the birth of a child whose genital sex was ambiguous. A comparable error, it now began to be claimed, could affect the development of the mind alone, causing aberrations in sexual orientation. Frank Sulloway has shown that these theories were part of a phylogenetic perspective on sexuality that developed in association with functionalist psychology in the United States.[21] Among the American investigators of the phylogeny of sex, the psychiatrist James G. Kiernan (1852–1923) and the urologist G. Frank Lydston (1857–1923) exerted great influence over Central European theorists of homosexuality.

This influence had its ironies. Kiernan's theory of homosexuality was an extension of the views of the German classicist and pioneering homosexual activist Karl Heinrich Ulrichs (1825–1895). Ulrichs, a vehement opponent of degenerationism, had written a series of pamphlets between 1864 and 1879 against the legal persecution and medical stigmatization of homosexuals.[22] His theory of homosexuality was based on his knowledge of embryology and on ideas articulated in Pausanias's speech in Plato's *Symposium*.[23] Ulrichs's central assertion was that the male homosexual represented "a female soul in a male body": *anima muliebris virili corpore inclusa*. Homosexuals made up a "third sex," neither wholly male nor wholly female.[24] Ulrichs's later views became convoluted in their attempt to explain female homosexuality and the different varieties of male homosexual desire, but none of those complexities were picked up by physicians.[25] Ulrichs's contribution to medical discourse was confined to the idea that homosexuality represented psychological gender transposition. In Central Europe, Westphal accepted the idea and so did Krafft-Ebing.[26] In France, Eugène Gley (1857–1930) and Valentin Magnan independently declared, in a neurological vein, that the male homosexual possessed a female brain.[27] The cause of the gender transposition, however, was attributed by all of these authors to degeneration, a concept to which Ulrichs himself was wholly opposed. His own causal hypothesis, detailed in letters to his relatives in 1862, had attributed homosexuality to an unexplained error in embryonic development.

Discussing embryological reports of sexual development in impressive detail, Ulrichs had speculated that "a double sexual germ" was present in each embryo. Normally, only one-half of this, the male or the female half, underwent development. Genital hermaphroditism resulted when both halves developed equally. In the homosexual, however, the male germ developed physically and the female germ "in all nonphysical directions."[28] These letters, however, were published only in 1899. Long before that, James Kiernan had come forward with his neo-Ulrichsian hypothesis, which no Central European sexologist had anticipated in spite of their familiarity with Ulrichs's work.

In 1884, Kiernan accepted Ulrichs's fundamental conception and, consigning questions of soul to theologians, argued that the male homosexual had a functionally female brain.[29] This was, of course, similar to the views of Magnan and Gley. Kiernan's innovation lay in his phylogenetic explanation of this phenomenon. Pointing out that males could be born with female external genitals and that many lower animals were hermaphroditic, he claimed that hermaphroditism was a reversion to the evolutionary ancestors of the human species.[30] If the genitalia could revert, he reasoned, so could the brain. A homosexual orientation would be the psychosexual consequence of such a reversion.[31] For Kiernan, therefore, homosexuality was essentially an atavistic phenomenon, a "functional if not organic" reversion to an earlier stage of phylogeny. G. Frank Lydston, too, saw homosexuality as atavistic, but for him the reversion was to the early embryonic stage of potential hermaphroditism. "The more nearly the individual approximates the type of fetal development which exists prior to the commencement of sexual differentiation," Lydston stated, "the more marked is the aberrance of sexuality."[32] The reversion caused homosexuality, but what caused the reversion? Neither Kiernan nor Lydston raised this question, an omission for which they were criticized by Albert Moll. Degeneration, obviously, was a possible cause for the reversion.[33]

Almost contemporaneously, a nonatavistic phylogenetic theory of homosexuality was proposed by Julien Chevalier in France. He portrayed the embryonic development of sex as an ontogenetic struggle between male and female elements. Although a predominantly male or predominantly female constitution was the usual outcome of that contest, Chevalier emphasized that the human species had not yet evolved sufficiently to attain complete individual monosexuality: the germ of the other sex still lurked within every human being, no matter how apparently monosexual s/he seemed, and could be activated by a variety of internal and external factors. Since everybody possessed some element of the other sex, it was obvious that all humans were potentially homosexual to varying degrees. Homosexuality thus was not atavistic but a consequence of the incomplete differentiation of the sexes at the present stage of evolution.[34] The manifestation of this universal trait was, however, not inevitable: it was dependent upon a host of facilitating circumstances, among which degeneration was prominent. Degeneration, as we saw earlier, could have a place within a developmental theory of homosexuality as an ultimate cause; Chevalier's theory shows that it could serve equally well as a secondary cause, provided an "error" of development was assumed to be universal.[35]

Weininger knew of Kiernan, Lydston, and Chevalier only from the fairly detailed reviews of their work by Krafft-Ebing, who had acknowledged the heuristic worth of their approach in an article published in 1895, which Weininger cited (498).[36] Agreeing with Kiernan and Lydston that the human embryo in its earliest weeks was hermaphroditic, Krafft-Ebing had also endorsed Chevalier's contention that the phylogenetic progress toward complete differentiation of the sexes was still incomplete in the human species. All females harbored latent male traits and all males had latent female traits, and these became overtly expressed in homosexuality. But what were the loci of these traits? How exactly did the latent sex overwhelm the dominant one?[37] Krafft-Ebing tried to find answers to these important questions by postulating (on the basis of negligible neuroanatomic evidence) the existence of cerebral centers determining sexual "personality."[38] The early embryo pos-

sessed rudiments of male and female sexual centers in its brain, just as it possessed rudiments of male and female genitals. Nature, however, tended to develop only the center generating heterosexual desire, but the . center
generating homosexual desire remained extant in a rudimentary form even in
"normal" persons. If both centers were well developed, the subject would be
sexually drawn to members of both sexes, and if the center for same-sex desire
gained the upper hand while the other center remained rudimentary, the subject's sexual orientation would be exclusively homosexual. Such a reversal,
Krafft-Ebing insisted, could be caused only by degeneration.[39]

There was, in short, no wholesale replacement of the degenerationist
model by the developmental one.[40] Indeed, one could not really replace the
other since the first essentially combined a theory of etiology with a mechanism of pathogenesis, whereas the second was concerned solely with pathogenesis. The two could even be quite compatible, although one might choose
to focus on etiology or on pathogenesis. If one wished to understand only *how*
homosexuality arose, as did Kiernan and Lydston, the developmental theory
was sufficient. If, however, one regarded the developmental deviation as
pathological, one necessarily had to look for the cause of the error, and degeneration (or one of its conceptual variants such as hereditary predisposition
or inherited taint) was still a suitable candidate.[41] The renowned German
sexologist Albert Moll, for instance, believed that homosexuality was the
manifestation of a disharmony between anatomy and sexual drive that was at
least as abnormal as physical pseudohermaphroditism and that needed to be
investigated and treated medically.[42]

### Congenitalism and the Politics of Identity

Albert Moll's warnings on the abnormal nature of homosexuality were often
directed against another prominent German researcher on homosexuality,
Magnus Hirschfeld (1868–1935).[43] Hirschfeld, like Karl Heinrich Ulrichs,
was himself homosexual.[44] Unlike Ulrichs, he was a physician. He believed
passionately that only through science could the legal and cultural injustices
against homosexuals be ended. In 1897, Hirschfeld and others established
the Scientific-Humanitarian Committee *(Wissenschaftlich-humanitären Komi-
tee)*, which became the most visible organization of homosexuals and their
supporters in contemporary Central Europe and which had the revealing
motto, "justice through science" *(per scientiam ad justitiam)*. The committee
sent regular petitions to the Reichstag for a repeal of Paragraph 175, the German statute against sodomy; held lectures and public meetings to disseminate "scientific" information on homosexuality; and published the *Yearbook
for Sexually Intermediate Forms (Jahrbuch für sexuelle Zwischenstufen)* from
1899 until inflation killed it in 1923.[45] The *Yearbook* was of great theoretical

utility to Weininger, and he was not uninfluenced by its emancipatory agenda, although he felt that the publication would have been even more valuable if it had addressed all the diverse expressions of sexual intermediacy rather than homosexuality and hermaphroditism alone (469).

The rationale for the committee's demands to end discrimination against homosexuals was unequivocally biological. Its very first petition to the Reichstag, sent in 1897 and eventually rejected, asserted that recent scientific research had determined that homosexuality stemmed from an inner, constitutional predisposition *(einer tief innerlichen constitutionellen Anlage)* related to the developmental hermaphroditism of the human embryo and that no legal or moral guilt could possibly attach to so involuntary a condition. Armed with this unshakable biological conviction, the committee ridiculed the common argument that homosexuals ought to be punished since they might seduce minors into homosexuality: nobody, they argued, could be seduced into an inborn condition, and there was therefore no necessity to "protect" society against homosexuals.[46] To argue that homosexuality was congenital was not enough, however, to justify the committee's political demand for emancipation. In an age that saw degenerates as enemies of the social and moral order, it was crucial to separate homosexuality from degeneration. This was where Hirschfeld spoke with his clinical voice, declaring with authority that his meticulous examination of thousands of homosexuals had established that only about 16 out of 100 homosexuals displayed physical signs of degeneration, whereas few unequivocal degenerates were homosexual.[47] But even Hirschfeld, whose political activism never quite overcame his medical Weltanschauung, let degenerationism in by the back door by arguing that homosexuality was a "substitute for degeneration" *(Degenerations-Ersatz)* and that homosexuals were used by Nature as a "prophylactic agent" *(Vorbeugungsmittel)* against degeneration.[48] Hirschfeld suspected that a homosexual was born when a family, without being manifestly degenerate, began to slide toward a degenerative sequence: since few homosexuals ever reproduced, "his" birth was Nature's way of halting the transmission of the taint beginning to affect the family.[49] This bow to degeneration notwithstanding, Hirschfeld's theory did offer something new by expanding upon Ulrichs's original concept of a female soul within a male body and by reconstructing homosexuality, as we shall see, as a pervasive but nongenital form of hermaphroditism.

A different kind of hermaphroditism had, of course, been implicit in the theory that homosexuality was a psychosexual gender transposition. Albert Moll had expressed this neatly by describing the homosexual, in the words of the philosopher Eduard von Hartmann (1842–1906), as a "body-mind hermaphrodite" *(Leibseelenzwitter).*[50] Neither the genitalia nor the brain of the homosexual, in other words, was necessarily sexually ambiguous, but "he" was hermaphroditic because male genitalia and a female psychosexual personality co-existed in him.[51] Explaining homosexuality as "body-mind hermaphroditism," however, soon became problematic. Franciszek Neugebauer (1856–1914)—who was Polish by birth but achieved pan-European influence with his polyglot contributions on hermaphroditism—reported that although orthodox medical opinion expected a person with testicular tissue anywhere in his body to be drawn psychosexually to women, many male pseudohermaphrodites—and no contemporary clinician could claim to have examined more of them than Neugebauer, the undisputed authority on hermaphroditism!—considered themselves to be women and wished to marry men.[52] This was, to say the least, surprising, because pseudohermaphrodites were, of course, supposed to be males with "normal" male brains, affected only by a genital ambiguity. If people hitherto supposed to be suffering only from a genital abnormality were also affected by psychosexual anomalies, then homosexual orientation and physical hermaphroditism could no longer be treated as entirely separate entities.

The conventional distinction between hermaphroditism and homosexuality had never had much meaning for Magnus Hirschfeld, and Neugebauer's observations strengthened his conviction that homosexuals were psychologically as well as morphologically gender-transposed. Hirschfeld conceded that the vast majority of homosexuals possessed normal genitalia, but he did not believe that the examination of the genitals alone was sufficient to decide upon a person's sexual morphology. If one took a more global approach and examined a sufficient number of "cases," one soon saw that the body of the homosexual, in overall terms, was neither clearly male nor clearly female. What Krafft-Ebing had considered possible in a small group of highly degenerate homosexuals, Hirschfeld claimed to be common to all homosexuals. "Of the 1,500 homosexuals that I have seen, each was physically and mentally distinct from a complete male," Hirschfeld declared in 1903, without pausing to define what exactly he meant by a "complete male."[53] That omission characterized all of Hirschfeld's writings—indeed, it characterized his entire perspective on the question of sexuality. He constantly referred to the "complete" or "average" man (or, on occasions, woman) but never defined that entity in any detail or with any conceptual rigor. Hirschfeld was (more or less) radical with regard to social attitudes on homosexuality, but he never seems to have felt any desire to challenge contemporary definitions of masculine and feminine norms, accepting virtually every conventional assumption about the "complete" male and female.

Homosexuality, as we have seen, was initially regarded by physicians as a disease or at least as a manifestation of the disease process of degeneration. By the end of the nineteenth century, however, physicians began to argue that homosexuality could well be a mere deviation from the norm (an anomaly). However, such a *deviation*, although not a disease, continued to be considered as pathological and, therefore, not merely as a *variation* of the human species, like having black or brown skin. A disease was a process, often progressive and usually noxious, whereas *any* deviation—whether structural or functional—from *any* biological norm was pathological in the broad sense: a cleft palate was a pathological entity because it deviated from the structural norm, but since it was neither progressive nor in itself noxious, it was not a disease. Similarly, medical sexologists continued to conceptualize sexuality with reference to a fixed, virtually uncontested norm—the mutual attraction of man and woman culminating in vaginal intercourse. With reference to this norm, *any* other form of sexual behavior—even between men and women—was pathological, though pathological did not necessarily mean diseased.

Medical sexologists never succeeded in formulating homosexuality as completely nonpathological, finding it relatively easy to jettison the idea of disease but not that of anomaly. Havelock Ellis, for instance, accepted that homosexuals were not diseased, while denying that they constituted "an anthropological human variety comparable to the Negro or the Mongolian man."[54] Citing no less an authority than Rudolf Virchow (1821–1902), Ellis argued that any deviation from the norm was pathological, without necessarily being a disease.[55] Hirschfeld, too, could not do without the idea of a universal heterosexual norm, in spite of all his rhetoric on the universality of sexual intermediacy. His classification of sexual intermediates was implicitly guided by the normative belief that although all humans were androgynous, most humans still belonged to one side of the spectrum or the other. "Male" or "female" were loose categories, to be sure, but they were far from meaningless, nor were "complete males" or "complete females" mere fictions for him. Homosexuality, similarly, was not a sin, vice, or disease, but it did represent an aberration from the usual pattern of human sexuality.

Otto Weininger used an early article by Hirschfeld, which presented his views clearly and concisely and which, predictably enough, was deeply marked by conceptual confusions on the question of gender.[56] In the article, Hirschfeld had argued that there was no absolute, qualitative distinction between male and female. Since everyone was partly male and partly female, it made no sense to classify genital hermaphrodites separately from the rest of humanity. The hermaphrodite was different only in degree from the male homosexual and the tomboyish girl. All belonged together, representing different grades of sexual intermediacy, and each group constituted a variety of the human species.[57] (In his 1914 treatise on homosexuality, Hirschfeld even cited Weininger in support of this contention.)[58]

Hirschfeld's pathological perspective was evident in the article that Weininger used: the title itself ("The Objective Diagnosis of Homosexuality") revealed a pathological bias. Hirschfeld's argument was prefaced by his analysis of sexual differences, which he categorized into five separate groups: (1) differences in the sex glands—testes in males, ovaries in females; (2) structural and functional differences in the internal and external genitals; (3) differences in sexual characteristics that emerge at puberty, e.g., development of breasts in females and growth of facial hair in males; (4) differences in psychology, e.g., women were kinder, men less so; and (5) differences in sexual orientation—women were attracted to men and men to women.[59] Hirschfeld accepted these differences as broadly valid, while denying them any status as absolute distinctions between the sexes. The earlier these differences were established in the life cycle, the more prominent and the more stable they were. The sex glands, for instance, developed from a hermaphroditic rudiment but differentiated into male or female gonads very early in the life of the organism. They were, consequently, relatively immune to developmental disturbances, as confirmed by the clinical rarity of "true" hermaphrodites possessing both ovaries and testes or a single ovotestis. Characters belonging to the second group were more prone to disturbances but less so than those of the last three groups, all of which developed around puberty.[60]

Homosexuality was a developmental disturbance of the fifth group of Hirschfeld's classification. Since the differences of the fifth group emerged at the same time as those of the third and the fourth, homosexuals usually also displayed developmental anomalies in the latter, with male homosexuals, for instance, being more or less feminized in physical as well as psychological attributes. Moreover, the more feminized a male homosexual, the stronger his homosexual desire, and the more masculine his preferred partners.[61] The intensity of desire was thus linked, on one hand, with the physical and psychological traits of the subject and with the physical and behavioral attributes of the sexual partner on the other. The partner, then, was chosen so as to complement the subject, an argument clearly resembling Weininger's Law of Sexual Relations.[62]

Weininger, nevertheless, approached the question of homosexuality very differently from Hirschfeld. The differences concerned their respective ideas on norms and deviations. Hirschfeld believed that homosexuality was caused by a developmental disturbance, which implied, of course, that he also believed in a developmental *norm*, which could be nothing other than heterosexuality, an idea that Hirschfeld challenged so strenuously in the political arena.[63] As a political activist, Hirschfeld presented the world as one full of sexually intermediate organisms, of whom the homosexual was only one kind. As a man of science, he argued that these intermediate forms had been

created by anomalous biological processes which needed to be understood—
in comparison to a norm, which he never problematized.[64] For Weininger,
however, the world was simply full of sexual intermediates, some of whom
were naturally homosexual: it was a simple fact of nature and not a pathological problem in any way.[65] Rigorously stripping away all notions of anomaly
or abnormality from the concept of variety, he argued that since all humans
were sexually intermediate between pure masculinity and pure femininity,
the laws of statistics ordained the existence of a cluster of individuals around
the middle of the spectrum who were almost equally male and female and
whose ideal partners belonged to the same genital sex (55–61).[66]

### The Question of Treatment

With views such as these, Weininger obviously had little interest in the treatment of homosexuality, and he referred sarcastically to the advice of an
anonymous professor of psychiatry that homosexuals should be simply castrated.[67] Other, less radical therapies, Weininger declared, had proved
equally useless and theoretically unsound: the vogue for hypnotherapy of homosexuality, for instance, had not led to any noteworthy success (59–60).
Hypnosis had been regularly used in the treatment of homosexuality at least
from the time of Krafft-Ebing, who had declared it to be "all that can really
benefit the patient."[68] By the early twentieth century, however, its benefits
had come to be seen as rather too transient, and the popularity of hypnotherapy was on the wane.[69] Magnus Hirschfeld, however, condemned it for reasons having nothing to do with its efficacy. Since hypnosis could affect sight
or menstruation, there was, he said, no reason to doubt that it could generate
heterosexual desire in a homosexual.[70] What he questioned was the need for
therapy. Since homosexuality was a "prophylactic" of degeneration, it might
actually be harmful from the perspective of race-hygiene *(Rassenhygiene)* to
enable homosexuals to procreate.[71]

Hirschfeld once proclaimed that only one agent could really extinguish
homosexual desire: death.[72] Albert Moll was less pessimistic, advocating an
unusual blend of cognitive psychotherapy and counselling, which he called
"association-therapy." Moll believed that even in strongly homosexual subjects, there was always a link, no matter how weak, to "normality." Association
therapy sought to strengthen this link by a variety of means, one of which was
to encourage the male homosexual to associate with masculine women.[73]
Weininger, to whom Moll did not refer, had already argued that if indeed the
treatment of homosexuality was ever essential, the only efficacious procedure
would be to urge the male homosexual to consort with his true complementary partner, the masculine woman, or even a lesbian (60). This was less a
therapeutic recommendation than an illustration of his Law of Sexual Rela-

tions. A male homosexual, possessing little masculinity in himself, would need an extremely masculine partner: this could be a man or a strongly masculine woman. Mutatis mutandis, the same principle applied to female homosexuals. If Weininger had said any more on the treatment of homosexuality, it would have been logically inconsistent with the notion of nonpathological variety that he propounded with such vigor.

He had not always been so careful. In his early outline "Eros und Psyche," where he had espoused the same theory of homosexuality, he had included a section on the therapy of homosexuality under the slender pretext that an effective treatment would enable homosexuals to reproduce.[74] Here, Weininger had recommended that the male homosexual's weak innate masculinity should be augmented with sex-gland extracts. This was not simply a theoretical recommendation. Weininger, otherwise the archetypal armchair-theorist, seems to have tested this idea in human experiments. In April 1901, he had sent this report to Hermann Swoboda:

> My agent to combat homosexuality seems to be successful!! Even though this only confirms my own theory, I have yet to recover from my amazement. If only I could be certain that no suggestion was involved. . . . In any case, the doses must be continued. . . . My patient is already preparing for his first coitus![75]

Although we have no unequivocal proof, it is strongly likely that this "patient" was Weininger himself. If that were indeed the case, it would explain much of the extreme fear of femininity that pervades *Geschlecht und Charakter*. The future of humanity, Weininger argued, depended upon the eradication of femininity—his attempt to "cure" male homosexuality, therefore, was not simply an eccentric experiment but an integral part of his entire project. Whether that project as a whole was inspired by his own homosexuality is a question that cannot be answered with the available evidence, and even if it could be proved beyond contention that Weininger himself was homosexual, that would not be self-sufficient in explaining his concern with gender.[76] Even such unambiguously heterosexual Viennese intellectuals as Karl Kraus, Rosa Mayreder, and Sigmund Freud, after all, were concerned with many of the same themes, expressing some similar anxieties over the fluidity of gender and the effeminacy of modern civilization. If their views cannot be explained by their personal homosexuality, then it follows that it would be unwise to try to explain Weininger's views solely in the light of a biographical possibility.

Weininger's enigmatic experiment, however, has other historical insights to offer. Weininger's experiments lead us into the early history of organotherapy, usually regarded as the precursor of modern endocrinology. Weininger injected his "patient" with testicular extract, which was commercially available under the proprietary name of Sequardine, a name inspired by none other than Brown-Séquard, who, as we saw earlier, had galvanized the medical world by claiming to have rejuvenated himself by injections of extracts of animal testicles.[77] Fully aware that after Brown-Séquard's announcement, treatment of all kinds of disorders, real or imagined, with extracts from all kinds of glands and organs had become immensely popular, Weininger wondered why organotherapists had not thought of administering sex-gland extracts in cases of homosexuality. As we have seen, he did his best to make up for this deficiency, and he seems to have been quite alone in this venture. Physicians, in fact, did not think of homosexuality in glandular terms at all during Weininger's lifetime. A mere twenty years after his death, however, the medical press of Central Europe hummed with claims and controversies regarding the glandular basis of homosexuality.[78]

At the height of this trend, male homosexuals were castrated by surgeons and testicles from "normal" donors implanted in them.[79] The procedure was based on the eminent Viennese physiologist Eugen Steinach's claim that male homosexuality was due to "feminine erotization" of the brain by female hormones secreted by aberrant cells in the testicle, which, according to Steinach, resembled the cells of the ovary.[80] It seemed obvious to him, therefore, that if testes with such aberrant cells were replaced by fully "male" gonads, homosexual desire would be replaced by heterosexuality. Magnus Hirschfeld was so overjoyed by the political utility of this demonstration of the biological basis of homosexuality that he declared that Ulrichs's celebrated formulation now had to be revised: rather than a female *soul,* the homosexual possessed a female *gland* in a male body.[81] In the event, the hope proved illusory: the operation produced no lasting effects and Steinach's glandular theory of homosexuality soon passed into oblivion.[82] It is important, however, to note that Weininger's unpublished idea was in tune with notions that would, however briefly, be considered as "good" science. Weininger was not, of course, a professional scientist, nor an uncritical admirer of science or even an invariably logical thinker. His knowledge of the scientific literature, however, was extensive and his responses to it often critical and well reasoned. There is no better evidence for this assertion than his analysis of homosexuality, which used biomedical discourse to affirm a distinct homosexual identity while rejecting the narrow pathological perspective of contemporary physicians and medically-trained emancipationists like Magnus Hirschfeld. He integrated his final theory of homosexuality with his broader thesis of universal bisexuality without falling prey to the contradictions marking the work of Hirschfeld and his associates. Even in his earlier, self-contradictory draft, Weininger's approach to the treatment of homosexuality was conceptually elegant—and in whiggish terms, prescient. These qualities do not, of course, make Weininger into a real scientist. They do establish, however, that Weininger was a more complex and unpredictable thinker than the one-dimensional bigot one encounters in his standard biographies.

Should we, then, see *Geschlecht und Charakter* as a "modern" text because of its approach to homosexuality? That, I think, would be just as untenable as the traditional view that the text contains nothing besides venom, prejudice, and pseudoscience. We must approach the text instead as a fundamentally fragmented and more than occasionally incoherent work, parts of which were malignantly prejudiced, parts merely dull and tedious, and yet other parts "modern," or indeed, more "modern" than the most radical statements on gender that one could find in fin-de-siècle Europe. This disunity of the text is one of its most striking features and it reflects not merely Weininger's own immaturity and haste, although those factors are not to be discounted. Turn-of-the-century discourses on gender and sexuality were almost invariably riven by similar contradictions and inconsistencies. Very traditional notions of masculinity and femininity, for example, could go hand in hand with radical claims on the healthiness of homosexuality, as one sees in the work of Magnus Hirschfeld. Similarly, very "modern" notions on (hetero)sexual relations could co-exist with explicitly conservative ideas about the meaning and worth of femininity, as with Karl Kraus. As far as gender and sexuality were concerned, fin-de-siècle debates were far too complex to be reified with anachronistic labels such as "modern" or "reactionary," and there exists no better example of such discursive complexity than *Geschlecht und Charakter*. Its attitude toward homosexuality is a component and a reflection of that complexity rather than a clear and unambiguous sign of the text's modernity.

## CHAPTER SIX

# Deconstructing Femininity: The Psychology of Hysteria

The late nineteenth century has been described as the golden age of hysteria. This puzzling condition, characterized by unexplained disturbances of consciousness and by dramatic physical symptoms having no organic basis, fascinated physicians, intellectuals, artists, and writers of the era and appeared to hold the keys to many enigmas. How did the mind affect the body? Was the human psyche one and indivisible or could it be split with ease? How was human perception regulated? Perhaps above all, however, hysteria was intimately associated with issues of gender. Some regarded hysteria as the royal road to the secrets of femininity. Others struggled to explain why men were rarely affected by it. Many condemned the hysteric as lying, cheating, and immoral; others detected hysteria in the great female saints of the past. All this has been extensively studied by recent historians, and the scholarly literature on hysteria continues to expand.[1] The importance of hysteria in Weininger's work, however, has not been sufficiently appreciated.[2] This is unfortunate, since Weininger's analysis of hysteria forms the core of his belief on the ontological nullity of Woman, and it is a particularly clear example of the intertwining of scientific, medical, and cultural discourses that is characteristic of *Geschlecht und Charakter* as a whole.[3]

Weininger used the medical discourse on hysteria very differently from that on homosexuality. Contemporary scientific theories of homosexuality harmonized, within limits, with Weininger's fundamental hypothesis that each human being was both male and female in different proportions. By analyzing hysteria, however, Weininger wished to prove his metaphysical theory of femininity, and a mere critique of psychological or psychiatric theories of hysteria would not have answered his needs. He followed a different path.

Despite the availability of many misogynistic theories of hysteria, no medical theory of the time reached the metaphysical depth that Weininger's theory demanded. Instead of refining, amplifying, or criticizing current theories, therefore, Weininger incorporated aspects of them into his political and metaphysical project by transforming their meaning. He selected one of the central concepts of Josef Breuer and Sigmund Freud's *Studies on Hysteria*—that of the "second consciousness" of hysterics—and overturned it. What had been a second consciousness for Breuer and Freud became the true consciousness for Weininger, and what had been genuine for them became a simulacrum for him. He exchanged the ontological status of the two selves, while leaving the structure of the concept intact. With the aid of this transformed concept, Weininger reinterpreted other medical theories of hysteria and placed the theory (now quite legitimately "his" theory) in the framework of Kantian ethics. As we saw earlier, Weininger believed that the intelligible self was the source of all logical or ethical thought. But hysteria, Weininger argued, was a state of crisis that revealed Woman's greatest secret: that Woman did not possess an intelligible or noumenal self.[4] Here we reach the heart of Weininger's answer to the Woman Question: Woman did not deserve autonomy because she had no intelligible self. Hysteria proved this.

Recent scholars have written much on Freud's alleged transmission of his friend Wilhelm Fliess's unpublished theories on universal sexual intermediacy to Weininger through Hermann Swoboda.[5] The rather more fascinating intellectual links between Freud's theory of hysteria and Weininger's have been largely ignored. Contemporaries of Weininger, however, had realized the importance of his theory of hysteria as an intellectual response to *Studies on Hysteria:* Ludwig Wittgenstein, for instance, observed that Weininger was one of the first people to take serious notice of the work of Breuer and Freud.[6] Other Viennese intellectuals who reacted enthusiastically to the *Studies* were the dramatist Hermann Bahr (1863–1934), who saw tragic heroines as hysterics, and Hugo von Hofmannsthal (1874–1929), the heroine of whose 1903 play *Elektra,* according to a recent historian, was based on Breuer's hysterical patient Anna O.[7] Breuer and Freud's notions on the dual personality of hysterics were also reflected in Robert Musil's 1911 novella, "The Temptation of Quiet Veronica."[8] While Weininger's discussion of hysteria belongs to this cluster, it is a far more complex and ambitious reading of the *Studies* than Bahr's or Hofmannsthal's, who simply *incorporated* some Breurian or Freudian concepts into their own work. Weininger, on the other hand, attempted to reconfigure those concepts into a new political and philosophical theory of femininity. Freud himself believed that Weininger's chapter on hysteria had been designed merely to win his favor.[9] There was undoubtedly some truth to this, since Weininger had approached Freud with an early draft of *Geschlecht und Charakter,* hoping for a favorable recommendation to a publisher.[10] The conceptual role of the Breuer-Freud theory in *Geschlecht und Charakter,* however, is too fundamental to be attributed solely to flattery. Weininger's reinterpretation of hysteria was *the* crucial component of his answer to the Woman Question, and the structural identity of his theory of hysteria with Freud's and Breuer's was a deeply ironic link between a legendary text of modern Western misogyny and a work famous for providing one of the least misogynistic portrayals of hysterical women.

*Hysteria: The Female Malady?*

Hysteria, Weininger claimed, provided evidence for his fundamental belief that Woman had no genuine attribute except sexuality (113–14). Every other quality that might seem to be associated with femininity was a simulation, although not necessarily a conscious one (355–57). The sole purpose of this "organic mendacity" was to win the esteem of Man. The actual inner being of Woman was exclusively preoccupied with thoughts of coitus, which was the "transcendental function of the female" (351).

For Weininger, hysteria was a disease of the feminine element alone (which he referred to in abbreviation as W, presumably for *Weib*), which he immediately conflated with individual women. Male hysteria, he stated, did not really exist. Pierre Briquet (1796–1881), a pioneering investigator of hysteria, had observed long ago that twenty hysterical females were encountered for each hysterical male.[11] Briquet's ratio, generally accepted by contemporary physicians, provided enough justification for assuming that hysteria was preponderantly a female malady.[12] Weininger, however, sought to establish hysteria as a pathology exclusively, not just preponderantly, of Woman. What then of the male hysterics who indubitably existed, albeit in fewer numbers than female hysterics?

The principle of sexual intermediacy came to Weininger's rescue. Male hysterics, Weininger claimed, were markedly effeminate: they frequently had undescended or maldeveloped testes, and, since Jean-Martin Charcot (1825–93) had identified undescended testes in males and ovaries in females as "hysterogenic zones," Weininger felt free to infer that undescended testes were analogous to ovaries (570).[13] Not that a man with normal testes was immune from hysteria—every male possessed some femininity and that feminine element in a man could, of course, succumb to hysteria. Since, however, hysteria affected only the feminine elements in his constitution, leaving the masculine bulk of his self unaffected, it would be incorrect to describe such a man as a *male* hysteric (359, 571).

Weininger's analysis was not quite as bizarre as it might seem. Nineteenth-century physicians had frequently regarded the male hysteric as feminized. Pierre Briquet had believed that hysteria affected only delicate, effeminate males. He declared that a hysterical man represented the overturning of social laws ("Un homme hystérique, c'est le renversement des lois constitutives de la societé").[14] Charcot had opposed this trend, arguing repeatedly that hysteria could arise in "robust men presenting all the attributes of the male sex . . . men in whom one would be very astonished, unless forewarned, to meet with an affection considered by most as an exclusively feminine disease."[15] Some of Charcot's own followers, however, rejected his strictures, continuing to see male hysterics as effeminate.[16] Weininger, too, ignored Charcot's emphasis on the masculinity of male hysterics, focusing exclusively on his observation that an undescended testis could be a hysterogenic zone.[17] The equation of an undescended testis with the ovary was Weininger's own, but it would not have seemed irrational to a contemporary physician: gynecologist Leopold Landau, for instance, had suggested in 1884 that a painful and "irritable" testis in male hysterics was the analogue of the well-known painful ovary in a female hysteric.[18]

Having identified hysteria exclusively with femininity, Weininger proceeded to his own theory that hysteria was the "crisis of the organic mendacity of Woman." Many contemporary physicians stressed the supposed mendacity of hysterics, but Weininger's theory addressed a different issue. To appreciate its novelty, we need to place it in the context of medical ideas on hysterical mendacity.

*"One Perpetual Falsehood": Mendacity, Hysteria, and Femininity*
Many late-nineteenth-century physicians saw deceit, imposture, and lying as integral to hysteria.[19] Hysteria was often defined as a pathological mental disposition, characterized by mendacity and dissimulation, rather than as a constellation of physical symptoms.[20] Since the dramatic physical symptoms of hysteria had no demonstrable physical basis, the condition itself seemed akin to a falsehood, and hysterics to liars.[21] Even Pierre Janet (1859–1947), although himself critical of such conflations, admitted in 1889 that most contemporary physicians regarded the idea of hysterical mendacity as an "axiom."[22]

The eminent German psychiatrist Wilhelm Griesinger (1817–68) had regarded "a tendency to deception and prevarication" as a prominent feature of "the peculiar hysteric disposition."[23] Jules Falret (1824–1902), physician at Charcot's Salpêtrière, had been more eloquent: "In one word, the life of the hysteric is nothing but one perpetual falsehood; [hysterics] affect airs of piety and devotion and let themselves be taken for saints while secretly abandoning themselves to the most shameful actions."[24] According to Henri Legrand du Saulle (1830–86), hysterics habitually resorted to lies and trickery to satisfy their "invincible craving for attention."[25] Charcot himself described hysteria as "the great simulatrix" *(la grande simulatrice)* and marvelled at the cunning and the "incredible persistence" with which hysterical women attempted to deceive their physicians.[26] Somewhat paradoxically, however, most contemporary authorities also considered hysteria to be a real disease and not simply a series of conscious simulations. The differentiation of hysteria from simulation was recognized as difficult but essential. Physicians, in short, believed in the reality of hysteria but feared the mendacity of hysterics.[27]

This, however, was not the kind of mendacity to which Weininger referred. For him, it was *normal* women who were mendacious because they concealed their real, pervasively sexual natures in everyday life. This was the "organic" or "ontological" mendacity that defined the feminine character. What sentimental men regarded as the true female self—modest, self-effacing, and sexually reticent—was false: women developed this false self because it attracted men, appealing to their romantic instinct. Usually, male gullibility about women went so deep that the deception continued undetected for life. It was hysteria, which was nothing other than an attempt by Woman's inner sexual essence to break through her false outer shell of modesty, that exposed this lie (356). A hysterical attack indicated an ontological emergency: "the organic crisis of the organic mendacity of woman" (358).

### The Hysteric's Two Selves

Weininger's contention was an intriguing variation on the common theme of hysterical dual personality.[28] From the late eighteenth century, physicians had come to regard hysteria, hypnosis, and dual personality as related because hysterical attacks were often accompanied by hypnotic or "magnetic" phenomena such as catalepsy, somnambulism, and multiple personalities. Moreover, magnetization or hypnosis could lead to (as well as cure) hysterical attacks and multiple personalities.[29] The link between hysteria and multiple personality remained strong in late-nineteenth-century medical psychology. Etienne Azam, a surgeon at the Bourdeaux medical school, had coined the term *dédoublement de la personnalité* to describe his famous hysterical patient Felida X.[30] Jean-Martin Charcot was convinced that hysterical symptoms originated in a "second consciousness," which was sealed off from the normal consciousness and could be reached only by hypnosis. Not everybody, according to Charcot, was susceptible to hypnosis: it could be induced only in people predisposed to hysteria.[31] Pierre Janet, the director of the laboratory for experimental psychology at the Salpêtrière, agreed that the formation of a second personality was fundamental to hysteria.[32] The psychologist Alfred Binet (1857-1911), who had once belonged to Charcot's circle, held essentially the same opinion; so did Richard von Krafft-Ebing, Josef Breuer and Sigmund Freud.[33] It should be emphasized that these authors agreed only on the simple postulation of a double personality in hysteria; the mechanism of its formation remained very much in dispute.[34]

### Hysteria and Female Sexuality

Weininger's notion that hysteria involved two personalities in one individual was thus in tune with the views of influential physicians, and even his stress on sexuality was only a little less orthodox.[35] Hysteria has always been related to sexuality, but the relationship has been interpreted in profoundly different

ways. The Viennese psychiatrist Ernst von Feuchtersleben (1806–49), echo-
ing an ancient notion, had taught that sexually unappeased women were the
likeliest victims of hysteria.[36] In Germany, Wilhelm Griesinger had considered hysteria to be a sexual disorder, but a somatic one: a sequel to pathological conditions of the uterus, ovary, or vagina.[37] For British physician Robert
Brudenell Carter (1828–1918), hysteria was brought about by the conflict
between female lust and the social need to conceal it: unmarried and chaste
women were particularly at risk and so were the salacious. "The greater the
salacity," he warned, "the greater the tendency to hysteria" *(Salacitas major,
major ad hysteriam proclivitas).*[38] Despite the obvious similarities between
their views, however, Weininger does not seem to have been familiar with
Carter's 1853 treatise on hysteria. Even more surprisingly, he ignored the
work of the Viennese neuropsychiatrist Moritz Benedikt (1835–1920), who
had long argued that female hysterics led a secret "second life" that was sexually oriented, whether in thought or in deed.[39]

Charcot and his associates, arguably the most prominent workers on hysteria in the late nineteenth century, did not, however, consider hysteria to be
caused by sexual factors. They followed Pierre Briquet, who had pointed out
that since hysteria was rare among nuns and rife among the prostitutes of
Paris, it was unlikely that erotic cravings or frustrations played any serious
role in its genesis.[40] While refusing an etiological role to sexuality, however,
Charcot did acknowledge that many of the *symptoms* of hysteria (hallucinations, for example, or reenactments of early traumas) were sexual in nature.[41]
Recently, scholars have shown how, in spite of Charcot's overt rhetoric, the
ways in which he and his associates regarded and portrayed hysterical women
were strongly erotized, and a famous anecdote recounted by Freud suggests
that the erotization of Charcot's hysterics might have been more intentional
than one would suspect from Charcot's published views. At a party, Freud had
overheard Charcot exclaim with regard to the cause of the hysteria in one of
his patients: "But in this sort of case it's always a question of the genitals—
always, always, always." On hearing this, Freud had wondered, "Well, but if
he knows that, why does he never say so?"[42]

Although subtly highlighting the sexual quality of hysterical symptoms
through their depictions of the patients, the widely disseminated writings of
Charcot and his school did temporarily eclipse traditional beliefs on the sexual
etiology of hysteria. Such a theory reemerged, however, in the work of Breuer
and Freud. Freud, ironically, had begun as a disciple of Charcot and, in his very
early work on hysteria, had claimed that the role of sexuality in the etiology of
hysteria was "as a rule over-estimated."[43] With increasing clinical experience,
however, he came to be convinced that the cause of hysteria was always sexual.[44] Breuer did not disagree.[45] In *Studies on Hysteria* (1895), the supposedly

puritanical Breuer asserted: "The unsophisticated observations of our prede-cessors, the residue of which is preserved in the term 'hysteria,' came nearer the truth than the more recent view which puts sexuality almost last."[46] In healthy young males, the sexual instinct was outgoing and aggressive, whereas young women's sexual thoughts were always strongly colored by apprehension.[47] Hysterical women tended to fend off sexual ideas to a pathological degree: "[Hysterics] fall ill . . . owing to their *defence* against sexuality."[48]

Otto Weininger praised Pierre Janet, Oskar Vogt (1870–1959), Breuer, and Freud for trying to reconstruct the psychological process that led to hys-teria (357–58). In presenting his own theory, Weininger referred frequently to these four authors, but it was to Breuer and Freud that his theory was most profoundly indebted.

### *Inverting Breuer and Freud: Appropriation and Transformation*
Freud and Breuer believed that hysteria resulted from psychic trauma, which itself was often trivial but which acquired pathological significance due to the emotions associated with it, most commonly fright or shame. The memory of this trauma and its associated emotions were not dissipated in the usual ways but formed a "foreign body" (*Fremdkörper*) within the psyche, remaining ac-tive for a long time.[49] The "foreign body" (equivalent to a second conscious-ness) was not accessible to normal consciousness but emerged "with the undiminished vividness of a recent event" under hypnosis. This vividness was due to the original emotions, which, instead of being dispersed through an adequate, immediate reaction, had been retained with the memory of the trauma.[50]

For Weininger, hysteria was a conflict between innate feminine sexuality and a false, superficial personality that women acquired under masculine in-fluence. He linked this contention with the notion of the "foreign body" but inverted the Breuer-Freud concept. According to Weininger, the "foreign body" was not a second consciousness but the genuine feminine self, which was repressed in normal life by a false, outer self. The latter was wrongly identified by most people (including Breuer and Freud) as the normal female consciousness. In hysteria, Weininger proclaimed, Woman's genuine self re-belled against repression and impinged on her consciousness. Breuer's pa-tient Anna O. had used the term "bad self" *(das schlimme Ich)* for her second consciousness.[51] This "bad" self, according to Weininger, was the real self of woman (358, 361).

Freud had spoken of a hysterical counter-will *(Gegenwille)*, which induced hysterics to act in ways opposed to their conscious intentions.[52] Every idea or intention, according to Freud, had its unconscious antithesis, even in health. In hysteria, however, the antithetic ideas entered the consciousness "like bad spirits" and took control of the mind.[53] Weininger found the term and the concept useful, but, once again, he inverted it ontologically. For Freud, the counter-will opposed the conscious self; both were equally genuine and neither was identifiable with femininity per se. Weininger's counter-will, on the other hand, represented inherent female nature attempting to break through the barrier of the false self. While agreeing with Breuer and Freud that asexual nervous shocks and psychic traumas could precipitate hysteria, Weininger insisted that the traumas did not induce the formation of a "foreign body," as maintained in *Studies on Hysteria*. Instead, they weakened the false self, thereby facilitating the emergence of the true (sexual) self, which was then misconstrued by the patient and the physician as "foreign." Hysteria signified the "bankruptcy" *(Bankerott)* of the false, outer self, which had hitherto cloaked the woman's inner sexuality (361).

Weininger also linked Freud's concept of defense with the false self (361, 572). "Defense" was the partially successful effort of the false self to halt the emergence of the true: it prevented the emerging sexual ideas, which could no longer be repressed completely by the false ego, from flooding the consciousness by converting them into physical symptoms (362). The idea that sexual ideas were converted into physical symptoms in hysteria came explicitly from Freud's 1894 article on the neuropsychoses of defense (572–73). For good measure, Weininger also threw in an allusion to Freud's concept of "screen memories." Freud had noticed that trivial childhood memories were often retained into adulthood while important but unpleasant events had been "forgotten": he had explained this phenomenon as an intrapsychic "compromise." The distressing experience was not retained in the conscious mind and was replaced by a closely related indifferent experience.[54] For Weininger, however, the screen memories represented efforts of the outer self to suppress Woman's natural sexuality (572).

Weininger denied that hysterical symptoms were conscious simulations, referring to Breuer's cathartic therapy as the surest evidence for their genuineness (573). In Breuer's therapy, the hysterical patient was hypnotized and asked to talk about her symptoms and what may have caused them. As the true precipitating cause of the illness (the trauma) was discovered and the emotions linked with it expressed ("abreacted"), the symptom disappeared.[55] The therapeutic success of catharsis proved, according to Weininger, that hysterical complaints were not consciously simulated (573). The symptoms of hysteria were genuine enough: the mendacity was at the very center of Woman's being (356, 363). The ultimate cause of hysteria was the mendacious masking of the true feminine self, but hysteria itself, by shattering that mask, offered the truest evidence of the nature of Woman. It was normal female existence that deceived; hysterics did not.

Emphasizing that the false self was not constructed consciously, Weininger defined it as "an entire system of ideas and values assimilated through education and interaction" (359).[56] The process of assimilation was entirely passive, and what was assimilated was not some general cultural code but a specifically masculine ethic (571).[57] For all its ontological falsity, this outer self of woman was complex and well entrenched and could be splintered only by a massive, overwhelming blow. Stunned by the shock of such a trauma, the woman usually lost all will and volition, becoming, in the language of nineteenth-century psychiatry, abulic.[58]

What, however, of the nature of the trauma itself? For Weininger, it could only be sexual in nature (358), and, in order to establish this contention, he reinterpreted Freud's "seduction" hypothesis of 1896, which had posited that every case of hysteria was ultimately due to sexual abuse by adults during childhood. According to Freud, the illness was only seemingly caused by a recent, often trivial, trauma; in reality, those slight traumas merely revived memories of childhood seduction, which were the actual precipitators of the hysterical attack.[59] Initially exultant about this hypothesis, Freud had described it as "the discovery of a *caput Nili* in neuropathology."[60] Within a year, however, he had rejected the theory, although only in his private correspondence with Wilhelm Fliess.[61] In blissful ignorance of its repudiation, Weininger enthusiastically endorsed the seduction hypothesis, while suggesting that what Freud called childhood "traumas" were not traumatic at all but pleasurable: the memory of that pleasure, however, was suppressed by the false ego. Postpubertal sexual experience often reactivated those suppressed memories of childhood pleasure, but they returned to consciousness transformed into *traumatic* memories of seduction. Even those transformed memories, however, were enough to weaken the false self, leading to the intrapsychic conflict of hysteria, which culminated in the emergence of the inner sexual self into consciousness (365–66).

### The False Self and Female Suggestibility

Failing to find a medical author sharing his belief in the false outer self of women, Weininger latched upon the rich nineteenth-century literature in which hysteria, hypnosis, and femininity were linked together under the rubric of "suggestibility." Women, in this discourse, were deeply susceptible to fashion, easily hypnotizable, and, of course, more at risk for hysteria.[62] The outer female self, Weininger asserted, was no more than a hitherto unrecognized consequence of female suggestibility.

He commenced his analysis by outlining Pierre Janet's description of the construction of a new, albeit fragile, personality during hypnosis.[63] By hypnotizing each subject repeatedly and studying her psychological and behavioral changes, Janet had sought to uncover the nature of the hypnotist's influence on the subject.[64] He had found that after repeated sessions of hypnosis with the same hypnotist, the hypnotist's influence persisted in the subject's psyche even between the sessions.[65] The subject's actual reaction to the hypnotist differed with external circumstances and personal traits, but fear, affection, or childlike submission were the commonest reactions. These were invariably accompanied, however, by a deep, continuous preoccupation with the hypnotist, which, Janet believed, was of great therapeutic utility.[66] In hysteria, the will was weak and the emotions headstrong: the hypnotist, by exploiting the patient's preoccupation with him, could impose his will on the subject, creating a "synthesis" of resolutions, beliefs, and emotions that the neurotic psyche could not create by itself.[67]

Weininger emphasized this last point: the false self of Woman, he argued, must be formed by a similar preoccupation with male preferences and expectations (571). And if so, Woman's outward morality was profoundly immoral. As Kant had declared long ago, any submission to the will of another person (or, indeed, to any extraneous influence) was heteronomous and, therefore, unethical. Moral beings were characterized by autonomy: they obeyed the moral law laid down by their own noumenal self. Heteronomous behavior might sometimes *look* moral, but whatever its appearance, it represented the ethical nadir of humanity.[68] Disagreeing vehemently with Breuer and Freud's observation that many hysterical patients were eminently moral people, Weininger asserted that the apparent moralism of some hysterics was nothing but an extreme form of heteronomy, a slavish adoption of extraneous moral imperatives.[69] The hysteric's self-accusations over trivial lapses (a phenomenon noted by Freud) were instances of unconscious hypocrisy. True guilt, Weininger averred, varied with the degree of the offense. Hysterical guilt could not be genuine since it was equally great for all offenses. And could genuine guilt ever be removed by hypnosis? (362–65)

The question boiled down, in short, to Woman's lack of autonomy. Hysterical women made the best hypnotic subjects, and to permit oneself to be hypnotized, Weininger proclaimed, implied giving oneself over to another person's will: the most immoral act a Kantian could imagine. Women enjoyed being hypnotized because their rapport with the hypnotist was essentially sexual, an idea going back to the days of Franz Anton Mesmer (1734–1815).[70] Weininger, however, confined himself to the observations of Albert Moll (1862–1939) and Janet on the theme.[71] Janet's chapter on the hypnotist's influence over the subject, again, proved to be the most useful source. Janet, as we have seen, had regarded the imposition of the hypnotist's will over the subject as a therapeutic procedure: it was a way of strengthening the weak will of the neurotic. Weininger, however, was not interested in therapy but in the genesis of hysteria and in what it revealed about the nature of femininity. Janet's hypnotic studies actually provided much material that could be fitted into such a project.

Janet had observed that subjects with no initial faith in hypnotic therapy soon developed a passionate desire to be hypnotized and grew preoccupied with the hypnotist in a "patently excessive manner." They insisted on being hypnotized by the particular hypnotist who had initiated them, often becoming acutely jealous of his other patients.[72] These observations, Weininger argued, allowed only one interpretation: hypnosis was analogous to sexual intercourse. The more women had it, the more they liked it, and the more they grew obsessed with their partner (573–74).[73] Weininger, however, was honest enough to acknowledge that Janet had warned against interpreting the hypnotic rapport in exclusively erotic terms (574). Without denying the analogies between erotic love and the rapport, Janet had emphasized their differences, pointing out that the attachment between the subject and the hypnotist could take filial or maternal forms, could be deeply respectful or wholly terrifying. Secondly, the same subject often developed an apparently passionate attachment to the hypnotist while harboring the keenest erotic feelings for a real-life lover. If the hypnotic rapport was indeed one of love, then that love was of a very peculiar kind.[74] Weininger found these arguments quite unsound: Woman's fear of man was only a camouflage for desire, and as for maternal feelings, they, too, were expressions of the sexual essence of woman, albeit confined to the reproductive sphere (574).[75]

Hysterics were often held to be skilled at introspection. But this supposed skill, Weininger argued, was another effect of extraneous masculine influence and provided further support for his own interpretation. In hypnotized subjects, the male hypnotist's will "impregnated" the woman and then observed her from within. Since the male element was now within the woman's psyche, its observations seemed to come from within. But that, of course, was untrue. Incorporating a foreign agent unconsciously did not make the agent any less foreign. Weininger stressed that Oskar Vogt (1870–1959), "the most respected figure" among German hypnotists and theorists of hypnotism around 1900, had observed that the exactitude of introspection could be heightened by hypnotic suggestion, which, of course, was a form of masculine influence.[76] The supposed "clairvoyance" *(Hellsehen)* of hysterical mediums was also due to male influence. It occurred only under male command, but the commands were more successful on women than on men. The male will acted so powerfully over women as to cause a transcendence of sensory limitations, and this transcendence appeared to be clairvoyance (373).

Woman, in a nutshell, was a slave to Man: she was "under the sway of the phallus" *(unter dem Banne des Phallus).*[77] On rare occasions, she could achieve a vague consciousness of this bondage. But how did she manage even this? The principle of universal sexual intermediacy—emphasized so greatly in earlier sections of *Geschlecht und Charakter*—reappeared now as a deus ex machina. Women's faint suspicions of being under male bondage stemmed from their scanty, inherited masculine elements, which, Weininger sternly emphasized, were too exiguous to permit women to actually liberate themselves from that bondage.[78]

But if all women were slaves, why did only some women develop hysteria? Because there were different degrees of servility. The hysterical woman, Weininger explained, was extraordinarily passive. She accepted male ethical principles so slavishly that she completely repressed her true feminine (i.e., sexual) self. In support of this contention, Weininger adduced the reports of Paul Sollier, a French physician who had once been an associate of Charcot's and who achieved some lasting fame with his theory that hysterics were in a perpetual condition of semi-somnambulism or "vigilambulism."[79] Sollier had argued that hysterics had an instinctive need to be guided and commanded and that they bonded preferentially with men because they admired masculine authority and reason. Weininger quoted these views with approval, while omitting Sollier's caveat that hysterical women's admiration for men was not necessarily sexual.[80] Sollier's belief in hysterical passivity, Weininger rightly insisted, was widely shared by contemporary physicians (367).[81] Supported by medical opinion, and guided by his love for typology, Weininger declared that the hysterical woman belonged to the psychological type "Maid" *(Magd)*. She was born, not made: psychological servitude had nothing to do with socioeconomic circumstances. The Maid was opposed to the Shrew *(Megäre)*, who represented the type of woman least susceptible to hysteria. The Shrew vented her wrath (deriving from lack of sexual satisfaction) on others; the Maid vented it on herself. The Shrew was insensitive to male reproach and never blushed when reproached by a man. She was, in other words, less open to male influence than the Maid and therefore had a weaker false self. The Maid, on the other hand, blushed when an impure thought came into her mind, even if she was alone. She had been completely impregnated by male values; her false self had fully enveloped her sexual essence (369–70).

Due to the powerful influence of masculine values, hysterics were often sexually anesthetic. Once again, Weininger quoted Paul Sollier, who had observed that most hysterics were completely frigid and terrified by the idea of coitus (575–76). While a minority of hysterics did show heightened sexual desire, frigidity was the commoner finding and could be so profound that a pregnant hysteric could not even feel the movements of her fetus. "The denial of sexuality," Weininger approvingly commented, "must lead to denial of the child" (370).[82] Hysterical frigidity, according to Weininger, was one of the many untrue anesthesias in hysteria, which were not due to any sensory impairment but stemmed from the psychical urge to exclude certain sensations from consciousness. Weininger appealed again to the experiments of Oskar Vogt to prove his point. Vogt had reported that if the arm of a subject was made anesthetic by suggestion, the subject could still say how many times the arm was pricked, even though she could not "feel" any of them.[83] Frigidity, Weininger argued, occurred by an analogous "external" command, not from a hypnotist but, rather, from the woman's own false self (370).

### The Meaning of Hysteria: "Woman is Nothing"

The deeper reasons for Weininger's interest in hysteria should now be clear. For him, hysteria was the major source of evidence for his philosophical and psychological deconstruction of femininity. Hysteria proved that Woman was sexuality alone and that this sexuality did not possess any ontological significance since it was supraindividual and not linked with individual men. Woman could not comprehend the individuality of men; she understood masculinity alone and her sexual desire was simply the urge to be impregnated by Man (397). The relation between Man and Woman, in epistemological terms, was of subject and object; ontologically, it was the Aristotelian one of form and matter. Woman was pure, unindividualized matter, on which Man conferred form. Woman existed because of Man's sexuality, and the sole reason why women should be acknowledged as human beings (as opposed to animals or plants) was because they complemented men (390). To be formed by Man was Woman's sole destiny and her greatest fulfillment (391–96). Since Woman did not exist as an autonomous individual but only as a sexual object for Man, "Woman is Nothing" (383, 394, 398). It was in hysteria that the falsity of the female self was exposed beyond doubt. As the outward trimmings of femininity fell away, female sexuality and ontological nullity were revealed to the world. Medical men might turn away from this terrifying truth but the philosopher could not.

Weininger's argument, of course, was philosophical only in its terminology and rhetoric. Based largely on medical discourse, which Weininger displaced, reinscribed, and transformed in order to align his "data" with his profoundly political ontology, Weininger's much-vaunted resolution of the Woman Question consisted of the demonstration that since Woman did not possess an individual identity and intelligible self, she could not demand freedom and autonomy. Her only valid identity was that of a sexual object for Man. The content of this view, needless to say, was ancient and forms the core of the vast majority of antifeminist philosophies. Weininger's demonstration of the assertion and the manner of its integration within his own antifeminist discourse were, however, novel and worthy of analysis.

There is no evidence that any turn-of-the-century psychologist or psychiatrist, with the exception of the dismissive Freud, even acknowledged the existence of Weininger's theory, and it is justly ignored in most histories of medical concepts of hysteria. But ideas regarding hysteria, as scholars are beginning to appreciate, were of far more than mere medical import in fin-de-siècle Europe. Weininger's theory of hysteria needs to be approached not as a medical theory of hysteria but as an example of antifeminism in a new, psychiatric key that was characteristic of the medicalized language of fin-de-siècle social thought and cultural politics. The medical language should not obscure the fact that Weininger reconfigured the boundaries of the female psyche not simply as a metaphysical or a scientific exercise, but in order to attain his ideological objective of demonstrating the impossibility and undesirability of female emancipation. It was a political act.

## CHAPTER SEVEN

# Impregnation and Autonomy: The Political Physiology of Motherhood

Weininger realized that critics would oppose his devaluation of femininity by pointing to the high moral status of Woman as Mother (281), and he was, no doubt, also well aware that for many contemporary Central European feminists, motherhood was *the* symbol of true, emancipated womanhood: the New Woman was the New Mother. No resolution of the Woman Question in contemporary Central Europe could afford to ignore the political and moral dimensions of maternity.

True to his style, Weininger approached the issue typologically, classifying all women into two fundamental categories: Mother and Prostitute. The distinction, in spite of its ancient terminology, was actually quite original. Weininger's Mother was not the saintly figure of tradition: maternity, for him, was essentially as sexual as prostitution. The Mother differed from the Prostitute only in the *way* she expressed her equally pervasive sexuality. Since sexuality, in Weininger's world, signified ontological and ethical nullity, there was nothing ethically admirable or politically emancipatory about motherhood.[1] Weininger's argument, as usual, was interwoven with biological and medical discourse. Uncharacteristically, however, he wholly rejected current theories of reproductive biology instead of building upon them, as with homosexuality, or transforming their content, as he had done for hysteria. Employing a new strategy, he returned to theories that, by 1903, were being progressively *rejected* by professional scientists. This was not due to ignorance: in his copious notes, Weininger demonstrated his awareness of the current status of those theories and discussed the reasons for their obsolescence. His larger goals, however, compelled him to incorporate these outmoded theories into his argument. By this point, Weininger had lost all of his early positivistic interest in science. Although still immersed in the discourse of science, he no longer spoke as a critic, let alone as a participant manqué. His only concern now was to demonstrate the ontological nullity of Woman and to expose the political futility of feminism: if obsolete scientific theories did that job better than current ones, then that was fine with him.

### The Prostitute and the Mother

In order to demolish the traditional concept of the Mother, Weininger opposed it with another—the Prostitute (281)—but transformed the entire meaning of this well-known dyad. Traditionally, the asexual, loving Mother served as the polar opposite of the sensual Prostitute, but for Weininger both were completely sexual beings differing in the expression and aims of their sexuality.

Weininger's interest in the Prostitute was influenced quite significantly by the situation in Europe. Rapid industrialization and urban expansion had led to a sharp increase in prostitution in Germany and Austria during the late nineteenth century, and prostitution was a part of everyday life in Vienna.[2] Novelists created a virtual "Cult of the Prostitute" *(Dirnenkult)*, filling their works with promiscuous, predatory, or mercenary women while ridiculing "the asexual bourgeois woman."[3] Physicians, social theorists, and cultural critics weighed in with theories about the causes of prostitution, triggering debates about its social consequences and about the possibility of its elimination. Weininger's analysis of prostitution was almost entirely rooted in this tradition, and his major source of data was the classic work on female criminality and prostitution by the Italian psychiatrist and criminologist Cesare Lombroso (1835–1909). The opposition of the Prostitute to the Mother, Weininger argued, was supported by Lombroso's observation that good housewives had many children, street prostitutes were usually sterile, and coquettish women, who obviously fell somewhere in between, had fewer children than the typical housewife. Lombroso believed that prostitutes and criminals were born, not made: they were instances of biological atavism. Their behavior was a sign of inborn "ethical idiocy" *(ethische Idiotie)*, other symptoms of which were alcoholism, incorrigible laziness, and total lack of maternal feelings.[4] Social or economic factors played no role in Lombroso's criminal anthropology, which, essentially, was based on the "anatomy of deviant and dangerous bodies, grounded in scientific measurements."[5] Weininger, however, was concerned with the Prostitute as a characterological rather than a physical type: *any* woman who enjoyed sex for its own sake— including, he emphasized, many outwardly virtuous maidens and housewives—was a Prostitute (283). Despite their differences on definitional matters, however, Weininger agreed with Lombroso that prostitution was a biological phenomenon and sharply criticized the socialist leader August Bebel's sociological explanation.

In the extensive debates on prostitution in Central Europe around the turn of the century, most participants espoused either the biological perspective of Lombroso and Weininger or the sociological approach of Bebel.[6] Bebel had argued in his popular treatise *Die Frau und der Sozialismus*, first published in 1883, that prostitution was "a necessary social institution of bourgeois society, just as the police, the standing army, the church and the capitalist class."[7] Appealing to Lombroso for data, Weininger countered Bebel's economic argument by arguing that many affluent women behaved like prostitutes and that many former prostitutes returned to their profession even after a stable marriage. Also, due to unknown constitutional factors, prostitutes were immune to many diseases that affected virtuous women. Finally, prostitution had existed throughout history, and the number of prostitutes had not risen significantly during the capitalistic era.[8] These points suggested that prostitution was caused by constitutional rather than environmental reasons. It was true, Weininger acknowledged, that women were often compelled to resort to prostitution after being left destitute by men. While men were responsible for women's destitution, however, the choice of prostitution, he doggedly maintained, was grounded in the very nature of the human female.[9] This remained a mere declamation: Weininger offered no biological evidence to prove his case.

The leaning toward prostitution, then, was organic and congenital—but only in some women. In others, the biological leaning was toward motherhood (284–85). Both types, however, showed equal lack of interest in the *individuality* of their sexual partners. The Prostitute accepted any man who could give her erotic pleasure (Weininger's Prostitute had no truck with money and apparently distributed her favors solely for the pleasure involved), while the Mother accepted any man who could give her a child. The Mother remained monogamous only because she required nothing other than a child from a man. The Prostitute was polygamous because she had an inner compulsion to be desired by all men. Coitus, for the Mother, was simply the means to an end: the child. For the Prostitute, intercourse was an end in itself.[10] The fundamental similarity, again, was that neither attached any importance to the individual qualities of particular males.

The Mother's fundamental sexual aim was to be impregnated. Receptive and submissive, she treated her partner's sperm as a deposit. She did experience pleasure during coitus but never the erotic abandon of the Prostitute.[11] The Mother's orgasmic cry, Weininger pointed out on the basis of undisclosed evidence, was short and stifled whereas the Prostitute's loud orgasmic shrieks revealed her desire to concentrate all her life-force into one endless moment of pleasure (304–307). The Mother ensured the conservation of the species and nothing else, but the Prostitute refused to be a mere "container" *(Behälter)* of life. Nor was she simply an instrument for men's erotic pleasure, however: diverging sharply from Lombroso, Weininger emphasized that

characterologically, intellectual women were often Prostitutes, and even
when not themselves intellectually gifted, many Prostitutes served as muses
to creative men. The Mother, however, was almost always intellectually negligible and concerned solely with caring for her children and for their father.
Only men lacking in spiritual productivity—men who could only father children of the flesh—could love a woman of the maternal type. Great and creative men, however, had always loved biologically sterile Prostitutes, because
the creative man found biological fatherhood worthless compared to father-
ing great creations of the spirit. The Prostitute often catalyzed the latter, the
Mother never. For the moral philosopher, therefore, the Prostitute was a wor-
thier being than the Mother (297–98). But this was a minor difference in
cosmic terms. Whether Mother or Prostitute, Woman was completely and
pervasively sexual and consequently had no ontological importance.

Did all women belong unequivocally to one type or the other? No, said
Weininger: Mother and Prostitute were ideal types like Man and Woman.
Just as real individuals were partly male and partly female, all women were
Mother as well as Prostitute to different degrees. One predisposition *(Veran-
lagung)* might be predominant in one individual, but the other predisposition
was never completely absent. No woman was completely without an instinct
for prostitution or a maternal instinct. Nevertheless, Weininger added characteristically, more women came close to being absolute Prostitutes than absolute Mothers: nobody who had seen how modern women moved around on
the streets in clinging, form-revealing clothes could, he avers, disagree with
his contention (286–87, 312). The motherly woman, then, could be partly a
Prostitute, and the Prostitute partly a Mother: the only thing Woman could
never be was an asexual, innocent maiden *(Jungfrau)*.

This last assertion was a vital point in Weininger's critique of motherhood,
but he did not supply any information on the rich literary and cultural seams
he was mining here. By the end of the nineteenth century, the literary types of
*femme fragile* and *femme fatale* had become well entrenched in Germanic cultures. The average bourgeois woman was expected to be an innocent, asexual,
weak, and ethereal creature in need of male protection. At the same time, active, erotic, and independent women found their own admirers among men
who were not exclusively bourgeois in their inclinations. Artists and writers
celebrated both types, but the *femme fragile* was the specific cult-object of
such eminent Austrian literati as Hugo von Hofmannstahl, Rainer Maria
Rilke, and Peter Altenberg. It was their idealization of the fragile, asexual
*Jungfrau* that Weininger opposed, and, without avowing it explicitly, he
equated the *Jungfrau* with his characterological type, the Mother.[12] It was
not an illogical conflation, since maternity as well as maidenhood were regarded in contemporary cultures almost as asexual and sacred.

## Mothers as Metaphors

Historians have demonstrated that the mother-child bond was reformulated in moral terms during the eighteenth century. Mothers had previously been under no cultural compulsion to be the primary nurturers of their children: until the end of the eighteenth century, it was the father-child bond that had been of major moral and pedagogical importance in Central Europe. The situation, however, changed quite radically in the next century, with women coming to be regarded and, even more importantly, coming to regard themselves as the natural guardians of the child.[13] The new pedagogical theories of Johann Heinrich Pestalozzi, for instance, emphasized the moral, cultural, and physical importance of the mother for the child, as did the later views of Friedrich Froebel, who introduced the concept of the Kindergarten and proposed that only women could teach in such institutions. The medical profession, too, emphasized that motherhood was a "calling" for women.[14] In German feminist politics, moreover, the idea of motherhood was invested with great moral and political significance. Concurrently, the evolution of the family from a center of production into a private sphere characterized by emotional intimacy created new roles for women. One was that of the submissive wife. The other was of the mother with authority over children, and this was emphasized by German feminists. Since child-rearing was one of the few subjects on which women were coming to be heard with respect, maternal metaphors were of great strategic importance in feminist political rhetoric. Most German feminists portrayed their social and political activities as extensions of the maternal role, arguing that motherhood was a social as well as a biological phenomenon. This rhetoric was soon infiltrated by biological and socialist tropes, and, to simplify a complex story, radical feminists argued that the mother-child bond was the primary source of the cooperative and altruistic traits driving human evolution.[15]

The theory of primeval matriarchy, argued most notably by Johann Jakob Bachofen (1815–87), intersected with and reinforced this view. Bachofen, who taught Roman law at the University of Basel in Switzerland, had published his treatise *Das Mutterrecht* (Mother-Right) in 1861. This immensely influential philological and historical study had argued that the first durable form of human society had been matriarchal; patriarchal forms had evolved much later. Bachofen had extolled mother-love in almost mystical terms but did not believe that matriarchal civilization had been superior to the later patriarchy.[16] Feminist thinkers appropriated some of Bachofen's arguments without endorsing his general evaluation of matriarchal civilization. Mother-love, many feminists suggested, should substitute for sexual love in the lives of women, since female sexuality inevitably led to domination and objectification by men.[17] In Vienna, Grete Meisel-Hess argued that motherhood was the supreme justification of a woman's life and much more important than mere sexual pleasure. The truly emancipated woman, Meisel-Hess believed, made the best mother and a powerful mother was the most effective adversary of patriarchy. Women should assert the ancient mother-right of Bachofen not simply to win self-respect but to rob the patriarchy of its ideological authority over the child.[18] Weininger did not live to read Meisel-Hess, but the antipatriarchal potential of motherhood was evident to him as well as to other intellectuals of the time. It had generated at least one artistic masterwork: August Strindberg's play, *The Father*, a work that is of the greatest importance in explicating *Geschlecht und Charakter*'s devaluation of motherhood. Before we can get to Strindberg, however, Weininger's analysis of motherhood must be dealt with in detail.

### Sexualizing Motherhood

Weininger began by denying that mother-love was asexual and, therefore, more ethically pure than romantic love. Since no woman was an absolute Mother, it was clear that a son exerted some sexual effect on his mother, no matter how little or how unconsciously.[19] Many adult males realized this when they had sexual dreams involving their mothers, which Weininger designated as "Oedipus-Dreams" (290–91). Given his keen interest in Freud's work and his almost obsessive habits of citation, it is surprising that he did not mention corroborating observations from *The Interpretation of Dreams*, which had been published late in 1899, where Freud had stated, without using the term "Oedipus Complex," that "being in love with the one parent and hating the other" were "among the essential constituents of the stock of psychical impulses" acquired in childhood. "It is the fate of all of us, perhaps," he had written, "to direct our first sexual impulse towards our mother. . . . Our dreams convince us that that is so. . . . To-day, just as [in the time of Sophocles], many men dream of having sexual relations with their mothers, and speak of the fact with indignation and astonishment."[20]

Instead of engaging explicitly with Freud, Weininger turned to physiology, emphasizing the voluptuous feelings experienced by lactating women. Anatomically, the nipples contained erectile tissue, and their stimulation by a suckling child led, he pointed out, to contractions of the uterus, an observation supported by the standard medical sources of the time.[21] Max Runge, Professor of Gynecology and Director of the University Clinic for Women at Göttingen, had mentioned in his well-known textbook that the uterine muscles contracted in response to stimulation of the nipples, a phenomenon long known to abortionists, who often attempted to abort a fetus by stimulating the mother's nipples.[22] Lactation and suckling, which constituted the very essence of maternity, were, then, also sources of sexual pleasure. Tailoring

Lombroso to his own typology, Weininger concluded that the more of the Prostitute a woman had in her, the less she enjoyed nursing her baby. It followed, therefore, that the mother's relation with her child was fundamentally sexual and could not claim the unique ethical distinction conferred upon it by society (291). This sexualization of mother-love, however, was only the first step toward dislodging it from its high cultural position.

The second and more important step was to prove that mother-love was not simply sexual but also contravened the fundamental principles of Kantian ethics. The Mother, Weininger argued, was indifferent to the individuality of the child and completely undiscriminating toward all the children she had carried in her womb. Mother-love was not love for an individual: in the light of Kantian ethics, therefore, it was immoral. The instinctive, almost reflexive love of the human mother for her children, Weininger asserted, was purely animal and not dictated by reason or by any moral imperative (295–97). He even rebuked Bachofen, whom he otherwise lauded as a "philosophically learned sociologist," for waxing eloquent on the glories of maternal love among humans without realizing that it was equally intense among cats and poultry (556).

Proving mother-love to be sexual and deeply unethical removed, Weininger believed, the last major objection to his thesis that Woman was amoral and exclusively sexual. Not stopping with that, however, he explored reproductive biology at length, looking for further evidence for his conviction that "Woman is Nothing." Hysteria had shown Weininger that Woman, psychologically, was infinitely impressionable and open to outer (male) influence. Would the biology of reproduction complement that "discovery" by showing that physiologically, too, Woman was permeable to exterior influences and thus not a monad deserving of autonomy?

### Impressions and Impregnability

Arthur Schopenhauer, declared Weininger, had been wrong to remark that a person's existence dated from the moment when his parents fell in love.[23] Instead, Weininger suggested, conception occurred when the mother first saw the father or heard his voice (547). Schopenhauer's somewhat egalitarian view of the matter was inadequate for Weininger, who wished to emphasize that Woman was impregnable and always open to the exterior regardless of actual love for any individual man. To establish this contention, Weininger turned first to the theory of maternal impressions *(Versehen)*, which, in its simplest form, held that the psychological experiences, fears, and desires of a pregnant woman could physically deform the embryo. This was an ancient idea, going back at least to Hippocrates.[24] According to a recent scholar, "the feminine imagination was the mistress of errors and behaved even more capriciously than normal during pregnancy. During this altered state, it was credited with the physical ability to materialize, by simulation, objects either wishfully or fearfully perceived."[25]

The idea of maternal impressionability had been especially popular in early modern medicine as a global explanation of birthmarks and more serious fetal malformations. The notion had reached its apotheosis in the theories of the French philosopher Nicolas Malebranche (1638–1715) and his followers.[26] Fright or shock, they had claimed, were responsible for congenital deformities, and the actual object that frightened the mother determined the precise nature of the malformation: the "concealed or surrogate passions" became visible on the bodies of one's offspring.[27] Discussing the case of a "young man who was born mad, and whose body was broken in the same places in which those of criminals are broken," Malebranche had attributed the deformities to the fact that his mother, when pregnant, had observed a criminal being broken on the wheel.[28]

Although maternal imagination produced deformities, it was also responsible for maintaining normality. Malebranche had taught that the "communication of the spirits" between mother and child ensured the perpetuation of species-characteristics in the progeny, and, although a preformationist, he had conceded that the mother's imagination modulated the further development of the preformed embryo.[29] Malebranche's views were influential but not universally accepted: in the course of a serious dispute over the role of the maternal imagination, the English physician James Blondel, for instance, had ridiculed them as "silly and absurd," resulting from "meer Enthusiasm and Bigotry."[30] Notwithstanding such disputes, however, Malebranchian notions of the maternal imagination's deforming power were so popular in the German-speaking lands during the nineteenth century that an authoritative German compendium of medical anthropology had observed at the end of the century that "it is not so long ago since that not only the cultivated public but even medical men were at pains to account for every monstrosity, every deformity, from the mother 'having had a shock' [aus dem Versehen]."[31]

This account is a trifle exaggerated, at least with respect to the elite physicians of mid-nineteenth-century Germany, who, led by the physiologist Johannes Müller (1801–58), had begun to question the theory of maternal impressions. In his celebrated textbook of physiology, Müller had described the belief in impressions as an "old and extremely popular superstition."[32] The relations between a mother and her fetus, he allowed, were of the most intimate kind, but that intimacy did not amount to a state of fusion: the two remained independent entities (zweier an und für sich ganz selbständiger Wesen). Agreeing that any significant psychological turbulence could disturb the organic interrelationship between mother and fetus and thus cause a developmental anomaly in the latter, Müller emphatically denied that the *specific* thoughts or fantasies of the mother had any causal connection with that anomaly.[33] Every woman, in any case, was bound to experience at least a few startling or frightening sensations during her pregnancy, and the theory of impressions could, therefore, be used to explain away any malformation in her eventual child.[34] Müller's views paralleled the older opinion of Pierre-Louis Moreau de Maupertuis (1698–1759) that while the maternal imagination could disturb the development of the fetus, this influence was not comparable to plastic art: the specific ideas or images troubling the mother were not mimetically reproduced on the fetus.[35] Müller was soon seconded by Theodor Ludwig Wilhelm Bischoff, Gabriel Gustav Valentin, Rudolph Wagner, Emil Du Bois-Reymond, and other prominent medical scientists.

Weininger devoted considerable attention to this collective critique. After discussing Müller's opinion, he appended long quotations from Theodor Bischoff, who had taught physiology and comparative anatomy at Heidelberg and Giessen. In an 1842 article on developmental anomalies written for an influential physiological encyclopedia, Bischoff had acknowledged that psychological events in the mother's life could cause fetal malformations, while denying, as had Müller, that such malformations could be linked directly to the phenomena that had caused the mother's psychological turmoil. That kind of direct influence, Bischoff argued, would require a direct nervous link between the mother and the fetus, which simply did not exist: the intermixing of blood was not enough. After raising many other objections, he had concluded rather ambivalently with the concession that the classical theory of maternal impressions might be worth retaining but only as an extremely rare cause of congenital anomalies.[36]

The theory of impressions was also rejected by many clinicians and animal breeders in Germany, of whom the gynecologist Max Runge and the breeding theorist Hermann Settegast (1819–1908) were quoted at length by Weininger (549–50). Runge had declared that most clinicians of the time did not believe in the reality of impressions and it was incumbent upon the profession to oppose lay beliefs that malformations were caused by maternal shocks.[37] Settegast had acknowledged that the belief in maternal impressions was primordial, but the facts contradicting the belief were so numerous that he felt any continued acceptance of the theory could only be described as superstitious.[38] The last influential skeptic cited by Weininger was none other than Charles Darwin, who, in *The Variation of Animals and Plants under Domestication,* had flatly rejected the theory of maternal impressions. The eighteenth-century surgeon William Hunter, Darwin recollected, had asked his clients just before delivery to describe their psychological experiences during pregnancy but had failed to establish any correspondence between those reports and the malformations he actually found in the occasional child. Yet, when the mother was informed of the malformation, "she frequently suggested some fresh [emotional] cause."[39]

Not all biologists of the nineteenth century, however, were so skeptical about maternal impressions. Perhaps the most eminent believer was Karl Ernst von Baer, who recounted an anecdote concerning his own sister who, during pregnancy, had been frightened by a fire and had eventually given birth to a daughter with a flame-shaped birthmark on her forehead.[40] Von Baer's account was part of a textbook discussion of maternal impressions that argued, despite his own belief, that while the maternal imagination could indeed cause specific malformations, not every malformation could be attributed to the imagination of the mother.[41] Weininger agreed that there was no evidence to attribute all malformations to maternal impressions: all he aimed to establish was the *possibility* of influencing progeny without having sexual intercourse with the mother. The theory of maternal impressions need not be a "superstition" simply because it challenged the theory that an individual was conceived solely by the union of an ovum and a spermatozoon. In a science like mathematics it was impossible that two times two might equal five on Jupiter, but the laws of biology were not that universal. As Kant had maintained, empirical laws (such as those of the biological sciences) could never aspire to anything higher than "comparative universality" or "extensive applicability."[42] The theory of maternal impressions, therefore, needed to be dealt with as a possibility instead of being dismissed out of hand as a superstition (285–86).

*The Plasticity of Woman: Sexual Impressions and Remote Impregnation*
Weininger then turned to the curious phenomenon of "telegony," which he classified as an especially intense form of maternal impression (308). This phenomenon, again, had been widely accepted by earlier biologists but had become quite controversial around 1900. Weininger was well aware of the current dubious status of the concept, but it was so crucial to his project of deconstructing the autonomy of Woman that he could not do without it.[43]

The term "telegony" had been coined in the 1890s by the biologist August Weismann from two Greek roots meaning "at a distance" and "offspring." The concept itself was much older: physicians, going back to the seventeenth-century Jan Baptista Van Helmont (1579–1644), had long been convinced that a woman, after having children by one man, continued to transmit the traits of that man to her subsequent children by a second male.[44] Richard Burkhardt has pointed out that three major explanations were available for the phenomenon, the reality of which was not seriously questioned by anybody before the late nineteenth century. The first explanation relied upon Albrecht von Haller's old belief that a female's reproductive organs were directly and permanently modified by intercourse with her first mate. Another hypothesis argued that the blood of the fetus "infected" the mother with the traits of the father, which were "stored" in the maternal system and subsequently transmitted to later children fathered by a different male. The third explanation, which Weininger upheld, regarded telegony as a special instance of maternal impressions.[45]

Charles Darwin had taken a dim view of maternal impressions but "believed absolutely in telegony," and Weininger, with almost palpable delight, filled page after page with quotations from Darwin attesting to the reality of telegony (558–61, 563–64).[46] In *The Variation of Animals and Plants under Domestication*, Darwin had observed that, although according to the laws of fertilization pollination should affect only the ovules, other parts of the female plant, such as the coats of the ovules, were often changed by pollination. The development of the embryo within the ovule was, of course, expected to show the traits of the fertilizing male, but the coats of the ovule were part and parcel of the female plant and not expected to be modified by the male. Darwin described this phenomenon as the "direct or immediate action of the male element on the mother form," observing that not only the seed-coats but "the ovarium or fruit, including even the calyx and upper part of the peduncle of the apple, and the axis of the ear in maize" were modifiable by male influence. This direct action of pollen on female tissues, although far from invariable, was one that Darwin considered to be of the greatest theoretical interest.[47]

Turning then to animals, Darwin had summarized what was probably the most widely cited report of telegony, a report that Weininger, too, quoted at length (561–62). In 1820, the Earl of Morton had reported to the President of the Royal Society of London that he had recently attempted to domesticate the quagga, a zebra-like species native to South Africa.[48] Having failed to find a female specimen of the species, he had been compelled to cross a male quagga with "a young chestnut mare of seven-eighths Arabian blood, and which had never been bred from." Later, he had given the mare away to a fellow peer, who had mated her with an Arabian horse. The progeny of that second union had "the character of the Arabian breed" but the color and the hair of their manes bore a "striking resemblance to the quagga." Lord Morton could offer no explanation for the phenomenon, declaring loftily that he was "not apt to build hypotheses in a hurry."[49] His report, however, was read and cited very widely, and increasing numbers of physicians and natural historians used the term "quagga taint" to refer to the traces in the offspring of the physical features of its mother's earlier mate.

Approaching Morton's phenomenon as the zoological counterpart of his botanical example, Darwin had remarked: "If we could imagine the same

flower to yield seeds during successive years, then it would not be very surprising that a flower of which the ovarium had been modified by foreign
pollen should next year produce, when self-fertilised, offspring modified by
the previous male influence."[50] Lord Morton's report apart, Darwin had referred to many independent observations of similar phenomena.[51] He had
denied, however, that these were illustrations of maternal impressions and
had refused to countenance the theory that it was the embryo that "infected"
the mother with paternal traits. Proceeding from the botanical example of
the direct influence of pollen on maternal tissue, Darwin had argued in a
Hallerian vein that "the male element acts directly on the female, and not
through the crossed embryo."[52] This was a passage that Weininger emphasized (563–64).

Darwin's interest in telegony was part of his wider biological project of explaining the inheritance of variations with his "provisional hypothesis of pangenesis." Ernst Mayr has pointed out that, although never accepted in its
entirety by other biologists, Darwin's hypothesis of pangenesis did exert a significant influence on later theories of heredity, including those proposed by
Francis Galton, Hugo de Vries, and August Weismann. Darwin's hypothesis,
which suggested, in essence, that various characters of the organism were determined by the inheritance of individually different particles, was heuristically valuable, since previous theories of particulate heredity—such as that of
Herbert Spencer—had not differentiated between the particles themselves.[53] According to Darwin, all the cells of the body emitted minute "gemmules" that circulated in the blood, travelling eventually to the germ-cells and
then to the embryo, where each gemmule developed into the specific kind of
cells they had stemmed from.[54] This explained inheritance of parental traits,
but what of telegony and allied phenomena? Tackling the botanical case first,
Darwin had argued that the gemmules in pollen multiplied after fertilization,
penetrating into "the closed embryonic sack within the ovule" and then into
the surrounding cells of the mother-plant, causing the "direct or immediate
action of the male element on the mother form." The "quagga taint" in animals, too, could be explained by the "diffusion, retention, and action of the
gemmules included within the spermatozoa of the previous male."[55]
Weininger, however, was less interested in the technical issues Darwin was
grappling with than in Darwin's insistence that the male element acted *directly* on the female organism and not just on the female germ cell. This, said
Weininger, should be perfectly obvious to anybody who had noticed the
enormous transformation affecting a woman immediately after marriage and
her growing physical resemblance to her husband with time (563).[56] The idea
that the male could influence the female constitution directly, needless to say,
dovetailed very neatly with Weininger's larger argument on Woman's lack of

individuality and autonomy. Man, remarked Weininger, was his own greatest creation, but he had not just formed himself: he had also created and modified Woman. The old myths in which Woman was created from Man were true in essence (396).

Weininger did not, however, ignore post-Darwinian criticisms of the concept of telegony. The leading critic of the concept was the same August Weismann who had given it its name. As Richard Burkhardt has demonstrated, telegony was "a threatening anomaly" for Weismann's theory of heredity, which wholly rejected the idea of the inheritance of acquired characteristics, a virtually omnipresent concept in nineteenth-century theories of heredity, including that of Darwin.[57] Weismann believed that the germ cells, which carried the hereditary material, were separate from the somatic cells: any modifications of the latter, therefore, could not be passed on to the progeny.[58] Contemporary biologists, Darwinian as well as non-Darwinian, criticized Weismann's theory with acerbity, and telegony was pivotal to this criticism. One of Weismann's most articulate and relentless opponents was the British polymath and self-taught biological theorist Herbert Spencer (1820–1903), who believed in the inheritance of acquired characters as fervently as Weismann opposed it.[59] Weininger quoted extensively from Weismann's *Germ-Plasm* as well as from Spencer's polemical articles against Weismann. It was not so much their dispute on inheritance that was of importance to Weininger as was the question whether telegony was possible, whereas for Weismann and Spencer, telegony was important only in relation to the broader issue of the inheritance of acquired characters.

In *The Germ-Plasm*, Weismann had devoted an entire chapter to "Doubtful Phenomena of Heredity," and telegony had been the first of those named therein. Reviewing the reports in the literature and Darwin's endorsements, Weismann had concluded that "even the best of these 'cases' are not reliable and actually convincing."[60] In assessing the reports, he had relied greatly on the opinions of German experts on animal husbandry, of whom Hermann Settegast was one of the most eminent. Settegast, who, as we saw earlier, had also rejected the theory of maternal impressions, dismissed telegony as "the sea-serpent of theories of inheritance" *(Die Seeschlange der Vererbungslehre)*.[61] Herbert Spencer, never overly thrifty with words, criticized Weismann's theory in numerous articles, of which two were translated into German and published in a leading biological journal, and which Weininger studied with great interest because of their forceful endorsement of telegony (557–58).[62] Spencer's discussion of telegony had commenced, predictably enough, with Lord Morton's quagga and had then reviewed all subsequent reports. Refusing to doubt the reality of the phenomenon, Spencer had asserted that during embryonic development some of the germ plasm of the embryo passed into the somatic cells of the mother, from whence it was eventually transmitted to her own germ plasm. The somatic traits of the first mate, then, were transferred to the mother by the embryo and "stored" in the mother's germ plasm. When she mated with a second male, these stored traits of the first mate were transmitted to the progeny of her second union. Telegony, therefore, demonstrated that the soma and the germ plasm were not separate and that the inheritance of acquired (somatic) characters was entirely possible. Telegony, Spencer had concluded, was "fatal to Weismann's hypothesis" of the autonomy of the germ plasm.[63]

Spencer subsequently provided further evidence for the reality of telegony, citing evidence from the United States concerning the interbreeding of whites and blacks. An unnamed American correspondent had reported to Spencer that the children of two white parents often showed traces of black features if the mother had previously had a child by a black man. Professor Othniel Marsh, the well-known paleontologist, had told Spencer that although he had not seen such a case himself, he had received dependable reports on them. Other Americans had expressed similar opinions. W. J. Youmans of New York had sent Spencer a passage from Austin Flint's renowned textbook of physiology making an identical assertion. Youmans had visited Flint, who had reaffirmed the accuracy of the passage. Armed with these attestations, Spencer declared that telegony provided "an absolute disproof of Prof. Weismann's doctrine that the reproductive cells are independent of, and uninfluenced by, the somatic cells." The inheritance of acquired characters was real and verifiable.[64]

Richard Burkhardt has shown that the concept of telegony did not suddenly disappear from biological discourse. After 1900, however, it became definitely passé, and was gradually replaced by new explanations of the phenomena. The "quagga taint" became an illustration of "reversion" and the "direct action of the male on the mother form" that had so impressed Darwin was shown to be due to double fertilization.[65] Weininger was well aware of some of the new developments.[66] He could not, however, do without telegony or maternal impressions: they were far too useful for his ideological project of negating female subjectivity.[67] But how could he, in the face of scientific opposition, establish that such phenomena really happened? First, he attempted to dispute the fairly standard objection that if telegony was at all possible, then it ought to be seen much more frequently. Weininger pointed out that when the two consecutive male mates were racially similar, the traits of the first mate would not be too apparent in the child of the second even when the child did bear them (308). His main strategy, however, was not to oppose the scientists on their own territory but, in a defiant and despairing gesture, to move into the altogether separate domain of literature, arguing that the literary evidence of telegony was more valid and ultimately of far greater relevance than the ridicule of a Weismann or a Settegast.

### Maternal Impressions and Telegony: The Literary Evidence

Weininger regarded telegony, we recall, as a special instance of maternal impressions. This is important because most of Weininger's "literary evidence" concerned impressions rather than telegony in the strict Weismannian sense.[68] Inheritance and its scientific explanations were, of course, recurrent motifs in nineteenth-century imaginative literature, playing significant roles in very different ways in the works of Emile Zola (1840–1902), Henrik Ibsen (1828–1906), and August Strindberg (1849–1912).[69] A less overtly biological concern with heredity had also been at the heart of Goethe's 1810 novel, *Elective Affinities,* which exerted a seminal influence on many later writers, and particularly on Weininger. In his discussion of impressions and telegony, Weininger appealed to Goethe, Ibsen, Strindberg, and Zola in an effort to authenticate his beliefs in the face of scientific criticism: scientific reason might doubt the reality of telegony, but it was validated, Weininger proclaimed, by the eternal wisdom of great literature (551, 557, 564).

Many interpretive studies have been written on the literary, moral, philosophical, and social aspects of Goethe's *Elective Affinities.*[70] Weininger, as we saw earlier, quoted from the novel in his analysis of the "chemical" basis of sexual affinity. He was also greatly impressed by Goethe's treatment of inheritance. The novel revolves around the married couple Eduard and Charlotte, their friend the Captain, and Charlotte's foster daughter Ottilie. Early on in it, future illicit attraction between the characters is foreshadowed by the Captain's speech on the formation and dissolution of chemical bonds.[71] As the story progresses, the Captain and Charlotte grow attracted to each other, and Eduard is drawn to Ottilie. All of them resist acting out their temptations, but their minds prove less obedient. While making love to his wife Charlotte, Eduard "clasped none other than Ottilie in his arms; Charlotte saw the Captain more or less distinctly before her mind's eye."[72] Charlotte conceives, and Eduard is away at war when she gives birth. The returning Eduard first sees his son in Ottilie's arms, and this encounter was specifically quoted by Weininger (551):

> Eduard looked at [the boy] in astonishment. "Good Lord," he exclaimed, "if I had cause to doubt my wife or my friend, would not these features bear terrible witness against them? Isn't this the Captain's face exactly? I've never seen such a likeness."[73]

But that is not all. Ottilie points out to Eduard that the baby, according to most people, looks like her. Startled, Eduard looks at the boy again and exclaims:

"It's you! . . . Those are your eyes. . . . Let me draw a veil over the unhappy hour which gave this little creature his existence. Shall I alarm your pure soul with the distressing thought that a husband and wife . . . can desecrate a legal bond by their vivid fantasies? . . . This child is the result of a double adultery!"[74]

Goethe's denouement highlighted the influence on the child of the paternal as well as the maternal imagination. This egalitarianism was unusual in medical theory, which always saw the maternal imagination as of far greater importance than the paternal in "shaping" or "distorting" the embryo.[75] Weininger did not address this issue, and Goethe's unorthodox gender-symmetrical viewpoint was absent from the other literary works he used.

Of the latter, Henrik Ibsen's 1888 play *The Lady from the Sea* was as useful to Weininger as was Goethe's novel. According to Marvin Carlson, "While European scientists debated about telegony, Ibsen produced a dramatic case study of the phenomenon in *The Lady from the Sea*."[76] The play, strictly speaking, turns upon maternal impressions rather than telegony. The heroine Ellida is the second wife of a physician, Dr. Wangel. Before meeting Wangel, Ellida had been in love with a sailor of mysterious origin. Their (probably) unconsummated relationship had been charged with obsessional intensity, and Ellida confesses to Wangel that her preoccupation with the mysterious man has not diminished over the years. The son she bears to Wangel dies in infancy, but not before she notices that it has the stranger's eyes. Fearful of committing psychological adultery again, Ellida chooses to break off all sexual relations with Wangel.[77] Soon, there ensue further complications—the chief being the sudden reappearance of the stranger—but the play ends on a note of reconciliation between Ellida and Wangel. Ibsen, characteristically, used the notion of maternal impressions to dramatize broader philosophical and social issues concerning individual freedom, free choice, and the position of women in society.[78] A recent critic has argued that the play "may stand as the last word on the question of Ibsen and feminism. . . . It does not present women with the choice between motherhood and solitary New Woman-hood, but rather powerfully advocates women's right to choose their destiny and combine roles as they desire."[79] Weininger, however, ignored these deeper issues, focusing only on Ibsen's brief, albeit pivotal, use of the concept of impressions. Ibsen's concern with feminine autonomy would, in any case, have been anathema to him.

One finds something closer to Weismann's concept of telegony in Weininger's third literary source: Emile Zola's early novel *Madeleine Férat*. Zola had been deeply influenced by the physician Prosper Lucas's treatise on heredity, and many of his novels were pervaded by a deep preoccupation with inheritance and its vicissitudes.[80] Laura Otis has shown that Zola was especially interested in the contemporary scientific belief that the events and traumas of life were indelibly imprinted on the body. The body "remembered" these biologically and passed them on to subsequent generations. Memory and heredity were indissolubly interrelated.[81] Otis does not mention *Madeleine Férat,* but the novel offers a fascinating portrayal of "organic memory."

The plot of *Madeleine Férat* centers upon the eponymous heroine, her husband Guillaume de Viargue, and her earlier lover Jacques Berthier.[82] Madeleine and Guillaume have a daughter, who, they discover, resembles Jacques. The narrator reflects:

> Little Lucie was like Jacques. Even though he had engendered this daughter of Madeleine, Guillaume had been powerless to give the child his image.... It was the woman who had given the child her features, and they were those of the man whose imprint she herself bore.[83]

Madeleine and Jacques, Zola emphasized, had been bound not just by emotions but by "ineluctable physiological forces." Jacques had almost literally imprinted himself on Madeleine's flesh, and

> when, after a year of this occult shaping of the blood and nerves, [Jacques] did leave her, what he left behind him was a young woman stamped for ever with the mark of his kisses, possessed to such a point that she was no longer merely mistress to his body, but in herself bore another being, those male essences which had completed her and in that new shape consolidated her. *It was a purely physical process at work. . . . She was shaped, fashioned by the male, for all time. . . . Her husband possessed merely her heart. Her body was no longer to be given, she could only lend it.*[84]

Fascinated by Zola's notion of feminine sexual plasticity, Weininger commented that Zola's views on women come very close to his own (564). This was indeed the case: Woman, in Weininger's scheme, was infinitely impressionable and modifiable by Man. Psychologically, Woman developed a false self under male influence, as we saw in the last chapter. If telegony and maternal impressions did exist, then Woman, one could argue, was also somatically impressionable—she was not a monad, not a genuinely distinct, autonomous individual. As for new doubts about the reality of telegony and maternal impressions, all one needed to say was that just as Goethe had been correct in his theory of color, regardless of the opposition of physicists, he had been right about maternal impressions too, even if his views were denounced by "all the medical faculties of the world" (286).[85]

*Mother-Right and the Uncertainty of Paternity: Bachofen and Strindberg*
Weininger's political agenda became even more explicit as he approached the work of August Strindberg, who, after Weininger's suicide, was to hail him as

a kindred spirit. Strindberg had not initially been hostile to feminism, but gradually, due to personal and cultural reasons too complex to address here, he developed into one of the most important and interesting antifeminists of the era.[86] Some of his dramatic masterpieces were also masterpieces of antifeminist polemic. Strindberg was as interested as Weininger in demonstrating the physical influence of the male over the female, and this was a major theme of his plays *The Great Highway, The Ghost Sonata,* and *To Damascus.* (All three, moreover, were influenced by Goethe's *Elective Affinities.*)[87] Weininger, however, did not refer to these plays but to the far more famous work, *The Father.* Although impressions or telegony did not feature in that play, it was crucial to Weininger's analysis of maternity; exploring this link, moreover, reveals some of the fundamental anxieties that shaped contemporary antifeminist thought and rhetoric.

Weininger cited *The Father* in his discussion of the uncertainty of paternity, which was one of Strindberg's preoccupations. The fundamental theme of *The Father* was the ancient notion that while the phenomenon of pregnancy ensured that the mother was always identifiable with absolute certainty, one could never be *absolutely* certain about the identity of a child's father. The play, first published in 1887, hinged on its protagonist's doubts about the parentage of his daughter, which are insinuated into his mind by his wife, who repeatedly insists that "no one can really know who the father of a child is." Ultimately, the "Father" is driven insane by his doubts and, at the end of the play, declares: "A man has no children; only women have children."[88]

Strindberg had written the play after reading an article on ancient matriarchy by a Marxist sociologist, who had claimed that the patriarchal family was, in historical terms, a fairly recent phenomenon and had been established after the brutal overthrow of an earlier matriarchal civilization. Such theories were common enough in the wake of Bachofen's *Mutterrecht.* (Bachofen's work had greatly influenced the ethnologist Lewis Henry Morgan, whose 1877 treatise *Ancient Society* had, in turn, influenced Friedrich Engels's 1884 work *The Origin of the Family, Private Property, and the State* and much of later Marxist theory.)[89] In the context of the feminist movements in Europe, the topic of ancient matriarchy was hardly a neutral one, and the article that Strindberg read had warned that the replacement of the current patriarchal civilization by a matriarchy would involve as many crimes and brutalities as had been committed at the rise of the patriarchy. This remark gave Strindberg the idea of a plot that would portray "the vast wheel of history turning backward, with women trying to gain ascendancy over men." Women could attain their goal, Strindberg believed, only by destroying man's faith in himself by making him doubt the one essential feature of patriarchy: fatherhood.[90]

Weininger, we have seen, aimed to resolve the "Woman Question" by demolishing the very concept of Woman as an autonomous subject with rights and obligations. He, therefore, demonstrated that Woman was sexuality incarnate and ontologically not an individual at all. His theory of hysteria proved that Woman had no mind of her own. (Again, the essence of this idea was ancient, but its demonstration and explication by Weininger were strikingly novel.) He then showed that the function for which Woman was honored by men as well by feminists—motherhood—was simply a sexual function. Finally, with the aid of the theory of maternal impressions and telegony, he established that even physically, Woman was formed and molded by male influence. Mentally and physically, Woman was "Nothing." Yet, Weininger's theoretical edifice was shaken, if not quite dislodged, by the Strindbergian motif of the uncertainty of paternity. As Weininger himself reiterated, the only natural, physical claim on the child was the right of the mother. Fatherhood was an illusion. Since Woman was completely and exclusively sexual, and since her sexuality was diffused all over the body, Woman related to the world constantly and exclusively on sexual terms. *Anybody* who made an impression on the Mother was at least partly the father of her children. There could, therefore, be no certainty that any particular man was the exclusive father of a woman's children (307). "The Father," as Bachofen had observed, "is always a juristic fiction, whereas motherhood is a physical fact" (557).[91]

Weininger's deconstruction of the subjectivity of Woman, then, succeeded only at the cost of the destruction of the ideal of the Father and the unintended apotheosis of the Mother, that very event which Strindberg had identified as the first step toward the reestablishment of a matriarchal civilization. Woman might be Nothing at the end of Weininger's discussion of maternity, but the Mother, clearly, was almost Everything. Weininger, of course, denied that biological reproduction had any ethical value, but even when he exalted spiritual fatherhood—the creation of great works of art and of philosophy—he had to concede that this glorious paternity was often facilitated by the Prostitute, which for him signified any woman who enjoyed sex and not simply a woman who sold her sexual favors.

Weininger's analysis, therefore, led to some rather piquant conclusions: the reproduction of the species was a sexual, and therefore, contemptible task; in this task, however, Woman was supreme. The only noble way to be a father was to engender great works; this fatherhood, however, was often facilitated by the promiscuous, biologically sterile Prostitute. While aiming to negate female subjectivity, then, Weininger actually affirmed the total power of Woman over physical reproduction and her significant power over the spiritual productivity of "great men." In the abstruse terms of Kantian ethics, Weininger might well have demonstrated that "Woman is Nothing." In more concrete terms, however, his complex, convoluted, and scholastic argument ended by attesting to female power over life, men, and creativity.[92] That, surely, was the greatest irony about *Geschlecht und Charakter.*

## CHAPTER EIGHT

# Echoes, Analyses, Critiques: Responses to Weininger

*Geschlecht und Charakter* did not cause an immediate stir on publication. The situation changed rapidly, however, after Weininger's dramatic suicide. Newspaper reports on the tragic death of a young genius contributed not a little toward the rapid rise in sales of Weininger's treatise. Some of Weininger's drafts and aphorisms were hastily collected by his friends and published as *Über die letzten Dinge* (On last things). Reviews of *Geschlecht und Charakter* appeared in profusion, many of them perpetuating the "tragic genius" motif. Weininger's life drew the attention of psychiatrists, and his work was championed by Vienna's most pugnacious cultural critic, Karl Kraus. Weininger's theories caused a permanent rift between Sigmund Freud and his intimate friend Wilhelm Fliess, inspired Nazis, provided topics for doctoral dissertations, influenced assorted literary figures from many nations, and played an important if somewhat obscure role in the philosophical development of Ludwig Wittgenstein. More recently, historians have used *Geschlecht und Charakter* as a "symptomatic" text of the fears and prejudices of fin-de-siècle Europe, and Weininger's short, unhappy life has been repeatedly pored over by psychobiographers. No analysis of Weininger's thought can afford to ignore the diverse uses to which it has been put over the years and the various meanings that succeeding generations have read into *Geschlecht und Charakter*. Attempting such an exhaustive survey would be far beyond the scope of the current work. All I wish to do here is to adumbrate, in very broad and rough strokes, the sheer diversity of responses to Weininger's work across generations, disciplines, and nations. Much of this story is still poorly known while other, important sections of it (such as the Italian or Russian readings of *Geschlecht und Charakter*) are omitted from my discussion simply because of my own lack of familiarity with the languages, ideologies, and locales of appropriation.

*Weininger, Swoboda, Freud, and Fliess: Friendship and its Vicissitudes*
Almost a year after Weininger's death, his work caused a major scandal that is usually referred to as the Freud-Fliess-Weininger-Swoboda affair. Probably the most spectacular, if unintentional, consequence of Weininger's work, this

episode has been exhaustively analyzed by historians of psychoanalysis and needs only the briefest recapitulation.[1]

Between 1887 and 1902, perhaps his most creative years, Sigmund Freud's closest friend was the Berlin otolaryngologist Wilhelm Fliess, who was greatly interested in the biology of sexuality. Freud and Fliess wrote long letters to each other and also met frequently to discuss their theories in sessions that Freud called "congresses." Fliess's interests and theories were complex and their relations to the emerging body of Freudian theory more so.[2] The Weininger episode, however, was centered only on Fliess's ideas on the universality of bisexuality. Fliess had argued that every human being, male or female, had a female physiological cycle of twenty-eight days and a male cycle of twenty-three days. Since both cycles occurred in everybody, all humans were constitutionally male as well as female, or bisexual. This notion was not radically different from the theory of universal sexual intermediacy, albeit Fliess's conviction that "the latent sex survives in a dynamic, biochemical, and unconscious form in every normal adult human being" was far more physiologically and psychodynamically oriented than, say, Magnus Hirschfeld's more morphological approach.[3] Freud accepted many of Fliess's ideas, including that of universal bisexuality, but gradually their relationship was strained by progressively wide divergences between their approaches to psychology, and their regular correspondence had ended by 1902.[4]

Then, in July 1904, Freud received a letter from Fliess asking him what he knew about the author of *Geschlecht und Charakter*, which Fliess had just read. The biological section of Weininger's work, said Fliess, seemed to be founded in his own ideas on bisexuality and "the nature of sexual attraction consequent upon it." Fliess noted that Weininger had been a friend of Hermann Swoboda's, who, he knew, had been a student of Freud's. "I have no doubt," charged Fliess, "that Weininger obtained knowledge of my ideas via you. . . . What do you know about it?"[5] After several rather equivocal replies, Freud admitted that there was more than a grain of truth in Fliess's accusation, but pointed out that Weininger could have obtained the idea of bisexuality from other sources "because it has figured in the literature for some time": one glance at Richard von Krafft-Ebing's *Psychopathia Sexualis* should convince Fliess that he had had many forerunners.[6] Far from being placated by Freud's reply, Fliess published an angry pamphlet on the affair and so did his supporter Richard Pfennig.[7] Freud swiftly sent defensive letters to Magnus Hirschfeld and to Karl Kraus, who had by then become a fervent admirer of Weininger.[8] Finally, Swoboda himself published a pamphlet in his defense and sued Fliess unsuccessfully for libel.[9]

Was Fliess right in his accusation? The idea that all humans were both male and female, as we have seen, was far from new, and Fliess himself stressed that Weininger had not "stolen" the idea of constant, universal bisexuality, which he had already mentioned in a work published in 1897 and which Weininger had cited with high praise.[10] What he had not published, however, was his conviction that the two cycles were constantly present in *all* vital processes, thus signifying that every organism was composed of two kinds of vital *substance:* male and female. Although he had not published these findings yet, Fliess had discussed them with Freud, who, he suspected, had divulged them to Swoboda.[11] Swoboda always denied unequivocally that Freud had told him anything except the simple statement that all humans were bisexual, and there is obviously no evidence to help us decide who was telling the truth in this dispute. Nevertheless, one must point out that Fliess's notion of the organism being constructed of male and female substances does remind one quite sharply of Weininger's concept of arrhenoplasm and thelyplasm. Although bisexuality was a common enough idea among biologists and medical scientists, this protoplasmic form of the theory was quite unusual: I do not know of a third example hailing from the turn of the century.

Despite the unpleasant associations Weininger's name must have had for him and despite his own distaste for Weininger's theories, Freud always acknowledged Weininger's gifts. After his suicide, he described him as a "a personality with a touch of the genius."[12] Freud, however, was far from reticent about Weininger's shortcomings as a thinker. The book itself he found "somewhat unbalanced," but Weininger's theories had even broader pathological significance. "The deepest unconscious root of anti-Semitism," Freud surmised, was the childhood belief that the Jews had a piece of their penis cut off at circumcision, and male feelings of superiority over women, too, stemmed from the childhood discovery that females did not possess a penis. The "highly gifted but sexually deranged" Weininger, Freud added, offered the best evidence for his contentions. Weininger's equally hostile description of women and Jews could only have originated from his castration complex: "Being a neurotic, Weininger was completely under the sway of his infantile complexes."[13]

*The Tragic Genius: Weininger's Image in the Early Twentieth Century*
Contemporary responses to *Geschlecht und Charakter* varied according to individual proclivities and cultural, professional, and ideological dispositions. Cultural critics, literati, feminists, antifeminists, scientists, and physicians all read the book differently. No comprehensive study of their responses to Weininger has ever been attempted, and I do not offer one here. My episodic and partial overview is intended only to establish the diversity of responses rather than to analyze their substance or specific contexts.

*Geschlecht und Charakter* created a sensation in the popular press of the time. This was not so much because of its incendiary content but because of the author's dramatic suicide. Many excerpts from these eulogies were distributed in a brochure compiled by Weininger's publisher.[14] A very early notice in the *Neues Wiener Tageblatt* recommended *Geschlecht und Charakter* as essential reading to biologists and psychologists, and to "those concerned with the great questions of emancipation."[15] Another anonymous review in the *Wiener Allgemeine Zeitung* declared that although the book was "marked by genius," Weininger's philosophy was nihilistic, destroying the idea of love and even of maternal love. It was this philosophical negativity that, according to the reviewer, had driven the young author to suicide.[16] Wilhelm Freiherrn von Appel's review for the literary magazine *Neue Bahnen* was entitled "A Great Book by a Great Human Being." Describing Weininger as a prophet, Appel wrote: "Each word of this book is saturated with the spirit of Plato." Count Gobineau and Weininger, Appel added, would one day be appreciated as the two figures who had best understood the epoch and prescribed the proper treatment for its ills: high ideals. Socialism and positive science, he added, were eroding man's personality, and Weininger's book should persuade people to "think again from the beginning." Just as Gobineau had extolled the cultural superiority of the Germanic race, Weininger had found the meaning of humanity in the platonic type Man. (Surprisingly, the reviewer did not even mention Weininger's views on race.)[17] The metaphysics of sexual love and feminine psychology, observed Richard Nordhausen in the *Münchener Neueste Nachrichten,* had never been treated with such monstrous brutality or acuity as in Weininger's book. "But," he said, "one must, must, must read this book."[18]

The reviewer for the *Deutsches Volksblatt* (identified only as Dr. H. F.) was less enthusiastic and censured Weininger for drawing untenable conclusions. "The rose had its thorns but was still the empress of flowers," he remarked. Women, too, for all their flaws, were not the amoral, soulless beings described in Weininger's treatise.[19] In the *Beilage zur Allgemeinen Zeitung,* published from Munich, the reviewer remarked that Weininger's hypothesis of universal sexual intermediacy could only have been formed in the city of Vienna, universally known for its innumerable effeminate men![20] The reviewer for the *Kölnischer Volkszeitung* found the book "contemptible" *(niederträchtiges)* and declared: "If Weininger had entrusted himself to a psychiatrist in time, the German book trade would have been spared a shame and the author would have been saved from the revolver."[21]

Such unequivocally negative assessments of *Geschlecht und Charakter* were rare in the press, and rarer still in the higher reaches of contemporary culture. The European literary intelligentsia of the fin de siècle did not always agree with Weininger, but they treated *Geschlecht und Charakter* with great respect. Describing the English translation of the work as "the most important, as it is the most singular, of contributions to the modern literature on the sex question," Ford Madox Ford reminisced that around 1906,

> in the men's clubs of England and in the cafés of France and Germany—one began to hear singular mutterings amongst men. . . . The idea was that a new gospel had appeared. I remember sitting with a table full of overbearing intellectuals in that year, and they at once began to talk—about Weininger. It gave me a singular feeling because they all talked under their breaths.[22]

In Central Europe, however, few intellectuals referred to Weininger "under their breaths": their response to *Geschlecht und Charakter* was open, enthusiastic, and loudly expressed, indicating, according to historian and critic Hans Meyer, "the traumatic states of consciousness of the bourgeois orders in central Europe."[23]

Perhaps the most significant champion of Weininger's work was the Viennese periodical *Die Fackel,* published and edited by the celebrated satirist Karl Kraus, who had a complex attitude toward women and no patience at all for feminism. Like Weininger, he did not believe that women and men could ever be politically or intellectually equal: both were convinced that women symbolized the primeval power of sexuality alone and that contemporary culture was becoming steadily more effeminate and degenerate. Unlike Weininger, however, Kraus endorsed female sexuality as a valuable stimulus for male intellection and creativity: female sensuality, he once wrote, was "the primal spring at which the intellectuality of man finds renewal."[24] But that difference (which was not that enormous if we recall Weininger's views on the Prostitute's role of providing spiritual stimuli to creative men) did not undermine Kraus's admiration for Weininger. For Kraus, who was deeply ambivalent about Freud and openly hostile to Freud's followers, *Geschlecht und Charakter* also served, in the words of Jacques Le Rider, as "an Anti-Freud-Compendium, an antidote against psychoanalysis." Weininger's theory of the ineffable, microcosmic genius endeared him to Kraus and his followers, who were infuriated by the "reductionist" and "pansexualist" analyses of great works of art then being attempted by Freud's more unrestrained disciples.[25]

But Weininger was valuable to Kraus and his followers not merely as an "anti-Freud"; there were broader cultural reasons for their appreciation of *Geschlecht und Charakter.* In his review of *Geschlecht und Charakter* in *Die Fackel,* Karl Bleibtreu opposed many of Weininger's contentions but hailed the author's "heroic worldview and compelling personality," referring with some distaste to "our feminine century."[26] The supposed effeminacy of the era was, in fact, a major theme of *Die Fackel:* Kraus himself described his age as a "vaginal epoch" *(vaginales Zeitalter),* a phrase that Weininger would surely have appreciated. Nike Wagner has demonstrated that the journal was ideologically antimodern and "masculine," and that it equated the feminine with the sexual. The *Fackel* writers blamed the effeminacy of modern culture for a multitude of sins, but especially for encouraging formlessness in art, language, and character. Their crusade was for a masculine reorientation of civilization, an impeccably Weiningerian goal.[27] Equally Weiningerian was their opposition to granting any intellectual role to women. Culture and civilization, argued a typical essay in the journal, had been created by males. Women had advanced or impeded cultural development solely by stimulating or inhibiting male efforts; their role in society was exclusively erotic and aesthetic.[28] Kraus agreed with Weininger that the male was intermittently sexual while the female was perpetually so.[29] Realizing, however, that Weininger would never have concurred with his own view that female sexuality revitalized the male intellect (Kraus might have not have paid adequate attention to Weininger's discussion of the Prostitute!), Kraus penned this epigram to Weininger's memory: "An admirer of women agrees enthusiastically with your arguments for misogyny."[30] Kraus's admiration for Weininger remained constant over the years. *Geschlecht und Charakter* became a "great classic" of the Viennese avant-garde, asserts Jacques Le Rider, only because it had been championed by Kraus. Kraus mentioned Weininger even in his love letters, and when Weininger's father wanted to protest against psychiatrist Ferdinand Probst's pathography of his son, Kraus printed Leopold Weininger's statement in *Die Fackel,* adding a caustic, antipsychiatric commentary in footnotes.[31]

August Strindberg contributed twice to *Die Fackel*'s engagement with Weininger. The first was a letter of July 1903 from Strindberg to his German translator Emil Schering, in which Strindberg informed Schering that Weininger had sent him a copy of *Geschlecht und Charakter,* which Strindberg had found to be a "frightening" *(furchtbares)* book that had "probably solved the hardest of all problems." To Weininger himself, Strindberg sent a postcard offering heartfelt thanks for at last solving the "Woman Problem."[32] Soon, however, it was time to write Weininger's obituary, and, in his deeply felt tribute, Strindberg declared that only the mentally retarded would doubt the superiority of the male sex over the female. All the spiritual and material riches of humanity had been created by males; woman was negative and passive, whereas man was positive and active. Woman's love for man, Strindberg opined, was "50% animal heat *(Brunst)* and 50% hate." Otto Weininger had rediscovered and reported this "well-known secret" in his "virile" book, and it was this discovery of the "essence and nature of woman" that, Strindberg surmised, had cost Weininger his life.[33] Strindberg did not, however, explain how the novelty of this "discovery" surpassed the insights into the "true nature" of woman found in his own works.

*Weininger as Source: The Literary Influence of Geschlecht und Charakter*

Weininger has long had an audience among European literati, but not all of their responses have been as emotional or as ideologically inflected as those of Kraus or Strindberg.[34] Many well-known literary figures have used selected ideas from *Geschlecht und Charakter* as guiding principles for their own work, while others have satirized and undermined Weininger's notions in very different ways. Collectively, they have tended to use Weininger's work as a source and stimulus instead of venerating it as a manifestation of the author's ineffable genius.

Let us begin with Franz Kafka. "Nowadays," according to Gerald Stieg, "decency would seem to forbid mentioning the names Kafka and Weininger in one breath, but historical truth forces one to commit such a sacrilege."[35] Kafka's biographer Heinz Politzer has suggested that Weininger's description of the Absolute Female "reads like a blueprint for the female figures in *The Trial*." Politzer detected Weininger's influence in the character known as the usher's wife in the novel, who is motherly as well as promiscuous. Another Weiningerian character in *The Trial* was Leni the nurse, whom Kafka portrayed, Politzer argues, in accordance with Weininger's opinion that females excelled at nursing because they had no real understanding of individuality and individual suffering.[36] More broadly, asserts Gerald Stieg, Kafka and Weininger "share a radicalness of experience in the world that is dictated to them by *angst:* they are afraid of the *others.* Their *others* are first of all women."[37]

*Geschlecht und Charakter* also drew the attention of a group of young writers affiliated with the literary magazine *Der Brenner,* published in Innsbruck and edited by Ludwig von Ficker. Profoundly influenced by the ideas of Karl Kraus, the *Brenner* was often seen as the "*Fackel* of the provinces" *(Provinzfackel).*[38] Kraus introduced Weininger's work to the *Brenner* circle, where it produced an even greater impact than in Kraus's own journal.[39] In the words of Gerald Stieg, "nearly all contributors to the *Brenner* were *infected* by Weininger."[40] Among these contributors were the fanatical anti-Semite Jörg Lanz von Liebenfels and the Jewish engineer Erich Messing, who had rejected his "effeminate" religion, converting, like Weininger, to "masculine" Protestantism. At a more sophisticated level within the *Brenner* group, the poet Georg Trakl recirculated such Weiningerian themes in his work as the belief that civilization was in terminal decline, that human beings could be reduced into types, that maternity and prostitution were not polar opposites, and that one must try to transcend sexuality.[41]

Other Brennerites, such as Carl Dallago and Ferdinand Ebner, rejected

Weininger's views on Jewishness and femininity. Dallago, indeed, celebrated the natural polygamousness of humans, in contradistinction to Weininger's idealization of celibacy. Ebner admitted the social necessity for monogamy, while stressing that humans (and particularly men) were polygamous by nature. As for Weininger's portrayal of the Absolute Male as the complete human being, Dallago and Ebner dismissed the very concept of "the complete human being," which for them could never be an individual but rather an entity emerging from the dialogue of self and other.[42] Ebner also pointed out that idealistic philosophy was a thoroughly male construct and that it was often overlooked that, when taken to its extreme, idealism led quite naturally to the exclusion of women and of the feminine in general. There was no place for the Other, whether feminine or divine, in philosophies founded exclusively in the Self.[43]

Weininger left many a trace in the work of novelist Hermann Broch, who was also an occasional contributor to *Der Brenner*. In 1914, he described Weininger as "the most passionate ethical thinker since Kant," while admitting, however, that Weininger had interpreted Kant's ethical principles with unacceptable rigidity. In Broch's trilogy of novels, *The Sleepwalkers*, echoes of Weininger were audible in the depiction of the "little whore" Ruzena, who was bereft of all will and intentionality except in erotic matters. Even more Weiningerian was Broch's description of Pasenow's "projection" of innocence and Madonna-like qualities onto Elisabeth von Baddensen, the woman he loved. At the end of the trilogy, Broch attempted to resolve Weininger's dualities by uniting the male Jew Nuchem with the Christian female Marie in spiritual love. In his later work, Broch continued to play with some of Weininger's themes while overturning Weininger's judgments and depicting their implications as "murderous." Indeed, Broch tried so hard to portray some of his female characters as pure and chaste that a recent critic has described them as clichéd.[44]

Critics have also seen Weininger's influence in Robert Musil's celebrated novel set in early-twentieth-century Vienna, *The Man without Qualities*. Without fully sharing Weininger's ethical viewpoint, Musil's novel frequently depicted women who were incapable of abstract thought and who expected men to analyze complicated situations for them: of these characters, the most dramatic was undoubtedly the adulterous Bonadea, consumed by lust and troubled by conscience only when she reflected that her conduct might ruin her marriage and thus rob her of worldly security. Many of Weininger's assertions on love and sexual relations were also reflected in the metaphors used by the mentally unbalanced Clarisse—which, perhaps, indicated Musil's own opinion of Weininger's beliefs![45]

Elias Canetti resurrected some of Weininger's concepts of masculinity and femininity in his 1935 novel *Die Blendung*.[46] Canetti, who won the Nobel Prize for literature in 1981, spent his youth in Vienna and throughout his life acknowledged the influence of Karl Kraus on his work. In his autobiography, he recalled that during the 1920s his intellectual friends continually discussed Kraus, Weininger, and Schopenhauer: "Pessimistic and misogynistic statements were particularly popular, although none of [my friends] was a misogynist or a misanthrope."[47] Canetti's *Blendung* has been seen as a sustained satirical recollection of these friends, who formed a virtual "Weiningercult."[48] The character Peter Kien represented the impossible Absolute Male, whereas his wife represented the Absolute Female. These and other characters from the novel, says Gerald Stieg, were "marionettes out of Weininger's world."[49] It should be emphasized that Canetti used Weininger without assenting to his views: in the last years of his life, he refused to write an introduction to a reprint of *Geschlecht und Charakter* because he considered it racist and sexist beyond redemption.[50]

Weininger's literary influence was not confined to Central Europe. James Joyce was greatly struck by the Viennese philosopher's portraits of the Woman and the Jew, and it has been suggested that Leopold Bloom in *Ulysses*, whom Joyce described as "a finished example of the new womanly man," was modelled partly on Weininger's description of the Jewish male: "feminine, will-less, and intellectually fuzzy."[51] Molly Bloom, predictably, was portrayed as the purely and exclusively sexual Absolute Female described by Weininger.[52] In Italy, the plot of Italo Svevo's novel *The Confessions of Zeno* turned upon a Weiningerian notion of telegony, and the protagonist of the novel was an avid reader of *Geschlecht und Charakter*, declaring it to be "excellent company if one ran after women."[53] In the United States, the poet William Carlos Williams decided to marry a woman he did not love because he had learned from *Geschlecht und Charakter* that sexual affinity, rather than love, was the most important bond between Man and Woman. Also influenced by Weininger's conviction that a man with sufficient power of will could develop into a genius, Williams believed that it was only his weakness for women that prevented him from attaining genius.[54]

Among other American writers, Gertrude Stein felt that Weininger's theories corroborated her own views on "character." She was especially drawn to Weininger's critique of experimental psychology because she had independently developed similar views during her work at the Harvard psychological laboratory. After reading *Geschlecht und Charakter*, Stein attempted, in her novel *The Making of Americans*, to portray action in such a way that each act would reveal the entire "character" of a person and, at a less rarefied level, shaped her female characters to fit the Weiningerian categories of Prostitute, Mother, and Maid.[55]

All in all, *Geschlecht und Charakter,* intended to be a philosophical resolution of a political question, had its most enduring success in the field of imaginative literature. Weininger's influence was not wholly insignificant on other fields, but with the exception of one philosopher, none of the people who found his work instructive or stimulating could match up to the stature of Kafka, Musil, Broch, or Joyce. It is all the more interesting, therefore, to note how piecemeal the literary appropriations of *Geschlecht und Charakter* were and how oblivious their authors were, by and large, to the political, scientific, and cultural contexts by which it had been shaped.

*Weininger, Feminists, and Antifeminists*

Since *Geschlecht und Charakter* was written to resolve the Woman Question, one might well wonder how feminist and antifeminist thinkers responded to its contentions. Around the turn of the century, Rosa Mayreder and Grete Meisel-Hess were among the most articulate Austrian writers on feminist issues, and both wrote much about Weininger.[56] Philosophically, Rosa Mayreder could be best described as a romantic individualist. Like Nietzsche, she believed in the worth of the exceptional individual and opposed "the tyranny of the norm"; her hero was Goethe.[57] Meisel-Hess, too, was drawn to Nietzschean individualism but was more concerned with reconstructing the image of the mother and freeing it from its patriarchal frame of reference. Interested in psychoanalysis and in the anti-Christian monist philosophy propagated by biologist Ernst Haeckel, Meisel-Hess fought for greater sexual liberty for women and against the "largely pathological nature of much of modern sexual life."[58] Mayreder celebrated the intellectual woman, Meisel-Hess the liberated mother.[59]

For Mayreder, Weininger's "sexualization" of the protoplasm was evasive, since the argument that the protoplasm existed in male and female forms did not explain the nature of male-female differences but merely pushed them down to a lower level. Mayreder did approve of the basic idea that there was no absolute distinction between the two sexes, but, she pointed out, Weininger had negated this notion by dealing solely with ideal types of Man and Woman in the second part of his book. As for his denial of a soul to Woman, Mayreder assumed that for Weininger the biological correlate of the soul was the arrhenoplasm, the male form of protoplasm. Now, since Weininger had argued that both men and women possessed male as well as female plasmas, although in different amounts, Mayreder asked: How much arrhenoplasm did one need to possess in order to have a soul?[60]

For all his talk of male and female protoplasm, observed Mayreder, Weininger still followed a genital scheme: the possession of a phallus implied the possession of a soul, regardless of how much female protoplasm the individual might possess. She lamented that despite having begun with a promisingly nuanced view of sexual differences, Weininger had concluded by upholding the crude, ancient perspective on male-female differences: sex was known from the genitals alone, and those with male genitalia were the polar opposites of those with female genitalia, even in the psychological sphere. The psychological differences between the sexes, Mayreder concluded, could never be adequately appreciated with such an essentialist scheme.[61]

Some of this analysis was rather simplistic, and Weininger's concept of masculinity was really not genitalist. Moreover, it should not be assumed that Mayreder had no use at all for Weininger's views. Many of her arguments seem to have been responses to his, even when she did not mention him by name. She denied, for instance, that genius represented "an intensification of masculine nature," declaring, instead, that genius represented a synthesis of the masculine elements with the feminine: male geniuses were more emotional and female geniuses possessed masculine traits.[62] This was a clear *Aufhebung* of Weininger: it negated his theory of genius—even imagining a female genius was enough to negate Weininger!—while preserving some of the microcosmic quality he had stipulated for the soul of a true genius.

Grete Meisel-Hess charged that Weininger had "rushed past the facts and his arguments have shattered at the first impact with reality. It has in truth nothing to do with 'woman and her question.'"[63] Despite her rejection of Weininger's overall thesis, Meisel-Hess did acknowledge, however, that as long as Weininger restricted himself to purely scientific or scholarly issues *(das rein Wissenschaftliche),* he displayed an impressive acuity.[64] In far-off America, for instance, Charlotte Perkins Gilman praised the "intense moral earnestness" and "lofty scope" of Weininger's work. Yet, she observed, to anybody with any understanding of the social aspects of women's status, Weininger's beliefs and recommendations were "so paralyzingly absurd . . . that the attitude of serious attention is difficult to maintain." For Gilman, the book's real importance lay "in its so fully concentrating and carrying to its logical conclusion the andro-centric view of humanity. . . . Never before in all our literature has the ultra-masculine view of woman been so logically carried out, so unsparingly forced to its conclusion." Gilman was confident, however, that the book would not find favor among Americans, because "with us the humanness of women is more compellingly visible than in older lands."[65]

As the feminist movement gathered strength in Central Europe, a strong antifeminist movement emerged in reaction to it.[66] Hans Blüher, one of its prominent theorists, distinguished between "bourgeois antifeminism," which opposed specific feminist aims, and "spiritual antifeminism," which opposed feminism from the ideological conviction of female inferiority.[67] Blüher fervently believed in the cultural superiority of an exclusive male community, the *Bund.* In the male (and the homoerotic) world of the Bund, women were by definition subordinate to men, and, as with most forms of Volkish ideology, women's emancipation was seen as a threat.[68] In one of his tracts, Blüher argued that the emancipation of Jews and slaves was logically admissible since Jews and slaves wanted emancipation. Women's emancipation, however, was a nonsensical concept since Otto Weininger had demonstrated that it was the nature of Woman to be a slave. Even the superficially masculine woman was inwardly a slave to Man.[69]

One fairly recent feminist reading of Weininger demands to be mentioned here because of its unique combination of a feminist with what one might conventionally label an antifeminist argument. In her well-known work *The Female Eunuch,* Germaine Greer described *Geschlecht und Charakter* as "a remarkably rigorous and committed book by a mere boy." According to her, "the most chastening reflection is that Weininger was simply describing what he saw in female behavior around him. . . . All the moral deficiencies Weininger detected masqueraded in Victorian society as virtues. Weininger is to be credited with describing them properly."[70] Agreeing with Weininger's contentions on the illogicality and emotionality of Woman, Greer argued that these traits, instead of being limitations, were actually advantageous. Alluding to Weininger's belief that the absolute female lacked an ego, Greer exclaimed: "If women had no ego, if they had no separation from the rest of the world, no repression and no regression, how nice that would be!"[71]

The feminist and antifeminist responses to Weininger are obviously far less impressive in range and depth than the literary reactions. Some of the most striking assertions of the book were either ignored or only superficially addressed by that very constituency which ought to have responded at the greatest depth. Although the topic needs further research, one might tentatively argue that Weininger's treatise was so abstruse and its antifeminism so baroque and overblown that it read more like a novel than a serious exposition that needed to be refuted in detail by feminists or that deserved to be accepted in toto by antifeminists. If this is correct, then Weininger clearly failed in his self-imposed task of resolving the Woman Question.

*Weininger among the Philosophers*

What then of philosophers, who might have been expected to evince some interest in this idiosyncratic text of neo-Kantian cultural analysis? With one quite remarkable exception, Weininger seems to have failed to impress his fellow philosophers. Even Weininger's *Doktorvater* Friedrich Jodl did not regard the book as a genuine contribution to philosophical literature. Although he praised Weininger's scholarship in a rueful article published after his student's suicide, he described most of the second part of *Geschlecht und Charak-*

*ter* as "shocking and repulsive." The key to Weininger's personality, observed Jodl, lay in his utopian vision of a world of asexual individuals. All his intellectual sophistication notwithstanding, Weininger had suffered from a schoolboyish horror of sex. Suspecting that Weininger's views on women had owed something to personal romantic disappointments, Jodl remarked: "What a person with poetic gifts would have turned into a play or a novel, [Weininger] turned into a psychological construct."[72]

Less sympathetic philosophers considered Weininger to be psychologically unbalanced, if not downright insane. In a comprehensive review published in the well-known philosophical journal established by Johann Gottlieb Fichte, Meta Jörges criticized Weininger for his "uncritical generalizations" and for the unabashed essentialism characterizing his views on the differences between male and female thought. "The author follows," exclaimed Jörges, "a delusion *[Wahnidee]*!"[73] The same note was struck more sharply by the editors of the leading journal of Kantian philosophy, *Kant-Studien*. When publishing Weininger's own description of *Geschlecht und Charakter,* the editors said in a cautionary footnote that the journal bore no responsibility for the contents of the book or the notice: their author had recently committed suicide due to nervous disturbances.[74] Some philosophers believed that there had been method in Weininger's madness. The German-Jewish Marxist philosopher Ernst Bloch (1885–1977), for example, defined *Geschlecht und Charakter* as driven by "bourgeois male hatred of the women's movement."[75] Weininger, suffering from "the most vehement misogyny known to history," had argued with "total obsession" that "only woman as hetaira is the truth, woman as madonna is a creation of man."[76]

The one striking exception I mentioned above was Ludwig Wittgenstein (1889–1951). Wittgenstein grew up in Vienna, and his adolescence coincided with the period when what Canetti called the Weininger "cult" was at its height.[77] Wittgenstein's respect for Weininger was quite strikingly profound. In 1931, he had written in a private notebook that he had never "invented" a novel line of thought: "I have always taken over from someone else," he observed, appending a list of his "sources," which included physicists Ludwig Boltzmann and Heinrich Hertz, cultural critic Karl Kraus, architect Adolf Loos, historian Oswald Spengler, and philosophers Arthur Schopenhauer, Gottlob Frege—and Otto Weininger.[78] This confession of his lack of originality, moreover, was part of a Weiningerian meditation on Jewishness. "Amongst Jews," Wittgenstein had written, "'genius' is found only in the holy man. Even the greatest of Jewish thinkers is no more than talented. (Myself for instance.)"[79] Biographer Ray Monk believes that Wittgenstein attributed his personal and intellectual flaws to his Jewishness, and it is indeed true that Wittgenstein's private writings were pervaded by ambivalence about his race:

when considering the Jewish presence in Europe, for instance, he had used the old metaphor (which was particularly popular with the Nazis) equating Jews with a "tumor" in the body politic.[80]

Wittgenstein's admiration for Weininger was not simply a private enthusiasm. He recommended *Geschlecht und Charakter* to his peers, and when philosopher G. E. Moore had reacted critically to the book, Wittgenstein responded:

> I can quite imagine that you don't admire Weininger very much, what with that beastly translation and the fact that W. must feel very foreign to you. It is true that he is fantastic but he is *great* and fantastic. It isn't necessary or rather not possible to agree with him but the greatness lies in that with which we disagree. It is his enormous mistake which is great. I.e. roughly speaking if you just add a "~" to the whole book it says an important truth.[81]

Wittgenstein never clarified what he meant by Weininger's great mistake, nor what he thought to be the "important truth" expressed in *Geschlecht und Charakter*. Ray Monk speculates that Wittgenstein was indicating his disagreement with Weininger's fundamental tenet that femininity was the source of all evil.[82] He is, indeed, reported to have exclaimed "How wrong he was, my God he was wrong" when an acquaintance had asked him about Weininger's ideas on women. However, we need to juxtapose that reported remark with the fact, also reported by Monk, that Wittgenstein was against the idea of women adopting philosophy as a profession. One does not know the reasons for the latter belief or its contexts, but considered purely by itself, it was vintage Weininger. Wittgenstein also greatly admired Weininger's conceptualization of the microcosmic genius and included this lapidary aphorism in his *Tractatus Logico-Philosophicus:* "I am my world. (The microcosm.)"[83]

There are other, somewhat less clear factors that may have endeared Weininger to Wittgenstein at a more existential level. Wittgenstein, it is well known, lived by impossibly high ethical standards, blaming himself frequently for his "baseness and rottenness" *(Niedrigkeit und Gemeinheit).*[84] Allan Janik has attributed this punitive, inexorable ethical stance to the influence of Weininger's views on one's duty to oneself.[85] In his philosophical theories, Wittgenstein may have been significantly influenced by Weininger's conviction that logic and ethics were one, and that, consequently, it was immoral to think illogically.[86] Once, when Wittgenstein was pacing up and down in Bertrand Russell's Cambridge rooms "like a wild beast for three hours in agitated silence," Russell asked him: "Are you thinking about logic or your sins?" "Both," replied Wittgenstein.[87] "A Weiningerian," remarks Janik, "could hardly do other than think of logic and his sins."[88]

Philosopher Rudolf Haller agrees that Weininger's views on the unity of logic and ethics induced Wittgenstein to assert in the *Tractatus* that logic, ethics, and aesthetics were one.[89] But the "deepest basis for the common ground between Weininger and Wittgenstein," according to Haller, "is their belief that one could not empirically establish or verify logical or ethical rules even though they had 'an essential connection to the world.'"[90] Barry Smith contests this analysis. While Weininger may indeed have exerted some early influence on Wittgenstein's ethical views, he argues, Wittgenstein was convinced by the time he wrote the *Tractatus* that one could not say or even think *anything* meaningful about ethics. Weininger's verbosity on ethical matters would, therefore, have seemed futile and nonsensical to him. To use Wittgenstein's own metaphor, he had thrown away Weininger's ladder after using it to climb up beyond Weininger's world.[91] This, again, does not dovetail very neatly with other, admittedly scattered pieces of evidence, which suggest that Wittgenstein might have climbed beyond only *some* parts of Weininger's world. Weininger's conviction of Jewish intellectual inferiority and cultural perniciousness seems to have stayed with him, as did, perhaps, the conviction of women's incapacity to think logically.

### Scientists and Physicians on Weininger

Although the work is a philosophical analysis of a political question, much of the material discussed in *Geschlecht und Charakter* was biological, psychological, or medical. How then, one might inquire, was Weininger's work received by professionals in these fields? Again, one encounters a wide range of opinions rather than any broad consensus.

We have already seen that Weininger's notion of idioplasmic sexuality was cited appreciatively by the physiologist Francis Marshall in his influential work, *The Physiology of Reproduction* and, less conspicuously, by the zoologist Edward Minchin in an article in the *Encyclopaedia Britannica*. In Vienna, gynecologist Josef Halban found *Geschlecht und Charakter* a thoughtful and stimulating work that had, however, drawn untenable conclusions from the data. Halban applauded Weininger's biological erudition as "astounding" but ignored Weininger's theory that the sexual characters were not produced solely by the internal secretions, which served only to accentuate the already existing sexual traits of the idioplasm. Now, although Halban was a pioneer in research on the effects of the internal secretions of the ovary on female sexual development, he had soon decided that the sexual characters were determined *ab ovo*, with the internal secretions exerting only a "protective influence" over them.[92] It is, therefore, more than a little odd that Halban found Weininger's biological knowledge "astounding" but paid no attention to the one topic about which Halban knew more than any other reviewer and on which Weininger's opinions were close to (although far from identical with) his own.

The other reviews were hardly more detailed or rigorous. An anonymous reviewer in another medical journal urged "every physician" to read *Geschlecht und Charakter* and marvelled at Weininger's mastery of the biomedical literature on sexuality—which was evident to the reviewer even from the second, "philosophical" part of the book. The concluding pages of the book, he added, revealed "a fiery philosophical spirit *[philosophische Feuergeist]*, thoroughly schooled in the natural sciences, embracing the world-renouncing mysticism of Leo Tolstoy."[93] Such hyperbole was not uncommon among scientists: the Viennese zoologist Karl Camillo Schneider, for instance, rejected Weininger's ethical evaluation of femininity but declared that Weininger, for all his errors, was destined for immortality as a psychologist, alongside Sigmund Freud and Hermann Swoboda.[94]

Occasionally, medical reviewers agreed with Weininger's moral and antifeminist contentions, while dismissing the book as a whole. In a gynecological journal, the reviewer described *Geschlecht und Charakter* as the timeliest of all books, full of astonishingly accurate observations and conclusions. Although the reviewer approved of Weininger's views on women, he found the vision of a sexless utopia utterly nihilistic. *Geschlecht und Charakter,* although brilliant in parts, would, he predicted, disappear from the literary horizon as meteorically as it had appeared.[95]

The *Jahrbuch für sexuelle Zwischenstufen,* devoted to the medical study of homosexuality and the political emancipation of homosexuals, considered Weininger's views on femininity to be largely wrong or overstated. All the same, the reviewer, not himself a physician, had high praise for Weininger's talent and emphasized the intellectual significance of *Geschlecht und Charakter.*[96] "Since the days of Schopenhauer," he observed, "this is the first time that a serious philosophical work has tried to solve the homosexual problem."[97] The reviewer was especially pleased that Weininger, in his theory of sexual intermediacy, had followed quite closely the views propagated in the *Jahrbuch.*[98] The criminologist Hans Groß, too, was greatly impressed by Weininger's analysis of homosexuality and femininity and recommended that every criminologist read *Geschlecht und Charakter.*[99]

Physicians outside Central Europe did not ignore *Geschlecht und Charakter.* In New York, Douglas McMurtrie hailed Weininger as "the writer who did most to bring the theory [of universal sexual intermediacy] before the public."[100] McMurtrie provided a detailed overview of Weininger's ideas on sexual intermediacy, stressing the importance of the Law of Sexual Relations. Weininger's biological chapters, he said, deserved medical attention, even though the sweeping assertions of the latter part of the book were nothing "other than fantastic."[101] In England, however, sexologist Havelock Ellis offered no appreciative words at all when *Geschlecht und Charakter* was published in an English translation. Calling Weininger "a radically morbid person," Ellis declared:

> Youth, certainly, is the time for ideas, but a youth who really had in him the mental force and calibre to grapple with a great problem would, like Darwin, have kept the secret to himself for thirty years of quiet investigation. But this neurotic young doctor of philosophy lived in an intellectual hot-house. . . . It thus came about that a highly gifted youth expended himself at the threshold of life in a pyrotechnical display which, however brilliant it may seem, can scarcely throw any illumination on the problems of the real world.[102]

German psychiatrist Paul Möbius was even more critical than Ellis. Möbius, author of the notorious *Physiological Feeble-Mindedness of Woman*, accused Weininger of plagiarizing his ongoing series of publications on sexuality. Noting that Weininger had dared to disagree with his own view that talent in women was a sign of degeneration, Möbius retorted: "So the man in a philosopher's cloak would determine what is normal and what is pathological!"[103] Despite his charge of plagiarism, Möbius would not, one feels, have been happy with the American psychologist Helen Thompson Woolley, who put his work on women's feeble-mindedness in the same category as *Geschlecht und Charakter,* stating that "there is perhaps no field aspiring to be scientific where flagrant personal bias, logic martyred in the cause of supporting a prejudice, unfounded assertions, and even sentimental rot and drivel, have run riot to such an extent" as in the study of sexual differences. Current research, she continued, suggested that there were few, if any psychological differences between the sexes that were of biological origin, "in spite of the continued popularity of such books as Möbius's *Physiologischer Schwachsinn des Weibes* and Weininger's *Geschlecht und Charakter.*"[104]

In Germany, too, psychologist William Stern grouped the two books together as cautionary examples of scientific bias. Both Möbius and Weininger, Stern wrote, had ignored empirical facts challenging their conviction of female inferiority.[105] Paul Hensel, writing in a leading German biological journal, went farther. He described Weininger's critique of experimental psychology as "childish" and his assertions on genius as worthy of nineteenth-century Naturphilosophie.[106] The physicist Wilhelm Ostwald, who found Weininger's book to be valuable only as "the case history of a precocious, unbalanced youth," also criticized Weininger's speculative, *naturphilosophisch* style of argumentation.[107]

There may, of course, be other scientific and medical responses to *Geschlecht und Charakter* that I have not succeeded in locating, but it is clear from my sample that even biologists and physicians who reacted quite critically to the book did not find any serious deficiencies in Weininger's scientific knowledge. Some (like Josef Halban) even found that knowledge "astounding." That, however, was just about all the praise that Weininger seems to have received from the scientific readers of his era. It is difficult to imagine that he would have been satisfied with this, but it does suggest that whatever historians and biographers might think today, the scientific content of *Geschlecht und Charakter* was not necessarily dismissed as pseudoscientific in its time.

### Weininger's Place in Recent Scholarship

"Weininger's name is no longer a household word, but his voice is still heard in texts by familiar authors who helped form modern and postmodern culture," say the editors of a recent collection of scholarly essays entitled *Jews and Gender: Responses to Otto Weininger.* "His text has rendered any boundaries between genre, nationality, or discipline obsolete; his influence, stemming from a work that today might be called 'popular science,' has been felt in literature, philosophy, science, and history."[108] Whether Weininger's work rendered intellectual or national boundaries "obsolete" is, of course, doubtful, but the content of his work as well as its influence undoubtedly transcend quite a few of them.

   Until very recently, however, this breadth was not reflected in the scholarship on Weininger. *Geschlecht und Charakter* tended to be approached largely as a "symptomatic text" of the fears and prejudices of fin-de-siècle Central European intellectuals, and some of the most prominent examples of such studies were mentioned in the Introduction.[109] Such approaches were questioned vigorously by Allan Janik in a series of essays published in the 1980s.[110] His fundamental point was that virtually none of the studies on Weininger then available was based on a really close reading of the text and its multiple, interwoven contexts. Pointing out that the task of contextualizing *Geschlecht und Charakter* was lightened by Weininger's detailed notes and references, Janik asserted that such a reading of *Geschlecht und Charakter* would find that "one could accuse Weininger of being precipitously speculative but not of being *unscientific* in his own time."[111] Very recently, scholars have begun to evolve more complex and contextual approaches to Weininger's work than were common when Janik's essays were published. The studies on various aspects of Weininger's thought, contexts, and influence collected, for example, in the volume *Jews and Gender* (most of which have been cited previously in this work) attest to the diversity, percipience, and methodological sophistication with which Weininger's work is currently being analyzed. Those qualities, of course, are not confined to the scholars represented in that particular collection: others have been contributing equally stimulating studies.[112] These recent explorations have begun to yield richly detailed analyses of various important aspects of Weininger's work and contexts, but there has, as yet, been no sufficiently comprehensive attempt to explore *Geschlecht und Charakter* as a whole and to analyze its polyphonic—more precisely, cacophonous!—multiplicity of themes in their diverse contexts.

This is what I have attempted to do in this work. In analyzing and contextualizing *Geschlecht und Charakter*, I have tried to establish the fragmented, incoherent, and occasionally contradictory nature of Weininger's treatise and to relate those elements to their respective contexts—discursive, cultural, and ideological. I have paid particularly close attention to Weininger's use of biological and medical discourse, a crucial theme that had been left virtually unexplored by scholars. This lack of interest in scientific and medical discourse was first pointed out by Allan Janik. As this book should demonstrate, I enthusiastically second Janik's call to rethink Weininger's work in the light of fin-de-siècle science and medicine.

Unlike Janik, however, I do not think that Weininger was an unrecognized scientist and I do not regard the question of Weininger's own scientificity as terribly important. True, Weininger was far more rational in parts of his book than he has been given credit for—the chapter on homosexuality, for example, seems progressive even today, as do some of Weininger's suggestions on pedagogical reforms in the light of differential psychology. In overall terms, however, Weininger was far from a scientist, whether defined narrowly as a professional who earns his living from scientific work or more broadly as a thinker trained in the sciences and working in accordance with principles and toward goals that would be accepted as legitimate by contemporary scientists. To *use* scientific discourse or even to criticize and build upon it intelligently is not necessarily to *be* a scientist. Except in the first part of *Geschlecht und Charakter*, Weininger used the discourse of science in different ways but always with the conscious and explicit goal of advancing his ideological antifeminist project. Janik's argument that he saw himself as a reformer of psychology is undoubtedly true but only up to a point. The reformed psychology Weininger aspired to was a *gendered* psychology in which the microcosmic male soul would be left to the philosopher while the typical experimental psychologist would be concerned solely with the rudimentary minds of women and, possibly, Jews. This was not so much a reform of psychology or an example of the cultural shaping of scientific research but simply another of Weininger's strategic deployments of scientific arguments in the explicit service of ideological antifeminism.

Weininger's use of science, in short, demands detailed historical exploration but not because he was an unappreciated scientist. Although well informed on contemporary science, his use of biomedical discourse, as I have shown, was governed not by the conventions of professional scientists and physicians but by the strategic demands of his larger project. The science of Weininger's time, of course, was frequently quite compatible with his own convictions of gender inequality. Compatibility, however, is not equivalence. For Weininger, the cultural-political aim of his work was *explicitly* paramount, and he moved through the discourse of science with an almost gleeful, childlike abandon, picking what was of use to him for his ideological argument, ignoring everything that was not, and, in the later parts of *Geschlecht und Charakter*, ridiculing all that seemed to challenge his ontological convictions on masculinity and femininity. A professional scientist may have *thought* like Weininger and shared his beliefs on the worth of womanhood, but, when communicating with his peers, he would have *argued* his case in accordance with different intellectual, stylistic, and professional conventions. If a scientist had wished to resurrect the rejected idea of telegony, for example, the conventions of his profession would not have permitted him to appeal exclusively to novels and plays for supportive evidence.

It is thus essential that we see *Geschlecht und Charakter* as a melange of science, bigotry, philosophy, personal anxiety, and cultural politics. The most fruitful way of approaching Weininger's notorious—and notoriously misconstrued—work is to read it as a disorganized, fragmented, and cacophonous text, analyzing each element with reference to its intellectual and cultural contexts. Such a close, comprehensive, and contextual reading helps us appreciate not only the importance of scientific doctrines and language in Weininger's work but also shows us how those ideas, themselves culturally shaped but in accordance with different conventions, were appropriated, reshaped, and integrated with Weininger's metaphysical and ideological analysis of gender and identity. Above all, a comprehensive study of Weininger's thought and his sources leads us beyond Weininger himself into the broader realms of fin-de-siècle debates, anxieties, and ideologies over identity, demonstrating the ways in which such anxieties and debates drew from and influenced contemporary scientific and medical theories.

## Introduction

1. See Edward Timms, *Karl Kraus, Apocalyptic Satirist: Culture and Catastrophe in Habsburg Vienna* (New Haven: Yale University Press, 1986), 18.

2. See Emil Lucka, *Otto Weininger: Sein Werk und seine Persönlichkeit*, 3d ed. (Vienna: Braumüller, 1921); Hermann Swoboda, *Otto Weiningers Tod* (Vienna: Deuticke, 1911); Moriz Rappaport, "Vorwort," in Otto Weininger, *Über die letzten Dinge*, 2d ed. (Vienna: Braumüller, 1907), v–xxiii; and Artur Gerber, "Ecce Homo!," in Otto Weininger, *Taschenbuch und Briefe an einen Freund* (Leipzig: Tal, 1919), 5–24.

3. See Barbara Hyams, "Weininger and Nazi Ideology," in Nancy A. Harrowitz and B. Hyams, eds., *Jews and Gender: Responses to Otto Weininger* (Philadelphia: Temple University Press, 1995), 155–68.

4. See George L. Mosse, ed., *Nazi Culture: Intellectual, Cultural and Social Life in the Third Reich*, trans. Salvator Attanasio et al. (New York: Grosset & Dunlap, 1966), 76, n. 1; and Mosse, *Nationalism and Sexuality: Respectability and Abnormal Sexuality in Modern Europe* (New York: Howard Fertig, 1985), 145–46. See also Mosse, *The Image of Man: The Creation of Modern Masculinity* (New York: Oxford, 1996), where Mosse describes *Geschlecht und Charakter* as "the most important source-book for the feminization of the Jews" (69) and as a response to the crisis of masculine identity induced by feminist activism (103).

5. W. M. Johnston, *The Austrian Mind: An Intellectual and Social History* (Berkeley: University of California Press, 1972), 160.

6. S. L. Gilman, "Otto Weininger and Sigmund Freud: Race and Gender in the Shaping of Psychoanalysis," in Harrowitz and Hyams, eds., *Jews and Gender*, 103–20, at 103; and Theodor Lessing, *Der jüdische Selbsthass* (Berlin: Jüdischer Verlag, 1930; rpt., Munich: Matthes & Seitz, 1984), 91.

7. J. Toews, "Refashioning the Masculine Subject in Early Modernism: Narratives of Self-Dissolution and Self-Construction in Psychoanalysis and Literature, 1900–1914," *Modernism/Modernity* 4, no. 1 (1997): 31–67, at 31.

8. See Jacques Le Rider, *Der Fall Otto Weininger: Wurzeln des Antifeminismus und Antisemitismus*, trans. Dieter Hornig (Vienna: Löcker, 1985). Le Rider has recently attempted a more nuanced psychoanalytic reading of *Geschlecht und Charakter*, in which the text is seen as representing a "crisis of masculinity and Jewishness" characteristic of fin-de-siècle Viennese culture. See J. Le Rider, "'The Otto Weininger Case' Revisited," trans. Kristie A. Foell, in Harrowitz and Hyams, eds., *Jews and Gender*, 21–33; and Le Rider, *Modernity and Crises of Identity: Culture and Society in Fin-de-Siècle Vienna*, trans. Rosemary Morris (New York: Continuum, 1993). See also D. Abrahamsen, *The Mind and Death of a Genius* (New York: Columbia University Press, 1946); and F. Probst, *Der Fall Otto Weininger: Eine psychiatrische Studie* (Wiesbaden: Bergmann, 1904). Probst believed that Weininger was

definitely deranged and probably manic-depressive. Abrahamsen was convinced, too, that Weininger had been insane but argued that Probst had misdiagnosed a clear-cut case of schizophrenia. See Abrahamsen, *Mind and Death,* 160–94. One must note, however, that in spite of its primarily psychoanalytic focus, Abrahamsen's study remains an indispensable source of information on Weininger's family life and his relations with Freud.

9. For trenchant critiques of current scholarly approaches to Weininger, see Allan Janik, "Therapeutic Nihilism: How Not to Write about Otto Weininger," in Barry Smith, ed., *Structure and Gestalt: Philosophy and Literature in Austria-Hungary and Her Successor States* (Amsterdam: Benjamins, 1981), 263–92; Janik, "Weininger and the Science of Sex: Prolegomena to Any Future Study," in Robert B. Pynsent, ed., *Decadence and Innovation: Austro-Hungarian Life and Art at the Turn of the Century* (London: Weidenfeld & Nicolson, 1989), 24–32; Janik, "Writing about Weininger," in his *Essays on Wittgenstein and Weininger* (Amsterdam: Rodopi, 1985), 96–115; and "Must Anti-Modernism be Irrational?" in Janik, *How Not to Interpret a Culture: Essays on the Problem of Method in the Geisteswissenschaften* (Bergen: Universitetet i Bergen, Filosofisk institutt, 1986), 66–84.

10. Previous attempts to resolve this *textual* question are surprisingly few in number. See, however, Peter Labanyi, "'Die Gefahr des Körpers': A Reading of Otto Weininger's *Geschlecht und Charakter,*" in G. J. Carr and Eda Sagarra, eds., *Fin-de-Siècle Vienna: Proceedings of the Second Irish Symposium in Austrian Studies* (Dublin: Trinity College, 1985), 161–86; and Chandak Sengoopta, "The Unknown Weininger: Science, Philosophy, and Cultural Politics in Fin-de-Siècle Vienna," *Central European History* 29 (1996): 453–93.

11. I provide a comprehensive reading, *not* a totalizing one. As Michel Foucault observed, a critical (in Foucault's terminology, genealogical) history is relentlessly comprehensive in order to demonstrate the fragmentation and multiplicity of the material. See M. Foucault, "Nietzsche, Genealogy, History," in Foucault, *Language, Counter-Memory, Practice: Selected Essays and Interviews,* ed. Donald F. Bouchard, trans. D. Bouchard and Sherry Simon (Ithaca: Cornell University Press, 1977), 139–64, especially 140, 152–53.

12. Every book, to quote Foucault again, is "a node within a network" of other texts. Texts like Weininger's, however, are especially large and conspicuously well-connected nodes. See Michel Foucault, *The Archaeology of Knowledge,* trans. A. M. Sheridan Smith (New York: Harper, 1972), 23; and Quentin Skinner's comments on the necessity of distinguishing between relatively autonomous and relatively heteronomous texts in his article, "Hermeneutics and the Role of History," *New Literary History* 7 (1995): 209–32, especially 222–24 and 227–28. Above all, see the voluminous endnotes in *Geschlecht und Charakter,* which comprise the section "Zusätze und Nachweise."

13. Janik, "Therapeutic Nihilism," 280, 282.

14. See Otto Weininger, "Vorwort," *Geschlecht und Charakter: Eine prinzipielle Untersuchung* (Vienna: Braumüller, 1903; rpt., Munich: Matthes & Seitz, 1980), viii; and O. Weininger, "Selbstanzeige: 'Geschlecht und Charakter,'" *Kant-Studien* 8 (1903): 484.

15. Christine Buci-Glucksmann, *Baroque Reason: The Aesthetics of Modernity,* trans. Patrick Camiller (London: Sage, 1994), 49.

16. See, for example, Christina von Braun, "'Der Jude' und 'Das Weib': Zwei Stereotypen des 'Anderen' in der Moderne," *Metis* (Pfaffenweiler) 1 (1992): 6–28, especially 6–9.

17. Nancy Harrowitz and Jacques Le Rider have independently accused contextualizers of Weininger of trying to "disinfect" or exculpate him by appealing to "the god of contextualization." See N. A. Harrowitz, "Weininger and Lombroso: A Question of Influence," in Harrowitz and Hyams, eds., *Jews and Gender,* 73–90, at 88; and J. Le Rider,

"Wittgenstein und Weininger," in Emil Brix and Allan Janik, eds., *Kreative Milieu: Wien um 1900* (Vienna: Verlag für Geschichte und Politik, 1993), 189–208, at 189–90. If, indeed, a historian is expected to condemn past prejudices and apportion blame for them, then I would have to condemn almost the entire fin-de-siècle Viennese intelligentsia *including* Otto Weininger, but I would refuse to condemn him alone.

18. J. G. A. Pocock, *Virtue, Commerce, and History: Essays on Political Thought and History, Chiefly in the Eighteenth Century* (Cambridge: Cambridge University Press, 1985), 9–10. Pocock's historiographic views are part of a continuing conversation among intellectual historians that began with the reflections of Quentin Skinner. Skinner's seminal articles, a sampling of the responses they evoked, and his reply to critics are conveniently available in James Tully, ed., *Meaning and Context: Quentin Skinner and his Critics* (Cambridge: Polity Press, 1988).

19. Pocock, *Virtue, Commerce, and History,* 5.

20. Ibid., 10.

21. H. White, "The Context in the Text: Method and Ideology in Intellectual History," in White, *The Content of the Form: Narrative Discourse and Historical Representation* (Baltimore: Johns Hopkins University Press, 1987), 185–213, at 212.

22. For the argument that Weininger was justified in regarding himself as a genuine scientist, see Allan Janik, "Weininger and the Science of Sex," 24. I am unpersuaded by this claim, although some parts of *Geschlecht und Charakter,* as I show in later chapters, do indeed espouse a scientistic viewpoint.

23. Le Rider, "'The Otto Weininger Case' Revisited," 32–33.

24. Weininger's attempt was seen as heuristically useful by as eminent a biological scientist as Francis H. A. Marshall. See chapter 4 for more on Marshall's response to Weininger.

25. Currently, the term "bisexuality" denotes psychological and/or behavioral manifestations of homo- and heterosexual desire in the same individual. In late-nineteenth-century biomedical discourse, however, "bisexuality" denoted the simultaneous possession of male and female attributes, be these traits anatomical, physiological, psychological, or behavioral. For Freud's testimonial, see chapter 8.

26. In fact, as Allan Janik has stated, it provided the rationale of Weininger's construction of the Male and Female ideal types. If individual men and women were both male and female, then, Weininger asked, what did masculinity and femininity consist of? His answer to this fundamental question occupied the larger part of *Geschlecht und Charakter* and drew upon a diverse range of sources from the metaphysical and ethical to the medical. See Janik, "Weininger and the Science of Sex," 28.

27. See Gert Hekma, "'A Female Soul in a Male Body': Sexual Inversion as Gender Inversion in Nineteenth-Century Sexology," in Gilbert Herdt, ed., *Third Sex, Third Gender: Beyond Sexual Dimorphism in Culture and History* (New York: Zone, 1994), 213–39; and Katrin Schmersahl, "Die Kreation des 'Mannweibes' im Spannungsfeld von Frauenemanzipation und bürgerlicher Gesellschaft," in Franziska Jenny, Gudrun Piller, and Barbara Rettenmund, eds., *Orte der Geschlechtergeschichte* (Zurich: Chronos, 1994), 37–55 for analyses of the historical importance and the cultural contexts of this theory. The ubiquity of the view that all human beings were situated somewhere between the two poles of absolute masculinity and absolute femininity supports Michel Foucault's observation that in modern times, absolute categorizations of humans have been replaced by "a whole range of degrees of normality . . . playing a part in classification, hierarchization and the distribution of rank." This "normalizing" perspective, according to Foucault, "individualizes by

making it possible to measure gaps, to determine levels, to fix specialties and to render the differences useful by fitting them one to another" (M. Foucault, *Discipline and Punish: The Birth of the Prison*, trans. Alan Sheridan [New York: Vintage, 1979], 184). Strangely, Foucault himself ignored this issue when discussing nineteenth-century medical sexology! See M. Foucault, *The History of Sexuality,* vol. 1, *An Introduction,* trans. Robert Hurley (New York: Vintage, 1980).

28. Although Ludwig Wittgenstein noted its importance long ago, biographers of Freud and historians of psychoanalysis have not explored Weininger's views on hysteria at any depth. Those same scholars, however, have written extensively on Weininger's role in causing a dispute between Freud and his close friend Wilhelm Fliess over plagiarism. For a brief sketch of this much-discussed episode, see chapter 8. For Wittgenstein's comments on Weininger's engagement with Freudian theory, see chapter 6.

*Chapter One*

1. The first edition of the work has recently been reprinted: Otto Weininger, *Geschlecht und Charakter: Eine prinzipielle Untersuchung* (Munich: Matthes & Seitz, 1980). This edition includes, in an appendix, Weininger's personal notes, some of his letters, and recent analyses of Weininger's importance by Annegret Stopczyk, Gisela Dischner, and Roberto Calasso. All references to *Geschlecht und Charakter* in this study, unless otherwise mentioned, are to this edition: page references are given in parentheses in the text. Quotations in English follow *Sex and Character* (New York: Scribner's, 1906) but rarely without significant emendations. All other unspecified translations are my own. Some of Weininger's draft writings and letters were published after his death by his friends as Moriz Rappaport, ed., *Über die letzten Dinge* (Vienna: Wilhelm Braumüller, 1907) and Artur Gerber, ed., *Taschenbuch und Briefe an einen Freund* (Leipzig: Tal, 1919). While these fragmentary texts are interesting in their own right and would be indispensable for a *biographer* of Weininger, they offer little of interest to those interested in the content and contexts of Weininger's views on *gender.* I have, therefore, omitted them from this study.

2. See David Abrahamsen, *The Mind and Death of a Genius,* 9, 204. While no definite information is available about Leopold Weininger's religious allegiance at the time of his death, it is possible that he had left Judaism. His death was not registered by the Israelitische Kultusgemeinde of Vienna (ibid., 10).

3. See Jacques Le Rider, *Der Fall Otto Weininger,* 18.

4. Abrahamsen, *Mind and Death,* 10–11.

5. Ibid., 14.

6. The essay itself is lost but a linguist has recently tried to reconstruct it on the basis of descriptions in Weininger's letters. See Manfred Mayrhofer, "Ein indogermanistischer Versuch Otto Weiningers," *Historische Sprachforschung (Historical Linguistics)* 104 (1991): 303–6.

7. See Hannelore Rodlauer, "Fragmente aus Weiningers Bildungsgeschichte (1895–1902)," in H. Rodlauer, ed., *Otto Weininger, Eros und Psyche: Studien und Briefe 1899–1902* (Vienna: Österreichischen Akademie der Wissenschaften, 1990), 13–53, at 13. This essay is now available in English translation: H. Rodlauer, "Fragments from Weininger's Education (1895–1902)," trans. Kristie A. Foell and Nancy Chadburn, in N. A. Harrowitz and B. Hyams, eds., *Jews and Gender,* 35–58. My references, however, are to the German original.

8. See Abrahamsen, *Mind and Death,* 17.

9. See Le Rider, *Der Fall Otto Weininger,* endpapers. Weininger's biomedical training

critically influenced his approach to gender and sexuality in *Geschlecht und Charakter*. Hans Kohn noted but did not explore the importance of biology in Weininger's Weltanschauung: see H. Kohn, *Karl Kraus, Arthur Schnitzler, Otto Weininger: Aus dem jüdischen Wien der Jahrhundertwende* (Tübingen: Mohr, 1962). More recently, Allan Janik has emphasized the importance of the biological connection. See A. Janik, "Therapeutic Nihilism: How Not to Write about Otto Weininger," in Barry Smith, ed., *Structure and Gestalt*, and Janik, "Weininger and the Science of Sex: Prolegomena to Any Future Study," in Robert B. Pynsent, ed., *Decadence and Innovation: Austro-Hungarian Life and Art at the Turn of the Century*.

10. Weininger's curriculum vitae is printed in facsimile in the endpapers of Le Rider, *Der Fall Otto Weininger* and reprinted in Rodlauer, ed., *Otto Weininger, Eros und Psyche*, 210-11.

11. See Maurice Mandelbaum, *History, Man, and Reason: A Study in Nineteenth-Century Thought* (Baltimore: Johns Hopkins University Press, 1971), 10-20; and Leszek Kolakowski, *The Alienation of Reason: A History of Positivist Thought*, trans. Norbert Guterman (New York: Anchor, 1969), 101-28. Avenarius and Mach themselves denied that they were positivists. Avenarius coined the term "Empiriocriticism," derived from "empiricism" and "criticism," to describe his philosophy. He argued that while empiriocriticism denied the existence of anything outside experience, it distinguished critically between the experience reported by an individual and experience that was universally valid. See Friedrich Carstanjen, "Richard Avenarius and His General Theory of Knowledge, Empiriocriticism," trans. H. Bosanquet, *Mind*, new ser., 6 (1897): 449-75, at 450-51.

12. Kolakowski, *Alienation*, 104, 106.

13. On Weininger's interest in Avenarius, see Emil Lucka, *Otto Weininger: Sein Werk und seine Persönlichkeit*, 3d ed. (Berlin: Schuster & Loeffler, 1921), 11-12. On Weininger's initial admiration for Mach, see Le Rider, *Der Fall Otto Weininger*, 23.

14. On Avenarius's views on the self, see Kolakowski, *Alienation*, 109-10. I discuss Mach's philosophical dissolution of the self in detail in chapter 2.

15. Abrahamsen, *Mind and Death*, 61.

16. Swoboda, *Otto Weiningers Tod*, 6-7.

17. H. Swoboda, "Gedenkrede für Otto Weininger," unpublished lecture at the PEN Club, Vienna, 4 October 1958, quoted in Le Rider, *Der Fall Otto Weininger*, 24.

18. E. Lucka, *Otto Weininger*, 13, 15. Swoboda denied this, saying that Weininger, initially, was no stranger to happiness. It was only later that his personality changed. See Swoboda, *Otto Weiningers Tod*, 9.

19. Rodlauer, "Fragmente," 16.

20. Ibid., 17-18.

21. See Paul M.-J. Joire, "De la nécessité de l'emploi de nouvelles méthodes et en particulier de méthodes expérimentales dans l'étude de la psychologie," in Pierre Janet, ed., *IVe Congrès international de psychologie tenu à Paris, du 20 au 26 Août 1900: Compte rendu des séances et texte des mémoires* (Paris: Alcan, 1901), 639-42. For Weininger's critique, see 642-43.

22. On Freud's early reputation within Central Europe, see Hannah S. Decker, *Freud in Germany: Revolution and Reaction in Science, 1893-1907* (New York: International Universities Press, 1977); and Michael Worbs, *Nervenkunst: Literatur und Psychoanalyse im Wien der Jahrhundertwende* (Frankfurt a.M.: Europäische Verlagsanstalt, 1983).

23. See *The Complete Letters of Sigmund Freud to Wilhelm Fliess 1887-1904*, trans. and

ed. Jeffrey Moussaieff Masson (Cambridge, Mass.: Harvard University Press, 1985). This friendship has been "psychoanalyzed" by several commentators. See, for instance, Patrick Mahony, "Friendship and its Discontents," *Contemporary Psychoanalysis* 15 (1979): 55–109.

24. After Weininger's death, the transmission of this idea (from Freud to Weininger through Swoboda) created a major controversy. I discuss this episode in chapter 8.

25. Letter to Swoboda, 14 February 1901, in H. Rodlauer, ed., *Otto Weininger, Eros und Psyche,* 68.

26. Swoboda, *Otto Weiningers Tod,* 44. Lesley Hall has pointed out to me that this "deviation" could well have been intense fear, guilt, and self-loathing over masturbation. For instances of such "deviations," see L. Hall, "Forbidden by God, Despised by Men: Masturbation, Medical Warnings, Moral Panic, and Manhood in Great Britain, 1850–1950," *Journal of the History of Sexuality* 2 (1992): 365–87.

27. See Abrahamsen, *Mind and Death,* 124–27 and, on Weininger's homosexuality, chapter 6 below. For Swoboda's denial, see his *Otto Weiningers Tod,* 42.

28. Abrahamsen, *Mind and Death,* 83–85.

29. Edward Timms, *Karl Kraus, Apocalyptic Satirist: Culture and Catastrophe in Habsburg Vienna,* 28–29.

30. D. Luft, "Science and Irrationalism in Freud's Vienna," *Modern Austrian Literature* 23, no. 2 (1990): 89–97.

31. Allan Janik argues that even Weininger's final, published treatise, *Geschlecht und Charakter,* was a plea for liberal social reform, although many of Weininger's beliefs seem repugnant today. See Janik, "Therapeutic Nihilism," 283. The published book does retain elements of such a reform program (such as the pedagogical differentiation between students on the basis of their psychological gender, the decriminalization of homosexuality, and the recognition of the "characterological" basis of prostitution), but, as I show below, they are overshadowed by different political aims.

32. Hannelore Rodlauer, "Von 'Eros und Psyche' zu 'Geschlecht und Charakter': Unbekannte Weininger-Manuskripte im Archiv der Österreichischen Akademie der Wissenschaften," *Österreichische Akademie der Wissenschaften, philosophisch-historische Klasse: Anzeiger* 124 (1987): 110–39, at 113. Weininger's manuscript was recently discovered in the archives of the academy and is reprinted in Rodlauer, ed., *Otto Weininger, Eros und Psyche,* 145–89. It contains many of the fundamental biological notions of *Geschlecht und Charakter,* much misogyny and cultural criticism, and some early signs of Weininger's subsequent turn toward metaphysical and quasi-mystical arguments.

33. The physiologist Ernst Fleischl von Marxow (1846–91), for example, deposited his 1883 report on the electrical activity of the brain with the academy, which, says Erna Lesky, "was quite usual in Vienna at the time." See Erna Lesky, *The Vienna Medical School of the 19th Century,* trans. L. Williams and I. S. Levij (Baltimore: Johns Hopkins University Press, 1976), 490.

34. "I was also quite alarmed by the chapter on hysteria," wrote Freud to Wilhelm Fliess, "which was written *ad captandam benevolentiam meam.*" Letter, 27 July 1904, in *The Complete Letters of Sigmund Freud to Wilhelm Fliess,* 466–68, at 466. For a detailed analysis of Weininger's theory of hysteria and its relations with Freudian ideas, see chapter 6 below.

35. "But how," Weininger wondered, "could I possibly *prove* facts? Facts can only be indicated." See Otto Weininger, letter to H. Swoboda, undated [probably October 1901], in Rodlauer, ed., *Otto Weininger, Eros und Psyche,* 86–88, at 87.

36. Letter to H. Swoboda, 6 November 1901, in ibid., 90–92.

37. Rodlauer, "Fragmente," 41–42.

38. Rodlauer, "Von 'Eros und Psyche' zu 'Geschlecht und Charakter'," 121. Weininger's thoughts on *Peer Gynt* were published posthumously. See O. Weininger, "Über Henrik Ibsen und seine Dichtung 'Peer Gynt' (Zum 75. Geburtstage des Dichters)," in *Über die letzten Dinge*, 3–47.

39. See Weininger, letter to H. Swoboda, 2 March 1902, in Rodlauer, ed., *Otto Weininger, Eros und Psyche*, 107–108.

40. Ibid.

41. O. Weininger, "Zur Theorie des Lebens," reproduced in Rodlauer, ed., *Otto Weininger, Eros und Psyche*, 191–208. This outline contains some of the ideas Weininger highlighted in the second part of *Geschlecht und Charakter*. One of these was that the female lacks memory, soul, and a unitary self. Females, Weininger asserted in the outline, "have no character!" The outline also attempted to construct "Jewish" and "Aryan" psychological types, attributing materialism to the Jewish mind and denying the Jew a self (ibid., 201). A notorious chapter of *Geschlecht und Charakter* was based on these concepts.

42. Otto Weininger, letter to H. Swoboda, 17 June 1902, in Rodlauer, ed., *Otto Weininger, Eros und Psyche*, 122–27, at 122. The disjunction between the two parts, although exaggerated by some commentators, is indeed a striking feature of *Geschlecht und Charakter*. For a deeper analysis, see chapter 3 below.

43. The examiners' reports on the dissertation have been reproduced in full in Rodlauer, ed., *Otto Weininger, Eros und Psyche*, 211–14. Jodl's report is on 211–13 and Müllner's on 213–14.

44. Ibid., 213.

45. Ibid., 212.

46. Ibid., 212–13.

47. Ibid., 213. A consistent empiricist, Jodl rejected metaphysical speculation and mind-body dualism. See Margarete Jodl, *Friedrich Jodl: Sein Leben und Wirken dargestellt nach Tagebüchern und Briefen* (Stuttgart: Cotta, 1920).

48. Rodlauer, ed., *Otto Weininger, Eros und Psyche*, 213.

49. Ibid., 214.

50. Ibid., 213, 214.

51. After obtaining his doctorate in July 1902, Weininger had asked the university to return the dissertation to him so that he could revise it for publication. The authorities had acceded to the request. See Rodlauer, ed., *Otto Weininger, Eros und Psyche*, 215. Rodlauer's publication of this correspondence corrects Allan Janik's belief that the dissertation was destroyed during World War II. See Janik, "Therapeutic Nihilism," 291, n. 12.

52. Hannelore Rodlauer ("Von 'Eros und Psyche'," 132) argues that the examiners would have commented on Weininger's anti-Semitism had the chapter been included in the doctoral thesis.

53. Jodl's sympathetic but reserved article on Weininger is discussed in chapter 8. This was written after Weininger's suicide.

54. J. Le Rider, *Der Fall Otto Weininger*, 36.

55. Two months before his conversion, Weininger had formally left the Jewish Congregation of Vienna. See David Abrahamsen, *Mind and Death*, 58. Sander Gilman notes that post-doctoral conversions were common among Jews of the time. He argues that turn-of-the-century anti-Semites considered an inability to express oneself in "proper" language to be a cardinal sign of "Jewishness." Gilman explains that "writing a dissertation, whether in Latin . . . or in academic German, was the supreme act of language mastery. Not only did

the doctorate provide entrance into the economic world of Christian Europe but it symbolized the student's command of the language of European intellectual discourse" (S. L. Gilman, *Jewish Self-Hatred: Anti-Semitism and the Hidden Language of the Jews* [Baltimore: Johns Hopkins University Press, 1986], 248).

56. Weininger's religiosity was obvious in *Geschlecht und Charakter* as well as in the posthumously published *Über die letzten Dinge.* Hans Kohn has pointed out that Weininger was far more deeply and openly religious than most leading intellectuals of the time (H. Kohn, *Karl Kraus, Arthur Schnitzler, Otto Weininger,* 33–34).

57. Steven Beller, *Vienna and the Jews, 1867–1938: A Cultural History* (Cambridge: Cambridge University Press, 1989), 153.

58. Le Rider, *Der Fall Otto Weininger,* 34. Weininger might have had an additional reason for choosing Protestantism. In *Geschlecht und Charakter,* he argued that although Catholicism was not truly effeminate, women found it easier to live by its tenets than by those of Protestantism (269). The choice of Protestantism, then, was not simply Germanic and Kantian but also masculine.

59. Otto Weininger, letter to A. Gerber, 5 August 1902, reprinted in *Geschlecht und Charakter: Eine prinzipielle Untersuchung* (Munich: Matthes and Seitz, 1980), 630.

60. Otto Weininger, letter to A. Gerber, 17 August 1902, ibid., 635.

61. Weininger also told Gerber that he could feel "the chill of the grave" within himself. Weininger seemed so depressed at this time that Gerber feared he might commit suicide immediately. See A. Gerber, "Ecce homo," in Otto Weininger, *Taschenbuch und Briefe an einen Freund,* 5–24, at 17, 20.

62. O. Weininger, letters to A. Gerber, 30 March and 23 April 1903, *Geschlecht und Charakter* (1980), 641.

63. Le Rider, *Der Fall Otto Weininger,* 41–44. Weininger's later, powerful supporter Karl Kraus seems to have read the book on the day of its publication but even he did not mention *Geschlecht und Charakter* in his widely read weekly *Die Fackel* until October. One important early review was by the psychiatrist Paul Möbius, who accused Weininger of plagiarism. Weininger threatened Möbius with legal proceedings unless he proved his allegation or made a public retraction. For further details, see chapter 8.

64. Quoted in Abrahamsen, *Mind and Death,* 135.

65. Le Rider, *Der Fall Otto Weininger,* 45–46.

66. Sander Gilman points out that the "most revealing" aspect of Weininger's suicide "is its location in the death chamber of Beethoven, the quintessential German artist, whose works by the beginning of the twentieth century had become identified with the 'German spirit.' It was with this mode of aesthetic articulation that Weininger wished to identify, at least in death" (Gilman, *Jewish Self-Hatred,* 248).

67. Le Rider, *Der Fall Otto Weininger,* 46.

68. Peter Gay, *Freud, Jews and Other Germans: Masters and Victims in Modernist Culture* (New York: Oxford University Press, 1978), 196.

*Chapter Two*

1. Christine Buci-Glucksmann, *Baroque Reason: The Aesthetics of Modernity,* 39.

2. R. Musil, *The Man without Qualities,* trans. Eithne Wilkins and Ernst Kaiser, 4 vols. (London: Picador, 1988), 1:31, 33. The name "Kakania" was derived from the official description of Austro-Hungarian institutions as "Imperial and Royal" *(Kaiserlich und Königlich).* Allan Janik and Stephen Toulmin point out that "to anyone familiar with Ger-

man nursery language, it [the name Kakania] carries also the secondary sense of 'Excre-mentia' or 'Shitland'" (A. Janik and S. Toulmin, *Wittgenstein's Vienna* [New York: Simon and Schuster, 1973], 13, footnote). See also Ilse Barea, *Vienna* (New York: Knopf, 1966), 84–85, on the symbolic importance of the K. K. formula in Viennese culture.

3. On the many nationalities in the Habsburg Empire, see Robert A. Kann, *A History of the Habsburg Empire 1526–1918* (Berkeley: University of California Press, 1974), 406–520; and Arthur J. May, *The Hapsburg Monarchy 1867–1914* (Cambridge, Mass.: Harvard University Press, 1951). The Empire was not even geographically united: its constituent lands were separated by natural barriers, and the rivers did not connect important regions. See Barbara Jelavich, *Modern Austria: Empire and Republic, 1815–1986* (Cambridge: Cambridge University Press, 1987), 77.

4. Janik and Toulmin, *Wittgenstein's Vienna*, 39–40.

5. See Carl E. Schorske, "Politics in a New Key: An Austrian Trio," in C. E. Schorske, *Fin-de-Siècle Vienna: Politics and Culture* (New York: Vintage, 1981), 116–80. Emperor Franz Joseph refused to ratify Lueger's election and, despite opposition, persisted in his re-fusal until 1897. It was quintessentially Kakanian that the liberals, including the staunch anti-autocrat Sigmund Freud, were the biggest supporters of this autocratic decision. Freud was so happy at the Emperor's rejection of Lueger that he forgot his recent vow not to smoke too many cigars! See Ernest Jones, *The Life and Work of Sigmund Freud*, vol. 1, *The Formative Years and the Great Discoveries, 1856–1900* (New York: Basic Books, 1953), 311. On Lueger's political background and achievements, see John W. Boyer, *Political Radicalism in Late Imperial Vienna: Origins of the Christian Social Movement, 1848–1897* (Chicago: University of Chicago Press, 1981).

6. See Jelavich, *Modern Austria*, 83.

7. See Schroske, "Politics and the Psyche," 6–7.

8. The feeling of doom was not limited to the liberal bourgeoisie; the imperial elite, too, was deeply pessimistic about the future of the empire. See Solomon Wank, "Pessimism in the Austrian Establishment at the Turn of the Century," in S. Wank et al., eds., *The Mir-ror of History: Essays in Honor of Fritz Fellner* (Santa Barbara: ABC-Clio, 1988), 295–314. The middle classes, however, expressed their pessimism in forms that have been seen as quintessentially Viennese. "Elsewhere in Europe," says Carl Schorske, "art for art's sake implied the withdrawal of its devotees from a social class; in Vienna alone it claimed the al-legiance of virtually a whole class.... The life of art became a substitute for the life of ac-tion. Indeed, as civic action proved increasingly futile, art became almost a religion, the source of meaning and the food of the soul" (C. Schorske, "Politics and the Psyche: Schnitz-ler and Hofmannstahl," in *Fin-de-Siècle Vienna*, 8–9).

9. Schorske, "Politics and the Psyche," 9.

10. Ibid., 10.

11. The quoted sentence is from Erich Heller, *The Disinherited Mind: Essays in Modern German Literature and Thought* (New York: Harcourt Brace Jovanovich, 1975), 252. On Kraus and his contexts, see Edward Timms, *Karl Kraus, Apocalyptic Satirist: Culture and Catastrophe in Habsburg Vienna*.

12. A. Loos, "Potemkin City," in Loos, *Spoken into the Void: Collected Essays 1897–1900*, trans. Jane O. Newman and John H. Smith (Cambridge, Mass.: The MIT Press, 1982), 95–97.

13. Musil, *The Man without Qualities*, 33–34.

14. See Le Rider, *Der Fall Otto Weininger*, 31.

15. E. Jones, *The Life and Work of Sigmund Freud,* 1:293. For a comprehensive analysis of Freud's attitude toward Vienna, see Marie-Louise Testenoire, "Freud et Vienne en 1900," *Critique,* nos. 339–40 (1975): 819–36.

16. C. Schorske, "Introduction," in *Fin-de-Siècle Vienna,* xxvi; see also Schorske, "Generational Tension and Cultural Change: Reflections on the Case of Vienna," *Daedalus* 107, no. 4 (1978): 111–22; and Wolf Wucherpfennig, "The 'Young Viennese' and their Fathers: Decadence and the Generation Conflict around 1890," *Journal of Contemporary History* 17 (1982): 21–49.

17. See Dagmar Barnouw, "Loos, Kraus, Wittgenstein, and the Problem of Authenticity," in Gerald Chapple and Hans H. Schulte, eds., *The Turn of the Century: German Literature and Art, 1890–1915* (Bonn: Bouvier, 1981), 249–73.

18. C. Schorske, "Politics and the Psyche: Schnitzler and Hofmannsthal," in *Fin-de-Siècle Vienna,* 4. The long and complex history of the concept of a rational, autonomous self lies far beyond the scope of this study. See Charles Taylor, *Sources of the Self: The Making of the Modern Identity* (Cambridge, Mass.: Harvard University Press, 1989); Roy Porter, ed., *Rewriting the Self: Histories from the Renaissance to the Present* (London: Routledge, 1997); and Roger Smith, *The Fontana History of the Human Sciences* (London: Fontana Press, 1997).

19. Schorske, "Politics and the Psyche," 4.

20. For the dramatic background to this unusual appointment, see Josef Mayerhöfer, "Ernst Machs Berufung an die Wiener Universität, 1895," *Clio Medica* 2 (1967): 47–55.

21. John T. Blackmore, *Ernst Mach: His Work, Life, and Influence* (Berkeley: University of California Press, 1972) is the standard biography. See also Robert S. Cohen and Raymond J. Seeger, eds., *Ernst Mach: Physicist and Philosopher* (Dordrecht: Reidel, 1970); Rudolf Haller and Friedrich Stadler, eds., *Ernst Mach: Werk und Wirkung* (Vienna: Hölder-Pichler-Tempsky, 1988); and Dieter Hoffmann and Hubert Laitko, eds., *Ernst Mach: Studien und Dokumente zu Leben und Werk* (Berlin: Deutscher Verlag der Wissenschaften, 1991).

22. See Blackmore, *Ernst Mach,* 31–33.

23. Ibid., 30.

24. Mach distinguished, however, between the physiological and the narrowly physical. On this important point, see ibid., 64–65.

25. Ibid., 35. The eighteenth-century philosopher Georg Lichtenberg, with whose work Mach had long been familiar, had argued similarly. So had David Hume. See ibid., 27. On Lichtenberg's views on the self, see Guenter Zoeller, "Lichtenberg and Kant on the Subject of Thinking," *Journal of the History of Philosophy* 30 (1992): 417–41. On Hume's attempt to deconstruct the concept of the self, see Terence Penelhum, *Hume* (New York: St. Martin's Press, 1975), 75–88.

26. E. Mach, *The Analysis of Sensations and the Relation of the Physical to the Psychical,* trans. C. M. Williams and Sydney Waterlow (New York: Dover, 1959), 17.

27. Ibid., 24, where Mach's sentence is translated somewhat unsatisfactorily as "the ego must be given up." For the German version, see E. Mach, *Analyse der Empfindungen und das Verhältniss des Physischen zum Psychischen,* 4th ed. (Jena: Fischer, 1903), 20.

28. Hermann Bahr, *Bilderbuch* (Vienna: Wila, 1921), 37, as cited and translated in Blackmore, *Ernst Mach,* 155.

29. For a comprehensive analysis of the influence of Mach's ideas on the arts, literature, and criticism, see Manfred Diersch, *Empiriokritizismus und Impressionismus: Über Beziehungen zwischen Philosophie, Ästhetik und Literatur um 1900 in Wien* (Berlin: Rütten

& Loening, 1977). See also Blackmore, *Ernst Mach*, 180–203, especially 187–89; Judith Ryan, "Die andere Psychologie: Ernst Mach und die Folgen," in Wolfgang Paulsen, ed., *Österreichische Gegenwart: Die moderne Literatur und ihr Verhältnis zur Tradition* (Bern: Francke, 1980), 11–24; Friedrich Stadler, *Vom Positivismus zur "wissenschaftlichen Weltauffassung": Am Beispiel der Wirkungsgeschichte von Ernst Mach in Österreich von 1895 bis 1934* (Vienna: Löcker, 1982), especially 13–132; and Patrizia Giampieri Deutsch, "Mach, Freud, Musil: Die Frage nach dem Subjekt," *Sigmund Freud House Bulletin* 14, no. 2 (1990): 47–56.

30. See Stadler, *Vom Positivismus*, 50–52.

31. On psychology in the nineteenth century, see William R. Woodward and Mitchell G. Ash, eds., *The Problematic Science: Psychology in Nineteenth-Century Thought* (New York: Praeger, 1982); and Graham Richards, *Mental Machinery: The Origins and Consequences of Psychological Ideas, Part I, 1600–1850* (Baltimore: Johns Hopkins University Press, 1992).

32. For Wundt, psychology was divided into a physiological/experimental part and an ethnopsychological or social-psychological one. The two were complementary but their methods were completely different. Wundt acknowledged the value of experimentation in the investigation of individual psychology; nevertheless, he believed that psychology was not a natural science but a human science, a Geisteswissenschaft. See K. Danziger, "The Positivist Repudiation of Wundt," *Journal of the History of the Behavioral Sciences* 15 (1979): 205–30, especially 205–208; Mitchell G. Ash, "Wilhelm Wundt and Experimental Psychology in Germany before 1914: Aspects of an Academic Identity Problem," *Psychological Research* 42 (1980): 75–86; and David E. Leary, "Wundt and After: Psychology's Shifting Relations with the Natural Sciences, Social Sciences, and Philosophy," *Journal of the History of Behavioral Sciences* 15 (1979): 231–41.

33. Danziger, "Positivist Repudiation," 209–10.

34. Ibid., 210–11. Külpe later turned into an outspoken opponent of Mach's psychological theories. See Blackmore, *Ernst Mach*, 229–30; and E. G. Boring, *A History of Experimental Psychology*, 2d ed. (New York: Appleton-Century-Crofts, 1957), 397, 409.

35. O. Külpe, *Outlines of Psychology* (New York: Macmillan, 1893), 12.

36. Danziger, "Positivist Repudiation," 213–14.

37. See Katherine Arens, *Structures of Knowing: Psychologies of the Nineteenth Century* (Dordrecht: Kluwer, 1989), 155–60. In his reply to Dilthey's rejection of "explanatory psychology," the experimentalist Hermann Ebbinghaus argued that Dilthey misrepresented the new psychology as mechanistic and Newtonian, whereas it was actually Machian, and, therefore, scientific without being mechanistic. See Danziger, "The Positivist Repudiation of Wundt," 214; H. Ebbinghaus, "Über erklärende und beschreibende Psychologie," *Zeitschrift für Psychologie* 9 (1896): 161–205. Weininger cited Dilthey's work with approval in *Geschlecht und Charakter*, 102, 501, 506.

38. See Kurt Danziger, *Constructing the Subject: Historical Origins of Psychological Research* (Cambridge: Cambridge University Press, 1990), 18–19; and William Lyons, *The Disappearance of Introspection* (Cambridge, Mass.: MIT Press, 1986).

39. See Danziger's discussion in *Constructing the Subject*, 19–20.

40. See ibid., 23; and David E. Leary, "The Philosophical Development of the Conception of Psychology in Germany," *Journal of the History of the Behavioral Sciences* 14 (1978): 113–21.

41. Danziger, *Constructing the Subject*, 35.

42. See Thomas E. Willey, *Back to Kant: The Revival of Kantianism in German Social and Historical Thought, 1860–1914* (Detroit: Wayne State University Press, 1978), 78–80;

and Klaus Christian Köhnke, *The Rise of Neo-Kantianism: German Academic Philosophy between Idealism and Positivism* (Cambridge: Cambridge University Press, 1991).

43. Willey, *Back to Kant*, 24–25. See also Frederick Gregory, *Scientific Materialism in Nineteenth-Century Germany* (Dordrecht: Reidel, 1977).

44. Willey, *Back to Kant*, 83–101.

45. K. C. Köhnke, *The Rise of Neo-Kantianism*, 137. A standard reference work on the history of philosophy listed seven distinct varieties of neo-Kantianism in 1912. See Willey, *Back to Kant*, 187.

46. Willey, *Back to Kant*, 102–52.

47. For an illuminating discussion of this issue, see Rudolf Haller, "Österreichische Philosophie," in R. Haller, *Studien zur Österreichischen Philosophie: Variationen über ein Thema* (Amsterdam: Rodopi, 1979), 5–22; and R. Haller, "Wittgenstein and Austrian Philosophy," in Haller, *Questions on Wittgenstein* (London: Routledge, 1988), 1–26. See also Roger Bauer, "Der Idealismus und seine Gegner in Österreich," Beiheft to *Euphorion*, no. 3 (Heidelberg, 1966).

48. On the Viennese tradition of language-criticism and its moral and philosophical dimensions, see Janik and Toulmin, *Wittgenstein's Vienna*, 67–91 and 120–66; and Peter Weibel, "Philosophie als Sprachkritik," *Monatshefte* 79 (1983): 64–73. William Warren Bartley III, *Wittgenstein*, 2d ed. (Chicago: Open Court, 1985), 51–57, rejects much of the standard view. For a critical response to Bartley, with the important warning that Viennese language-criticism was not a homogeneous phenomenon and is best approached as a "family of related phenomena," see A. Janik, "The Crises of Language," in Janik, *How Not to Interpret a Culture: Essays on the Problem of Method in the Geisteswissenschaften*, 85–104.

49. Haller, "Wittgenstein and Austrian Philosophy," 4.

50. See Le Rider, *Modernity and Crises of Identity: Culture and Society in Fin-de-Siècle Vienna*, 159. Sigmund Freud, incidentally, was an admiring student of Brentano's and was encouraged by Brentano to translate the works of John Stuart Mill. See Haller, "Wittgenstein and Austrian Philosophy," 7–9.

51. See Haller, "Wittgenstein and Austrian Philosophy," 4–5; Haller, "Brentanos Sprachkritik oder daß 'man unterscheiden muß, was es (hier) zu unterscheiden gibt,'" in Haller, *Studien zur Österreichischen Philosophie*, 23–36; and K. Arens, *Structures of Knowing*, 172–94.

52. Haller, "Wittgenstein and Austrian Philosophy," 10.

53. Le Rider, *Modernity and Crises of Identity*, 12. On the relations between Brentano and Mach, see F. Stadler, *Vom Positivismus zur "wissenschaftlichen Weltauffassung,"* 74–77. After 1900, however, many Austrian intellectuals and artists, disillusioned by the political failure of liberalism, turned increasingly to the theories of Arthur Schopenhauer on "sexuality, mysticism, art, and ethics." See D. S. Luft, "Schopenhauer, Austria, and the Generation of 1905," *Central European History* 16 (1983): 53–75. This return to speculative philosophy, if not to Kant, was commoner among literary intellectuals than among university professors of philosophy. Otto Weininger's doctoral advisor Friedrich Jodl, for instance, was a staunch positivist unmarked by Schopenhauerian traits.

54. He criticized Brentano and his followers in the psychological sections of *Geschlecht und Charakter* (182–83) and aligned himself with representatives of the Marburg and Heidelberg neo-Kantians. Allan Janik has pointed out that Weininger's orientation was closer to that of the Heidelberg School. See A. Janik, "Philosophical Sources of Wittgenstein's Ethics," in Janik, *Essays on Wittgenstein and Weininger* (Amsterdam: Rodopi, 1985), 74–95, at 94.

55. H. Rodlauer, "Fragmente," 23. On the weak Idealist tradition in Austrian philosophy, see William M. Johnston, "Neo-Idealists from Austria," *Modern Austrian Literature* 4, no. 2 (1971): 7–17.

56. Rodlauer, "Fragmente," 49–50. Rodlauer emphasizes a passage from Kant's introduction, which declared that "*true* science is only that whose certainties are apodictic; knowledge that contains only empirical certainty is not truthfully called *knowledge.*"

57. It is likely, however, that Weininger subsequently reconsidered his allegiance to Kant. In a posthumously published aphorism, he says that Kant's hyperempirical (intelligible) self is a product of vanity. "There is no self, there is no soul," Weininger declares. "The highest, the most complete reality is that of the Good" (O. Weininger, *Über die letzten Dinge*, 175). Rappaport adds a note to this aphorism denying that Weininger retracted his earlier views; according to Rappaport, the aphorism refers to ontological reality and not to the expression of the intelligible world in the empirical (ibid.). This is quite inadequate, since in *Geschlecht und Charakter* Weininger argues repeatedly for the ontological reality of the intelligible self.

58. For general discussions, see Lorenne M. G. Clark and Lynda Lange, eds., *The Sexism of Social and Political Theory: Women and Reproduction from Plato to Nietzsche* (Toronto: Toronto University Press, 1979); Ute Frevert, "Bürgerliche Meisterdenker und das Geschlechterverhältnis: Konzepte, Erfahrungen, Visionen an der Wende vom 18. zum 19. Jahrhundert," in U. Frevert, ed., *Bürgerinnen und Bürger: Geschlechterverhältnisse im 19. Jahrhundert* (Göttingen: Vandenhoeck & Ruprecht, 1988), 17–48; Nancy Tuana, *Woman and the History of Philosophy* (New York: Paragon House, 1992); and N. Tuana, *The Less Noble Sex: Scientific, Religious, and Philosophical Conceptions of Woman's Nature* (Bloomington, Ind.: Indiana University Press, 1993).

59. See Kant, *Anthropologie in pragmatischer Hinsicht*, in Kant, *Gesammelte Schriften*, ed. Königlich Preussischen Akademie der Wissenschaften (Berlin: Reimer, 1902), 7:305–306. For analyses of Kant's views on gender, see Heidemarie Bennent, *Galanterie und Verachtung: Eine philosophiegeschichtliche Untersuchung zur Stellung der Frau in Gesellschaft und Kultur* (Frankfurt a.M.: Campus, 1985), 96–108; Susan Mendus, "Kant: An Honest but Narrow-Minded Bourgeois?" in Ellen Kennedy and Susan Mendus, *Women in Western Political Philosophy: Kant to Nietzsche* (Brighton: Wheatsheaf Books, 1987), 21–43; and Pauline Kleingeld, "The Problematic Status of Gender-Neutral Language in the History of Philosophy: The Case of Kant," *Philosophical Forum* 25 (1993): 134–50. For a different reading of Kant's position on women, see Ursula Pia Jauch, *Immanuel Kant zur Geschlechterdifferenz: Aufklärerische Vorurteilskritik und bürgerliche Geschlechtsvormundschaft* (Vienna: Passagen, 1988).

60. See Frevert, "Bürgerliche Meisterdenker;" and Karin Hausen, "Die Polarisierung der 'Geschlechtscharaktere': Eine Spiegelung der Dissoziation von Erwerbs- und Familienleben," in Werner Conze, ed., *Sozialgeschichte der Familie in der Neuzeit Europas* (Stuttgart: Klett, 1976), 363–93.

61. Hausen, "Polarisierung," 369. See also Marianne Weber, *Ehefrau und Mutter in der Rechtsentwicklung* (Tübingen: Mohr, 1907; rpt., Aalen: Scientia, 1971), 300–301. On the role of scientists in establishing this "natural" order of sexual inequality, and the necessity of such a basis for the justification of women's inferior status in liberal political philosophy, see Londa Schiebinger, *The Mind Has No Sex? Women in the Origins of Modern Science* (Cambridge, Mass.: Harvard University Press, 1989), 215–16.

62. Schopenhauer, "Über Weiber," in Arthur Hübscher, ed., *Arthur Schopenhauer: Sämtliche Werke*, 7 vols. (Wiesbaden: Brockhaus, 1972), 6:650–63. Schopenhauer may,

however, have changed his mind later. Shortly before his death, he observed to a woman that "if a woman succeeds in withdrawing from the mass, or rather raising herself above the mass, she grows ceaselessly and more than a man." See Rüdiger Safranski, *Schopenhauer and the Wild Years of Philosophy*, trans. Ewald Osers (Cambridge, Mass.: Harvard University Press, 1990), 348.

63. For Nietzsche's comment on Schopenhauer, see Nietzsche, *Untimely Meditations*, trans. R. J. Hollingdale (Cambridge: Cambridge University Press, 1983), 146.

64. See Carol Diethe, "Nietzsche and the Woman Question," *History of European Ideas* 11 (1989): 865–75; and David Booth, "Nietzsche's 'Woman' Rhetoric," *History of Philosophy Quarterly* 8 (1991): 311–25. On the importance of Nietzsche's views on women to his philosophy, see Peter J. Burgard, ed., *Nietzsche and the Feminine* (Charlottesville: University Press of Virginia, 1994). Perhaps paradoxically, Nietzsche's general iconoclasm and individualism have always appealed to feminists. In fin-de-siècle Vienna, Rosa Mayreder was an admirer of Nietzsche and so was her German contemporary Helene Stöcker. Many radical feminists of our time have also "deployed" Nietzsche in their work. For overviews of the feminist appropriations of Nietzsche, see R. Hinton Thomas, *Nietzsche in German Politics and Society, 1890–1918* (Manchester: Manchester University Press, 1983), 80–95; and Keith Ansell-Pearson, *An Introduction to Nietzsche as Political Thinker: The Perfect Nihilist* (Cambridge: Cambridge University Press, 1994), 180–98. Recently, Jacques Derrida has "deconstructively" undermined Nietzsche's antifeminism: see J. Derrida, *Spurs: Nietzsche's Styles*, trans. Barbara Harlow (Chicago: University of Chicago Press, 1978).

65. "When a woman has scholarly inclinations there is usually something wrong with her sexually. Sterility itself disposes one toward a certain masculinity of taste; for man is, if I may say so, 'the sterile animal.'" See Nietzsche, *Beyond Good and Evil*, trans. Walter Kaufmann, §144 and §239, in W. Kaufmann, ed., *Basic Writings of Nietzsche* (New York: Modern Library, 1968), 279, 359. Weininger argued similarly but, unlike Nietzsche, did not construe female sexuality in exclusively reproductive terms. He separated womankind "typologically" into the Mother and the Prostitute. *Both* types, he said, were equally sexual but in different ways: the maternal type desired sex out of a reproductive urge, whereas the Prostitute craved the pleasure of coitus alone. For a detailed analysis, see chapter 7 below.

66. Nietzsche, *Beyond Good and Evil*, §238, in Kaufmann, ed., *Basic Writings*, 356–57. For all his misogyny, Weininger denounced this belief of Nietzsche's as profoundly unethical.

67. T. Roszak, "The Hard and the Soft: The Force of Feminism in Modern Times," in Betty Roszak and T. Roszak. eds., *Masculine/Feminine: Readings in Sexual Mythology and the Liberation of Women* (New York: Harper & Row, 1969), 87–104, at 87–88.

68. See Susan Sleeth Mosedale, "Science Corrupted: Victorian Biologists consider 'The Woman Question,'" *Journal of the History of Biology* 11 (1978): 1–55; Janet Sayers, *Biological Politics: Feminist and Anti-Feminist Perspectives* (London: Tavistock, 1982); Cynthia Eagle Russett, *Sexual Science: The Victorian Construction of Womanhood* (Cambridge, Mass.: Harvard University Press, 1989); and Nancy Tuana, *The Less Noble Sex*. Almost all these studies have an Anglo-American focus. The Central European discourse remains insufficiently explored, but see Claudia Honegger, *Die Ordnung der Geschlechter: Die Wissenschaften vom Menschen und das Weib, 1750–1850* (Frankfurt a.M.: Campus, 1991).

69. P. J. Möbius, *Über den physiologischen Schwachsinn des Weibes* (Halle a.S.: Marhold, 1912). On Möbius, see Francis Schiller, *A Möbius Strip: Fin-de-Siècle Neuropsychiatry and Paul Möbius* (Berkeley: University of California Press, 1982). Although Möbius and

Weininger have often been pigeon-holed together, and although both considered women to be intellectually and morally inferior to men, we shall see later that their beliefs and social agendas were significantly different.

70. See C. Lombroso and Guglielmo Ferrero, *Das Weib als Verbrecherin und Prostituirte: Anthropologische Studien gegrundet auf eine Darstellung der Biologie und Psychologie des normalen Weibes,* trans. Hans Kurella (Hamburg: Verlagsanstalt und Druckerei A-G, 1894); and Nancy A. Harrowitz, *Anti-Semitism, Misogyny, and the Logic of Cultural Difference: Cesare Lombroso and Matilde Serao* (Lincoln: University of Nebraska Press, 1994).

71. Weininger shared most of these views, and Allan Janik has long emphasized the importance of Lombroso among Weininger's sources. See Janik, "Weininger and the Science of Sex: Prolegomena to Any Future Study," in Robert B. Pynsent, ed., *Decadence and Innovation: Austro-Hungarian Life and Art at the Turn of the Century,* 24–32, at 28. Lombroso and Weininger also shared similar views on the nature of Jewishness that Nancy Harrowitz has begun to analyze. See N. A. Harrowitz, "Weininger and Lombroso: A Question of Influence," in Harrowitz and Hyams, eds., *Jews and Gender: Responses to Otto Weininger,* 73–90.

72. See Terry R. Kandal, *The Woman Question in Classical Sociological Theory* (Miami: Florida International University Press, 1988), especially 89–185; Silvia Bovenschen, *Die imaginierte Weiblichkeit: Exemplarische Untersuchungen zu kulturgeschichtlichen und literarischen Präsantationsformen des Weiblichen* (Frankfurt a.M.: Suhrkamp, 1979); and Nike Wagner, *Geist und Geschlecht: Karl Kraus und die Erotik der Wiener Moderne* (Frankfurt a.M.: Suhrkamp, 1981).

73. Richard J. Evans, *The Feminist Movement in Germany 1894–1933* (London: Sage, 1976), 22. See also Karin Hausen, "Die Polarisierung der 'Geschlechtscharaktere,'" 363–93.

74. Gordon A. Craig, *Germany 1866–1945* (New York: Oxford University Press, 1978), 212.

75. For organizational details and statistics, see Martha S. Braun et al., eds., *Frauenbewegung, Frauenbildung und Frauenarbeit in Österreich* (Vienna: Bundes österreichischer Frauenvereine, 1930).

76. It was first published as *Die Befreiung der Frau und der sozialistischen Staat* (Leipzig, 1879), and then, from Zurich as *Die Frau und der Sozialismus* in the same year. Although banned by the Anti-Socialist Law, the book was sold in the major cities of Germany. The second edition was entitled *Die Frau in Vergangenheit, Gegenwart und Zukunft* (1883), the title it has carried ever since. See William H. Maehl, *August Bebel: Shadow Emperor of the German Workers* (Philadelphia: American Philosophical Society, 1980), 123.

77. W. Maehl, *August Bebel,* 124.

78. Many women socialists did believe, however, that women's lot could be improved before the revolution and fought for radical reforms in working women's training, working conditions, and treatment at workplace. See Jean H. Quataert, *Reluctant Feminists in German Social Democracy, 1885–1917* (Princeton: Princeton University Press, 1979), especially 12, 99–100. Conversely, many bourgeois feminists believed that individual liberties could flourish only after a more equitable restructuring of the social and political order. Late-nineteenth-century feminists rarely demanded equal rights alone. They saw their struggles as part of a larger crusade to transform society and politics. See Harriet Anderson, *Utopian Feminism: Women's Movements in Fin-de-Siècle Vienna* (New Haven: Yale University Press, 1992), 10. On socialist feminism, see Werner Thönnessen, *The Emancipation of Women: The Rise and Decline of the Women's Movement in German Social Democracy*

*1863-1933*, trans. Joris de Bres (London: Pluto, 1973); and on fin-de-siècle Social Democracy in general, see Guenther Roth, *The Social Democrats in Imperial Germany: A Study in Working-Class Isolation and National Integration* (Totowa, N.J.: Bedminster, 1963); and Melanie A. Sully, *Continuity and Change in Austrian Socialism: The Eternal Quest for the Third Way* (New York: Columbia University Press, 1982). The literature on socialist feminism in Austria remains rather scanty. See, however, Alida Mirella Hueller and Helmut Konrad, "Die Frau in der Österreichischen Arbeiterbewegung, 1900–1918," in Gerhard Botz and Hans Schafranek, eds., *Die Frau in der Arbeiterbewegung, 1900–1939*, 2 vols. (Vienna: Europaverlag, 1980), 1:283–96; and Murielle Martiny, "Adalheid Popp: Hoffnungen und Enttäuschungen," in ibid., 311–20. On Austrian working women in general, see Edith Rigler, *Frauenleitbild und Frauenarbeit in Österreich vom ausgehenden 19. Jahrhundert bis zum Zweiten Weltkrieg* (Munich: Oldenbourg, 1976), especially 47–53.

79. Anderson, *Utopian Feminism*, 93.

80. Evans, *Feminist Movement*, ix–xi, 1–3.

81. Ibid., 12. The promulgation of a new Uniform Civil Code for the entire German Empire in 1900 actually worsened matters by removing the liberal provisions on divorce. It recognized women as "legal persons," but the position of women in the family and the state remained basically unchanged. See ibid., 13–15.

82. Ibid., 17–20.

83. Anderson, *Utopian Feminism*, 21, 63–64.

84. Evans, *Feminist Movement*, 24; Anderson, *Utopian Feminism*, 25.

85. Anderson, *Utopian Feminism*, 24–26.

86. See Herrad U. Bessemer, "Bürgerliche Frauenbewegung und männliches Bildungsbürgertum 1860–1880," in Ute Frevert, ed., *Bürgerinnen und Bürger*, 190–205; and Irene Stoehr, "'Organisierte Mütterlichkeit': Zur Politik der deutschen Frauenbewegung um 1900," in Karin Hausen, ed., *Frauen suchen ihre Geschichte: Historische Studien zum 19. und 20. Jahrhundert* (Munich: Beck, 1983), 221–49.

87. Evans, *Feminist Movement*, 27–30.

88. See A. T. Allen, *Feminism and Motherhood in Germany, 1800–1914* (New Brunswick, N.J.: Rutgers University Press, 1991).

89. Anderson, *Utopian Feminism*, 190–91. This is particularly relevant to Weininger. Unlike most antifeminists of the time, Weininger did not venerate mothers. Although he did not mention feminist views on the subject, it is clear that Weininger's negative analysis of maternity was part of his resolution of the Woman Question. See chapter 7 for a detailed analysis.

90. Evans, *Feminist Movement*, 35–44. Disturbed by the new, radical turn of the movement, some older leaders retreated, labelling themselves as "moderates." On the differences between the "moderates" and the "radicals," see Bärbel Clemens, *"Menschenrechte haben kein Geschlecht!": Zum Politikverständnis der bürgerlichen Frauenbewegung* (Pfaffenweiler: Centaurus, 1988).

91. In Austria, women's suffrage was not a major issue until well after Weininger's death. See Anderson, *Utopian Feminism*, 83. Even the German suffrage movement at its height was much weaker than its Anglo-American counterparts. See Amy Hackett, "The German Women's Movement and Suffrage, 1890–1914: A Study of National Feminism," in Robert J. Bezucha, ed., *Modern European Social History* (Lexington, Mass.: Heath, 1972), 354–86. For a comparative perspective on early suffrage movements, see the articles in Caroline Daley and Melanie Nolan, eds., *Suffrage and Beyond: International Feminist Perspectives* (New York: New York University Press, 1994).

92. See Evans, *Feminist Movement*, 115–43; Amy Hackett, "Helene Stöcker: Left-Wing Intellectual and Sex Reformer," in Renate Briedenthal, Atina Grossmann, and Marion Kaplan, eds., *When Biology Became Destiny: Women in Weimar and Nazi Germany* (New York: Monthly Review Press, 1984), 109–30; and Christl Wickert, *Helene Stöcker (1869–1943), Frauenrechtlerin, Sexualreformerin und Pazifistin: Eine Biographie* (Bonn: Dietz, 1991).

93. See the classic description of prostitution in Vienna in Stefan Zweig's autobiography, *The World of Yesterday*, anonymous translation (New York: Viking, 1939), 83–91.

94. Anderson, *Utopian Feminism*, 72–73. Weininger may or may not have known of this petition; in any case, it would certainly have supported his allegation that modern women were conspiring to sexualize the world. After his death, Grete Meisel-Hess would urge the acceptance of "temporary" sexual relations (and of resulting illegitimate children) much more openly than had the petition. See ibid., 187.

95. See Bernd Nowacki, *Der Bund für Mutterschutz (1905–1933)* (Husum: Matthiesen, 1983).

96. Among the league's male supporters were people as different as the National Liberal Party's Friedrich Naumann, sociologist Max Weber, sexologist Iwan Bloch, and in Austria, Sigmund Freud. Many of the more conventional liberals, however, shunned the league and condemned its sexual ideology as insupportably Nietzschean. See Evans, *Feminist Movement*, 120–23.

97. See Richard J. Evans, *Comrades and Sisters: Feminism, Socialism and Pacifism in Europe, 1870–1945* (Sussex: Wheatsheaf, 1987), 52–53. Even without formal links, some socialist feminists had views on love and sexual ethics that paralleled those of the league. Nevertheless, the overall sexual philosophy of the Social Democrats was fairly conservative. See R. P. Neuman, "The Sexual Question and Social Democracy in Imperial Germany," *Journal of Social History* 7 (1974): 271–86.

98. See, for instance, the views of socialist Lily Braun, in J. Quataert, *Reluctant Feminists*, 103–105.

99. See Neuman, "The Sexual Question," 272. Around the turn of the century, there was a debate in German medical circles over the physiological effects of sexual abstinence. Orthodox physicians denied any harmful effect, whereas liberals such as Max Marcuse or a socialist such as Magnus Hirschfeld considered abstinence to be harmful. For further details, see Andreas Hill, "'May the Doctor advise Extramarital Intercourse?': Medical Debates on Sexual Abstinence in Germany c. 1900," in Roy Porter and Mikuláš Teich, eds., *Sexual Knowledge, Sexual Science: The History of Attitudes to Sexuality* (Cambridge: Cambridge University Press, 1994), 284–302.

100. See Neuman, "Sexual Question."

101. Evans, *Feminist Movement*, 175–205.

102. In reality, however, Jewish women had their own organizations, and these were more or less conservative with regard to the Woman Question. See ibid., 180–81.

103. Ibid., 175–77.

104. See *Strindberg's Letters*, selected, edited, and translated by Michael Robinson, 2 vols. (London: Athlone, 1992), 1:154; Strindberg, *The Confession of a Fool*, trans. Ellie Schleussner (London: Swift, 1912), 252–53; and Strindberg, Preface, *Miss Julie: A Naturalistic Tragedy*, trans. Helen Cooper (London: Methuen, 1992), xvi. On Strindberg's complex relations with feminism, see Declan Kiberd, *Men and Feminism in Modern Literature* (New York: St. Martin's Press, 1985), 34–60; Gail Finney, *Women in Modern Drama: Freud, Feminism, and European Theater at the Turn of the Century* (Ithaca, N.Y.: Cornell

University Press, 1989), 207–26; and Evert Sprinchorn, "Ibsen, Strindberg, and the New Woman," in Michael Bertin, ed., *The Play and its Critic: Essays for Eric Bentley* (Lanham, Md.: University Press of America, 1986), 45–66.

105. R. v. Krafft-Ebing, *Psychopathia Sexualis: A Medico-Forensic Study*, 12th ed. (1901), anonymous translation (New York: Pioneer, 1939), 399. See also Gudrun Schwarz, "'Viragos' in Male Theory in Nineteenth-Century Germany," trans. Joan Reutershan, in Judith Friedlander et al. eds., *Women in Culture and Politics: A Century of Change* (Bloomington, Ind.: Indiana University Press, 1986), 128–43.

106. See I. Bloch, *Das Sexualleben unserer Zeit in seinen Beziehungen zur modernen Kultur* (Berlin: Marcus, 1907), 580–81.

107. A. Rüling, "Welches Interesse hat die Frauenbewegung an der Lösung der homosexuellen Problems?" *Jahrbuch für sexuelle Zwischenstufen* 7 (1905): 129–51, at 133.

108. Ibid., 134–35, 143. This was also Weininger's recommendation. He explained that he was against *organized movements,* not against talented women finding their right niche in society. But Weininger sharply restricted his recommendation by arguing that even the most masculine woman was less masculine than the average man and therefore could not excel in any intellectual or professional field to the same extent as men. Also, he completely ruled out *political* equality, comparing women with children and the insane (450). Rüling cited Weininger's view that all talented women were homosexual, and thought that it was essentially correct, albeit too extreme (144–45).

109. Ibid., 144–45. As far as I know, Käthe Schirmacher was the only German feminist *leader* who was openly lesbian. See Ilse Kokula, *Weibliche Homosexualität um 1900 in zeitgenössischen Dokumenten* (Munich: Frauenoffensive, 1981), 31. For a simplistic, uncritical account based entirely on Rüling's opinion, see Lillian Faderman and Brigitte Eriksson, "Introduction," in Faderman and Eriksson, eds., *Lesbians in Germany, 1890's–1920's* (Tallahassee, Fl.: Naiad, 1990), ix–xxi, at xii–xiii. Rüling's views were not universally shared among feminists. In the same year as her lecture, the activist Johanna Elberskirchen asked: "How can the love of one woman for another woman show a propensity for the masculine? It is the masculine which is being excluded.... If we women in the movement for emancipation are homosexual, then let it be so!" (quoted in G. Schwarz, "'Viragos' in Male Theory," 139–40). On the diverse ideological uses of and debates over this notion, see Katharina Rowold, "A Male Mind in a Female Body: Sexology, Homosexuality, and the Woman Question in Germany, 1869–1914," in Kurt Bayertz and Roy Porter, eds., *From Physico-Theology to Bio-Technology: Essays in the Social and Cultural History of the Biosciences. A Festschrift for Mikuláš Teich* (Amsterdam: Rodopi, 1998), 153–79.

110. Quoted in Anderson, *Utopian Feminism,* 16. Mayreder, however, was not oblivious to male opposition. In her diary, she castigated Karl Kraus as "a characterless worm who nourishes himself off the leprous growths of others" (see ibid., 246).

111. Ibid., 17–19. Even Otto Weininger's *Doktorvater* Friedrich Jodl was sympathetic, albeit on a moral rather than political level. At the founding of the Viennese Ethical Society in 1894, Jodl declared that "without women no deeper changes in the moral spirit are possible.... It is precisely woman who must be won for our ideas, and... once she is won, she will be their most effective exponent" (ibid., 18). Less than a decade later, Jodl's own student, who may not even have been aware of this statement, would devote hundreds of pages to the argument that women were completely and irrevocably amoral.

112. Le Rider, *Modernity and Crises of Identity;* and Bernd Widdig, *Männerbünde und Massen: Zur Krise männlicher Identität in der Literatur der Moderne* (Opladen: Westdeutscher Verlag, 1992).

113. Le Rider, *Modernity and Crises of Identity*, 88. Le Rider points out that Freud, too, believed that true masculinity had to be laboriously acquired. "The majority of men," he had observed, "are far behind the masculine ideal." This, incidentally, was a courteous addition to Freud's statement that females were not as ethical as males. "We must not allow ourselves to be deflected from such conclusions by the denials of feminists, who are anxious to force us to regard the two sexes as completely equal in position and worth," Freud had asserted, and then "willingly" agreed that most men, too, fell short of the male norm. See S. Freud, "Some Psychical Consequences of the Anatomical Distinction between the Sexes," in James Strachey, ed., *The Standard Edition of the Complete Psychological Works of Sigmund Freud* (London: Hogarth, 1961), 19:248–58, at 258.

114. R. Lothar, "Kritik in Frankreich" (1891), in Gotthart Wunberg, ed., *Das junge Wien: Österreichische Literatur- und Kunstkritik, 1887–1902* (Tübingen: Niemeyer, 1976), 1:211.

115. Bloch, *Das Sexualleben unserer Zeit*, 527. The "third sex," of course, denoted homosexuals. This description was in common use around the turn of the century, and originated from the theory that homosexuals had the body of one sex and the mind of another. See chapter 5 below for details.

116. R. Mayreder, *Zur Kritik der Weiblichkeit: Essays* (Jena: Diederichs, 1910), 102–105.

117. Ibid., 102. Le Rider attributes the statement to Mayreder herself (*Modernity and Crises of Identity*, 155).

118. Cultural critics felt threatened by the goals of feminism, not by its (few) successes. For Weininger or Kraus, the meaning of feminism was that the traditional distinctions between the sexes was breaking down. And it was this realization that generated their anxiety and opposition. The actual "strength" of the Viennese feminist movement, *pace* Le Rider, was of secondary importance. There is, in any case, no reason to assume that Viennese intellectuals were oblivious to the dramatic feminist activities in neighboring Germany.

119. There is an enormous literature on German and Austrian anti-Semitism. For an excellent survey, see Peter Pulzer, *The Rise of Political Anti-Semitism in Germany and Austria*, rev. ed. (Cambridge, Mass.: Harvard University Press, 1988). For the specifically Viennese context, see John W. Boyer, *Political Radicalism in Late Imperial Vienna*; and Carl Schorske, "Politics in a New Key: An Austrian Trio," in Schorske, *Fin-de-Siècle Vienna*.

120. Exactly *how* one could transcend it, however, was a difficult question to answer. Certainly, conversion to Christianity was not universally accepted as satisfactory. The Jewish character, critics argued, could not be "washed away" by baptismal water. See Paul Lawrence Rose, *Revolutionary Anti-Semitism in Germany from Kant to Wagner* (Princeton: Princeton University Press, 1990), 14–15.

121. Ibid., xvi.

122. Ibid., 12. Weininger observed that among intellectuals, only Friedrich Nietzsche and dramatist Gotthold Ephraim Lessing were philo-Semitic. Nietzsche's philo-Semitism, Weininger argued, merely reflected his personal dislike for Wagner and Schopenhauer, while the views of the "greatly overrated" Lessing did not really merit a critique (586).

123. Rose, *Revolutionary Anti-Semitism*, 18.

124. Cited in ibid., 94–95.

125. Ibid., 96.

126. Cited in ibid., 99–100.

127. See Alexander Bein, "'Der jüdische Parasit': Bemerkung zur Semantik der Juden-frage," *Vierteljahrshefte für Zeitgeschichte* 13 (1965): 121–49.

128. For Schopenhauer, the eternal symbol of the Jewish people is Ahasverus, the "wan-dering Jew" of legend, who mocked Jesus and was cursed to roam the world for eternity. See Nathan Rotenstreich, *Jews and German Philosophy: The Polemics of Emancipation* (New York: Schocken, 1984), 185–86.

129. See Schopenhauer, *Parerga und Paralipomena: Kleine philosophische Schriften*, 2, ar-ticle 132, in Arthur Hübscher, ed., *Arthur Schopenhauer: Sämtliche Werke*, 7 vols. (Wies-baden: Brockhaus, 1972), 6:278–81, especially 279. Unlike Kant, Schopenhauer was also a fierce critic of the basic presuppositions of Christianity: theism and monotheism. See Rotenstreich, *Jews and German Philosophy*, 169.

130. "Wagner," remarked Nietzsche, "is Schopenhauerian in his hatred of the Jews" (Nietzsche, *The Gay Science*, trans. Walter Kaufmann [New York: Vintage, 1974], 154). On Wagner in general, see R. W. Gutman, *Richard Wagner: The Man, His Mind, and His Music* (New York: Harcourt, Brace, and World, 1968); and Ernest Newman, *The Life of Richard Wagner*, 4 vols. (New York: Knopf, 1937–46). On Wagner's anti-Semitism, see Ja-cob Katz, *The Darker Side of Genius: Richard Wagner's Anti-Semitism* (Hanover, N.H.: Uni-versity Press of New England, 1986); and Marc A. Weiner, *Richard Wagner and the Anti-Semitic Imagination* (Lincoln: University of Nebraska Press, 1995). On the Euro-pean impact of "Wagnerism," see David C. Large and William Weber, eds., *Wagnerism in European Culture and Politics* (Ithaca, N.Y.: Cornell University Press, 1984); and Carl Schorske, "Wagner and Germany's Cultures in the Nineteenth Century," in Solomon Wank et al., eds., *The Mirror of History: Essays in Honor of Fritz Fellner*, 171–80.

131. See R. Wagner, "Art and Revolution," in *Richard Wagner's Prose Works*, trans. William Ashton Ellis, 6 vols. (London: Kegan Paul, 1892–99), 1:59, 65; "The Artwork of the Future," ibid., 1:147, 177; "Judaism in Music," ibid., 3:79–82.

132. "Judaism in Music," *Richard Wagner's Prose Works*, 3:79–82.

133. See Michael Biddiss, *Father of Racist Ideology: The Social and Political Thought of Count Gobineau* (New York: Weybright and Talley, 1970). On Gobineau's influence in Central Europe, see Gunther Deschner, *"Gobineau und Deutschland": Der Einfluss von J. A. de Gobineau's 'Essai sur inégalité des races humaines' auf die deutsche Geistesgeschichte 1853–1917* (Erlangen: Hogl, 1967). On the Wagner circle's dissemination of Gobineau's theo-ries, see Geoffrey G. Field, *Evangelist of Race: The Germanic Vision of Houston Stewart Chamberlain* (New York: Columbia University Press, 1981), 154.

134. See Field, *Evangelist of Race*, 152–53.

135. This is not the only possible reading of *Parsifal*. For a Freudian analysis claiming that "the political world is completely absent" from *Parsifal*, see Carl Schorske, "The Quest for the Grail: Wagner and Morris," in Kurt H. Wolff and Barrington Moore Jr., eds., *The Critical Spirit: Essays in Honor of Herbert Marcuse* (Boston: Beacon, 1967), 216–32.

136. See Rose, *Revolutionary Anti-Semitism*, 373–74.

137. See David C. Large, "Wagner's Bayreuth Disciples," in D. C. Large and William Weber, eds., *Wagnerism in European Culture and Politics*, 72–133, at 129; and Anne Dzamba Sessa, "At Wagner's Shrine: British and American Wagnerians," in the same vol-ume, 246–77.

138. Field, *Evangelist*, 3.

139. The book was first conceived as a three-part cultural history of Western civilization for a popular audience, to be published in 1900 to mark the passing of the nineteenth cen-

tury. Only the first part was ever completed. Chamberlain's literary career soared after the publication of the *Foundations*, and a circle of followers formed around him. One member of this circle was Rudolf Kassner, a friend of Otto Weininger. See Field, *Evangelist*, 168–277; and H. Rodlauer, "Fragmente aus Weiningers Bildungsgeschichte," 45.

140. Chamberlain did not, however, define the term "race" with any precision. See Field, *Evangelist*, 215–16.

141. See ibid., 186; and H. S. Chamberlain, *The Foundations of the Nineteenth Century*, trans. John Lees, 2 vols. (London: Lane, 1913), 1:299–300.

142. Chamberlain, *Foundations*, 1:331.

143. Ibid., 1:201–13, 221–28; and Field, *Evangelist*, 183–84. Weininger cited Chamberlain frequently, though not always in agreement, in *Geschlecht und Charakter* (586, 588–91). Weininger accepted that Judaism and Christianity are mutually opposed but rejected the idea that Christ was an Aryan. It was crucial for Weininger that Jesus be Jewish, because he could then be portrayed as the symbol of a Jew's inner victory over his own Jewishness (420–21, 440).

144. See Field, *Evangelist*, 217–18, 155–56.

145. See Timms, *Karl Kraus*, 238.

146. Field, *Evangelist*, 95.

147. See Marsha L. Rozenblit, *The Jews of Vienna, 1867–1914: Assimilation and Identity* (Albany: State University of New York Press, 1983). Around 1900, only about twenty percent of all Jews living in the city had been born there. Among Jews themselves, the Galician immigrants tended to retain a more visible Eastern European identity "in a sea of Central European Jews" and were regarded contemptuously by the more Germanized Jews (ibid., 18, 43). The Jewish migration to Vienna was part of a larger European trend of Jewish migration to cities from outlying provinces (ibid., 15–16).

148. See Steven Beller, *Vienna and the Jews 1867–1938: A Cultural History* (Cambridge: Cambridge University Press, 1989), 33, 52, 38–40.

149. N. Stone, *Europe Transformed 1878–1919* (Cambridge, Mass.: Harvard University Press, 1984), 404–11.

150. Beller, *Vienna and the Jews*, 3. For the relationship with Stone, see ibid., x. For Beller's views on the problematic question of how to define who was Jewish and who was not, see ibid., 11–13.

151. Ibid., 41–42.

152. Ibid., 73–78.

153. Ibid., 102–103. While some of the Jewish interest in higher education may have been due to practical ambitions for upward social mobility, Beller pointed out that the Viennese Jewish elite was generally more deeply absorbed in Germanic culture than were the city's German-speaking gentiles.

154. Ibid., 106–13. Of all who left Judaism, as many as a quarter converted to Protestantism, including Victor Adler, Alfred Adler, Peter Altenberg, Arnold Schoenberg, and, of course, Otto Weininger. See ibid., 153.

155. Ibid., 114–21.

156. L. Wittgenstein, *Tractatus Logico-Philosophicus*, trans. C. K. Ogden (London: Routledge, 1922), 183.

157. Beller, *Vienna and the Jews*, 120–21.

158. See Beller's persuasive analysis of Otto Weininger as an "intolerant liberal" of this kind: S. Beller, "Otto Weininger as Liberal?" in Harrowitz and Hyams, eds., *Jews and Gender*, 91–101.

159. See Robert S. Wistrich, *The Jews of Vienna in the Age of Franz Joseph* (Oxford: Oxford University Press, 1989), 131–63.

160. See ibid., 205–37; and Michael Pollak, "Cultural Innovation and Social Identity in Fin-de-Siècle Vienna," in Ivar Oxaal, M. Pollak, and Gerhard Botz, eds., *Jews, Anti-Semitism, and Culture in Vienna* (London: Routledge, 1987), 59–74. On Herzl and Zionism, see Wistrich, *The Jews of Vienna*, 421–93; and Steven Beller, *Herzl* (London: Halban, 1991).

161. See Beller, *Vienna and the Jews*, 201–203.

162. When a young Jew in Arthur Schnitzler's novel *The Road into the Open* (Der Weg ins Freie) declares that he "never felt like a Jew," an older man with Zionist sympathies retorts: "If someone knocks your hat off once on the Ringstrasse because you have . . . a rather Jewish nose, you will feel hit like a Jew, you can rely on it" (A. Schnitzler, *The Road into the Open*, trans. Roger Byers [Berkeley: University of California Press, 1992], 52).

163. John E. Toews, "Refashioning the Masculine Subject in Early Modernism: Narratives of Self-Dissolution and Self-Construction in Psychoanalysis and Literature, 1900–1914," *Modernism/Modernity* 4, no. 1 (1997): 31–67, at 48–49 and 50. See also Beller, *Vienna and the Jews*, 220–21.

164. T. Lessing, *Der jüdische Selbsthass*. Lessing himself had been strongly anti-Semitic in his early years. See Lawrence Baron, "Theodor Lessing: Between Jewish Self-Hatred and Zionism," *Leo Baeck Institute Yearbook* 26 (1981): 323–40.

165. For a recent, widely-read example, see Sander L. Gilman, *Jewish Self-Hatred: Anti-Semitism and the Hidden Language of the Jews*, especially 244, where Gilman proclaims that Weininger offers "the best example of Jewish self-hatred." See also Michael Pollak, "Otto Weiningers Antisemitismus," in Jacques Le Rider and Norbert Leser, eds., *Otto Weininger: Werk und Wirkung* (Vienna: Österreichischer Bundesverlag, 1984), 109–22.

166. See A. Janik, "Viennese Culture and the Jewish Self-Hatred Hypothesis: A Critique," in Oxaal, Pollak, and Botz, eds., *Jews, Anti-Semitism, and Culture in Vienna*, 75–88.

167. For a strained attempt to biologize Weininger's racial psychology, see Gilman, *Jewish Self-Hatred*, 294.

168. Janik, "Viennese Culture and the Jewish Self-Hatred Hypothesis," 83–84, Janik's emphasis.

169. See Beller, *Vienna and the Jews*, 240. At the end of his life, with Nazism on the horizon, Kraus declared that his "spiritual scorn" stemmed from "an incorruptible Judaism . . . untouched by race, money, class, ghetto, or the masses." See K. Kraus, "Warum die Fackel nicht erscheint," *Die Fackel*, nos. 890–905 (1934): 38. Translation from Beller, *Vienna and the Jews*, 228–29.

170. S. P. Scheichl, "The Contexts and Nuances of Anti-Jewish Language: Were all the 'Antisemites' Antisemites?" in Oxaal, Pollak, and Botz, eds., *Jews, Anti-Semitism and Culture*, 89–110.

171. Ibid., 94.

*Chapter Three*

1. A. Janik, "Weininger and the Science of Sex: Prolegomena to Any Future Study," in Robert B. Pynsent, ed., *Decadence and Innovation: Austro-Hungarian Life and Art at the Turn of the Century*, 24–32, at 26.

2. Hermann Swoboda believed that *Geschlecht und Charakter* could be divided into three parts: a scientific, a philosophical, and an antifeminist one. See H. Swoboda, *Otto Weiningers Tod*, 4. Although not entirely unjustified, such an approach strikes me as too

schematic—the whole treatise, after all, is antifeminist and was avowed as such by its author.

3. There was no substantive separation of scientific and extrascientific discourse between the first and second parts. As examples, one may cite chapter 6 of part 1, which dealt with feminism, and chapter 12 of part 2, dealing, among other issues, with medical views of hysteria. Such examples may be easily multiplied.

4. Weininger's conception of "differential psychology" was his own, but he obtained the term from L. William Stern, *Psychologie der individuellen Differenzen*, Schriften der Gesellschaft für psychologische Forschung, 12 (1900).

5. This is a classic instance of what Michel Foucault called "normalizing judgment." See Introduction, note 27.

6. In his notes to these passages, Weininger heaped praise on Wilhelm Fliess and his 1897 monograph, *Die Beziehungen zwischen Nase und weiblichen Geschlechtsorganen* (The Connections between the Nose and the Female Sexual Organs). Weininger remarked that Fliess's "extraordinarily original treatise," although inappropriately titled, contained the "most interesting and most stimulating" observations on periodic phenomena in human life (499–500). Briefly, Fliess had argued that all human beings had two vital cycles, one male and one female. See Frank J. Sulloway, *Freud, Biologist of the Mind: Beyond the Psychoanalytic Legend* (New York: Basic Books, 1979), 138–41. After Weininger's death, Fliess would charge him with plagiarizing his unpublished work. I discuss this controversy in chapter 8.

7. Weininger's friend Hermann Swoboda observed that in the first part of the treatise, Weininger did not speak malevolently of women, even when there was ample opportunity for it, as in the chapter on women's emancipation. See Swoboda, *Otto Weiningers Tod*, 6. On contemporary medical and scientific views of woman's nature, see Cynthia Eagle Russett, *Sexual Science: The Victorian Construction of Womanhood;* and Nancy Tuana, *The Less Noble Sex: Scientific, Religious, and Philosophical Conceptions of Woman's Nature.*

8. That article was: Arduin, "Die Frauenfrage und die sexuellen Zwischenstufen," *Jahrbuch für sexuelle Zwischenstufen* 2 (1900): 211–23. Arduin believed that many of the leaders of the women's emancipation movements were masculine and lesbian (ibid., 216). These masculine women were biologically driven to masculine occupations, and should be permitted to do so (ibid., 220–21). Since, however, there was no practicable way to determine the masculinity of women on a societal scale, Arduin advocated the opening of all fields and professions to all women. Nature would then direct the true women to the "naturally feminine occupations" of mother and housewife, while masculine women could follow their chosen paths (ibid., 221–22). Arduin was the pseudonym of the physiologist and psychologist K. F. Jordan. See Peter Gorsen, "Nachwort," in W. J. Schmidt, ed., *Jahrbuch für sexuelle Zwischenstufen: Auswahl aus den Jahrgängen 1899–1923*, 2 vols. (Frankfurt: Qumran, 1984), 2:257–84, at 259.

9. Weininger quotes historian Jakob Burckhardt's statement that masculine intelligence and independence was a prized feature in women during the Renaissance (88, 504). See J. Burckhardt, *Die Kultur der Renaissance in Italien,* ed. Horst Günther (Frankfurt a.M.: Deutscher Klassiker Verlag, 1989), 388, 434.

10. Ottokar Lorenz, *Lehrbuch der gesammten wissenschaftlichen Genealogie, Stammbaum und Ahnentafel in ihrer geschichtlichen, soziologischen und naturwissenschaftlichen Bedeutung* (Berlin: Hertz, 1898), 54–55.

11. If feminist movements were really caused by the birth of masculine women and feminine men in higher numbers during specific periods, then, Weininger pointed out, it fol-

lowed that the current women's movement would disappear spontaneously and reappear again after many years (91).

12. C. Darwin, *The Variation of Animals and Plants under Domestication*, 2 vols. (New York: Appleton, 1897), 2:26.

13. A. Weismann, *The Germ-Plasm: A Theory of Heredity*, trans. W. N. Parker and H. Rönnfeldt (New York: Scribner's, 1893), 363–64.

14. Weininger cited the gynecologist Alfred Hegar's view that women had a weaker sex drive than men (508). See A. Hegar, *Der Geschlechtstrieb: Eine social-medicinische Studie* (Stuttgart: Enke, 1894), 5–6. This was standard medical teaching at the time. In his influential work on sexual pathology, Richard von Krafft-Ebing declared that "woman . . . if physically and mentally normal, and properly educated, has but little sensual desire. . . . Her need of love is greater, it is continual not periodical, but her love is more spiritual than sensual" (Krafft-Ebing, *Psychopathia Sexualis: A Medico-Forensic Study*, 14).

15. A. Moll, *Untersuchungen über die Libido sexualis* (Berlin: Fischer's medicinische Buchhandlung, 1897), 8–10. The British sexologist Havelock Ellis described Moll's distinction as "undoubtedly true," although he felt that Moll had not sufficiently appreciated how intimately the two component impulses were interrelated in real life. See H. Ellis, *Studies in the Psychology of Sex*, 2 vols. (New York: Random House, 1936), 1, pt. 2:20–21.

16. Rudolf Chrobak and Arthur von Rosthorn, *Die Erkrankungen der weiblichen Geschlechtsorgane*, 2 vols. in 1 (Vienna: Holder, 1900), 1:423–24.

17. Weininger linked his views on female sexual passivity with that of Aristotle, whose theory of reproduction assigned the active role to the male principle and the passive role to the female. Weininger lamented that Aristotle, like all Greek authors except Euripides, restricted himself to the reproductive sphere alone while discussing female sexuality (240, 537).

18. In its essence, the idea that woman was completely sexual has, of course, been a venerable component of many misogynistic theories over the centuries. What was unique to Weininger was the *kind* of "proof" he provided for this assertion (an idiosyncratic combination of the biomedical, the psychiatric, and the metaphysical) and, as we shall see, the manner in which he used this supposed truth to argue for universal chastity and the morally sanctioned extinction of humankind.

19. C. Darwin, *On the Origin of Species by means of Natural Selection*, 6th ed, (New York: Appleton, 1876), 119.

20. See C. Buci-Glucksmann, *Baroque Reason: The Aesthetics of Modernity*, 118.

21. Weininger derived this argument from Havelock Ellis, who had suggested that women respond more readily to stimuli but that men have greater sensibility: they perceive stimuli with greater precision and intensity. Women, then, were more irritable, while men were more sensible. Ellis had added that women might be less sensible because their senses are "habitually subject to a less thorough education." See H. Ellis, *Man and Woman: A Study of Human Secondary Sexual Characters* (London: W. Scott, 1904), 148–49. Weininger ignored Ellis's qualification.

22. The word was coined from the Greek *hen* (a single thing) to suggest an entity that did not permit the distinction of feeling from thought. (My thanks to Vivian Nutton for helping me with the translation and transliteration.) The "absolute henid," Weininger warned, was an abstract concept: it was uncertain how often real psychical experience in adult humans was so undifferentiated as to deserve the description of henid (125). Nor could Weininger provide an exact description of a henid. His explanation of this inability was ingenious: "The very idea of a henid," he declared, "forbids its description: it is merely

a something . . . one cannot describe particular henids; one can only be conscious of their existence" (126). Nevertheless, the concept of henid, he emphasized, was theoretically important for a psychological study of the sexes.

23. To describe the "proto-thought" or "henid," Weininger distinguished between "elements" and "characters," a distinction derived from Richard Avenarius, *Kritik der reinen Erfahrung*, 2 vols., 2d ed. (Leipzig: Reisland, 1907), 1:16. An element, roughly, was a perception *(Empfindung, Perzeption)* or the content of a perception: an entire tree could be an element; so could a single leaf, or even its color, and the causal factors of that color (119). Each element was accompanied by a character or a certain feeling-tone *(Gefühlston)*. This did not simply involve pleasantness or unpleasantness, but also whether the element was "surprising," "recognizable," or "dependable" (120). Although element and character were always linked even in the clearest thought, they were fused indistinguishably when the thought first took form. This "proto-thought," in which perception and feeling had not yet been resolved into distinct analytic moments, was a "henid" (125).

24. This psychic distinction between the sexes, Weininger remarked, was reflected in physical differences: the male body and features were sharply defined while the female body and physiognomy were rounded and indistinct (128).

25. Describing the difference between talent and genius as fundamental and qualitative, Weininger rejected Cesare Lombroso's definition of genius as an extreme degree of talent (521). See Cesare Lombroso, *The Man of Genius,* anonymous trans. (London: Walter Scott, 1891), viii.

26. Kant had excluded even philosophers from the category of "genius," reserving it solely for artists. See Kant, *Critique of Judgment*, trans. J. H. Bernard (New York: Hackett, 1951), 161. Weininger opposes Kant on this point.

27. This protean ability, Weininger emphasized, need not be simultaneous. As with masculinity and femininity in the same individual, the manifestations of genius might well be sequential.

28. Weininger did not identify a target for his remark on the Unconscious, but if he did have a specific figure in mind, it was more likely to be the philosopher Eduard von Hartmann (1842–1906), author of the popular treatise, *Philosophy of the Unconscious* (1869), than Sigmund Freud. Weininger described von Hartmann elsewhere as "extremely superficial and unoriginal" (555), whereas Freud, of course, was important to him for theoretical as well as pragmatic reasons that I discuss in chapters 1 and 8. On Hartmann and his philosophy of the Unconscious, see Theodor Schwarz, "Eduard von Hartmann," *Deutsche Zeitschrift für Philosophie* 17 (1969): 1469–77.

29. Weininger claimed (514–15) that only one previous thinker, Arthur Schopenhauer, had observed that genius might be rooted in the completeness and vividness of one's recollection of one's own life. See A. Schopenhauer, *Neue Paralipomena: Vereinzelte Gedanken über vielerlei Gegenstände,* vol. 4 of Edward Grisebach, ed., *Arthur Schopenhauers handschriftliche Nachlass,* 2d ed. (Leipzig: Reclam, 1896), §143, 114.

30. Here, Weininger launched into a caustic attack on experimental psychologists who used "letters, long rows of figures, unconnected words" to test memory: such experiments were worthless because they placed their subjects, regardless of their individuality, under the same experimental conditions, treating them "merely as good or bad recording devices *(Registrierapparat)*" (146–47). Weininger argued that people remembered only what interested them, and different people, needless to say, were interested in different things. Psychologists who failed to take this elementary fact into account, Weininger suggests, did not really know anything about the mind.

31. The lack of clear consciousness and perfect memory, according to Weininger, were also responsible for women's deficiencies in creative imagination. Men, said Weininger, had traditionally regarded women as more imaginative solely on account of the female preoccupation with sexual fantasies (151). True fantasies, however, could find a legitimate place only in the male psyche, which always had a clear view of the present and the past. Women succeeded only in those imaginative arts where vague and unformed sentiments could produce some small effect, such as painting, poetry, and pseudo-mysticism (152).

32. See Ewald Hering, *Über das Gedächtnis als eine allgemeine Funktion der organisierten Materie* (Leipzig: Engelmann, 1905); and E. Mach, *The Analysis of Sensations and the Relation of the Physical to the Psychical*, 235–44. For a stimulating discussion of nineteenth-century theories of memory and their cultural contexts and implications, see Laura Otis, *Organic Memory: History and the Body in the Late Nineteenth and Early Twentieth Centuries* (Lincoln: University of Nebraska Press, 1994).

33. Associationists, Weininger added, confused memory with recollection, overlooking that mere *recognition* of a situation does not imply the complete reproduction of a specific past situation (185). Animals, he pointed out, could recognize people and situations but did not possess any memory in the human sense, a distinction ignored by biologist G. J. Romanes, who had attributed genuine memory to animals (186, 524). On Romanes and his views on animal psychology, see Robert J. Richards, *Darwin and the Emergence of Evolutionary Theories of Mind and Behavior* (Chicago: University of Chicago Press, 1987), 331–408. Weininger's critique was based on the views of philosophers Richard Avenarius and Harald Höffding. See Avenarius, *Kritik der reinen Erfahrung*, 2:43–45; and H. Höffding, "Über Wiedererkennen, Association und psychische Activität," *Vierteljahrsschrift für wissenschaftliche Philosophie* 13 (1889): 420–58; 14 (1890): 27–54.

34. Since she did not possess any moral sense whatever, Woman could not be expected to act morally or be blamed when she did not (252). Weininger read the criminological literature of the late nineteenth century quite accurately in stating that women committed fewer crimes than men. See Havelock Ellis, *Man and Woman*, 364–66; Cesare Lombroso and Guglielmo Ferrero, *Das Weib als Verbrecherin und Prostituirte*, 193–95. Many of Weininger's other beliefs on the relations between gender and criminality, however, were entirely his own. He said, for instance, that the male criminal never really felt his punishment was unjust. Criminals may be born with a "criminal drive" *(verbrecherischen Triebe)* but, despite all fashionable theories about moral insanity, male criminals were always conscious that they had debased themselves by their crime. Women criminals, on the other hand, were always convinced that they were in the right (253).

35. On Kant's views on the origin of morality, see Roger J. Sullivan, *Immanuel Kant's Moral Theory* (Cambridge: Cambridge University Press, 1989), 126–29.

36. See D. Hume, *A Treatise of Human Nature*, ed. L. A. Selby-Bigge and P. H. Nidditch (Oxford: Clarendon, 1978), 251–63.

37. Mach, *Beiträge zur Analyse der Empfindungen*, 1–24.

38. Weininger later changed his mind on this point. In a long note (530–31), added during the printing of *Geschlecht und Charakter*, he stated that the axiom A = A did not allow one to infer the existence of the ego but only of absolute, hyperempirical Being *(Sein)*. The inference of the ego, he now said, was possible only on psychological, and not logical, grounds. Nevertheless, a denial of A = A implied a denial of Being. An entity that did not recognize that A was equal to A could not exist. Woman, Weininger argued repeatedly in later parts of the book, was "Nothing"; here, we have one basis of that assertion.

39. The portrayal of the human being as a microcosm was an ancient topos with a com-

NOTES TO PAGES 56–58

plex and fascinating history. See Rudolf Allers, "Microcosmos from Anaximandros to Paracelsus," *Traditio* 1 (1944): 319–408, and Walther Kranz, "Kosmos," *Archiv für Begriffsgeschichte* 2 (1955): 1–282. During the Renaissance, the theme was resurrected by Italian humanists to establish that man, because he possessed a "universal" nature, occupied a privileged position in the universe. See P. O. Kristeller, *Renaissance Concepts of Man and Other Essays* (New York: Harper & Row, 1972), 13. Weininger, too, provided a brief history of the concept (533–34).

40. On Pico's historical context, see Paul Oskar Kristeller, *Eight Philosophers of the Italian Renaissance* (Stanford: Stanford University Press, 1964), 54–71. For a somewhat different analysis, see William G. Craven, *Giovanni Pico della Mirandola, Symbol of His Age: Modern Interpretations of a Renaissance Philosopher* (Geneva: Droz, 1981).

41. See Paul Oskar Kristeller's analysis of Pico in Ernst Cassirer, P. O. Kristeller, and John Herman Randall, Jr., eds., *The Renaissance Philosophy of Man* (Chicago: University of Chicago Press, 1948), 219. Elsewhere, Kristeller added that Pico's removal of man from the hierarchy of nature was an early move toward "dissolving the notion of the great chain of being that had dominated Western thought for so many centuries." See P. O. Kristeller, *Renaissance Concepts of Man and Other Essays*, 13–14.

42. Giovanni Pico della Mirandola, "Oration on the Dignity of Man," trans. Elizabeth Livermoore Forbes, in Cassirer, Kristeller, and Randall, Jr., eds., *Renaissance Philosophy of Man*, 223–54, at 225.

43. Weininger reminded his reader that this was not a novel contention; he had merely discovered the philosophical foundations of an old truism. The Chinese, he pointed out, had denied women a soul in ancient times, and the prophet Mohammed had barred women from paradise on similar grounds. In the Western tradition, Aristotle had used the word "soul" only for the active masculine principle, thus indicating that females had no soul (240). Weininger cited numerous other thinkers, ranging from Tertullian to August Strindberg, who considered women to be soulless (240–41).

44. Women's lack of individuality, he pointed out, was evinced most commonly in their willingness to assume their husband's name after marriage. Women had no attachment to the personal name, although the name is integral to the personality. Moving back to the language of types, Weininger concluded that Woman is fundamentally nameless (*im Grund namenlos,* 266–67).

45. The description itself, as Weininger recorded (545), was coined by F. A. Lange, *Geschichte der Materialismus,* 6th ed., 2 vols. in 1 (Leipzig: Baedeker, 1898), 2:381.

46. Women, says Weininger, developed mental capacities only at puberty and lost them with the decline of their physical sexuality in old age (278). The male, on the contrary, never lost his mental capacities in old age. Man was never fully divisible, unlike Woman, who was always a mere aggregate and thus easily split. As evidence for this assertion, Weininger mentioned multiple and double personalities, found almost exclusively among women (277). Weininger cited Albert von Schrenck-Notzing, *Über Spaltung der Persönlichkeit (sogenanntes Doppel-ich)* (Vienna: Holder, 1896). On the history of the concept of multiple personality, see Ian Hacking, *Rewriting the Soul: Multiple Personality and the Sciences of Memory* (Princeton, N.J.: Princeton University Press, 1995). The few similar cases in men were negligible in comparison, said Weininger, and, in any case, he had already explained how Man could become *anything,* including Woman! (546).

47. Weininger acknowledged that even Kant had believed that love was simply a refined expression of sexuality. But Kant, he commented, was personally unacquainted with love or sexuality—his only passion had been metaphysics!

48. In fact, said Weininger, women were drawn only to the phallus, which exerted a hypnotizing influence on them: it was the penis that made Woman completely and fundamentally unfree (339).

49. Le Rider, *Modernity and Crises of Identity,* 165, 186, 291–92.

50. Allan Janik argues that the ideal type Weininger called the Jew could be better described as the Conformist who represented "the counterfeit (i.e. unreflective) pseudorationality of conventional mores." See A. Janik, "How did Weininger influence Wittgenstein?" in Harrowitz and Hyams, eds., *Jews and Gender: Responses to Otto Weininger,* 61–71, at 66. I find such a reinterpretation problematic. While Weininger did charge the Jewish type with slavish adherence to moral and social codes, he also, incoherently, depicted the Jew as the complete unbeliever. Woman, he remarked, at least believed in Man but "the Jew believes in nothing, within him or without him" (431).

51. Weininger provided a long list of anti-Semitic geniuses ranging from Tacitus, Pascal, and Voltaire to Goethe, Kant, and Wagner (406).

52. According to Weininger, communists, exemplified by Karl Marx, wished to abolish private property, whereas socialists encouraged co-operation between individuals and recognize human individuality. Modern social democracy, Weininger complained, had retreated from the classical socialism of Owen, Carlyle, Ruskin, and Fichte due to Jewish influence (410).

53. Weininger compared this submission to external authority to Woman's passive submission to Man (430–31).

54. Sensuousness, Weininger clarified, was not immoral because it was voluptuous. Asceticism, he emphasized, was equally immoral. First, it took a negative approach to the issue: a person was declared moral if he simply abandoned the pursuit of pleasure. More importantly, the ascetic imperative came from outside the individual and was thus, in Kantian terms, heteronomous and not genuinely moral (448).

55. Nietzsche, *Beyond Good and Evil,* trans. Walter Kaufmann, §238, in Kaufmann, ed., *Basic Writings of Nietzsche,* 356–57.

56. Weininger cited only one source for his statement (595), and that source dealt only with Pythagoras's views on woman's claim to equal rights: J. J. Bachofen, *Das Mutterrecht: Eine Untersuchung über die Gynaikokratie der alten Welt nach ihrer religiösen und rechtlichen Natur* (Basel: Schwabe, 1897), 381. On the importance of Bachofen's ideas on ancient matriarchy to Weininger's argument on woman's nature, see chapter 7.

57. See Richard D. Chessick, "Studies in Feminine Psychology, 6: Kundry," *American Journal of Psychoanalysis* 53 (1993): 237–45; and Sandra Corse, "Parsifal: Wagner, Nietzsche, and the Modern Subject," *Theatre Journal* 46 (1994): 95–110.

58. The sight of a pregnant woman, Weininger observed (596), was found revolting by most men, even if they were sometimes sexually excited by it. Describing the phenomenon as an indication of the link between ethics and aesthetics, he quoted a line from Charles Baudelaire on "les hideurs de la fécondité." See C. Baudelaire, *Les Fleurs du Mal,* ed. Jacques Dupont (Paris: Flammarion, 1991), poem V, 64.

59. "Did Weininger know," wonders Hans Meyer, "that he had almost literally paraphrased Sarastro in *The Magic Flute,* who had put it to Pamina that 'a man must guide your hearts, for without him every woman is wont to proceed out of her own sphere of action.'" *Geschlecht und Charakter,* Meyer suggests, upholds the Viennese Enlightenment tradition of bourgeois male hegemony over education. See H. Meyer, *Outsiders: A Study in Life and Letters,* trans. Denis M. Sweet (Cambridge, Mass.: MIT Press, 1982), 98–99.

60. As the argument progressed, however, the "ideal type" Woman became increasingly

conflated with individual women. Moreover, Weininger's conception of masculinity included the possibility that Man, being microcosmic, might even acquire some of the traits of Woman. The two opposed types, therefore, fused into each other at this point.

*Chapter Four*

1. A. Janik, "Weininger and the Science of Sex: Prolegomena to Any Future Study," in Robert B. Pynsent, *Decadence and Innovation: Austro-Hungarian Life and Art at the Turn of the Century,* 24–32.

2. J. Hunter, *Observations on Certain Parts of the Animal Oeconomy,* edited by Richard Owen, vol. 4 of James F. Palmer, ed., *The Works of John Hunter, F.R.S.* (London: Longman, Rees, 1837), 45. On the intellectual context of Hunter's views, see S. J. Cross, "John Hunter, The Animal Oeconomy, and Late-Eighteenth-Century Physiological Discourse," *Studies in History of Biology* 5 (1981): 1–110.

3. C. Darwin, *On the Origin of Species by means of Natural Selection,* 119. Darwin also upheld Hunter's distinction in another work that Weininger knew well, *Variation of Animals and Plants under Domestication,* 1:188.

4. C. Darwin, *The Descent of Man and Selection in Relation to Sex,* 2 vols. (New York: Appleton, 1872), 1:247–48.

5. H. Ellis, *Man and Woman: A Study of Human Secondary Sexual Characters,* 18.

6. Ibid., 19.

7. Ibid., 20.

8. Weininger referred to two typical case reports: Andrew Clark, "A Case of Spurious Hermaphroditism (Hypospadias and Undescended Testes in a Subject who had been brought up as a Female and been Married for Sixteen Years)," *Lancet,* 12 March 1898, 718–19; and L. Siebourg, "Ein Fall von Pseudohermaphroditismus masculinus completus," *Deutsche medizinische Wochenschrift* 24 (1898): 367–68.

9. Instead of multiplying examples of such differences, however, he referred the reader to a number of monographs and papers (469–72) and to two standard compendia on the subject: Havelock Ellis's *Man and Woman* and Cesare Lombroso and Guglielmo Ferrero's *Das Weib als Verbrecherin und Prostituirte,* both of which provided ample surveys of differences between the sexes in numerous areas, ranging from the shape of the pelvis to moral character.

10. This belief was shared by numerous biologists of the time and played a significant role in the application to human sexuality of the rule that ontogeny recapitulated phylogeny. In the next two chapters, we shall see that the "natural hermaphroditism" of lower animals was one of the premises of many turn-of-the-century theories regarding human sexual development and the origin of homosexuality.

11. Steenstrup's definition of hermaphroditism was extraordinarily strict. He would consider an organism to possess both male and female genitals only when (1) reproductive cells (spermatozoa or ova) of both sexes were present in the reproductive organs, and (2) when it had been demonstrated that these reproductive cells had been formed in the organs in which they were found. See J. J. S. Steenstrup, *Untersuchungen über das Vorkommen des Hermaphroditismus in der Natur,* trans. C. F. Hornschuch (Greifswald: Otte, 1846), 14–15.

12. Ibid., 9–10.

13. See T. W. Laqueur, *Making Sex: Body and Gender from the Greeks to Freud* (Cambridge, Mass.: Harvard University Press, 1990).

14. R. Leuckart, "Zeugung," in Rudolf Wagner, ed., *Handwörterbuch der Physiologie mit*

*Rücksicht auf physiologische Pathologie,* 4 vols. in 5 (Braunschweig: Vieweg, 1853), 4:707–1000, at 742–43.

15. The most concise and comprehensive discussion of Nägeli's multifaceted career is still that of Erik Nordenskiöld, *The History of Biology: A Survey* (New York: Tudor, 1928), 552–57.

16. C. v. Nägeli, *Mechanisch-physiologische Theorie der Abstammungslehre* (Munich: Oldenbourg, 1894). On the theory of the idioplasm, see Gloria Robinson, *A Prelude to Genetics, Theories of a Material Substance of Heredity: Darwin to Weismann* (Lawrence, Kan.: Coronado, 1979), 109–30; and Hans-Jörg Rheinberger, "Naudinn, Darwin, Nägeli: Bemerkungen zu den Vererbungsvorstellungen des 19. Jahrhunderts," *Medizinhistorisches Journal* 18 (1983): 198–212, 206–11.

17. C. v. Nägeli, *Mechanisch-physiologische Theorie,* 27.

18. Ibid., 24, 26.

19. E. B. Wilson, *The Cell in Development and Heredity* (New York: Macmillan, 1896), 300–301.

20. Ibid., 302. While acknowledging his importance in his own time, biologist and historian Ernst Mayr has pointed out that except for Nägeli's emphasis on the separation of the idioplasm and the nourishing plasm, "almost every detail of his theory was radically wrong and almost none of it based on any known fact" (E. Mayr, *The Growth of Biological Thought: Diversity, Evolution, and Inheritance* [Cambridge, Mass.: Harvard University Press, 1982], 671).

21. Nägeli, *Mechanisch-physiologische Theorie,* 531. Weininger quoted and discussed these passages on 479 of *Geschlecht und Charakter.*

22. Weininger declared that he had found Hertwig's treatise to be the richest source of information on biology apart from Charles Darwin's *Variation of Animals and Plants under Domestication* (479).

23. O. Hertwig, *Die Zelle und die Gewebe: Grundzüge der allgemeinen Anatomie und Physiologie,* 2 vols. in 1 (Jena: Fischer, 1893), 1:278–79. Hertwig emphasized that although the cells of higher animals were unable to regenerate entire organisms, these cells nevertheless may carry the species characters in their idioplasm. The inability of animal cells to regenerate was probably due to nonidioplasmic factors such as greater functional differentiation of the cells.

24. Weismann, it is well known, believed that the germ cells were autonomous and that no modification of the soma could affect the germ plasm. This was the foundation of Weismann's controversial insistence that acquired characteristics (i.e., changes in the soma) could never be inherited (i.e., passed on through the germ plasm). On the controversy and Weismann's role in it, see Frederick B. Churchill, "The Weismann-Spencer Controversy over the Inheritance of Acquired Characters," in E. G. Forbes, ed., *Human Implications of Scientific Advance: Proceedings of the 15th International Congress of the History of Science, Edinburgh, 10–15 August 1977* (Edinburgh: Edinburgh University Press, 1978), 451–68. On Weismann's life and work, see Ernst Gaupp, *August Weismann: Sein Leben und sein Werk* (Jena: Fischer, 1917); Frederick B. Churchill, "August Weismann and a Break from Tradition," *Journal of the History of Biology* 1 (1968): 91–112; and Klaus Sander, ed., *August Weismann (1834–1914) und die theoretische Biologie des 19. Jahrhunderts: Urkunden, Berichte und Analysen,* special issue of *Freiburger Universitätsblätter* 87–88 (July 1985).

25. A. Weismann, *Die Continuität des Keimplasma's als Grundlage einer Theorie der Vererbung* (Jena: Fischer, 1885), 46. Weininger quoted this statement (480). Nägeli, al-

though not a great believer in the transmissibility of acquired characters, had accepted that the idioplasm and the nutritive plasm were interconvertible. See Gloria Robinson, *A Prelude to Genetics*, 122–27.

26. Weismann's argument, Weininger claimed, had been negated by Friedrich Miescher's demonstration that in female salmon the ovaries grew enormously during the breeding season at the expense of muscular tissue. Miescher himself had merely drawn an empirical and statistical correlation based on anatomical measurements without making any references to idioplasm or inheritance. Weininger, however, transformed it into evidence for the convertibility of somatic idioplasm into germ plasm (480). See F. Miescher, "Statistische und biologische Beiträge zur Kenntniss vom Leben des Rheinlachses im Süsswasser," in Miescher, *Die histochemischen und physiologischen Arbeiten*, 2 vols. in 1 (Leipzig: Vogel, 1897), 2:116–91, 132–52. Weininger also briefly cited reports of regeneration in lower species to refute Weismann's claim that germ cells could not develop from somatic cells. Among those studies were Hermann Vöchting, "Über die Regeneration der Marchantieen," *Jahrbücher für wissenschaftlichen Botanik* 16 (1885): 367–414; and Jacques Loeb, *Untersuchungen zur physiologischen Morphologie der Tiere*, vol. 2: *Organbildung und Wachstum* (Würzburg: Hertz, 1892), 34–37.

27. A. Biedl, *The Internal Secretory Organs: Their Physiology and Pathology*, trans. Linda Forster (London: Bale, Sons & Danielsson, 1913), 360–70.

28. A few researchers continued to deny that the sex glands played any role at all in the development of secondary sexual characters. Weininger cited two such skeptics: Konrad Rieger, Professor of Psychiatry at Würzburg, and Arthur W. Johnstone, an American gynecologist (476). See K. Rieger, *Die Castration in rechtlicher, socialer und vitaler Hinsicht betrachtet* (Jena: Fischer, 1900); and A. W. Johnstone, "Internal Secretion of the Ovary," *Transactions of the American Gynecological Society* 25 (1900): 269–79. On the general contexts of endocrinological research in the nineteenth and early twentieth centuries, see Victor C. Medvei, *The History of Clinical Endocrinology: A Comprehensive Account of Endocrinology from Earliest Times to the Present Day* (Lancaster: Parthenon, 1993), 123.

29. C.-E. Brown-Séquard, "Des effets produits chez l'homme par des injections sous-cutanées d'un liquide retiré des testicules frais de cobaye et de chien," *Comptes rendus hebdomadaires des séances de la Societé de Biologie (Paris)*, 9th ser., 1 (1889): 415–19. Although acquainted with his 1849 report (477), Weininger paid very little attention to the experiments of the physiologist Arnold Adolph Berthold (1803–61) of Göttingen, which are almost always mentioned in traditional histories of endocrinology as the true beginning of research on the internal secretions of the sex glands. For details on Berthold's experiments, which proved difficult to replicate, see C. Barker Jørgensen, *John Hunter, A. A. Berthold, and the Origins of Endocrinology* (Odense: Odense University Press, 1971).

30. On organotherapy, see Merriley Borell, "Origins of the Hormone Concept: Internal Secretions and Physiological Research, 1889–1905" (Ph.D. dissertation, Yale University, 1976); Borell, "Brown-Séquard's Organotherapy and its Appearance in America at the End of the Nineteenth Century," *Bulletin of the History of Medicine* 50 (1976): 309–20; Borell, "Organotherapy and the Emergence of Reproductive Endocrinology," *Journal of the History of Biology* 18 (1985): 1–30. Similar general accounts of organotherapy in the Central European context are not available. See, however, these medical surveys, which exemplify the late-nineteenth- and the early-twentieth-century perspectives: Georg Buschan, "Organsafttherapie," in Albert Eulenburg, ed., *Real-Encyclopädie der gesammten Heilkunde*, 3d ed., 26 vols. (Vienna: Urban and Schwarzenberg, 1894–

1901), 18 (1898): 22–82; and Julius Wagner von Jauregg and Gustav Bayer, eds., *Lehrbuch der Organotherapie mit Berücksichtigung ihrer anatomischen und physiologischen Grundlagen* (Leipzig: Thieme, 1914).

31. Hertwig, *Die Zelle und die Gewebe*, 2:162.

32. E. Ziegler, *Lehrbuch der allgemeinen Pathologie und der pathologischen Anatomie für Ärzte und Studierende*, 9th ed., 2 vols. (Jena: Fischer, 1898), 1:79–80.

33. F. Goltz and A. Freusberg, "Über den Einfluss des Nervensystems auf die Vorgänge während der Schwangerschaft und des Gebärakts," *Archiv für die gesammte Physiologie* 9 (1874): 552–65.

34. Ibid., 557–58. If one refused to surrender the neural perspective, the only available option, said Goltz, was to assume that the sex glands and the brain were not connected through the spinal cord but through that portion of the autonomic nervous system which originated from the spinal cord above the level of transection and did not "travel" with it. Such a hypothesis was plausible, but the chemical theory, he believed, was more reasonable. Hans Simmer has pointed out that despite its acuity, Goltz's hypothesis was virtually ignored. This, says Simmer, may have been caused by the lack of a theoretical basis, which became available only after Brown-Séquard's expansion of Claude Bernard's concept of internal secretion into a system of regulation akin to the nervous system. See H. H. Simmer, "Bilaterale Oophorektomie der Frau im späten 19. Jahrhundert: Zum methodologischen Wert der Kastration für die Entdeckung ovarieller Hormone," *Geburtshilfe und Frauenheilkunde* 43, Sonderheft (1983): 54–59, at 57.

35. Medvei, *History of Clinical Endocrinology*, 43.

36. On oophorectomy for hysteria and other "feminine complaints" in the Central European context, see Edward Shorter, "Medizinische Theorien spezifisch weiblicher Nervenkrankheiten im Wandel," in Alfons Labisch and Reinhard Spree, *Medizinische Deutungsmacht im sozialen Wandel des 19. und frühen 20. Jahrhunderts* (Bonn: Psychiatrie-Verlag, 1989), 171–80, here 173–76. On the importance of these operations in inducing endocrinologic investigations, see Hans H. Simmer, "Bilaterale Oophorektomie der Frau."

37. R. Chrobak, "Über Einverleibung von Eierstocksgewebe," *Centralblatt für Gynäkologie* 20 (1896): 521–24, at 522. Chrobak referred to an earlier report by F. Mainzer, "Vorschlag zur Behandlung der Ausfallserscheinungen nach Castration," *Deutsche medizinische Wochenschrift* 22 (1896): 188. Mainzer had reported on the successful treatment of post-oophorectomy symptoms with ovarian extracts and had suggested the same analogy with hypothyroidism. The sequelae of thyroidectomy were well documented by the 1880s and were being treated with thyroid extracts by 1891. Transplants of the thyroid had been attempted by the 1890s. See Medvei, *History of Clinical Endocrinology*, 160–62. On the use of ovarian preparations in turn-of-the-century medicine, see George W. Corner, "The Early History of the Oestrogenic Hormones," *Journal of Endocrinology* 31 (1964–65): iii–xvii, vi; and Hans H. Simmer, "Organotherapie mit Ovarialpräparaten in der Mitte der neunziger Jahre des 19. Jahrhunderts: Medizinische und pharmazeutische Probleme," in Erika Hickel and Gerald Schröder, eds., *Neue Beiträge zur Arzneimittelgeschichte: Festschrift für Wolfgang Schneider zum Geburtstag* (Stuttgart: Wissenschaftliche Verlagsgesellschaft, 1982), 229–64.

38. E. Knauer, "Einige Versuche über Ovarientransplantation bei Kaninchen: Vorläufige Mitteilung," *Centralblatt für Gynäkologie* 20 (1896): 524–28; Knauer, "Zur Ovarientransplantation (Geburt am normalen Ende der Schwangerschaft nach Ovarien-

transplantation beim Kaninchen)," *Centralblatt für Gynäkologie* 22 (1898): 201–203; Knauer, "Über Ovarientransplantation," *Wiener klinische Wochenschrift* 12 (1899): 1219–22. The most comprehensive report issued by Knauer was the one cited by Weininger (478): "Die Ovarientransplantation: Experimentelle Studie," *Archiv für Gynäkologie* 60 (1900): 322–75. On Knauer, see Hermann Knaus, "Emil Knauer, Graz," *Archiv für Gynäkologie* 159 (1935): 429–31. An American gynecologist had already attempted to graft ovaries from one woman to another with some putative success. See Robert T. Morris, "The Ovarian Graft," *New York Medical Journal* 62 (1895): 436–37. Another early report on ovarian transplantation in humans also came from the United States. See James Glass, "An Experiment in Transplantation of the Entire Human Ovary," *Medical News* 74 (1899): 523–25. Glass was acquainted with Knauer's experiments, but Morris apparently was not.

39. Ovarian transplantation became a very popular experiment among European biologists soon after the publication of Knauer's reports. Most results were compatible with Knauer's: grafting was highly successful when the glands were reimplanted in the same animal from which they had been removed (autoplastic grafts). Transplantation of ovaries in a second animal of the same species (homoplastic grafting) was far more difficult, and transplantation in a member of a different species (heteroplastic grafting) virtually always unsuccessful. For a review of these results and of the technical terminology, see W. E. Castle and John C. Phillips, *On Germinal Transplantation in Vertebrates* (Washington, D.C.: Carnegie Institution, 1911), 2–6.

40. J. Halban, Comments on E. Knauer, "Über Ovarientransplantation," *Wiener klinische Wochenschrift* 12 (1899): 1243–44; and Halban, "Über den Einfluss der Ovarien auf die Entwicklung des Genitales (Transplantation von Uterus, Tube, Ovarium)," *Monatsschrift für Geburtshülfe und Gynäkologie* 12 (1900): 496–506. Weininger cited the latter paper (478). On Halban, see Hans H. Simmer, "Josef Halban (1870–1937): Pionier der Endokrinologie der Fortpflanzung," *Wiener medizinische Wochenschrift* 121 (1971): 549–52. Without repudiating his results, Halban later qualified his views on the causal relationship between the internal secretions of the sex glands and the development of secondary sexual characters. See J. Halban, "Die Entstehung der Geschlechtscharaktere: Eine Studie über den formativen Einfluss der Keimdrüse," *Archiv für Gynäkologie* 70 (1903): 205–308, especially 296–304.

41. See George Corner, "Early History of the Oestrogenic Hormones," vi–vii. Weininger points out, however, that these experiments, while strongly indicative of a chemical explanation, did not totally exclude the possibility that the grafts produced their effects due to the reestablishment of nervous connections following revascularization. The strongest evidence against the neural hypothesis, he says, is not the success of ovarian grafts but the fact that one-sided castration had never been shown to produce any effect on the secondary sexual characters (477–78).

42. Aristotle, *History of Animals* 5.14.545a21, trans. D'Arcy W. Thompson, in Jonathan Barnes, ed., *The Complete Works of Aristotle: The Revised Oxford Translation*, 2 vols. (Princeton: Princeton University Press, 1984), 1:861.

43. W. Yarrell, "On the Influence of the Sexual Organ in Modifying External Character," *Journal of the Proceedings of the Linnean Society (Zoology)* 1 (1857): 76–82, at 81. On Yarrell, see Thomas R. Forbes, "William Yarrell, British Naturalist," *Proceedings of the American Philosophical Society* 106 (1962): 505–15.

44. Darwin, *Variation of Animals and Plants under Domestication*, 2:26–27.

45. Ibid., 2:27.

46. A. Weismann, *The Germ-Plasm: A Theory of Heredity*, trans. W. Newton Parker and Harriet Rönnfeldt (New York: Scribner's, 1893), 358–59.

47. H. Sellheim, "Zur Lehre von den sekundären Geschlechtscharakteren," *Beiträge zur Geburtshilfe und Gynäkologie* 1 (1898): 229–55.

48. Ibid., 237.

49. Citing the passage from Aristotle mentioned earlier, Rieger commented that the more one read Aristotle's works, the more one realized the extent of his responsibility for the errors of science. In many ways, remarked Rieger, Aristotle could be described as "the Great Impostor" (K. Rieger, *Die Castration*, 33–34).

50. A. Foges, "Zur Lehre von den secundären Geschlechtscharakteren," *Archiv für die gesammte Physiologie* 93 (1903): 39–58.

51. Biedl, *Internal Secretory Organs*, 378.

52. W. Yarrell, "On the Change in the Plumage of Some Hen-Pheasants," *Philosophical Transactions of the Royal Society of London* 117 (10 May 1827): 268–75, at 269.

53. Ibid., 275.

54. See Darwin, *Variation of Animals and Plants under Domestication*, 2:26; and Hertwig, *Die Zelle und die Gewebe*, 2:162.

55. R. v. Krafft-Ebing, *Psychopathia Sexualis: A Medico-Forensic Study*, 12th ed., 304–24, at 314.

56. Ibid., 324–26.

57. The failure of experimental efforts to transplant testes into female animals suggested, according to Weininger, that the sex glands could not act upon an inappropriate idioplasmic substrate (484). This was a fairly well-known phenomenon among biologists at the time, and concepts of tissue-typing and graft-rejection were not yet available. Artur Foges recorded his own graft failures in "Zur Lehre von den secundären Geschlechtscharakteren," 53–54. Much later, however, another Viennese scientist, Eugen Steinach (1861–1944) claimed success in such cross-gender transplantations. Between 1910 and 1920, Steinach claimed to have created a series of feminized males, masculinized females, and artificial hermaphrodites among rats and guinea pigs by castration and transplantation of sex glands. Although there is no adequate study of Steinach's work, see his intellectual autobiography, *Sex and Life: Forty Years of Biological and Medical Experiments* (New York: Viking, 1940); and Artur Biedl, *Innere Sekretion: Ihre physiologischen Grundlagen und ihre Bedeutung für die Pathologie*, 2d ed., 2 vols. (Berlin: Urban and Schwarzenberg, 1913), 2:199–343. Generally on historical issues of transplantation and immunity, see Michael F. A. Woodruff, *The Transplantation of Tissues and Organs* (Springfield, Ill: Thomas, 1960).

58. Weininger's theory (or even his name) is not mentioned in any well-known Central European work on the biology or endocrinology of sexuality published between 1900 and 1930. I have examined the following: Julius Tandler and Siegfried Grosz, *Die biologischen Grundlagen der sekundären Geschlechtscharaktere* (Berlin: Springer, 1913); Artur Biedl, *Innere Sekretion*, 2d ed. (1913); Hermann Zondek, *Die Krankheiten der endokrinen Drüsen: Ein Lehrbuch für Studierende und Ärzte* (Berlin: Springer, 1926); Julius Bauer, *Innere Sekretion: Ihre Physiologie, Pathologie und Klinik* (Berlin: Springer, 1927); and all publications of Eugen Steinach. Scientists' silence on Weininger can, of course, be attributed to a number of reasons, ranging from their lack of acquaintance with a "philosophical" work to revulsion at the metaphysical tenor of its later pages. Most importantly however, as Allan Janik points out, Weininger's stress on idioplasmic sexuality was scientifically obsolescent by

1903 and his treatment of the internal secretions would not have been impressive enough in the rapidly changing scientific climate. From an "internalist" perspective, the historian of science can safely dismiss Weininger's biological theory of sex as a failure, or, at best, a curiosity.

59. F. H. A. Marshall, *The Physiology of Reproduction*, 2d ed. (London: Longmans, 1922), 690. It is ironic that Marshall criticized Weininger's views as "somewhat too morphologically conceived" and did not mention Weininger's ideas on the role of the internal secretions. There is a simple reason for this. Marshall seems to have been familiar only with the English translation of *Geschlecht und Charakter*. Most of Weininger's endocrinologic hypotheses were presented in long endnotes, all of which were omitted from the English version.

60. E. A. Minchin, "Protozoa," *Encyclopaedia Britannica*, 11th ed. (1911), 22:479–89, at 486.

61. Weininger borrowed the term "sexual affinity" from biologists Oscar and Richard Hertwig. The Hertwigs had used the term as a chemical metaphor to indicate the factor determining successful fertilization of gametes in cross-breeding experiments. They believed that this affinity depended upon the "constitution or the inner organization of the gametes." See O. and R. Hertwig, *Experimentelle Untersuchungen über die Bedingungen der Bastardbefruchtung*, vol. 4 of *Untersuchungen zur Morphologie und Physiologie der Zelle* (Jena: Fischer, 1885), 44. See also Oscar Hertwig, *Die Zelle und die Gewebe*, 1:240–41. Weininger emphasized that he defined the term much more broadly.

62. See Peter O'Donald, *Genetic Models of Sexual Selection* (Cambridge: Cambridge University Press, 1980). The theory of sexual selection remained marginal to evolutionary biology until the 1970s. See ibid., 15–22; and Bernard G. Campbell, ed., *Sexual Selection and the Descent of Man, 1871–1971* (Chicago: Aldine, 1972).

63. Darwin, *Descent of Man*, 2:95–96. Darwin consistently maintained that male choice, even if it was a factor in sexual selection, was less important than female choice (ibid., 2:260). "The general impression among breeders," he remarked, "seems to be that the male accepts any female; and this, owing to his eagerness, is in most cases probably the truth. Whether the female as a general rule indifferently accepts any male is much more doubtful" (ibid., 2:256).

64. Darwin's insistence on female choice was controversial from the beginning. Even his otherwise staunch supporter Alfred Russel Wallace rejected the hypothesis. Aesthetic choice, said Wallace, was an exclusively human trait. Moreover, even if females preferred certain kinds of ornamentation, that did not directly influence their choice of mate. Wallace pointed out anthropomorphically that women preferred their lovers to be well dressed but that had not determined the variety of human male costumes through history. Other critics of Darwin, such as St. George Jackson Mivart, were overtly misogynistic: even if females chose their mates on aesthetic grounds, female taste was too fickle—Mivart spoke of the "instability of a vicious feminine caprice"—to cause any lasting biological change in the male. On these issues, see Helena Cronin, *The Ant and the Peacock: Altruism and Sexual Selection from Darwin to Today* (Cambridge: Cambridge University Press, 1991), 165–81, at 172.

65. His Law, Weininger clarified, did not indicate a force drawing individuals together. It was merely an empirical expression of a relation observable in each strong sexual bond (35). Technically, the Law indicated an "invariant" (490). Nineteenth-century geometricians had begun to put figures, as it were, in motion, to determine their mutual relations. After such "projections," certain relations of the figures remained unchanged ("invariant")

while others, expectedly enough, changed. The study of such invariant relations and the metaphor of the invariant soon became common in economics and even political science. See John T. Merz, *A History of European Thought in the Nineteenth Century,* 4 vols. (Edinburgh: Blackwood, 1928), 2:676–77.

66. Weininger firmly separated sex from love. As we have seen, he considered love to be an exclusively mental and exclusively male phenomenon, in which a man projected the image of his own ideal (not necessarily real) self on to a woman and unconsciously loved "himself" in her (49–50). This psychological conception of love had little to do with biological sexuality, but Weininger did occasionally point out analogies between the two, without spelling out the criteria for determining the legitimacy of such analogies (322–23).

67. "Physiologists," Schopenhauer had argued, "know that manliness and womanliness admit of innumerable degrees. . . . Accordingly, the neutralization, here under discussion, of the two individualities by each other requires that the particular degree of his manliness shall correspond exactly to the particular degree of her womanliness, so that the one-sidedness of each exactly cancels that of the other. Accordingly, the most manly man will look for the most womanly woman and vice versa" (A. Schopenhauer, *The World as Will and Representation,* trans. E. F. J. Payne, 2 vols. [New York: Dover, 1966)] 2:546, emphases in the original). On Schopenhauer's analysis of sexuality, see Wolfram Bernhard, "Schopenhauer und die moderne Charakterologie," *Schopenhauer-Jahrbuch* 44 (1963): 25–133, especially 74–85. Albert Moll's statement was much more cursory than Schopenhauer's. He had merely observed that there were all possible transitional forms (*alle möglichen Übergänge*) between the typically female desire for fully developed males and the typically male desire for fully developed females. See A. Moll, *Untersuchungen über die Libido sexualis* (Berlin: Fischer's medicinische Buchhandlung, 1897), 193.

68. This hypothesis has been rejected by contemporary botanists, who agree, however, that heterostyly reinforces existing physiological barriers to self-fertilization. See S. C. H. Barrett, ed., *Evolution and Function of Heterostyly* (Berlin: Springer-Verlag, 1992), especially R. Ornduff, "Historical Perspectives on Heterostyly," 31–39; and H. L. K. Whitehouse, "Cross- and Self-Fertilization in Plants," in R. Bell, ed., *Darwin's Biological Work: Some Aspects Reconsidered* (Cambridge: Cambridge University Press, 1959), 207–61.

69. C. Darwin, *The Different Forms of Flowers on Plants of the Same Species* (New York: Appleton, 1877), 1–277; and J. Sachs, *Vorlesungen über Pflanzen-Physiologie* (Leipzig: Engelmann, 1882), 968–71. Julius Sachs (1832–97) was Professor of Botany at the University of Würzburg and was "the central figure in German botany from the mid-1860s to the mid-1880s." See Eugene Cittadino, *Nature as the Laboratory: Darwinian Plant Ecology in the German Empire, 1880–1900* (Cambridge: Cambridge University Press, 1990), 18–25, at 18.

70. Darwin, *Different Forms of Flowers,* 256, 287, 296. Having found that the small anthers of the short-stamened (and long-styled) form of one flower produced "bad pollen-grains," Darwin had concluded that "this form is tending to become female." Such an evolutionary sequence, Darwin felt, was by no means the rule among heterostyled flowers but, he observed, "they offer singular facilities . . . for such conversion; and this appears occasionally to have been the case" (258).

71. Weininger was merely following Darwin in correlating larger pollen size with masculinity, but the idea of the "selectivity" of the stigma was his own. See Darwin, *Different Forms of Flowers,* 186. For novelist Marcel Proust's similar use of botanical metaphors to

explain the diversity of human sexual choice, see Rina Viers, "Évolution et sexualité des plantes dans 'Sodome et Gomorrhe,'" *Europe: Revue Mensuelle*, nos. 502–503 (February–March 1971): 100–113.

72. Although Weininger did not emphasize his originality in framing human sexual attraction in algebraic terms, no biologist or medical sexologist of the time seems to have attempted anything similar. Ian Hacking has observed that in the nineteenth century, "the numbering of the world was occurring in every branch of human inquiry." Weininger's Law and equations, of course, had less to do with numbers than with a more general urge for quantification and mathematical expression. Nevertheless, Weininger's Law would fall within Hacking's definition of a law: "Any equations with some constant numbers in them. They are positivist regularities, the intended harvest of science" (I. Hacking, *The Taming of Chance* [Cambridge: Cambridge University Press, 1990], 60, 63).

73. Biologists Oscar and Richard Hertwig, Weininger remarked, had found that if an ovum was brought into contact with spermatozoa immediately on its release from the ovary, the chances of fertilization were poor. The later the fertilization was attempted (up to about thirty hours after the expulsion of the ovum from the ovary), the higher the rate of successful fertilization. See O. and R. Hertwig, *Experimentelle Untersuchungen über die Bedingungen der Bastardbefruchtung,* 37–38. This, to say the least, was a very strange choice of supporting material. Weininger's thesis turned on the time of interaction between the two hypothetical individuals. The Hertwigs, on the other hand, reported that the entities had to be kept apart for a certain period in order to ensure successful reproduction.

74. W. Pfeffer, "Lokomotorische Richtungsbewegungen durch chemische Reize," *Untersuchungen aus dem botanischen Institut zu Tübingen* 1 (1885): 363–482, especially 474. On the significance of Pfeffer's experiments on irritability, see H. Kniep, "Wilhelm Pfeffer's Bedeutung für die Reizphysiologie," *Die Naturwissenschaften* 3 (1915): 124–29.

75. See chapter 7, note 71.

76. On Mendel's work, its rediscovery, and its impact, see Robert Olby, *Origins of Mendelism,* 2d ed. (Chicago: University of Chicago Press, 1985); and Peter J. Bowler, *The Mendelian Revolution: The Emergence of Hereditarian Concepts in Modern Science and Society* (Baltimore, Md.: Johns Hopkins University Press, 1989), 110–27. On the identification of the sex chromosome, see John Farley, *Gametes and Spores: Ideas about Sexual Reproduction, 1750–1914* (Baltimore, Md.: Johns Hopkins University Press, 1982), 220–21.

77. J. Maienschein, "What Determines Sex? A Study of Convergent Research Approaches, 1880–1916," *Isis* 75 (1984): 457–80, especially 476–80. See also T. H. Morgan, "Recent Theories in Regard to the Determination of Sex," *Popular Science Monthly* 64 (1903): 97–116; Garland E. Allen, "Thomas Hunt Morgan and the Problem of Sex Determination, 1903–1910," *Proceedings of the American Philosophical Society* 110 (1966): 48–57; and John Farley, *Gametes and Spores,* 218–51. References to sex chromosomes and their role in sex-determination were rare in the work of Central European scientists during the first decade of the twentieth century. For an excellent overview of the many controversies among Central European biologists regarding the determination and inheritance of sex around 1900, see M. von Lenhossék, *Das Problem der geschlechtsbestimmenden Ursachen* (Jena: Fischer, 1903).

78. Darwin, *Variation,* 2:2, 25. For terminological and contextual information on the concepts of "dormancy" and "latency" as used by Darwin and other contemporary biolo-

gists, see Margaret Campbell, "The Concepts of Dormancy, Latency, and Dominance in Nineteenth-Century Biology," *Journal of the History of Biology* 16 (1983): 409–31.

79. Darwin, *Variation,* 2:35–36. Later in the treatise, Darwin explained latency with his controversial "provisional hypothesis of pangenesis" (2:393–94).

80. Weismann, *The Germ-Plasm,* 357–59.

81. For a vehemently "presentist" but magnificently erudite commentary, see Howard B. Adelmann, *Marcello Malpighi and the Evolution of Embryology,* 5 vols. (Ithaca: Cornell University Press, 1966), 4:1758–2057. See also Walther Felix and Anton Bühler, "Die Entwicklung der Keimdrüsen und ihrer Ausführungsgänge," in Oscar Hertwig, ed., *Handbuch der vergleichenden und experimentellen Entwickelungslehre der Wirbelthiere,* 3 vols. in 4 (Jena: Fischer, 1906), 3, pt. 1:619–896. On nineteenth-century embryological research in general, see Frederick B. Churchill, "The Rise of Classical Descriptive Embryology," in Scott F. Gilbert, ed., *A Conceptual History of Modern Embryology* (New York: Plenum, 1991), 1–29.

82. Weininger relied greatly on the historical sections of W. Nagel, "Über die Entwickelung des Urogenitalsystems des Menschen," *Archiv für mikroskopische Anatomie* 34 (1889): 269–385, especially 299–305 on the testes and the ovary and 375–81 on the external genitalia.

83. Weininger's recent biographer, Jacques Le Rider, has accused him of relying on the outmoded views of earlier scientists such as Rathke (*Der Fall Otto Weininger,* 68). A closer examination of the notes in *Geschlecht und Charakter* shows that Weininger did not rely on Rathke or on other earlier embryologists for evidence. Rather, he used their views to chart the development of the current consensus on the subject, as given in Hertwig's textbook.

84. F. Tiedemann, *Anatomie der kopflosen Missgeburten* (Landshut: Thomann, 1813), 79–80, 83–84.

85. See T. Lenoir, *The Strategy of Life: Teleology and Mechanics in Nineteenth-Century German Biology* (Dordrecht: Reidel, 1982), 54–111.

86. H. Rathke, "Beobachtungen und Betrachtungen über die Entwicklung der Geschlechtswerkzeuge bei den Wirbelthieren," *Neueste Schriften der naturforschenden Gesellschaft in Danzig* 1 (1825): 1–145, at 120–21.

87. W. Waldeyer, *Eierstock und Ei: Ein Beitrag zur Anatomie und Entwicklungsgeschichte der Sexualorgane* (Leipzig: Engelmann, 1870), 152–53. On his versatile career, see J. Sobotta, "Zum Andenken an Wilhelm von Waldeyer-Hartz," *Anatomischer Anzeiger* 56 (1922): 1–53. Debates over the sexual status of the early embryo did not, of course, cease after Waldeyer, nor was there any immediate, universal revision of "neutralist" terminology. For a concise review of continuing disagreements over embryonic sexual development, see Gustav Born, "Die Entwickelung der Geschlechtsdrüsen," *Ergebnisse der Anatomie und Entwickelungsgeschichte* 4 (1894): 592–616. One contentious point concerned the differentiation of the testes and the ovaries. Were these glands distinct from the time they first appeared or was the first gonad an undifferentiated one from which either the testis or the ovary developed gradually? See ibid., 615–16.

88. See, for example, these leading popular and technical texts: Oscar Hertwig, *Lehrbuch der Entwicklungsgeschichte des Menschen und der Wirbeltiere,* 8th ed. (Jena: Fischer, 1906), 320; Patrick Geddes and J. Arthur Thomson, *The Evolution of Sex* (New York: Scribner's, [1889]), 32–33, 78–79; Robert Müller, *Sexualbiologie* (Berlin: Marcus, 1907), 177; and Artur Biedl, *The Internal Secretory Organs: Their Physiology and Pathology,* 358, 363.

89. O. Hertwig, *Lehrbuch der Entwicklungsgeschichte des Menschen und der Wir-beltiere,* 8th ed., 446. Weininger used the 7th edition of 1902, which was not available to me.

90. "One would be justified in saying that female genitals are male genitals that did not reach full development [die weiblichen Genitalien sind nicht zur Ausbildung gelangte männliche Genitalien] and are stuck at a lower stage of development, which would be normal only in the early life of the embryo" (Tiedemann, *Anatomie der kopflosen Missgeburten,* 83–84).

91. H. Rathke, "Beobachtungen und Betrachtungen," 127–30. Borrowing the concept and the phrase of the Naturphilosoph Gotthilf Heinrich von Schubert, Rathke remarked that it was as if the male had undergone one extra metamorphosis. See G. H. v. Schubert, *Ahndungen einer allgemeinen Geschichte des Lebens,* 2 vols. in 3 (Leipzig: Carl Heinrich Reclam, 1806–21), 1:182.

92. O. Hertwig, *Lehrbuch der Entwicklungsgeschichte,* 460. My discussion here parallels Anne Fausto-Sterling's approach to current biological theories and texts. See her study, *Myths of Gender: Biological Theories about Women and Men* (New York: Basic Books, 1985).

### Chapter Five

1. See Vern L. Bullough, *Homosexuality: A History* (New York: New American Library, 1979); Jeffrey Weeks, *Sex, Politics, and Society: The Regulation of Sexuality since 1800,* 2d ed. (London: Longman, 1989), especially 96–121; and Martin Bauml Duberman, Martha Vicinus, and George Chauncey Jr., eds., *Hidden from History: Reclaiming the Gay and Lesbian Past* (New York: New American Library, 1989). For the sake of convenience, I use the word "homosexuality" throughout as a generic term including homosexual acts, psychological orientation, and sexual preference. This does not reflect the complexities of nineteenth-century terminology and conceptualization, for a comprehensive review of which see Havelock Ellis, *Studies in the Psychology of Sex,* 2 vols. (New York: Random House, 1936), 1, pt. 4 *(Sexual Inversion):* 310–17.

2. See John Lauritsen and David Thorstad, *The Early Homosexual Rights Movement (1864–1935)* (New York: Times Change Press, 1974); James D. Steakley, *The Homosexual Emancipation Movement in Germany* (New York: Arno, 1975); Steakley, "Iconography of a Scandal: Political Cartoons and the Eulenburg Affair in Wilhelmine Germany," in Duberman, Vicinus, and Chauncey Jr., eds., *Hidden from History,* 233–57; and John C. Fout, "Sexual Politics in Wilhelmine Germany: The Male Gender Crisis, Moral Purity, and Homophobia," *Journal of the History of Sexuality* 2 (1992): 388–41. For a first-hand account of the movement by one of its leading figures, see Magnus Hirschfeld, *Von einst bis jetzt: Geschichte einer homosexuellen Bewegung 1897–1922,* ed. Manfred Herzer and James Steakley (Berlin: Verlag Rosa Winkel, 1986). On homosexual subcultures in Weininger's Vienna, see Magnus Hirschfeld, "Die Homosexualität in Wien," *Wiener klinische Rundschau* 15 (1901): 788–90; and Hanna Hacker and Manfred Lang, "Jenseits der Geschlechter, zwischen ihnen: Homosexualitäten im Wien der Jahrhundertwende," in Neda Bei et al., eds., *Das lila Wien um 1900: Zur Ästhetik der Homosexualitäten* (Vienna: Promedia, 1986), 8–18.

3. On medical theories of homosexuality in Central Europe, see Frank J. Sulloway, *Freud, Biologist of the Mind: Beyond the Psychoanalytic Legend* (New York: Basic Books, 1979), 277–319; David F. Greenberg, *The Construction of Homosexuality* (Chicago: University of Chicago Press, 1988), 397–433; and Arnold I. Davidson, "Closing Up the

Corpses: Diseases of Sexuality and the Emergence of the Psychiatric Style of Reasoning," in George Boolos, ed., *Meaning and Method: Essays in Honor of Hilary Putnam* (Cambridge: Cambridge University Press, 1990), 295–325; and the essays in Vernon A. Rosario, ed., *Science and Homosexualities* (London: Routledge, 1997).

4. Female homosexuality assumed importance for Weininger only when he discussed feminist movements and the Woman Question. On female homosexuality in fin-de-siècle Central Europe, see Ilse Kokula, ed., *Weibliche Homosexualität um 1900 in zeitgenössischen Dokumenten* (Munich: Frauenoffensive, 1981), 9–79; and Katharina Rowold, "A Male Mind in a Female Body: Sexology, Homosexuality, and the Woman Question in Germany, 1869–1914," in Kurt Bayertz and Roy Porter, eds., *From Physico-Theology to Bio-Technology: Essays in the Social and Cultural History of Biosciences*, 153–79.

5. Weininger misread a reference to Féré in Albert Moll's *Untersuchungen über die Libido sexualis*, 651, n. 3. Moll's passage discussed Féré's belief that homosexuality was a congenital phenomenon caused by degeneration. See the article mentioned by Moll, which Weininger cited without consulting: C. Féré, "La Descendance d'un inverti: Contribution à l'hygiene de l'inversion sexuelle" *Revue génerale de clinique et de thérapeutique*, 2d ser., 10 (1898): 561–65. Weininger did consult Féré's monograph, *L'Instinct sexuel: Evolution et dissolution* (Paris: Alcan, 1899) and, rather surprised by its stress on congenital factors in homosexuality, assumed that Féré had changed his views (497).

6. The psychologist Alfred Binet (1857–1911), whom Weininger did not cite, was one of the leading proponents of the view that sexual "perversions" were not innate but arose due to "accidental" psychological associations. Dealing primarily with the phenomenon he christened fetishism, Binet traced the "perversions" to early childhood experiences. Even Binet conceded, however, that a generalized *predisposition* to perversion (as opposed to the specific perversion itself) could well be inherited. See A. Binet, "Le Fétichisme dans l'amour," *Revue philosophique* 24 (1887): 143–67, 252–74; especially 153, 164, and, on homosexuality, 164–67.

7. A. von Schrenck-Notzing, *Die Suggestions-Therapie bei krankhaften Erscheinungen des Geschlechtssinnes mit besonderer Berücksichtigung der conträren Sexualempfindung* (Stuttgart: Enke, 1892), 150, 157–59, 193. See also Havelock Ellis, *Studies in the Psychology of Sex*, 1, pt. 4:271.

8. E. Kraepelin, *Psychiatrie: Ein kurzes Lehrbuch für Studierende und Ärzte*, 4th ed. (Leipzig: Abel, 1893), 689–92. Kraepelin reiterated this belief even in the last edition of his famous textbook. See Kraepelin, *Psychiatrie: Ein Lehrbuch für Studierende und Ärzte*, 8th ed., 4 vols (Leipzig: Barth, 1909–15), 4 (1915): 1952–60.

9. This point is made without adequate historical substantiation by Ruth Leys, "The Real Miss Beauchamp: Gender and the Subject of Imitation," in Judith Butler and Joan W. Scott, eds., *Feminists Theorize the Political* (New York: Routledge, 1992), 167–214, at 209.

10. I. Bloch, *Das Sexualleben unserer Zeit in seinen Beziehungen zur modernen Kultur*, 590–91; M. Hirschfeld, *Die Homosexualität des Mannes und des Weibes*, 2d ed. (Berlin: Marcus, 1920), 187, 193–94; and Hirschfeld, "Die Ursachen und Wesen des Uranismus," *Jahrbuch für sexuelle Zwischenstufen* 5 (1903): 1–193, at 5. Hirschfeld also constructed a separate category of "bisexuality": while a pseudohomosexual was simply capable of being potent with members of his own sex, the bisexual possessed an inner sexual drive directed toward both sexes. See Hirschfeld, *Die Homosexualität*, 199–200. Michel Foucault described the construction of a "genuine" homosexual identity in a memorable passage: "The nineteenth-century homosexual became a personage, a past, a case history, and a child-

hood, in addition to being a type of life, a life form, and a morphology, with an indiscreet anatomy and possibly a mysterious physiology" (Foucault, *The History of Sexuality,* vol. 1: *An Introduction,* 43).

11. M. Dessoir, "Zur Psychologie der Vita sexualis," *Allgemeine Zeitschrift für Psychiatrie* 50 (1894): 941–75, especially 941–42; Ellis, *Studies,* 1, pt. 4:79–81; A. Moll, *Untersuchungen über die Libido sexualis,* 420–28; Moll, *The Sexual Life of the Child* (original publication 1908), trans. Eden Paul (New York: Macmillan, 1929), 60–63. Moll was one of the most prominent sexologists of the period, even though he has been largely forgotten today. On Moll, see Frank Sulloway, *Freud,* 299–305; and Christina Schröder, "Ein Lebenswerk im Schatten der Psychoanalyse? Zum 50. Todestag des Sexualwissenschaftlers, Psychotherapeuten und Medizinethikers Albert Moll (1862–1939)," *Wissenschaftliche Zeitschrift, Karl-Marx-Universität, Mathematisch-naturwissenschaftliche Reihe* 38 (1989): 434–44.

12. Sigmund Freud would later offer a similar argument. See S. Freud, *Fragment of an Analysis of a Case of Hysteria* (1905 [1901]), *Standard Edition,* 7:1–122, at 60; Freud, *Three Essays on the Theory of Sexuality* (1905), *Standard Edition,* 7:123–245, at 229.

13. He did not cite authorities, but he would have been familiar with them from Albert Moll's *Untersuchungen über die Libido sexualis,* assuming that he had read it with greater care than in the case of Féré.

14. Ellis, *Studies,* 1, pt. 4:83. The situation was even more complicated than Ellis's analysis might suggest. Albert Moll, who believed that homosexuality could not be acquired late in life, denied, nevertheless, that all cases of homosexual behavior occurring for the first time late in life were due to a latent inborn homosexuality. For Moll, what was inborn in such cases was a weakness of *heterosexuality.* This weakness could lead to homosexual behavior in conducive circumstances. In other cases, he argued, homosexuality was both congenital and acquired: the innate factor was a generalized predisposition or nervous lability, while the homosexual orientation itself was learnt. With different life experiences, the same general nervous lability could give rise to other "perversions" (such as sadism) instead of homosexuality. This argument was essentially identical to that of Binet, Schrenck-Notzing, and Kraepelin, the putative believers in acquired homosexuality. See A. Moll, *Untersuchungen über die Libido sexualis,* 485; Moll, *Behandlung der Homosexualität: Biochemisch oder psychisch?* (Bonn: A. Marcus and E. Weber, 1921), 22.

15. This simplified account should be supplemented by Annemarie Wettley and Werner Leibbrand, *Von der "Psychopathia sexualis" zur Sexualwissenschaft* (Stuttgart: Enke, 1959), 45–55; Annemarie Wettley, "Zur Problemgeschichte der 'Dégénérescence,'" *Sudhoffs Archiv für Geschichte der Medizin und der Naturwissenschaften* 43 (1959): 193–212; Françoise Castel, "Dégénérescence et structures: Réflexions méthodologiques à propos de l'oeuvre de Magnan," *Annales médico-psychologiques* 125 (1967): 521–36; and Ian Dowbiggin, "Degeneration and Hereditarianism in French Mental Medicine, 1840–90: Psychiatric Theory as Ideological Adaptation," in W. F. Bynum, Roy Porter, and Michael Shepherd, eds., *The Anatomy of Madness: Essays in the History of Psychiatry,* 3 vols. (London: Tavistock, 1985–88), 1:188–232.

16. On the sociocultural dimensions of the "degeneration" diagnosis, see Daniel Pick, *Faces of Degeneration: A European Disorder, c. 1848–c. 1918* (Cambridge: Cambridge University Press, 1989); and the essays in J. E. Chamberlin and S. L. Gilman, eds., *Degeneration: The Dark Side of Progress* (New York: Columbia University Press, 1985).

17. C. F. O. Westphal, "Die conträre Sexualempfindung: Symptom eines neuropathischen (psychopathischen) Zustandes," *Archiv für Psychiatrie und Nervenkrankheiten* 2

(1869): 73–108, 107. Westphal's nomenclature (*Die conträre Sexualempfindung*, often translated as "antipathic sexuality" by English-speaking physicians of the nineteenth century) was suggested to him by an unidentified classicist (see ibid., 107) and was accepted by the majority of German-speaking physicians in the subsequent decades. The term *Homosexualität* (homosexuality), coined in the same year by the Hungarian writer and physician Karl Maria Kertbeny (1824–1882), became the preferred term only much later. On Kertbeny and his coinage, see Manfred Herzer, "Kertbeny and the Nameless Love," *Journal of Homosexuality* 12, no. 1 (1985): 1–26; Jean-Claude Féray and Manfred Herzer, "Homosexual Studies and Politics in the 19th Century: Karl Maria Kertbeny," trans. Glen W. Peppel, *Journal of Homosexuality* 19, no. 1 (1990): 23–47.

18. R. v. Krafft-Ebing, "Über gewisse Anomalien des Geschlechtstriebs und die klinisch-forensische Verwerthung derselben als eines wahrscheinlich functionellen Degenerationszeichens des centralen Nerven-Systems," *Archiv für Psychiatrie und Nervenkrankheiten* 7 (1877): 291–312, especially 305–12. "Functional" was, of course, opposed to the standard "physical" stigmata of degeneration, such as cleft-lip or misshapen ears. Other "functional" signs of degeneration were an abnormally early awakening of sexual desire, extraordinarily strong sexual urges, or, surprisingly from today's perspective, epilepsy.

19. The 12th edition of *Psychopathia Sexualis*, published posthumously in 1902, continued to describe homosexuality as a functional sign of degeneration. See R. v. Krafft-Ebing, *Psychopathia Sexualis: A Medico-Forensic Study*, 12th ed., anonymous trans. (New York: Pioneer, 1939), 347–50. In the year before his death Krafft-Ebing had declared that homosexuality, "in and of itself," was neither a disease nor a degeneration. He did not, however, reject degenerate heredity as the *ultimate cause* of homosexuality. See Krafft-Ebing, "Neue Studien auf dem Gebiete der Homosexualität," *Jahrbuch für sexuelle Zwischenstufen* 3 (1901): 1–36, at 5–7. Albert Moll maintained that Krafft-Ebing had always regarded homosexual orientation as the product of an abnormal organic predisposition. See Wettley and Leibbrand, *Von der "Psychopathia sexualis,"* 67, 96. Havelock Ellis and Iwan Bloch, on the other hand, believed that Krafft-Ebing had recanted degenerationism in toto. See Ellis, *Studies*, 1, pt. 4:70; and Bloch, *Das Sexualleben unserer Zeit*, 538–39. For a recent argument favoring the latter interpretation, see Frank Sulloway, *Freud*, 295–96. Generally on Krafft-Ebing's career and sexological theories, see Renate Hauser, "Sexuality, Neurasthenia, and the Law: Richard von Krafft-Ebing (1840–1902)" (Ph.D. diss., University College London, 1992); and Harry Oosterhuis, "Richard von Krafft-Ebing's 'Step-Children of Nature': Psychiatry and the Making of Homosexual Identity," in Rosario, ed., *Science and Homosexualities*, 67–88.

20. See Krafft-Ebing, *Psychopathia Sexualis*, 245–46.

21. Sulloway, *Freud*, 290–96.

22. See Hubert Kennedy, *Ulrichs: The Life and Works of Karl Heinrich Ulrichs, Pioneer of the Modern Gay Movement* (Boston: Alyson, 1988).

23. Pausanias had distinguished between two kinds of love associated with two Aphrodites. The "heavenly" Aphrodite was the daughter of Uranus alone and had no mother. She inspired the love of male youths (but not immature boys) by men. The "common" Aphrodite was the daughter of Zeus and Dione: she moved "the meaner sort of men," and the love she inspired did not discriminate between women and youths. It also "preferred the body rather than the soul." See Plato, *Symposium*, in Benjamin Jowett trans. and ed., *The Dialogues of Plato*, 4th ed., 4 vols. (Oxford: Clarendon Press, 1953), 1:503–55, at 512–13. Ulrichs named his homosexual men "Urnings" and his heterosexual men

"Dionings." This dichotomy, evidently, is absent from the Platonic conception. Ulrichs's Dioning, unlike Plato's, was exclusively heterosexual and his Urning was far from being interested only in the soul.

24. K. H. Ulrichs, *Memnon* (1868), 184; *Formatrix* (1865), 62–78, both in Ulrichs, *Forschungen über das Rätsel der mannmännliche Liebe* (Leipzig: Spohr, 1898; rpt., New York: Arno, 1975).

25. See Hubert C. Kennedy, "The 'Third Sex' Theory of Karl Heinrich Ulrichs," in Salvatore Licata and Robert Petersen, eds., *Historical Perspectives on Homosexuality* (New York: Haworth Press/Stein and Day, 1981), 103–11.

26. See Westphal, "Die conträre Sexualempfindung," 92–94; Krafft-Ebing, *Psychopathia Sexualis: Eine klinisch-forensische Studie*, 1st ed. (Stuttgart: Enke, 1886), 58.

27. E. Gley, "Les Aberrations de l'instinct sexuel d'après des travaux récents," *Revue philosophique* 17 (1884): 66–92, at 92; V. Magnan, "Des anomalies, des aberrations et des perversions sexuelles," *Annales médico-psychologiques*, 7th ser., 1 (1885): 447–74, at 462; J.-M. Charcot and V. Magnan, "Inversion du sens génital," *Archives de neurologie* 3 (1882): 53–60; 4 (1882): 296–322, at 301–302.

28. K. H. Ulrichs, "Vier Briefe von Karl Heinrich Ulrichs (Numa Numantius) an seine Verwandten," *Jahrbuch für sexuelle Zwischenstufen* 1 (1899): 36–70, 64–69.

29. J. G. Kiernan, "Insanity. Lecture XXVI: Sexual Perversion," *Detroit Lancet* 7 (1884): 481–84.

30. Kiernan defined masculinity by the standard nineteenth-century criterion: the presence of testicular tissue in *any* location. See Franz Ludwig von Neugebauer, *Hermaphroditismus beim Menschen* (Leipzig: Klinkhardt, 1908), for many examples of such "males" with female external genitals, or "male pseudohermaphrodites." Conversely, a female pseudohermaphrodite possessed ovarian tissue but had "male" external genitalia. Michel Foucault has commented that in the nineteenth century, "everybody was to have one and only one sex." The physician, when faced with a hermaphrodite, aimed to uncover "the true sex that was hidden beneath ambiguous appearances. . . . For someone who knew how to observe and to conduct an examination, these mixtures of sex were no more than disguises of nature: hermaphrodites were always 'pseudohermaphrodites'" (M. Foucault, "Introduction," in Foucault, ed., *Herculine Barbin, being the Recently Discovered Memoirs of a Nineteenth-Century French Hermaphrodite*, trans. Richard McDougall [New York: Pantheon, 1980], vii–xvii., at viii–ix).

31. Kiernan, "Sexual Perversion and the Whitechapel Murders," *Medical Standard* 4 (1888): 129–30, 170–72, at 129–30.

32. G. F. Lydston, "A Lecture on Sexual Perversion, Satyriasis and Nymphomania," in Lydston, *Addresses and Essays*, 2d ed. (Louisville, Ky: Renz and Henry, 1892), 243–64, at 247.

33. Moll, *Untersuchungen über die Libido sexualis*, 670.

34. Julien Chevalier, *Une maladie de la personnalité: L'Inversion sexuelle* (Paris: Masson, 1893), 409–11.

35. Ibid., 422.

36. R. v. Krafft-Ebing, "Zur Erklärung der conträren Sexualempfindung," *Jahrbücher für Psychiatrie und Neurologie* 13 (1895): 1–16. Krafft-Ebing also reviewed these theories in his *Psychopathia Sexualis*, 12th ed., 342–46. Interestingly, a patient of his had also worked out a very similar theory. See Krafft-Ebing, *Psychopathia Sexualis mit besonderer Berücksichtigung der conträren Sexualempfindung: Eine klinisch-forensische Studie*, 8th ed. (Stuttgart: Enke, 1893), 227–30.

37. R. v. Krafft-Ebing, "Zur Erklärung der conträren Sexualempfindung," 3–4.

38. Krafft-Ebing believed that each sex had a "normal" psychosexual personality characterized by heterosexual desire. Even senility or castration in adult life could not change this "personality." On the other hand, the "psychosexual personality" could be "abnormal" (i.e., homosexual) even when the sex glands and the genitalia were perfectly normal.

39. See Krafft-Ebing, "Zur Erklärung der conträren Sexualempfindung," 5–6, 14–16. In the 1901 article where he denied that homosexuality was a degeneration in and of itself, he described the developmental process in identical terms, without indicating why it broke down in homosexuals. See Krafft-Ebing, "Neue Studien auf dem Gebiete der Homosexualität."

40. "After 1900," Frank Sulloway emphasizes, "the theory of degeneration was retained by many theorists as a subsidiary concept" (Sulloway, *Freud*, 297). Once again, the views of Albert Moll attest to the complexity of the situation. Moll agreed with the essentials of the developmental theory, denied that every homosexual came from tainted stock, and criticized the tendency to conceptualize hereditary predisposition so widely that virtually every human being could be shown to possess one. See A. Moll, *Die konträre Sexualempfindung*, 1st ed. (Berlin: Fischer's medicinische Buchhandlung, 1891), 162. And yet Moll maintained that in most cases of homosexuality, he had found severe hereditary taints, indicated by high incidences of insanity, suicide, hysteria, and epilepsy in the family; see Moll, "Die Behandlung der Homosexualität" *Jahrbuch für sexuelle Zwischenstufen* 2 (1900): 1–29, at 9; and Moll, ed., *Handbuch der Sexualwissenschaften*, 3d ed., 2 vols. (Leipzig: F. C. W. Vogel, 1926), 2:772. French psychiatrists, however, remained explicitly committed to degenerationism well into the twentieth century. Valentin Magnan reiterated in 1914 that homosexuality was a disease and that homosexuals were degenerates. See R. A. Nye, "The History of Sexuality in Context: National Sexological Traditions," *Science in Context* 4 (1991): 387–406, at 398.

41. These three terms were closely related but not synonymous. In the classic Morel-Magnan concept of degeneration, for example, the presence of physical stigmata was the sine qua non of diagnosis. The concepts of "predisposition" or "taint" did not attach so much importance to physical stigmata, while not excluding them from consideration. Nor was the idea of generational amplification as important to the latter as to the former. It should be noted that Krafft-Ebing's "functional" interpretation of degeneration was closer to the idea of "predisposition" than to the theories of Morel and Magnan. For some useful comments on this complex issue, see Havelock Ellis, *Studies*, 1, pt. 4:320–21.

42. Whether homosexuality was inborn or acquired was irrelevant for Moll: a mentally subnormal person, he pointed out, was pathological, whether the subnormality was due to congenital or acquired factors. See Moll, "Die Behandlung der Homosexualität," 3–6; Moll, "Sexuelle Zwischenstufen," *Zeitschrift für ärztliche Fortbildung* 1 (1904): 706–709, at 708.

43. On the acrimonious relations between Moll and Hirschfeld, see Charlotte Wolff, *Magnus Hirschfeld: A Portrait of a Pioneer in Sexology* (London: Quartet, 1986), 80–81, 243–49; and Erwin J. Haeberle, "Swastika, Pink Triangle, and Yellow Star: The Destruction of Sexology and the Persecution of Homosexuals in Nazi Germany," in Duberman, Vicinus, and Chauncey Jr., eds., *Hidden from History*, 365–79. See also Moll's sharp critique of the popular movement led by Hirschfeld for the emancipation of homosexuals: A. Moll, "Inwieweit ist die Agitation zur Aufhebung des §175 berechtigt?" *Deutsche medizinische Wochenschrift* 33 (1907): 1910–12. Moll also attacked Hirschfeld's theoretical views in A. Moll, ed., *Handbuch der Sexualwissenschaften*, 3d ed., 2:772–76.

44. In the homosexual/transvestite circles of Berlin, Hirschfeld was well known as "Tante Magnesia" (Aunt Magnesia). See Harry Benjamin, "Reminiscences," *The Journal of Sex Research* 6, no. 1 (1970): 3-9, at 4.

45. See James D. Steakley, *The Homosexual Emancipation Movement in Germany*; Steakley, "*Per scientiam ad justitiam:* Magnus Hirschfeld and the Sexual Politics of Innate Homosexuality," in Rosario, ed., *Science and Homosexualities*, 133-54; Charlotte Wolff, *Magnus Hirschfeld;* John Lauritsen and David Thorstad, *The Early Homosexual Rights Movement (1864-1935);* John C. Fout, "Sexual Politics in Wilhelmine Germany"; and Manfred Herzer, *Magnus Hirschfeld: Leben und Werk eines jüdischen, schwulen und sozialistischen Sexologen* (Frankfurt a/M: Campus, 1992).

46. See the "Petition an die gesetzgebenden Körperschaften des deutschen Reiches behufs Abänderung des §175 des R.-Str.-G. B. und die sich daran anschliessenden Reichstags-Verhandlungen," composed by Hirschfeld and signed by the members and numerous supporters of the committee, in *Jahrbuch für sexuelle Zwischenstufen* 1 (1899): 239-66. Some members (belonging to the anarchist/antifeminist wing of the movement) felt that the committee's scientistic position portrayed homosexual males as weak and feminized. In 1907, the committee split into two over this issue. The splinter group, called the "Sezession des Wissenschaftlich-humanitären Komitees," described the committee's biological argument as "a non-masculine way to effect the abolition of the law which hangs over our heads." See Gunter Schmidt, "Allies and Persecutors: Science and Medicine in the Homosexuality Issue," *Journal of Homosexuality* 10, nos. 3/4 (1984): 127-40, at 131-32. Many articles by members of this group were published between 1896 and 1931 in the magazine *Der Eigene*. Apart from the zoologist Benedict Friedländer (1866-1908), there were few biologists or physicians in this circle, and it never posed a serious challenge to the committee, which was numerically stronger, financially better off, and supported from outside by such leading physicians as Krafft-Ebing and Havelock Ellis. See Harry Oosterhuis, "Homosexual Emancipation in Germany before 1933: Two Traditions," *Journal of Homosexuality* 22, nos. 1/2 (1992): 1-27, and the translations of selected articles from *Der Eigene* in the same issue.

47. Hirschfeld, "Die Ursachen und Wesen des Uranismus," 145-51; Hirschfeld acknowledged that homosexuals possessed characteristic physical features (such as fine hands, full breasts, and sparse beards in men), but these he excluded as nondegenerative "Uranian stigmata" (146). For a list of the degenerative stigmata he looked for, see ibid., 146-48.

48. See Wettley and Leibbrand, *Von der "Psychopathia sexualis,"* 73-74.

49. Neuroses of all kinds, Hirschfeld claimed, were most common among relatives of homosexuals. These conditions, without being degenerate in themselves, presaged future degeneration of the line. When homosexuals did reproduce, their offspring were frequently affected by full-blown degenerative conditions such as psychoses, mental subnormality, or epilepsy. See Hirschfeld, *Die Homosexualität*, 385-86, 391-92. For a similar view, holding that the birth of a homosexual enabled the "regeneration" of a tainted family, see L. S. A. M. von Römer, "Die erbliche Belastung des Zentralnervensystems bei Uraniern, geistig gesunden Menschen und Geisteskranken," *Jahrbuch für sexuelle Zwischenstufen* 7 (1905): 67-84, at 78-81.

50. Moll, *Untersuchungen über die Libido sexualis*, 477. See also E. v. Hartmann, *Philosophie des Schönen*, in Hartmann, *Ausgewählte Werke* (Leipzig: Hermann Haacke, 1887) 4:237-38. The concept had been implied by Ulrichs, by Westphal, by Krafft-Ebing, and by Kiernan. Later, the Viennese gynecologist Josef Halban argued that if a person with

normal male genitals and full breasts was considered a "secondary male pseudohermaphrodite," there was every reason to classify the homosexual male as an example of psychic
male pseudohermaphroditism. See J. Halban, "Die Entstehung der Geschlechtscharaktere: Eine Studie über den formativen Einfluss der Keimdrüse," *Archiv für Gynäkologie* 70
(1903): 205–308, at 290–91, 295–96. Despite the new terminology, this was still a model
of body-mind hermaphroditism. The basic conceptualization of homosexual orientation
as psychosexual gender transposition continues to this day among physicians and biologists. See William Byne and Bruce Parsons, "Human Sexual Orientation: The Biologic
Theories Reappraised," *Archives of General Psychiatry* 50 (1993): 228–39, at 229.

51. Genital hermaphroditism and homosexuality, Krafft-Ebing had emphasized,
"stand in no relation to each other." Pseudohermaphrodites, he had claimed, were not homosexual, and genital hermaphroditism had never been observed in homosexuals. Generalized feminization or masculinization of the body (with the exception of the genitals) was
possible, but only in a rare, advanced stage of homosexuality, which he designated as "an-
drogyny," and even in those rare instances, he emphasized, "actual transitions to hermaphrodites never occur, but, on the contrary, completely differentiated genitals; so that, just as
in all pathological perversions of the sexual life, the cause must be sought in the brain"
(Krafft-Ebing, *Psychopathia Sexualis,* 336–37, 347–48, 389–94). In her otherwise illuminating study of hermaphroditism, Alice Dreger seems to misinterpret Krafft-Ebing's observations as pertaining to all homosexuals rather than to one very small group of them.
See Alice Domurat Dreger, *Hermaphrodites and the Medical Invention of Sex* (Cambridge,
Mass.: Harvard University Press, 1998), 134. On Krafft-Ebing's division of homosexuality into stages, which were linked with the degree of degeneration and which differed between the congenital and acquired varieties, see *Psychopathia Sexualis,* 286, 297, 304, 328,
336–37.

52. F. L. v. Neugebauer, "50 Missehen wegen Homosexualität der Gatten und einige
Ehescheidungen wegen 'Erreur de sexe,'" *Centralblatt für Gynäkologie* 23 (1899): 502–12.
Weininger cited a review of this article. See also Neugebauer, *Hermaphroditismus beim
Menschen,* 697–702. Like most physicians of his time, Neugebauer did not regard the sex
of rearing as an important determinant of sexual orientation and behavior. A person with
testicular tissue was male and should feel attracted toward females, even if he was reared as
a female. For an astute and superbly detailed history of medical studies of hermaphroditism, see Alice Dreger, *Hermaphrodites and the Medical Invention of Sex.*

53. Hirschfeld, "Ursachen und Wesen des Uranismus," 79–86.

54. H. Ellis, *Studies in the Psychology of Sex,* 1, pt. 4: 321.

55. Ellis's distinction between *pathos* (an anomaly, i.e., any deviation from the norm)
and *nosos* (disease) was drawn from R. Virchow, "Eröffnungsrede, XXV. Allgemeine Ver-
sammlung und Stiftungsfest der Deutschen anthropologischen Gesellschaft in Innsbruck vom 24.–28. August 1894," *Correspondenz-Blatt der deutschen Gesellschaft für
Anthropologie, Ethnologie und Urgeschichte* 25 (1894): 80–87, at 84; and from L. Aschoff,
"Pathos und Nosos," *Deutsche medizinische Wochenschrift* 36 (1910): 201–204.

56. Hirschfeld, "Die objektive Diagnose der Homosexualität," *Jahrbuch für sexuelle
Zwischenstufen* 1 (1899): 4–35.

57. Hirschfeld agreed with Iwan Bloch that the homosexual was "an important anthropological variety of the genus *Homo.*" See Hirschfeld, *Die Homosexualität,* 2d ed., 389; and
Bloch, *Das Sexualleben unserer Zeit,* 553.

58. Hirschfeld, *Die Homosexualität,* 389.

59. Hirschfeld, "Die objektive Diagnose der Homosexualität," 8–9.

60. Ibid., 15-17.

61. Ibid., 25-26.

62. See chapter 4 above. Weininger did not comment on this similarity.

63. Discussing degeneration, Hirschfeld had once asked: "But what is the type? What is the norm? What are the limits of physiological variability?" See Hirschfeld, "Die Ursachen und Wesen des Uranismus," 151. He did not raise the same questions with regard to his own notion of homosexuality.

64. On this point, see M. Herzer, *Magnus Hirschfeld*, 98-99.

65. For a medical view approaching that of Weininger's, see A. Aletrino, "Uranisme et dégénérescence," *Archives d'anthropologie criminelle* 23 (1908): 633-67, especially 649-53. According to Havelock Ellis (*Studies*, 1, pt. 4:321), Aletrino's position was quite singular among physicians, and I have found no evidence to challenge that assessment. Interestingly, Aletrino, like Weininger, described the proportions of masculinity and femininity in homosexuals numerically, which does not seem to have been a popular convention with other physicians writing on sexual intermediacy. Aletrino did not, however, refer to Weininger.

66. Weininger admitted, however, that his theory could not explain why some virile males felt sexually attracted toward other virile males (61-62). Hirschfeld, too, failed to explain the problem of "virile homosexuality."

67. The professor was merely old fashioned. On the castration of male homosexuals in the effort to "cure" them, see Charles Féré, "La Castration contre l'inversion sexuelle," *Revue de Chirurgie* 31 (1905): 293-98; Havelock Ellis, *Studies*, 1, pt. 4:327-28; and Magnus Hirschfeld, *Die Homosexualität*, 425. Ellis observed that no leading physician believed any longer in the applicability of castration to homosexuality. "Sexual inversion," Ellis remarked, "is not a localized genital condition. It is a diffused condition, and firmly imprinted on the whole psychic state. . . . Castration of the body in adult age cannot be expected to produce castration of the mind" (Ellis, 327). By the 1920s, the perspective would change again, and Hirschfeld would play a major role in the transition.

68. Krafft-Ebing had emphasized, however, that hypnotic suppressions of homosexual desire were "marvellous *artefacta* . . . but by no means *transformations*" (Krafft-Ebing, *Psychopathia Sexualis*, 450-51). Havelock Ellis (*Studies*, 1, pt. 4:329-30) believed that hypnosis was useful only in the most superficial cases.

69. By this time, Albert von Schrenck-Notzing was the only leading advocate of the use of hypnosis in homosexuality. He routinely used hypnotic suggestion to arouse heterosexual desire in homosexuals, then advising them to consort with female prostitutes. See Schrenck-Notzing, *Die Suggestions-Therapie*, 198-211. This, Hirschfeld commented, was comparable to a heterosexual male being compelled, by hypnotic suggestion, to have sex with a man. Hirschfeld as well as Albert Moll also rebuked Schrenck-Notzing for helping spread syphilis and other sexually transmitted diseases. See Hirschfeld, *Die Homosexualität*, 414; Moll, "Behandlung der Homosexualität," 21-22.

70. Hirschfeld, *Die Homosexualität*, 396.

71. Ibid., 398. Albert Moll, however, was in favor of encouraging treatment and marriage when the chances of degenerate offspring were low. See Moll, "Die Behandlung der Homosexualität," 11.

72. Hirschfeld, *Die Homosexualität*, 436.

73. A. Moll, "Die Behandlung sexueller Perversionen mit besonderer Berücksichtigung der Assoziationstherapie," *Zeitschrift für Psychotherapie und medizinische Psychologie* 3 (1911): 1-29, at 16.

74. See H. Rodlauer, ed., *Otto Weininger, Eros und Psyche: Studien und Briefe 1899–1902*, 173.

75. "Mein Mittel zur Bekämpfung der Homosexualität scheint Erfolg zu haben!! Trotzdem es ja zu meiner Theorie nur stimmen würde, habe ich mich doch von meinem Staunen darüber noch nicht erholt. Wenn ich nur sicher wäre, daß keine Suggestion vorliegt! . . . Jedenfalls werden die Dosen fortgesetzt werden müssen. . . . Mein Patient bereitet sich schon auf den ersten Koitus vor!" (ibid., 73).

76. See J. Le Rider, *Der Fall Otto Weininger*, 25–26. I am indebted to Richard Allen for an illuminating discussion of the importance of this issue.

77. See Le Rider, *Der Fall Otto Weininger*, 72.

78. See Wettley and Leibbrand, *Von der "Psychopathia sexualis,"* 74–76.

79. For further details on this procedure and its many contexts, see Chandak Sengoopta, "Glandular Politics: Experimental Biology, Clinical Medicine, and Homosexual Emancipation in Fin-de-Siècle Central Europe," *Isis* 89 (1998): 445–73.

80. See Eugen Steinach, *Sex and Life: Forty Years of Biological and Medical Experiments* (London: Faber and Faber, 1940), 87–88; E. Steinach and R. Lichtenstern, "Umstimmung der Homosexualität durch Austausch der Pubertätsdrüsen," *Münchener medizinische Wochenschrift* 65 (1918): 145–48; and E. Steinach, "Histologische Beschaffenheit der Keimdrüse bei homosexuellen Männern," *Archiv für Entwicklungsmechanik* 46 (1920): 29–37.

81. M. Hirschfeld, *Die Homosexualität des Mannes und des Weibes*, 2d ed., xiv. See also M. Hirschfeld, "Die Untersuchungen und Forschungen von Professor E. Steinach über künstliche Vermännlichung, Verweiblichung und Hermaphrodisierung," *Vierteljahrsberichte des Wissenschaftlich-humanitären Komitees/Jahrbuch für sexuelle Zwischenstufen* 17 (1917): 3–21.

82. See C. Sengoopta, "Glandular Politics."

*Chapter Six*

1. On the history of hysteria, see Ilza Veith, *Hysteria: The History of a Disease* (Chicago: University of Chicago Press, 1965); and Étienne Trillat, *Histoire de l'hysterie* (Paris: Éditions Seghers, 1986). For a comprehensive analysis of historiograhic approaches to hysteria, see Mark S. Micale, *Approaching Hysteria: Disease and its Interpretations* (Princeton: Princeton University Press, 1995). On German medical discourse on hysteria, see Hannah S. Decker, *Freud in Germany: Revolution and Reaction in Science, 1893–1907* (New York: International Universities Press, 1977), 73–87; and K. Codell Carter, "Germ Theory, Hysteria, and Freud's Early Work in Psychopathology," *Medical History* 24 (1980): 259–74. The cultural importance of hysteria around the turn of the century is addressed by Jacqueline Carroy-Thirard, "Hystérie, théâtre, littérature au dix-neuvièm203e siècle," *Psychanalyse à l'université* 7 (1982): 299–317; and Marianne Schuller, "'Weibliche Neurose' und Identität: Zur Diskussion der Hysterie um die Jahrhundertwende," in Dietmar Kamper and Christoph Wulf, eds., *Die Wiederkehr des Körpers* (Frankfurt a/M: Suhrkamp, 1982), 180–92. For references to more specialized studies, consult M. Micale, "Hysteria and its Historiography: A Review of Past and Present Writings," 2 parts, *History of Science* 28 (1989): 223–61, 319–51.

2. Esther Fischer-Homberger, "Hysterie und Misogynie—ein Aspekt der Hysteriegeschichte," *Gesnerus* 26 (1969): 117–27 provides an adequate summary of Weininger's conception of hysteria but ignores Weininger's medical sources. Regina Schaps, *Hysterie und Weiblichkeit: Wissenschaftsmythen über die Frau* (Frankfurt: Campus,

1982) devotes a few sketchy paragraphs (61–62) to Weininger. Marianne Schuller, "'Weibliche Neurose' und Identität," analyzes Weininger's theory of hysteria in the context of his philosophy of consciousness but does not explore the medical sources. Jacques Le Rider makes a few references to Weininger's theory of hysteria while concentrating on general parallels and divergences between Weininger's thought and psychoanalytic theory (Le Rider, *Der Fall Otto Weininger,* 169–88).

3. For similar interminglings of medical and "cultural" concepts of hysteria in nineteenth-century France, see Mark Micale, *Approaching Hysteria,* 179–284. "From its origins in medicine," says Micale, "hysteria—the word, image, theory, and diagnosis—penetrated one cultural area after another, including fiction, poetry, dramaturgy, historical writing, social and political criticism, sociology, criminology, and anthropology" (217). No comparably detailed study exists for fin-de-siècle Vienna, but for a suggestive overview, see Manfred Schneider, "Hysterie als Gesamtkunstwerk," in Alfred Pfabigan, ed., *Ornament und Askese im Zeitgeist des Wien der Jahrhundertwende* (Vienna: Brandstätter, 1985), 212–29.

4. The "intelligible" self, in Kant's philosophy, is the self *as it is in itself,* and thus distinct from the self *as it is known in/from experience.* The existence of the intelligible self can be inferred but not demonstrated. This distinction follows from Kant's fundamental differentiation of "things in themselves" ("noumena") from "phenomena." See Vincent M. Cooke, "Kant's Godlike Self," *International Philosophical Quarterly* 28 (1988): 313–23; and C. Thomas Powell, *Kant's Theory of Self-Consciousness* (Oxford: Clarendon, 1990), 52–54.

5. See chapter 8, below.

6. See Rush Rhees, ed., *Ludwig Wittgenstein: Personal Recollections* (Totowa, N.J.: Rowman & Littlefield, 1981), 106. My thanks to Allan Janik for this reference.

7. See Michael Worbs, *Nervenkunst: Literatur und Psychoanalyse im Wien der Jahrhundertwende* (Frankfurt a.M.: Europäische Verlagsanstalt, 1983), 139–43, 280–95.

8. See Lorna Martens, "Musil and Freud: The 'Foreign Body' in 'Die Versuchung der stillen Veronika,'" *Euphorion* 81 (1987): 100–18.

9. "I was also quite alarmed by the chapter on hysteria," wrote Freud to Wilhelm Fliess, "which was written *ad captandam benevolentiam meam.*" Letter dated 27 July 1904, in *The Complete Letters of Sigmund Freud to Wilhelm Fliess, 1887–1904,* 466–68, at 466. Thirty-five years later, Freud wrote to a biographer of Weininger that Weininger "had to a large extent given consideration to my views on hysteria." See D. Abrahamsen, *The Mind and Death of a Genius,* 207–208.

10. H. Rodlauer, "Von 'Eros und Psyche' zu 'Geschlecht und Charakter': Unbekannte Weininger-Manuskripte im Archiv der Österreichischen Akademie der Wissenschaften," 120.

11. Briquet, *Traité clinique et thérapeutique de l'hystérie* (Paris: Baillière, 1859), 36, 51. On Briquet, see François M. Mai and Harold Merskey, "Briquet's *Treatise on Hysteria:* A Synopsis and Commentary," *Archives of General Psychiatry* 37 (1980): 1401–1405; Micale, "Hysteria and its Historiography," pt. 1:242–44.

12. Many physicians made this assumption as a matter of course. See, for instance, Havelock Ellis, *Man and Woman: A Study of Human Secondary Sexual Characters,* 284.

13. Hysterogenic zones were small, circumscribed regions of the body which, when pressed, might trigger off an hysterical attack *or* stop one. The regions over the ovaries or, in men, the region over the inguinal canal were commonly identified as hysterogenic zones. See J.-M. Charcot, *Oeuvres complétes,* vol. 3: *Leçons sur les maladies du système*

*nerveux* (Paris: Progrès médical, 1890), 86–88. On Charcot's life and career, see Christopher G. Goetz, Michel Bonduelle, and Toby Gelfand, *Charcot: Constructing Neurology* (New York: Oxford University Press, 1995), especially 172–216, which deal with his research on hysteria. On the long historical association of the ovary with hysteria, see Ilza Veith, *Hysteria,* 173, 210, 232; and on the removal of ovaries to treat hysteria, Edward Shorter, "Medizinische Theorien spezifisch weiblicher Nervenkrankheiten im Wandel," in Alfons Labisch and Reinhard Spree, *Medizinische Deutungsmacht im sozialen Wandel des 19. und frühen 20. Jahrhunderts* (Bonn: Psychiatrie-Verlag, 1989), 171–80, at 173–76. Weininger briefly noted that the removal of the ovaries would radically attenuate innate sexuality and thus diminish the intensity of its conflict with the false outer modesty of Woman (574–75). But since sexuality was, in his view, a feature of every cell of the body, the removal of the sex glands could never wholly eradicate sexuality.

14. Briquet, *Traité clinique,* 101.

15. See Charcot, *Oeuvres complètes,* 3:115. Weininger used this volume of Charcot's lectures in the German translation by Sigmund Freud: *Neue Vorlesungen über die Krankheiten des Nervensystems insbesondere über Hysterie* (Vienna: Toeplitz and Deuticke, 1886). I have consulted both versions. The French original, incidentally, was published *after* Freud's German version. On Charcot's approach to male hysteria, see Mark S. Micale, "Charcot and the Idea of Hysteria in the Male: Gender, Mental Science, and Medical Diagnosis in Late Nineteenth-Century France," *Medical History* 34 (1990): 363–411, especially 380–81; Micale, "Hysteria Male/Hysteria Female: Reflections on Comparative Gender Construction in Nineteenth Century France and Britain," in Marina Benjamin, ed., *Science and Sensibility: Gender and Scientific Enquiry, 1780–1945* (Oxford: Basil Blackwell, 1991), 200–39. For a different perspective on the issue, see Jan Goldstein, "The Uses of Male Hysteria: Medical and Literary Discourse in Nineteenth Century France," *Representations* 34 (1991): 134–65.

16. See Elaine Showalter, *The Female Malady: Women, Madness, and English Culture, 1830–1980* (New York: Penguin, 1987), 112; and Showalter, *Sexual Anarchy: Gender and Culture at the Fin de Siècle* (New York: Penguin, 1991), 105–106. My thanks to Mark Micale for clarifications on this point.

17. Actually, Charcot had said that an undescended testis could often turn into a "partial" hysterogenic zone *(une partie de zone hystérogene).* See Charcot, *Oeuvres complètes,* 3:88. In Freud's translation, this qualification was removed: "Beim Manne sieht man nicht selten den Hoden, besonders wenn er der Sitz einer Lage- oder Entwickelungsanomalie ist, in eine hysterogene Zone einbezogen" *(Neue Vorlesungen,* 70). Since Weininger did not use the French version, this specific distortion, if distortion it was, must be attributed to Freud.

18. E. Mendel, "Über Hysterie beim männlichen Geschlecht," *Berliner klinische Wochenschrift* 21 (1884): 314–17, 330–31, 347–48. Landau's comments appear on 330. See also H. Decker, *Freud in Germany,* 80–82.

19. See Veith, *Hysteria,* 210–12.

20. See Micale, "Hysteria and its Historiography," pt. 1, 245.

21. See Esther Fischer-Homberger, *Die traumatische Neurose: Vom somatischen zum sozialen Leiden* (Bern: Hans Huber, 1975), 124–28; and Martha Noel Evans, *Fits and Starts: A Genealogy of Hysteria in Modern France* (Ithaca: Cornell University Press, 1991), 31. Psychologist Pierre Janet was one of the rare authorities who denied that hysterics were more dishonest than "normal" people. See Janet, *The Mental State of Hystericals* (original publication 1892–94), trans. Caroline Rollin Corson (New York: Putnam's, 1901; rpt.,

Washington, D.C.: University Publications of America, 1977), 216. On Janet's long and versatile career, see Henri F. Ellenberger, *The Discovery of the Unconscious: The History and Evolution of Dynamic Psychiatry* (New York: Basic Books, 1970), 331–417.

22. Janet, *L'Automatisme psychologique*, 214.

23. W. Griesinger, *Mental Pathology and Therapeutics*, 2d ed., trans. C. L. Robertson and J. Rutherford (London: New Sydenham Society, 1867; rpt., New York: Hafner, 1965), 179. On Griesinger and his work, see Otto M. Marx, "Wilhelm Griesinger and the History of Psychiatry: A Reassessment," *Bulletin of the History of Medicine* 46 (1972): 519–44.

24. J. Falret, *Études cliniques sur les maladies mentales et nerveuses* (Paris: Bailliére, 1890), 502. The translation is slightly modified from that in Ilza Veith, *Hysteria*, 211.

25. H. Legrand du Saulle, *Les hystériques: État physique et état mental* (Paris: Baillière, 1883), 345–46.

26. See Fischer-Homberger, *Die traumatische Neurose*, 125; and J.-M. Charcot, *Oeuvres complétes*, vol. 1: *Leçons sur les maladies du système nerveux* (Paris: Progrès médical, 1890), 281–82.

27. See Fischer-Homberger, *Die traumatische Neurose*, 126–27.

28. Without equating the two, one might note the parallels between Weininger's views on hysteria and those of Luce Irigaray, the dissident Lacanian psychoanalyst and feminist philosopher. Hysteria, according to Irigaray, is a "privileged dramatization of feminine sexuality" that is "stopped short, impeded, *controlled by a master-signifier*, the Phallus, and by its representative(s) . . . stigmatized as a place where fantasies, ghosts, and shadows fester and must be unmasked, interpreted" (L. Irigaray, *Speculum of the Other Woman* [original publication 1974], trans. Gillian C. Gill [Ithaca: Cornell University Press, 1985], 59–60, emphasis in the original). For general introductions to Irigaray's difficult work, see Carolyn Burke, "Irigaray through the Looking Glass," *Feminist Studies* 7 (1981): 288–304; and Toril Moi, *Sexual/Textual Politics: Feminist Literary Theory* (New York: Methuen, 1985), 127–49.

29. See Ellenberger, *Discovery of the Unconscious*, 142–44.

30. See ibid., 136.

31. On Charcot's theory of hysteria and hypnosis, see A. R. G. Owen, *Hysteria, Hypnosis and Healing: The Work of J. M. Charcot* (London: Dennis Dobson, 1971), 104–105; and Ellenberger, *Discovery of the Unconscious*, 89–101. Charcot's belief that only hysterics could be hypnotized drew fire from Hippolyte Bernheim (1840–1919), who represented what historians usually call the Nancy School of Hypnosis. Bernheim contended that hypnosis was not pathological but simply an effect of suggestibility, which, to varying degrees, was a universal human trait. See Ellenberger, *Discovery*, 87–89; and Alan Gauld, *A History of Hypnotism* (Cambridge: Cambridge University Press, 1992), 306–36.

32. Janet, *L'automatisme psychologique*, 417–31; Janet, *The Mental State of Hystericals*, 489–96; A. Gauld, *History of Hypnotism*, 369–81.

33. See A. Binet, *On Double Consciousness: Experimental Psychological Studies*, new ed. (Chicago: Open Court, 1896), 10–29; Binet, *Alterations of Personality*, trans. Helen G. Baldwin (New York: D. Appleton, 1896), 91–139; and R. v. Krafft-Ebing, *An Experimental Study in the Domain of Hypnotism*, 2d ed., trans. C. G. Chaddock (New York: Putnam's, 1889), 115. On Breuer, Freud, and their work on hysteria, see Ola Andersson, *Studies in the Prehistory of Psychoanalysis: The Etiology of Psychoneuroses and Some Related Themes in Sigmund Freud's Scientific Writings and Letters, 1886–1896* (Stockholm: Svenska Bokförlaget, 1962); F. Sulloway, *Freud*, 22–69; Albrecht Hirschmüller, *The Life and Work of Josef Breuer: Physiology and Psychoanalysis* (New York: New York University Press, 1989), 165–

69; and B. B. Rubinstein, "Freud's Early Theories of Hysteria," in R. S. Cohen and L. Laudan, eds., *Physics, Philosophy, and Psychoanalysis* (Dordrecht: Reidel, 1983), 169–90. Elin Diamond suggests that the idea of the dual personality became so popular because it "reinforced the popular epistemology of the doubleness of women. . . . The notion that a good woman contained within her a bad woman . . . permitted physicians to see women as simultaneously innocent and guilty, pitiable but meriting severe correction" (E. Diamond, "Realism and Hysteria: Toward a Feminist Mimesis," *Discourse: Theoretical Studies in Media and Culture* 13 [1990–91]: 59–92, at 70).

34. Breuer and Freud, for example, accepted Janet's view that a dual personality was always present in hysteria. They did not, however, agree with Janet that this splitting of the consciousness was due to inherent psychic "weakness." The "split," according to them, was caused by a traumatic experience during a spontaneous hypnosis-like condition ("hypnoid state"). The hypnoid state, and not the splitting of consciousness, was the primary condition for the development of hysteria. See Breuer's remarks in *Studies on Hysteria*, in *Standard Edition*, 2:230–35, and Freud's in ibid., 104. Freud subsequently rejected the idea of the hypnoid state, emphasizing other factors in the causation of hysteria.

35. Sexuality, particularly feminine sexuality, had long been central to theories on hysteria. For a succinct review, see Havelock Ellis, "Hysteria in Relation to the Sexual Emotions," *Alienist and Neurologist* 19 (1898): 599–615.

36. E. v. Feuchtersleben, *The Principles of Medical Psychology*, trans. H. E. Lloyd and B. G. Babington (London: New Sydenham Society, 1847), 228–29. On Feuchtersleben, see Otto M. Marx, "German Romantic Psychiatry," pt. 2, *History of Psychiatry* 2 (1991): 1–25, at 22–25.

37. See Griesinger, *Mental Pathology and Therapeutics*, 201.

38. R. B. Carter, *On the Pathology and Treatment of Hysteria*, as quoted in Ilza Veith, *Hysteria*, 202. On Carter, see Micale, "Hysteria and its Historiography," pt. 1, 238–42.

39. See Moritz Benedikt, "Second Life: Das Seelenbinnenleben des gesunden und kranken Menschen," *Wiener Klinik* 20 (1894): 127–38. On Benedikt, see H. F. Ellenberger, "The Pathogenic Secret and its Therapeutics" (1966) and "Moritz Benedikt (1835–1920): An Insufficiently Appreciated Pioneer of Psychoanalysis" (1973)" both in Mark S. Micale, ed., *Beyond the Unconscious: Essays of Henri F. Ellenberger in the History of Psychiatry* (Princeton: Princeton University Press, 1993), 341–59 and 110–18, respectively.

40. See Ellenberger, *Discovery of the Unconscious*, 42. According to Jacqueline Carroy-Thirard, one encounters two basic types of hysterical women in nineteenth-century medical literature: the "bad" (lascivious) and the "idealized" (fragile, asexual). Briquet's image of the hysteric, she argues, belonged to the latter type. See J. Carroy-Thirard, "Figures de femmes hystériques dans la psychiatrie française au 19e siècle," *Psychanalyse à l'université* 4 (1979): 313–24, especially 313–17.

41. Ellenberger, *Discovery of the Unconscious*, 143.

42. Michel Foucault argued that Charcot's clinical approach to hysteria was characterized by an "interplay of incitement and elision" of sexuality. Charcot's school, according to Foucault, "constructed around and apropos of sex an immense apparatus for producing truth, even if this truth was to be masked at the last moment" (Foucault, *The History of Sexuality*, vol. 1: *An Introduction*, 56). On the erotization of hysteria by Charcot and his followers, see Georges Didi-Huberman, *Invention de l'hystérie: Charcot et l'iconographie photographique de la Salpêtrière* (Paris: Macula, 1982); J. Carroy-Thirard, "Figures de femmes hystériques," 317–23; and the illustrations in Désiré-Magloire Bourneville and Paul Régnard, *Iconographie photographique de la Salpêtrière*, 3 vols. (Paris: Delahaye and

Lecrosnier, 1876–80). For Freud's anecdote, see Freud, "On the History of the Psychoanalytic Movement," in *Standard Edition*, 14:1–66, at 13–14. This sensuous image of the hysteric, however, was questioned at the time from within Charcot's own institution by Pierre Janet. While endorsing the importance of sexual hallucinations and fantasies in hysterical symptomatology, Janet argued that hysterics thought no more about sex than normal women of the same age and class. They were, in fact, more often frigid than normal women (Janet, *The Mental State of Hystericals*, 214–16).

43. Freud, "Hysteria" (1888), *Standard Edition*, 1:37–59, at 50. In *Studies on Hysteria*, Freud reminisced thus on his early attitude: "I had come fresh from the school of Charcot, and I regarded the linking of hysteria with the topic of sexuality as a sort of insult" (*Standard Edition*, 2:260).

44. The development of Freud's views on the relations between hysteria and sexuality is surveyed in Renate Schlesier, *Konstruktionen der Weiblichkeit bei Sigmund Freud: Zum Problem von Entmythologisierung und Remythologisierung in der psychoanalytischen Theorie* (Frankfurt a/M: Europäische Verlagsanstalt, 1981), 41–74. Malcolm Macmillan, *Freud Evaluated: The Completed Arc* (Amsterdam: North Holland, 1991), 33–73, demonstrates that Charcot's influence remained strong in *Studies on Hysteria*, despite the heretical focus on sexual etiology.

45. According to traditional histories of psychoanalysis, Breuer insisted that sexual factors be "kept in the background" in the *Studies on Hysteria*. See, for example, Ernest Jones, *The Life and Work of Sigmund Freud*, 1:250–54. This view is no longer tenable. Breuer agreed that the "root" of hysteria was always sexual but did not agree with Freud's later view that each hysterical *symptom* was interpretable as sexual. On this point, see Frank Sulloway, *Freud*, 88–89; and A. Hirschmüller, *Josef Breuer*, 174–75. Breuer's stress on the sexual etiology of hysteria in the *Studies* does not seem to have originated from his *recorded* clinical experience with hysterics, which was confined to the single case of Bertha Pappenheim (1860–1936), known as Anna O. "The element of sexuality," Breuer wrote, "was astonishingly undeveloped in her. . . . During her illness that element of mental life never emerged" (*Studies, Standard Edition*, 2:21–22).

46. *Studies on Hysteria, Standard Edition*, 2:247. The first chapter ("On the Psychical Mechanism of Hysterical Phenomena") of the *Studies* was published in a medical journal in 1893 under joint authorship. The other chapters were prepared expressly for the book and none was written jointly. By 1895, Freud's views had begun to differ from Breuer's, and these differences were politely expressed in their respective contributions to the *Studies*. See J. Strachey, "Editor's Introduction," ibid., ix–xxviii; and Sulloway, *Freud*, 64–65.

47. "The girl," wrote Breuer, "senses in Eros the terrible power which governs and decides her destiny and she is frightened by it" (*Studies, Standard Edition*, 2:246). Superficial similarities of expression notwithstanding, Breuer's views on female sexuality were entirely opposed to Weininger's. According to Weininger, boys experienced puberty as a crisis. The first erection was puzzling and disturbing since it was independent of the boy's will. For girls, on the other hand, puberty represented fulfillment; it was the moment the girl has been looking forward to from childhood (113–14).

48. *Studies, Standard Edition*, 2:247, Breuer's emphasis. The concept of "defense" came from Freud: see Freud, "The Neuro-Psychoses of Defense" (1894), in *Standard Edition*, 3:43–68, at 48–50. In this early formulation, "defense" was similar to the later concept of "repression," without being identical with it. For more information on this point, see Jean Laplanche and J.-B. Pontalis, *The Language of Psycho-Analysis*, trans. David Nicholson-Smith (New York: Norton, 1973), 390–94, especially 391.

49. *Studies, Standard Edition,* 2:6.

50. Ibid., 6–9, 12. The notion of a conflict remained strong in Freud's later views on hysteria. In 1905, he argued that hysteria was characterized by "the enigmatic contradiction" between "exaggerated sexual craving and excessive aversion to sexuality." Torn by this conflict, the patient chose illness as "a way of escape." See Freud, *Three Essays on the Theory of Sexuality* (1905), *Standard Edition,* 7:125–245, at 164–65. Weininger, if he had lived to read this, would have agreed. Later still, however, Freud emphasized the bisexuality of hysterics and saw the "exaggerated sexual craving" of the hysterical woman as masculine in nature. Hysteria still represented a conflict between the ego and repressed sexuality, but the former was feminine and the latter masculine. See Freud, "Hysterical Phantasies and their Relation to Bisexuality" (1908), *Standard Edition,* 9:157–66; and Sarah Kofman, *The Enigma of Woman: Woman in Freud's Writings,* trans. Catherine Porter (Ithaca: Cornell University Press, 1985), 123–26. This hypothesis did not refer to Weininger, but one cannot imagine a more complete inversion of Weininger's view.

51. *Studies, Standard Edition,* 2:46.

52. Ibid., 92–93.

53. Freud, "A Case of Successful Treatment by Hypnotism with Some Remarks on the Origin of Hysterical Symptoms through 'Counter-Will'" (1892–93), *Standard Edition,* 1:115–28, especially 127. See also M. Macmillan, *Freud Evaluated,* 92–93.

54. Freud, "Screen Memories" (1899), *Standard Edition,* 3:300–22.

55. *Studies on Hysteria, Standard Edition,* 2:30–35. Breuer's patient Anna O. had referred to this therapy as her "talking-cure" and, jokingly, as "chimney-sweeping." She used English in both instances (ibid., 30). Breuer's therapy was hardly as successful as he had claimed in the *Studies.* Bertha Pappenheim relapsed repeatedly and had to be hospitalized. Breuer himself once told Freud that death would be a kinder fate for her. She recovered much later, eventually becoming a leading figure in the Jewish feminist movement. See A. Hirschmüller, *Josef Breuer,* 114–16.

56. Weininger's "false self" bore some similarities with the Freudian concept of the "super-ego," which was formally presented twenty years after Weininger's death in *The Ego and the Id* (1923). Although the super-ego and the false self both represented internalizations of external agents, it is important to note their dissimilarities. Freud's super-ego was present (though not equally strong) in males and females whereas Weininger's false self was unique to women. Freud, however, did believe that women's super-ego was "never so" inexorable, so impersonal, so independent of its emotional origins as we require it in men" (S. Freud, "Some Psychical Consequences of the Anatomical Distinction Between the Sexes" [1925], *Standard Edition,* 19:248–58, at 257). Freud's super-ego has been seen as "an inner agent that transcends and acts on the experienced self": a naturalistic counterpart of Kant's ethical legislator, the noumenal self. In Weininger's world, Woman lacked this self. On the concept of the super-ego, see Jennifer Church, "Morality and the Internalized Other," in Jerome Neu, ed., *The Cambridge Companion to Freud* (Cambridge: Cambridge University Press, 1991), 209–23, especially 220.

57. At one point, Weininger used the interesting adjective *aufgeprägten* (stamped, embossed) to describe the false self (361). Platonic conceptions of mimesis involve the notion of "stamping" the plastic infant soul with language. The relation between plasticity and stamping, according to Philippe Lacoue-Labarthe, is gendered: plasticity, of course, is feminine and the process of stamping masculine. See Philippe Lacoue-Labarthe, *Typography: Mimesis, Philosophy, Politics* (Cambridge, Mass.: Harvard University Press, 1989), 126. This was exactly what Weininger claimed concerning the formation of the false self

in women under male influence (see below). In Luce Irigaray's reading of Plato's philosophy, woman is mimesis personified: she is "always a clean slate ready for the father's impressions. . . . She is pure mimicry" (Irigaray, *Speculum of the Other Woman*, 307–10).

58. On the concept of abulia, see John H. Smith, "Abulia: Sexuality and Diseases of the Will in the Late Nineteenth Century," *Genders*, no. 6 (Fall 1989): 102–24. Weininger pointed out that Pierre Janet, along with most leading psychiatrists of the time, believed that abulia was virtually constant in hysteria (359). He cited Pierre Janet, "Un cas d'aboulie et d'idées fixes," in Janet, *Névroses et Idées fixes*, vol. 2: *Études expérimentales sur les troubles de la volonté, de l'attention, de la mémoire, sur les émotions, les idées obsédantes et leur traitement* (Paris: Alcan, 1898), 1–68.

59. Freud, "The Aetiology of Hysteria" (1896), *Standard Edition*, 3:187–221.

60. Ibid., 203.

61. Freud's repudiation of the seduction hypothesis is a controversial topic in the historiography of psychoanalysis. According to the orthodox view, Freud's self-analysis revealed that "memories" of childhood seduction by parents were fantasies, an insight that led to the formulation of the Oedipus Complex. See Ernest Jones, *The Life and Work of Sigmund Freud*, 1:263–67. For a comprehensive review of recent controversies over the interpretation of Freud's change of heart, see Han Israëls and Morton Schatzman, "The Seduction Theory," *History of Psychiatry* 4 (1993): 23–59.

62. See E. A. Ross, *Social Psychology: An Outline and Source Book* (New York: Macmillan, 1908), 17; and H. Ellis, *Man and Woman*, 258–96, especially 258–61. The assumption of greater feminine suggestibility was widespread, but it was explained in different ways. Edward Ross (ibid.) emphasized, for instance, that "much of woman's exaggerated impressionability disappears once she enjoys equal access with men to such individualizing influences as higher education, travel, self-direction, professional pursuits, participation in intellectual and public life."

63. Janet, "L'Influence somnambulique et le besoin de direction," in Janet, *Névroses et Idées fixes*, 1:423–80.

64. Ibid., 423.

65. Ibid., 452.

66. Ibid., 446–52.

67. Ibid., 446–77.

68. On the Kantian concepts of autonomy and heteronomy, see "Autonomy," in James Mark Baldwin, ed., *Dictionary of Philosophy and Psychology*, 2d ed. (Gloucester, Mass.: Peter Smith, 1960), 1:95; and Roger J. Sullivan, *Immanuel Kant's Moral Theory*, 46–47.

69. In the first, jointly written, chapter of the *Studies*, Breuer and Freud had observed that hysterics possessed "the clearest intellect, strongest will, greatest character and highest critical power" (*Standard Edition*, 2:13). Later, in a case-history, Freud had remarked upon the "morally oversensitive personality" of his patient (ibid., 65–66). Freud's early respect for hysterics, according to Elaine Showalter, was replaced by a more abrasive and antagonistic attitude from the case of Dora (1899/1900) onwards (Showalter, *Female Malady*, 158–61).

70. For an overview of this history, see Ellenberger, *Discovery of the Unconscious*, 152–55.

71. A. Moll, *Der Rapport in der Hypnose: Untersuchungen über den tierischen Magnetismus* (Leipzig: Abel, 1893), 403–404. For Janet's views, see below.

72. Janet, *Névroses et Idées fixes*, 425–28, 447.

73. Weininger again quoted an anecdote from Freud to establish that even without hyp-

nosis, there was an erotic component in the relationship between the hysteric and her physician (574). Freud had reported that as he had massaged an agitated patient, she had become calmer and clearer, and was able to identify the cause of her current problem without hypnosis. Freud does not seem to have interpreted this phenomenon as sexual. See *Studies on Hysteria, Standard Edition,* 2:56.

74. Janet, *Névroses et Idées fixes,* 456–57.

75. See chapter 7 for Weininger's expansion of this notion.

76. On Vogt's reputation, see Alan Gauld, *A History of Hypnotism,* 421, 537–43. Today, Vogt is remembered primarily as a neuroanatomist, not least because he helped found the Brain Research Institute in Moscow and, between 1925 and 1929, presided over the microscopic study of Lenin's brain. See Rolf Hassler, "Cécile und Oskar Vogt," in Kurt Kolle, ed., *Grosse Nervenärzte,* 3 vols. (Stuttgart: Thieme, 1959), 2:45–64; and the recent novel by Tilman Spengler, *Lenin's Brain,* trans. Shaun Whiteside (New York: Farrar, Straus & Giroux, 1993). In a series of papers published between 1897 and 1899, Vogt had argued for rigorous experimental investigations of hypnotic phenomena. His most important papers were: "Die direkte psychologische Experimentalmethode in hypnotischen Bewußtseinszuständen," *Zeitschrift für Hypnotismus* 5 (1897): 7–30, 180–218; "Zur Methodik der ätiologischen Erforschung der Hysterie," ibid., 8 (1899): 65–83; "Normalpsychologische Einleitung in die Psychopathologie der Hysterie," ibid., 208–27; and "Zur Kritik der psychogenetischen Erforschung der Hysterie," ibid., 342–55. Weininger cited all of these publications.

77. This "phallus" was not a Lacanian abstraction but the actual organ. Weininger was convinced that the penis exerted a mesmerizing influence on women; it represented their "destiny" and made them absolutely and definitely unfree (339). He quoted the description in Zola's *Germinal* of bourgeois women looking at Maigrat's castrated genitals being paraded down the streets by a mob. After initial puzzlement about the object, the ladies "stood stock still, open mouthed. The girls, deathly pale, asked no more questions, but their eyes watched the red vision disappear into the darkness" (Emile Zola, *Germinal,* trans. Leonard Tancock [New York: Knopf/Everyman's Library, 1991], 353). Weininger ignored the inconvenient fact that the castration had been performed by an angry mob of working-class women: "They pointed out to each other the bloody piece of flesh as though it were some nasty animal that had hurt them all and which they had at last squashed to death and now had lying there inert in their power" (ibid., 352).

78. What was the relation between woman's false outer self and this inherited (and, therefore, biological) masculinity? Weininger did not address this question. If the individual woman was composed of an innate core of pure sexuality, cloaked by an *acquired* (masculine) outer self, there was simply no space for any *inherited* masculinity anywhere.

79. Paul Sollier, *Genèse et nature de l'hystérie: Recherches cliniques et expérimentales de psycho-physiologie,* 2 vols. (Paris: Alcan, 1897), 1:7–12. Vigilambulism, according to Sollier, was a characteristically hysterical phenomenon in which an apparently wide-awake individual was actually in an inner state of somnambulism. On Sollier, see Ellenberger, *Discovery of the Unconscious,* 145. Havelock Ellis supported the notion of vigilambulism, describing Sollier as "one of the ablest of the more recent investigators of hysteria" (Ellis, "Hysteria in Relation to the Sexual Emotions," 599).

80. Sollier, *Genèse et nature de l'hystérie,* 1:460–61.

81. Pierre Briquet had stated that the principal predisposing factor in hysteria was the excessive impressionability of women. See Briquet, *Traité clinique,* 102. Georges Gilles de la Tourette (1857–1904), a prominent associate of Charcot's at the Salpêtrière, wrote in

1891 that the hysteric "is a passive being, a photographic plate which registers and displays its impressions as it has received them, sometimes amplified indeed, but always with the good faith of unconsciousness" (G. Gilles de la Tourette, *Traité clinique et thérapeutique de l'hystérie d'après l'enseignement de la Salpêtrière*, 2 vols. in 3 [Paris: Plon, 1891–95], 1 [1891]: 527). The translation is by Havelock Ellis, who had added that hysteria "may be summed up in one word—suggestibility" (Ellis, *Man and Woman*, 281).

82. Sollier, *Genèse et nature de l'hystérie*, 1:211, 458–59. Janet (see above) had already emphasized the frequency of sexual anesthesias in hysterics, and so had Pierre Briquet. On the basis of an examination of Briquet's work, Jacqueline Carroy-Thirard has argued that the idea of sexual anesthesia was indispensable for his "idealized" portrait of the hysteric as fragile and asexual (Carroy-Thirard, "Figures de femmes hystériques," 316–17).

83. Vogt, "Normalpsychologische Einleitung," 215.

*Chapter Seven*

1. David Abrahamsen suggested, without providing any concrete evidence, that Weininger's negative portrayal of the maternal type may have been influenced by his relationship with his own mother. See D. Abrahamsen, *The Mind and Death of a Genius*, 10–11.

2. See Stefan Zweig, *The World of Yesterday*, 83–91, for a famous, if exaggerated, account of prostitution in Vienna; and for a broader historical overview, see Karin J. Jusek, "Sexual Morality and the Meaning of Prostitution in Fin-de-Siècle Vienna," in Jan Bremmer, ed., *From Sappho to De Sade: Moments in the History of Sexuality* (London: Routledge, 1989), 123–42.

3. See Nancy McCombs, *Earth Spirit, Victim, or Whore? The Prostitute in German Literature, 1880–1925* (New York: Peter Lang, 1986).

4. C. Lombroso and G. Ferrero, *Das Weib als Verbrecherin und Prostituirte: Anthropologische Studien*, 540, 576–77. On the broader contexts of Lombroso's criminological project, see Robert Nye, "Heredity or Milieu: The Foundations of Modern European Criminological Theory," *Isis* 67 (1976): 335–55. On Lombrosian themes in Weininger's work, see Nancy A. Harrowitz, "Weininger and Lombroso: A Question of Influence," in Harrowitz and Hyams, eds., *Jews and Gender: Responses to Otto Weininger*, 73–90. For an overview of the fin-de-siècle German response to Lombroso, see Mariacarla Gadebusch Bondio, *Die Rezeption der kriminalanthropologischen Theorien von Cesare Lombroso in Deutschland von 1880–1914* (Husum: Matthiesen, 1995), 101–22, 150–240. On Lombroso's theories on sexual difference, see Klaus Hofweber, "Die Sexualtheorien des Cesare Lombroso" (Inaugural Dissertation, University of Munich, 1969); and David G. Horn, "This Norm Which Is Not One: Reading the Female Body in Lombroso's Anthropology," in Terry and Urla, eds., *Deviant Bodies: Critical Perspectives on Difference in Science and Popular Culture*, 109–28. On Lombroso's place in the history of criminology, see Ysabel Rennie, *The Search for Criminal Man: A Conceptual History of the Dangerous Offender* (Lexington, Mass.: D. C. Heath, 1978), 67–78. On the literary impact of Lombroso's views, see Barbara Spackman, *Decadent Genealogies: The Rhetoric of Sickness from Baudelaire to D'Annunzio* (Ithaca, N.Y.: Cornell University Press, 1989).

5. D. Horn, "This Norm Which Is Not One," 111.

6. See McCombs, *Earth Spirit, Victim, or Whore?* 44–49.

7. A. Bebel, *Woman and Socialism*, trans. Meta L. Stern Hebe (New York: Socialist Literature Co., 1910), 174.

8. Weininger acknowledged Lombroso as the source of these observations (546). See Lombroso and Ferrero, *Das Weib*, 228–64.

9. The genuine male, Weininger pointed out, never resorted to prostitution after a reversal of fate: only biologically feminized males did so (284).

10. "Everything about woman is a riddle," Friedrich Nietzsche had written, "and everything about woman has one solution: that is pregnancy. Man is for woman a means: the end is always the child" (Nietzsche, *Thus Spoke Zarathustra,* trans. Walter Kaufmann, in W. Kaufmann, ed., *The Portable Nietzsche,* 178). Weininger shared this view and expressed it in very similar terms, but only for *one* type of woman. Nietzsche, unlike Weininger, conceptualized the sexuality of *all* females in exclusively reproductive terms.

11. Sexually anesthetic or frigid women, Weininger stressed, were not necessarily Mothers. Many so-called frigid women, he argued, merely seemed to be so because an unattractive or sexually unskilled male partner could not arouse them (304). This opinion was opposed to the medical dogma of the time. Richard von Krafft-Ebing, to take the most famous example, was convinced that women who did not enjoy coitus were neuropathic or hysterical. The husband's responsibility was never even mentioned. See Krafft-Ebing, *Psychopathia Sexualis,* 12th ed., 68.

12. See Nike Wagner, *Geist und Geschlecht: Karl Kraus und die Erotik der Wiener Moderne,* 133–40; and Barbara Z. Schoenberg, "'Woman-Defender' and 'Woman-Offender,' Peter Altenberg and Otto Weininger: Two Literary Stances vis-à-vis Bourgeois Culture in the Viennese 'Belle Époque,'" *Modern Austrian Literature* 20, no. 2 (1987): 51–61.

13. See Elisabeth Badinter, *Mother Love, Myth and Reality: Motherhood in Modern History,* anonymous trans. (New York: Macmillan, 1981).

14. Claudia Honegger, "Frauen und medizinische Deutungsmacht im 19. Jahrhundert," in Alfons Labisch and Reinhard Spree, eds., *Medizinische Deutungsmacht im sozialen Wandel des 19. und frühen 20. Jahrhunderts* (Bonn: Psychiatrie-Verlag, 1989), 181–94, especially 191–92.

15. See Ann Taylor Allen, *Feminism and Motherhood in Germany, 1800–1914.*

16. J. J. Bachofen, *Das Mutterrecht: Eine Untersuchung über die Gynaikokratie der alten Welt nach ihrer religiösen und rechtlichen Natur* (Stuttgart: Krais and Hoffman, 1861). On the broader contexts of Bachofen's work, see Lionel Gossman, "Basle, Bachofen, and the Critique of Modernity in the Second Half of the Nineteenth Century," *Journal of the Warburg and Courtauld Institutes* 47 (1984): 136–85.

17. See Annette Kliewer, *Geistesfrucht und Leibesfrucht: Mütterlichkeit und "weibliches Schreiben" im Kontext der ersten bürgerlichen Frauenbewegung* (Pfaffenweiler: Centaurus, 1993), 241–54.

18. See Harriet Anderson, *Utopian Feminism: Women's Movements in Fin-de-siècle Vienna,* 200–201.

19. Hence, Weininger suggested, mother-love could be better gauged by a mother's relations with her daughter. He did not, however, explore this theme any further.

20. Freud, *The Interpretation of Dreams,* in *Standard Edition,* 4:260–64. The term "Oedipus Complex" formally appeared in Freud's writings only in 1910: see Freud, "A Special Type of Choice of Object Made by Men" (1910), *Standard Edition,* 11:164–75, at 171.

21. On erectile tissue in the nipples, Weininger cited Joseph Hyrtl, *Handbuch der topographischen Anatomie und ihrer praktisch medicinisch-chirurgischen Anwendungen,* 7th ed., 2 vols. (Vienna: Braumüller, 1882), 1:629–30; and Leonard Landois, *Lehrbuch der Physiologie des Menschen,* 9th ed. (Vienna: Urban and Schwarzenberg, 1896), 441–42.

22. M. Runge, *Lehrbuch der Geburtshilfe,* 3d ed. (Berlin: Springer, 1896), 177. Later, Freud, too, would sexualize the nursing of a baby, but from the child's perspective: "No one

who has seen a baby sinking back satiated from the breast and falling asleep with flushed cheeks and a blissful smile can escape the reflection that this picture persists as a prototype of the expression of sexual satisfaction in later life" (Freud, *Three Essays on the Theory of Sexuality,* in *Standard Edition,* 7:182).

23. A. Schopenhauer, *The World as Will and Representation,* trans. E. F. J. Payne, 2 vols. (New York: Dover, 1966), 2:536–37.

24. For a concise historical overview, see Havelock Ellis, *Studies in the Psychology of Sex,* 2 vols. (New York: Random House, 1936), vol. 2, pt. 1, *Erotic Symbolism, The Mechanism of Detumescence, The Psychic State in Pregnancy,* 218–27. Documenting fourteen case reports of unverified accuracy published in the *British Medical Journal* and *The Lancet,* Ellis observed that although the theory had little empirical validation, "we are not entitled to reject it with any positive assurance. Even if we accept it, however, it must remain, for the present, an inexplicable fact" (218–20, 225). See also Marie-Hélène Huet, *Monstrous Imagination* (Cambridge, Mass.: Harvard University Press, 1993), 1–123, and Dennis Todd, *Imagining Monsters: Miscreations of Life in Eighteenth-Century England* (Chicago: University of Chicago Press, 1995). For a fairly recent attempt at experimental validation of this idea, see G. Farkas and G. Farkas, Jr., "Is the Popular Belief about 'Maternal Impression' in Pregnancy Unscientific?" in *Proceedings of the XXIIIrd International Congress of the History of Medicine, London, 2–9 September 1972* (London: Wellcome Institute for the History of Medicine, 1974), 2:1303–1304.

25. Barbara Maria Stafford, *Body Criticism: Imaging the Unseen in Enlightenment Art and Medicine* (Cambridge, Mass.: MIT Press, 1991), 308.

26. Ibid., 311, 313–15; and M.-H. Huet, *Monstrous Imagination,* 45–55.

27. Stafford, *Body Criticism,* 312.

28. See Huet, *Monstrous Imagination,* 48–49, and Todd, *Imagining Monsters,* 62–63.

29. Huet, *Monstrous Imagination,* 50.

30. Ibid., 63–67.

31. Hermann Heinrich Ploss and Max Bartels, *Das Weib in der Natur- und Völkerkunde: Anthropologische Studien,* 1:614. The translation is from H. Ploss, M. Bartels, and P. Bartels, *Woman: An Historical, Gynaecological, and Anthropological Compendium,* trans. Eric J. Dingwall, 3 vols. (St. Louis: Mosby, 1936), 2:460.

32. J. Müller, *Handbuch der Physiologie des Menschen für Vorlesungen,* 2 vols. in 3 (Coblenz: Hölscher, 1833–40), 2, pt. 3 (1840): 574.

33. Ibid.

34. Ibid., 575.

35. See Huet, *Monstrous Imagination,* 73–74.

36. T. L. W. Bischoff, "Entwicklungsgeschichte mit besonderer Berücksichtigung der Missbildungen," in R. Wagner, ed., *Handwörterbuch der Physiologie mit Rücksicht auf physiologische Pathologie,* 4 vols. in 5 (Braunschweig: Vieweg, 1842–53), 1 (1842): 860–928, at 885–89.

37. M. Runge, *Lehrbuch der Geburtshilfe,* 6th ed. (Berlin: Springer, 1902), 82–83.

38. H. Settegast, *Die Tierzucht,* 4th ed., 2 vols. in 1 (Breslau: Korn, 1878), vol. 1, *Die Züchtungslehre,* 219.

39. Darwin, *The Variation of Animals and Plants under Domestication,* 2:251–52. Darwin added that beliefs in the power of the maternal imagination might have originated from "the children of a second marriage resembling the previous father, as certainly sometimes occurs" (ibid.). This latter belief would subsequently play a stellar role in Weininger's deconstruction of female subjectivity.

40. K. F. Burdach, K. E. von Baer, H. Rathke, and E. H. Meyer, *Die Physiologie als Erfahrungswissenschaft*, 2d ed., 3 vols. (Leipzig: Voss, 1837), 2:129.

41. Ibid., 125.

42. In the *Critique of Pure Reason,* Kant had argued that the concept of cause demanded "that something, A, should be such that something else, B, follows from it *necessarily and in accordance with an absolutely universal rule.* Appearances do indeed present cases from which a rule can be obtained according to which something usually happens, but they never prove the sequence to be *necessary*. . . . Empirical rules can acquire through induction only comparative universality [*comparative Allgemeinheit*], that is, extensive applicability [*ausgebreitete Brauchbarkeit*]" (Kant, *Critique of Pure Reason*, 125).

43. Weininger's engagement with theories of telegony has been explored from a very different angle by Alberto Cavaglion, "Svevo and Weininger (Lord Morton's Mare)," trans. Nancy A. Harrowitz, in Harrowitz and Hyams, eds., *Jews and Gender,* 237–43.

44. See Richard W. Burkhardt, Jr., "Closing the Door on Lord Morton's Mare: The Rise and Fall of Telegony," *Studies in History of Biology* 3 (1979): 1–21; and Prosper Lucas, *Traité philosophique et physiologique de l'hérédité naturelle,* 2 vols. (Paris: Baillière, 1847–50), 2 (1850): 58.

45. See Burkhardt, "Closing the Door," 5–6. Many nineteenth-century endorsements of the "fetal infection" theory were cited in William B. Carpenter, *Principles of Human Physiology* (Philadelphia: Blanchard and Lea, 1862), 781–82; and for the view that telegony was an example of maternal impression, see Alexander Walker, *Intermarriage, or the Natural Laws by which Beauty, Health and Intellect result from Certain Unions, and Deformity, Disease and Insanity, from Others* (London: Churchill, 1841), 274–78.

46. The quoted phrase is from Karl Pearson, *The Life, Letters and Labours of Francis Galton,* 3 vols. in 4 (Cambridge: Cambridge University Press, 1924), 2:159.

47. Darwin, *Variation,* 1:427–28, 432–33. This phenomenon was later named "xenia" by the German botanist Wilhelm Focke. Focke, whom Weininger cites, was actually quite undecided about the nature of "xenia" and its causation, and August Weismann later considered him to be a disbeliever in telegony. See Wilhelm Olbers Focke, *Die Pflanzen-Mischlinge: Ein Beitrag zur Biologie der Gewächse* (Berlin: Borntraeger, 1881), 510–18, especially 511. For Weismann's opinion, see A. Weismann, *The Germ-Plasm: A Theory of Heredity,* 384. For the ways in which the study of "xenia" may have stimulated early research on genetics, see L. C. Dunn, "Xenia and the Origin of Genetics," *Proceedings of the American Philosophical Society* 117 (1973): 105–11.

48. The Earl of Morton, "A Communication of a Singular Fact in Natural History," *Philosophical Transactions of the Royal Society of London* 111 (1821): 20–22. See also Daniel Giles, "Particulars of a Fact, Nearly Similar to that related by Lord Morton," ibid., 23–24. The quagga became extinct by the end of the nineteenth century.

49. Morton, "Communication of a Singular Fact," 20.

50. Darwin, *Variation,* 1:435.

51. Ibid., 436–37.

52. Ibid., 437.

53. E. Mayr, *The Growth of Biological Thought: Diversity, Evolution, Inheritance* (Cambridge: Harvard University Press, 1982), 694. See also Gerald L. Geison, "Darwin and Heredity: The Evolution of His Hypothesis of Pangenesis," *Journal of the History of Medicine and Allied Sciences* 24 (1969): 375–411. On the many theories of inheritance that crowded the biological literature before the rediscovery of Mendel's work in 1900, see Gloria Robinson, *A Prelude to Genetics: Theories of a Material Substance of Heredity.*

54. Darwin, *Variation*, 2: 370–71.

55. Darwin, *Variation of Animals and Plants under Domestication*, 1st ed., 2 vols. (New York: Orange Judd, 1868), 2:463–64. These passages were removed in the second edition; cf. Darwin, *Variation*, 2d ed., 2:381–83.

56. Lest these remarks be dismissed as typical examples of Weininger's pseudoscientific speculations, one should add that Darwin himself wrote the following words in 1870: "I remember formerly speculating . . . on the assertion that wives grow like their husbands." Nevertheless, Darwin was not Weininger. Immediately after that sentence, he had added: "But how impossible to eliminate effects of imitation and same habits of life, etc." See Darwin's letter of 17 March 1870 to J. Jenner Weir in Francis Darwin, ed., *More Letters of Charles Darwin*, 2 vols. (London: John Murray, 1903), 1:319–20.

57. R. W. Burkhardt Jr., "Closing the Door," 10.

58. See E. Mayr, *Growth of Biological Thought*, 700. Mayr points out that while Weismann's basic intuition was accurate in today's terms, "we now know that the crucial separation is that between the DNA program of the nucleus and the proteins in the cytoplasm of each cell." See also G. Robinson, *Prelude to Genetics*, 133–85. For the historical context in which Weismann developed his maverick hypothesis, see Frederick B. Churchill, "Weismann's Continuity of the Germ-Plasm in Historical Perspective," in Klaus Sander, ed., *August Weismann (1834–1914) und die theoretische Biologie des 19. Jahrhunderts: Urkunden, Berichte und Analysen*, special issue of *Freiburger Universitätsblätter* 87–88 (1985): 107–24.

59. On Spencer's life and work, see J. D. Y. Peel, *Herbert Spencer: The Evolution of a Sociologist* (New York: Basic Books, 1971); and on Spencer's biological theories, Derek Freeman, "The Evolutionary Theories of Charles Darwin and Herbert Spencer," *Current Anthropology* 15 (1974): 211–21.

60. Weismann, *Germ-Plasm*, 385.

61. Settegast, *Die Tierzucht*, 1:223–34. Weininger quoted this passage without comment (561). For more information on the breeders' assault on telegony, see Burkhardt, "Closing the Door," 9.

62. The original articles were: "The Inadequacy of 'Natural Selection,'" *Popular Science Monthly* 42 (1892–93): 799–812; 43 (1893): 21–28, 162–73; and "Professor Weismann's Theories," *Popular Science Monthly* 43 (1893): 473–90. Both articles had been published initially in the British periodical *Contemporary Review* 63 (1893). The German translation fused the two articles into one: "Die Unzulänglichkeit der 'natürlichen Zuchtwahl,'" *Biologisches Zentralblatt* 13 (1893): 696–704, 705–19, 737–53, and 14 (1894): 230–40, 259–69. For a list of all of Spencer's articles against Weismann, Weismann's rejoinders, and the contributions of other biologists to the debate, see Robert G. Perrin, *Herbert Spencer: A Primary and Secondary Bibliography* (New York: Garland, 1993), 257. For an analysis of the debate, see Frederick B. Churchill, "The Weismann-Spencer Controversy over the Inheritance of Acquired Characters," in Eric G. Forbes, ed., *Human Implications of Scientific Advance: Proceedings of the XVth International Congress of the History of Science, Edinburgh, 10–15 August 1977* (Edinburgh: Edinburgh University Press, 1978), 451–68. Generally on the fortunes of the idea of the inheritance of acquired characters, see L. I. Blacher, *The Problem of the Inheritance of Acquired Characters: A History of A Priori and Empirical Methods used to Find a Solution*, trans. Noel Hess, ed. F. B. Churchill (New Delhi: Amerind, 1982), especially 79–119.

63. Spencer, "Unzulänglichkeit," 748; "Inadequacy," 168.

64. Spencer, "Unzulänglichkeit," 262–63; "Professor Weismann's Theories," 485.

See also Austin Flint, *A Textbook of Human Physiology* (New York: Appleton, 1876), 894.

65. See Burkhardt, "Closing the Door," 14. Regarding double fertilization: Two male gametes are involved in the fertilization process in most flowering plants. One male gamete from the pollen grain unites with the egg nucleus to form the zygote, which develops into the embryo. A second male gamete unites with two "polar nuclei" in the embryo sac to form the endosperm, which contains nutritive material.

66. He was particularly familiar with the critiques of Weismann and Settegast but not with negative experimental studies, such as those of James Ewart (1851–1933), Regius Professor of Natural History at the University of Edinburgh. On Ewart's experiments, see Burkhardt, "Closing the Door," 12–14.

67. Concluding his survey of the historical aspects of the scientific concept of telegony, Richard Burkhardt lamented that scientists' writings on the subject do not clearly indicate the sociocultural underpinnings of the concept, although nineteenth-century ideas of racial purity and female subordination would seem to have been consonant with it ("Closing the Door," 16–17). It is all the more important, therefore, to demonstrate the social and cultural dimensions of the concept by investigating its use by thinkers beyond the professional world of science. Such an exploration would demonstrate not simply the existence of the potential cultural meaning that Burkhardt intuits but also show how it was utilized for specific cultural and political purposes.

68. Telegony, for Weismann, could occur only when one female has children by two different males. Psychological attraction to two males or even a nonreproductive sexual relationship with one followed by a reproductive relationship with another does not qualify.

69. See Marvin Carlson, "Ibsen, Strindberg, and Telegony," *PMLA: Publications of the Modern Language Association of America* 100 (1985): 774–82.

70. For an overview and bibliography of this literature, see John Winkelman, *Goethe's "Elective Affinities": An Interpretation* (New York: Lang, 1987).

71. "Think of a substance A," the Captain says, "existing as a compound with substance B, unable to be sundered from B by force or any other means; and then think of a substance C, related in the same way to substance D. Now bring the two compounds together: A will combine with D and C will combine with B in such a way that it will be impossible to say which elements separated or recombined first.... In this kind of separation and combination, repulsion and attraction, some higher destiny really does seem to manifest itself" (J. W. von Goethe, *Elective Affinities*, trans. Judith Ryan, in *Goethe's Collected Works*, 12 vols. [New York: Suhrkamp, 1988], 11:116.

72. Ibid., 147.

73. Ibid., 238.

74. Ibid.

75. The Renaissance natural philosopher and obstetrician Fortunii Liceti had observed in 1616 that the mother's imagination was more important in influencing the offspring because "though the father's imagination can affect him during the sexual act, the woman's is always at work, after copulation and during conception.... In any case, women's imaginations are stronger and more ardent" (quoted in Huet, *Monstrous Imagination*, 15).

76. Carlson, "Ibsen, Strindberg, and Telegony," 776.

77. *The Plays of Ibsen*, trans. Michael Meyer, 4 vols. (New York: Washington Square Press, 1986), 4:373.

78. For analyses of some of these issues, see Yvonne Shafer, "The Liberated Woman in Ibsen's *The Lady from the Sea*," *Theatre Annual* 40 (1985): 65–76; and Elinor Fuchs, "Mar-

riage, Metaphysics and *The Lady from the Sea* Problem," *Modern Drama* 33 (1990): 434–44.

79. Gail Finney, "Ibsen and Feminism," in James McFarlane, ed., *The Cambridge Companion to Ibsen* (Cambridge: Cambridge University Press, 1994), 89–105, at 103. See also Declan Kiberd, *Men and Feminism in Modern Literature* (New York: St. Martin's Press, 1985), 61–84.

80. On Zola and heredity, see Laura Otis, *Organic Memory: History and the Body in the Late Nineteenth and Early Twentieth Centuries*, 53–75; and Carlson, "Ibsen, Strindberg, and Telegony," 775–76.

81. Otis, *Organic Memory*, 4–5.

82. *Madeleine Férat*, in Emile Zola, *Oeuvres complètes*, ed. Henri Mitterand, 15 vols. (Paris: Cercle du Livre Precieux, 1966–70), 1:683–903; in English: *Madeleine Ferat*, trans. Alec Brown (London: Elek, 1957).

83. Zola, *Oeuvres complètes*, 1:813. Translation modified from Brown, 164.

84. Zola, *Oeuvres complètes*, 1:812–13; Brown's translation, 163–64, emphasis added.

85. On Goethe's anti-Newtonian theory of color, see Dennis L. Seper, *Goethe contra Newton: Polemics and the Project for a New Science of Color* (Cambridge: Cambridge University Press, 1988). Schopenhauer as well as Hegel had supported Goethe against the physicists. See F. H. Lauxtermann, "Hegel and Schopenhauer as Partisans of Goethe's Theory of Color," *Journal of the History of Ideas* 51 (1990): 599–624.

86. On the evolution of Strindberg's attitude toward feminism, see Evert Sprinchorn, "Ibsen, Strindberg, and the New Woman," in Michael Bertin, ed., *The Play and its Critic: Essays for Eric Bentley* (Lanham, Md.: University Press of America, 1986), 45–66.

87. See Carlson, "Ibsen, Strindberg, and Telegony," 777.

88. *The Father*, in August Strindberg, *Selected Plays*, trans. Evert Sprinchorn (Minneapolis: University of Minnesota Press, 1986), 163, 197. For an analysis of the personal and political motifs in the play, see Gail Finney, *Women in Modern Drama: Freud, Feminism, and European Theater at the Turn of the Century* (Ithaca, N.Y.: Cornell University Press, 1989), 207–26.

89. On Bachofen's influence on later social thought, see Harvey Greisman, "Matriarchate as Utopia, Myth, and Social Theory," *Sociology* 15 (1981): 321–36; Daniel Burston, "Myth, Religion, and Mother Right: Bachofen's Influence on Psychoanalytic Theory," *Contemporary Psychoanalysis* 22 (1986): 666–87; and Carolyn Fluehr-Lobban, "Marxism and the Matriarchate: One Hundred Years after *The Origin of the Family, Private Property, and the State*," *Critique of Anthropology* 7 (1987): 5–14.

90. See John Ward, *The Social and Religious Plays of Strindberg* (London: Athlone, 1980), 47–57.

91. See Bachofen, *Mutterrecht*, 77. This notion was the basis of an old legal tag quoted by Sigmund Freud: "'pater semper incertus est,' while the mother is 'certissima.'" See S. Freud, "Family Romances," *Standard Edition*, 9:235–41, at 239.

92. For a different, Lacanian interpretation of how Weininger's antifeminism led to an affirmation of the power of Woman, see Slavoj Žižek, "Otto Weininger, or, 'Woman Doesn't Exist,'" *New Formations*, no. 23 (Summer 1994): 97–113, especially 112–13.

## Chapter Eight

1. The most cogent and well-informed overview of the episode is provided by Frank J. Sulloway, *Freud, Biologist of the Mind*, 223–29. See also Kurt R. Eissler, *Talent and Genius: The Fictitious Case of Tausk contra Freud* (New York: Macmillan, 1971); Peter Heller, "A

Quarrel over Bisexuality," in Gerald Chapple and Hans H. Schulte, eds., *The Turn of the Century: German Literature and Art, 1890–1915* (Bonn: Bouvier, 1981), 87–115; Gustav Lebzeltern, "Zu Unrecht vergessene Freud-Briefe," *Dynamische Psychiatrie* 15 (1982): 97–113; and Sander L. Gilman, "Otto Weininger and Sigmund Freud: Race and Gender in the Shaping of Psychoanalysis," in Harrowitz and Hyams, eds., *Jews and Gender: Responses to Otto Weininger,* 103–20.

2. For an excellent discussion, see Sulloway, *Freud, Biologist of the Mind,* 135–237. An earlier account attempting to establish Freud's theories as essentially independent of Fliess, was Ernst Kris, "Einleitung," in Marie Bonaparte, Anna Freud, and E. Kris, eds., *Aus den Anfängen der Psychoanalyse: Briefe an Wilhelm Fliess, Abhandlungen und Notizen aus den Jahren 1887–1902* (London: Imago, 1950), 7–56.

3. See Sulloway, *Freud,* 140–44, 152–58, 160–69, 231, note 67. Sulloway has also shown that Fliess's notion of periodicity was hardly eccentric in the contemporary context of research on vital periodicity.

4. For an analysis of these differences, see ibid., 217–23.

5. *The Complete Letters of Sigmund Freud to Wilhelm Fliess,* 463.

6. See ibid., 464, 467. According to David Abrahamsen, Freud, after reading Weininger's manuscript, had accused him of plagiarism: "Sie haben das Schloss geöffnet mit einem gestohlenem Schlüssel!" (You have opened the lock with a stolen key). See Abrahamsen, *Mind and Death of a Genius,* 54, footnote. Weininger does not mention any such confrontation in his extant letters to Swoboda.

7. W. Fliess, *In eigener Sache: Gegen Otto Weininger und Hermann Swoboda* (Berlin: Goldschmidt, 1906); R. Pfennig, *Wilhelm Fliess und seine Nachentdecker: O. Weininger und H. Swoboda* (Berlin: Goldschmidt, 1906).

8. See Sulloway, *Freud,* 229. Hirschfeld published a brief article pointing out that the bisexuality of all humans was an idea going back to ancient times. See M. Hirschfeld, "Die gestohlene Bisexualität," *Wiener klinische Rundschau* 20 (1906): 706–707. For Freud's letter to Kraus, see Ernst L. Freud, ed., *Letters of Sigmund Freud,* trans. Tania and James Stern (New York: Basic Books, 1960), 249–51.

9. See Sulloway, *Freud,* 229; and H. Swoboda, *Die gemeinnützige Forschung und der eigennützige Forscher: Antwort auf die von Wilhelm Fliesz* [sic] *gegen Otto Weininger und mich erhobenen Beschuldigungen* (Vienna: Braumüller, 1906).

10. The work was W. Fliess, *Die Beziehungen zwischen Nase und weiblichen Geschlechtsorganen in ihrer biologischen Bedeutung dargestellt* (Leipzig: Deuticke, 1897). I discuss Weininger's remarks on it in chapter 3, above.

11. See Fliess, *In eigener Sache,* 11–12.

12. Quoted in Abrahamsen, *Mind and Death of a Genius,* 55.

13. Freud, *Standard Edition,* 7:143; 10:36.

14. *Geschlecht und Charakter: Eine prinzipielle Untersuchung von Dr. Otto Weininger* (Vienna: W. Braumüller, 1905). I am indebted to Allan Janik for providing me with a copy of this brochure.

15. Ibid., 37–38.

16. Ibid., 39–41.

17. Ibid., 11–13.

18. Ibid., 19.

19. Ibid., 20–23.

20. Ibid., 23–28. I do not know whether this statement is merely idiosyncratic or indicates a contemporary German stereotype about Viennese men.

21. Ibid., 36.

22. Ford Madox Hueffer [Ford Madox Ford], "Women and Men, II: The Literature of the Subject," *The Little Review*, no. 11 (March 1918): 36–51, at 40–41. Quite ill informed about Weininger's life and career, Ford believed that he had been a young physician of Jena who had written *Geschlecht und Charakter* (and shot himself) after being spurned by a woman.

23. H. Meyer, *Outsiders: A Study in Life and Letters,* trans. Denis M. Sweet (Cambridge, Mass.: MIT Press, 1982), 100.

24. See Edward Timms, *Karl Kraus, Apocalyptic Satirist: Culture and Catastrophe in Habsburg Vienna,* 83. On Kraus's views on women and sexuality, see Nike Wagner, *Geist und Geschlecht: Karl Kraus und die Erotik der Wiener Moderne.*

25. Jacques Le Rider, "Otto Weininger als Anti-Freud," in *Traum und Wirklichkeit: Wien, 1870–1930* (Vienna: Eigenverlag der Museen der Stadt Wien, 1985), 248–51, at 249. By far the most comprehensive and nuanced analysis of Kraus's position on Freud and psychoanalysis is Edward Timms, *Karl Kraus: Apocalyptic Satirist,* 95–114. Italian intellectuals of the fin de siècle, too, used Weininger's theories to oppose psychoanalytic pansexualism; this, however, was just one strand in the complex Italian response to *Geschlecht und Charakter.* See Alberto Cavaglion and Michel David, "Weininger und die italienische Kultur," in Jacques Le Rider and Norbert Leser, eds., *Otto Weininger: Werk und Wirkung* (Vienna: Österreichischer Bundesverlag, 1984), 37–49, at 40.

26. K. Bleibtreu, "Otto Weininger's *Geschlecht und Charakter,*" *Die Fackel,* no. 157 (1904): 12–20.

27. *Die Fackel,* nos. 389–90 (1913): 38; Nike Wagner, *Geist und Geschlecht,* 152–57.

28. Karl Hauer, "Weib und Kultur," *Die Fackel,* no. 213 (1906): 5–10. See also Ludwig Erik Tesar, "Die Wissenschaft und der einzelne Mensch," ibid., nos. 324–25 (1911): 34, 36.

29. See Nike Wagner, *Geist und Geschlecht,* 157.

30. *Die Fackel,* no. 229 (1907): 14. Although Kraus was himself anti-Semitic, he never addressed Weininger's anti-Semitism. On Kraus's attitude toward Jews and "Jewishness," see Timms, *Karl Kraus, Apocalyptic Satirist,* 237–41, 338–41. None of the early Central European responses to Weininger seem to have recognized his anti-Semitism. The situation in Russia, according to Laura Engelstein, was quite different. There, Weininger's anti-Semitism was noted and widely endorsed from the publication of the first Russian translation of *Geschlecht und Charakter* in 1909. See L. Engelstein, *The Keys to Happiness: Sex and the Search for Modernity in Fin-de-Siècle Russia* (Ithaca: Cornell University Press, 1992), 310–11, 317–18. In Germany, Weininger's anti-Semitism was highlighted only after the coming of the Nazis. Adolf Hitler recollected a mentor telling him that history recorded "only one decent Jew, Otto Weininger, who took his life when he realized that the Jew lives from the destruction of other peoples." Numerous other Nazis regarded Weininger's denunciation of Jews as the insights of a genius. See B. Hyams, "Weininger and Nazi Ideology," in Harrowitz and Hyams, eds., *Jews and Gender,* 155–68. Hyams points out that Nazis downplayed Weininger's antifeminism in order to conceal the antifeminism of their own, ostensibly exclusively racial, political agenda.

31. Le Rider states that architect Adolf Loos, composers Arnold Schönberg and Alban Berg, painter Oskar Kokoschka and poet Georg Trakl were all introduced to Weininger's work by Kraus (Le Rider, *Der Fall Otto Weininger,* 147). See also K. Kraus, *Briefe an Sidonie Nádherny von Borutin: 1913–1936,* ed. Heinrich Fischer and Michael Lazarus in consultation with Walter Methlagl and Friedrich Pfäfflin, 2 vols. (Munich: Kosel, 1974), 1:243;

2:193; F. Probst, *Der Fall Otto Weininger: Eine psychiatrische Studie;* and Leopold Weininger, "Der Fall Otto Weininger: Erklärung und Berichtigung," with a commentary in footnotes by Karl Kraus, *Die Fackel,* no. 169 (23 November 1904): 6–14.

32. *Die Fackel,* no. 144 (1903): 17. For comprehensive analyses of Strindberg's encounter with Weininger and Kraus, see Erich Unglaub, "Strindberg, Weininger und Karl Kraus: Eine Überprüfung," *Recherches Germaniques* (Strasbourg) 18 (1988): 121–50, and Hugh Salvesen, "The Disappointed Idealist: August Strindberg in Karl Kraus's Periodical *Die Fackel,*" *New German Studies* 9, no. 3 (1981): 157–79.

33. A. Strindberg, "Idolatrie, Gynolatrie," *Die Fackel,* no. 144 (1903): 1–3. This obituary is reproduced in Le Rider, *Der Fall Otto Weininger,* 51–52.

34. This audience, however, is not always an admiring one. In Günter Grass's 1963 novel *Hundejahre,* for instance, *Geschlecht und Charakter* is described as "a satanic work" *(Teufelswerk)* and used as a "document of German anti-Semitism." See Wesley V. Blomster, "The Documentation of a Novel: Otto Weininger and *Hundejahre* by Günter Grass," *Monatshefte* 61, no. 2 (1969): 122–38.

35. Gerald Stieg, "Kafka and Weininger," trans. Barbara Hyams, in Harrowitz and Hyams, eds., *Jews and Gender,* 195–206, at 195.

36. Heinz Politzer, *Franz Kafka: Parable and Paradox,* rev. ed. (Ithaca, N.Y.: Cornell University Press, 1966), 197–98. See also Rainer Stach, "Kafka's Egoless Woman: Otto Weininger's *Sex and Character,*" trans. Neil Donahue, in Mark Anderson, ed., *Reading Kafka: Prague, Politics, and the Fin de Siècle* (New York: Schocken, 1989), 149–69. Incidentally, writer Gottfried Benn remarked in 1949 that Weininger was one of the three Jewish figures he recognized as geniuses, whereas Kafka just possessed a "talent of the first order" (G. Benn, "Doppelleben," in *Autobiographische und vermischte Schriften,* vol. 4 of G. Benn, *Gesammelte Werke* [Wiesbaden: Limes, 1961], 72).

37. G. Stieg, "Kafka and Weininger," 196, emphases in the original.

38. See Gerald Stieg, *Der Brenner und Die Fackel: Ein Beitrag zur Wirkungsgeschichte von Karl Kraus* (Salzburg: O. Müller, 1976).

39. See Ursula Heckmann, *Das verfluchte Geschlecht: Motive der Philosophie Otto Weiningers im Werk Georg Trakls* (Frankfurt a.M.: Lang, 1992), 128.

40. Gerald Stieg, "Otto Weiningers 'Blendung': Weininger, Karl Kraus und der Brenner-Kreis," in J. Le Rider and N. Leser, eds., *Otto Weininger: Werk und Wirkung,* 59–68, on 63, emphasis in the original.

41. U. Heckmann, *Das verfluchte Geschlecht,* 237–40.

42. See Daniel Eckert, "Der gespiegelte Spiegel: Sexualphilosophie und Subjekttheorie bei Otto Weininger und Ferdinand Ebner," in Walter Methlagl, Peter Kampits, Christoph König, and Franz Josef Brandfellner, eds., *Gegen den Traum vom Geist: Ferdinand Ebner* (Salzburg: Müller, 1985), 182–90.

43. See F. Ebner, "Fragment 16: Otto Weininger. Geist und Sexualität. Die Juden. Christus," in Ebner, *Das Wort und die geistigen Realitäten: Pneumatologische Fragmente* (Frankfurt a.M.: Suhrkamp, 1980), particularly 219. See also D. Eckert, "Der gespiegelte Spiegel," 186.

44. See Gisela Brude-Firnau, "Wissenschaft von der Frau? Zum Einfluß von Otto Weiningers 'Geschlecht und Charakter' auf den deutschen Roman," in Wolfgang Paulsen, ed., *Die Frau als Heldin und Autorin: Neue kritische Ansätze zur deutschen Literatur* (Bern: Francke, 1979), 136–49, especially 139–42.

45. Ibid., 142–46.

46. See the English version, E. Canetti, *Auto-da-fé*, trans. C. V. Wedgwood (New York: Continuum, 1982).

47. E. Canetti, *Die Fackel im Ohr: Lebensgeschichte 1921–1931* (Munich: C. Hauser, 1980), 90, 136.

48. See Stieg, "Otto Weiningers 'Blendung,'" 61.

49. Ibid., 62.

50. See A. Janik, "Writing about Weininger," in Janik, *Essays on Wittgenstein and Weininger*, 96–115, at 97. For a recent argument that Weininger's "fascist" treatise should never have been reprinted, see Hannelore Schröder, "Anti-Semitism and Anti-Feminism Again: The Dissemination of Otto Weininger's *Sex and Character* in the Seventies and Eighties," in Erik C. W. Krabbe et al., eds., *Empirical Logic and Public Debate: Essays in Honour of Else M. Barth* (Amsterdam: Rodopi, 1993), 305–18.

51. See Robert Byrnes, "Bloom's Sexual Tropes: Stigmata of the 'Degenerate' Jew," *James Joyce Quarterly* 27 (1990): 303–23; Marilyn Reizbaum, "Weininger and the Bloom of Jewish Self-Hatred in Joyce's *Ulysses*," in Harrowitz and Hyams, eds., *Jews and Gender*, 207–13; and Natania Rosenfeld, "James Joyce's Womanly Wandering Jew," in ibid., 215–26. For Joyce's own description of Bloom's effeminacy, see J. Joyce, *Ulysses* (New York: Modern Library, 1961), 493.

52. See Elfriede Pöder, "Molly *is* Sexuality: The Weiningerian Definition of Woman in Joyce's *Ulysses*," in Harrowitz and Hyams, eds., *Jews and Gender*, 227–35.

53. See A. Cavaglion and M. David, "Weininger und die italienische Kultur," 38–39; A. Cavaglion, "Svevo and Weininger (Lord Morton's Mare)," in Harrowitz and Hyams, eds., *Jews and Gender*, 237–43; and Nancy A. Harrowitz, *Anti-Semitism, Misogyny, and the Logic of Cultural Difference: Cesare Lombroso and Matilde Serao*, 9.

54. See Mike Weaver, *William Carlos Williams: The American Background* (Cambridge: University Press, 1971), 17–22. My thanks to Gert Brieger for drawing my attention to Williams.

55. See Leon Katz, "Weininger and 'The Making of Americans,'" *Twentieth Century Literature* 24, no. 1 (1978): 8–26.

56. Weininger was well known to feminists beyond Central Europe. On British feminist and anarchist responses to Weininger, see Judy Greenway, "It's What You Do With It That Counts: Interpretations of Otto Weininger," in Lucy Bland and Laura Doan, eds., *Sexology in Culture: Labelling Bodies and Desires* (Cambridge: Polity, 1998), 27–43.

57. See Harriet Anderson, *Utopian Feminism: Women's Movements in Fin-de-Siècle Vienna*, 145–46.

58. Ibid., 147.

59. Ibid., 191. See also Ellinor Melander, "Toward the Sexual and Economic Emancipation of Women: The Philosophy of Grete Meisel-Hess," *History of European Ideas* 14 (1992): 695–713.

60. R. Mayreder, *Zur Kritik der Weiblichkeit: Essays* (Jena: Diederichs, 1910), 33.

61. Ibid.

62. Ibid., 276.

63. Margarethe Gellert [G. Meisel-Hess], *Weiberhass und Weiberverachtung: Eine Erwiderung auf die in Dr Otto Weiningers Buche "Geschlecht und Charakter" geäusserten Anschauungen über "die Frau und ihre Frage,"* as quoted in Anderson, *Utopian Feminism*, 150.

64. G. Meisel-Hess, *Weiberhass und Weiberverachtung*, as quoted in Le Rider, *Der Fall Otto Weininger*, 167.

65. C. Gilman, "Dr. Weininger's 'Sex and Character,'" *The Critic* 48, no. 5 (May 1906): 414–17.

66. See Richard J. Evans, *The Feminist Movement in Germany 1894–1933* (London: Sage, 1976), 175–205.

67. H. Blüher, *Der bürgerliche und der geistige Antifeminismus* (Tempelhof-Berlin: Verlag Hans Blüher, 1916).

68. See George L. Mosse, *The Crisis of German Ideology: Intellectual Origins of the Third Reich* (New York: Schocken, 1964), 176–77, 212–14.

69. H. Blüher, *Der bürgerliche und der geistige Antifeminismus*, 14.

70. G. Greer, *The Female Eunuch* (New York: McGraw Hill, 1971), 99–100.

71. Ibid., 104–105.

72. F. Jodl, "Otto Weininger," *Neues Wiener Journal*, 25 October 1903, reprinted in the brochure of reviews issued by Weininger's publisher, 6–10. Weininger's close friend Hermann Swoboda denied that Weininger had ever suffered any romantic disappointment but agreed with Jodl that many of the themes of Weininger's treatise would have been transformed by other authors into poems, plays, or movements of a symphony (Swoboda, *Otto Weiningers Tod*, 31).

73. M. Jörges, "Geschlecht und Charakter," *Zeitschrift für Philosophie und philosophische Kritik* 135 (1909): 200–216, especially 204–205, 214.

74. *Kant-Studien* 8 (1903): 484.

75. E. Bloch, *The Principle of Hope*, translated by Neville Plaice, Stephen Plaice, and Paul Knight, 3 vols. (Cambridge, Mass.: MIT Press, 1986), 2:593. On Bloch, see Wayne Hudson, *The Marxist Philosophy of Ernst Bloch* (London: Macmillan, 1982).

76. Bloch, *Principle of Hope*, 2:593.

77. On Wittgenstein's Viennese context, see Allan Janik and Stephen Toulmin, *Wittgenstein's Vienna*. For more specialized works on Wittgenstein and his philosophy, consult Guido Goody and Brian McGuinness, *Wittgenstein: A Bibliographical Guide* (Cambridge, Mass.: B. Blackwell, 1990).

78. L. Wittgenstein, *Vermischte Bemerkungen: Eine Auswahl aus dem Nachlaß*, ed. G. H. von Wright and Heikki Nyman (Frankfurt a.M.: Suhrkamp, 1977), 43. The translation is from L. Wittgenstein, *Culture and Value*, trans. Peter Winch (Chicago: University of Chicago Press, 1980), 18–19. Among those who influenced Wittgenstein, Karl Kraus and Oswald Spengler were open admirers of Weininger. Spengler regarded *Geschlecht und Charakter* as "the only serious attempt to revive Kant" in recent times and included it on his list of "real landmarks" of modern philosophy. See O. Spengler, *The Decline of the West*, trans. Charles F. Atkinson, 2 vols. (New York: Knopf, 1929), vol. 1, *Form and Actuality*, 374. Spengler described Weininger's suicide as "one of the noblest spectacles ever presented by a Late religiousness" (ibid., vol. 2, *Perspectives of World History*, 322). On Spengler, see H. Stuart Hughes, *Oswald Spengler* (New Brunswick, N.J.: Transaction, 1992); and Alexander Demandt and John Farrenkopf, *Der Fall Spengler: Eine kritische Bilanz* (Köln: Bohlau, 1994).

79. L. Wittgenstein, *Vermischte Bemerkungen*, 43. For philosophical analyses of Wittgenstein's views on "Jewishness," see Yuval Lurie, "Jews as a Metaphysical Species," *Philosophy* 64 (1989): 323–47; and Gerhard D. Wassermann, "Wittgenstein on Jews: Some Counter-examples," *Philosophy* 65 (1990): 355–65.

80. See the excellent analysis in R. Monk, *Ludwig Wittgenstein: The Duty of Genius* (New York: Free Press, 1990), 313–19. For a different and somewhat too defensive analysis of Wittgenstein's anti-Semitism, see Rush Rhees, "Postscript," in R. Rhees, ed., *Lud-*

*wig Wittgenstein: Personal Recollections* (Totowa, N.J.: Rowman and Littlefield, 1981), 195–98.

81. L. Wittgenstein, *Letters to Russell, Keynes, and Moore* (Ithaca, N.Y.: Cornell University Press, 1974), 159.

82. Monk, *Ludwig Wittgenstein*, 313. Monk argues that the negation of this belief could not reveal any fundamental truth. "The negation of an absurdity," he says, "is not an important truth, but a platitude."

83. See Rhees, ed., *Ludwig Wittgenstein: Personal Recollections*, 106–107; and L. Wittgenstein, *Tractatus Logico-Philosophicus*, trans. C. K. Ogden (London: Routledge, 1922), Proposition 5.63, 151. On the Weiningerian provenance of this statement, see Rudolf Haller, "What Do Wittgenstein and Weininger Have in Common?" in Haller, *Questions on Wittgenstein* (London: Routledge, 1988), 90–99, at 95.

84. See Paul Engelmann, *Letters from Wittgenstein with a Memoir*, trans L. Furtmüller and ed. B. F. McGuinness (New York: Horizon, 1967), 33.

85. A. Janik, "Wittgenstein and Weininger," in Janik, *Essays on Wittgenstein and Weininger*, 64–73, 68.

86. For an extended analysis of Wittgenstein's views on the connection between logic and ethics, see Philip R. Shields, *Logic and Sin in the Writings of Ludwig Wittgenstein* (Chicago: University of Chicago Press, 1993).

87. *The Autobiography of Bertrand Russell 1914–1944* (Boston: Little, Brown, 1968), 137.

88. Janik, "Wittgenstein and Weininger," 64, 73.

89. Haller, "What Do Wittgenstein and Weininger Have in Common?" 93.

90. Ibid., 97.

91. See B. Smith, "Weininger und Wittgenstein," *Teoria: Rivista semestrale* 5 (1985): 227–37.

92. J. Halban, "Geschlecht und Charakter: Eine prinzipielle Untersuchung von Dr. Otto Weininger," *Wiener klinische Wochenschrift* 16 (1903): 1282–83. On Halban's theory of the "protective influence" of the internal secretions, see Norbert Pecher, "Halbans Lehre von der protektiven Wirkung der Sexualhormone: Eine frühe Konzeption über den Wirkungsmechanismus der Hormone" (Inaugural dissertation, Medical Faculty, University of Erlangen-Nürnberg, 1985).

93. Excerpted from *Allgemeine Wiener medizinische Zeitung* no. 8 (1904) in the publicity brochure *Geschlecht und Charakter*, 32–33.

94. K. C. Schneider, "Wiener Psychologie," *Wiener klinische Rundschau* 24 (1910): 516–18, at 517. Anything but happy at being immortalized with Weininger and Swoboda, Freud wrote testily to Sándor Ferenczi that Schneider, "that philosophical animal skinner, who naively distributes immortalities . . . is probably a personal friend of Swoboda's and substitutes liking for understanding" (Eva Brabant, Ernst Falzeder, and Patricia Giampieri-Deutsch, eds., *The Correspondence of Sigmund Freud and Sándor Ferenczi*, trans. Peter T. Hoffer, vol. 1: 1908–1914 [Cambridge, Mass.: Harvard University Press/Belknap Press, 1993], 211).

95. Friedrich Kleinwächter Jr., "Geschlecht und Charakter," *Der Frauenarzt: Monatshefte für Gynäkologie und Geburtshilfe* 19 (1904): 266–69.

96. Numa Praetorius, "Weininger, Dr. Otto. Geschlecht und Charakter," *Jahrbuch für sexuelle Zwischenstufen* 6 (1904): 520–27.

97. Ibid., 526.

98. Ibid.

99. H. Groß, "Otto Weininger, Geschlecht und Charakter. Eine prinzipielle Untersuchung," *Archiv für Kriminal-Anthropologie und Kriminalistik* 22 (1906): 92.

100. D. C. McMurtrie, "The Theory of Bisexuality—A Review and a Critique," *Lancet-Clinic* 109 (1913): 370–72, at 370. This statement was no exaggeration. Even Sigmund Freud had conceded that "in lay circles the hypothesis [of sexual intermediacy] . . . is regarded as being due to O. Weininger, the philosopher" (*Standard Edition,* 7:143).

101. McMurtrie, "The Theory of Bisexuality," 372.

102. H. Ellis, "Sex and Character," *Mind: A Quarterly Review of Psychology and Philosophy* 16 (1907): 446–47. Ellis condemned Weininger for expressing "the ideas of others as his own" (ibid., 447). The polyglot Ellis must for once have neglected to examine the German original with its extensive annotations, among which Ellis's own work received numerous, respectful mentions.

103. [P. J.] Möbius, "Geschlecht und Charakter," *Schmidt's Jahrbücher der in- und ausländischen gesammten Medicin* 279 (1903): 213. Weininger was deeply affronted by the review and asked Möbius to prove his charges or tender a public apology. "He gave me," said Möbius, "three weeks, then he would make public the malicious slander and force me to bring a law suit against him." Möbius responded by expanding his review into an even more critical pamphlet, *Geschlecht und Unbescheidenheit: Beurteilung des Buches von O. Weininger "Ueber* [sic] *Geschlecht und Charakter,"* 3d ed. (Halle a. S.: Marhold, 1907). See also Abrahamsen, *Mind and Death of a Genius,* 138.

104. H. T. Woolley, "The Psychology of Sex," *Psychological Bulletin* 7 (1910): 335–42, at 340–41. On Woolley's importance in the history of American psychology and social reform, see Rosalind Rosenberg, *Beyond Separate Spheres: Intellectual Roots of Modern Feminism* (New Haven: Yale University Press, 1982), 54–83.

105. W. Stern, *Die Differentielle Psychologie in ihren methodischen Grundlagen* (Leipzig: Barth, 1911), 196–97. Weininger would have found Stern's dismissal particularly painful. His dearest ambition, after all, was to found a science of the "differential psychology of the sexes," and, as we saw in chapter 3, he had been inspired in this by the early work of Stern himself.

106. Paul Hensel, "Dr. Otto Weininger: Geschlecht und Charakter, Derselbe: Über die letzten Dinge, Emil Lucka: Otto Weininger, sein Werk und seine Persönlichkeit," *Biologisches Centralblatt* 25 (1905): 588–92.

107. W[ilhelm] O[stwald], "Geschlecht und Charakter. Eine prinzipielle Untersuchung," *Annalen der Naturphilosophie* 3 (1904): 342–43.

108. B. Hyams and N. A. Harrowitz, "A Critical Introduction to the History of Weininger Reception," in Hyams and Harrowitz, eds., *Jews and Gender,* 3–20, at 5.

109. This statement is inapplicable, however, to doctoral dissertations, which continue to have a largely literary focus. See, for instance, William Walter Jaffe, "Studies in Obsession: Otto Weininger, Arthur Schnitzler, Heimito von Doderer" (Yale University, 1979); Helga Krizmanic, "Emil Lucka und Otto Weininger" (University of Graz, 1969); and Ingeborg E. Marlock, "Otto Weininger's 'Geschlecht und Charakter' and Hermann Broch's 'Die Schlafwandler'" (Washington University, St. Louis, Mo., 1993).

110. See Janik, "Therapeutic Nihilism: How Not to Write about Otto Weininger," in Barry Smith, ed., *Structure and Gestalt: Philosophy and Literature in Austria-Hungary and Her Successor States,* 263–92; Janik, "Weininger and the Science of Sex: Prolegomena to Any Future Study," in Robert B. Pynsent, ed., *Decadence and Innovation: Austro-Hungarian Life and Art at the Turn of the Century,* 24–32; and Janik, "Writing about Weininger," in his *Essays on Wittgenstein and Weininger,* 96–115. See also A. Janik, "Must

Anti-Modernism be Irrational?" in Janik, *How Not to Interpret a Culture: Essays on the Problem of Method in the Geisteswissenschaften,* 66–84.

111. Ibid., 283, 287.

112. See, for example, Susan C. Anderson, "Otto Weininger's Masculine Utopia," *German Studies Review* 19 (1996): 433–53; Gottfried Gabriel, "Solipsismus: Wittgenstein, Weininger und die Wiener Moderne," in Helmut Bachmaier, ed., *Paradigmen der Moderne* (Philadelphia: Benjamin, 1990), 29–47; Misha Kavka, "The 'Alluring Abyss of Nothingness': Misogyny and (Male) Hysteria in Otto Weininger," *New German Critique* 66 (1995): 123–45; Dietrich Löffler, "Otto Weiningers 'Geschlecht und Charakter,'" in Karol Sauerland, ed., *Melancholie und Enthusiasmus: Studien zur Literatur- und Geistesgeschichte der Jahrhundertwende* (New York: Lang, 1988), 121–33; John E. Toews, "Refashioning the Masculine Subject in Early Modernism: Narratives of Self-Dissolution and Self-Construction in Psychoanalysis and Literature, 1900–1914," *Modernism/Modernity* 4 (1997): 31–67; and Patricia Vertinsky, "Body Matters: Race, Gender, and Perceptions of Physical Ability from Goethe to Weininger," in Norbert Finzsch and Dietmar Schirmer, eds., *Identity and Intolerance: Nationalism, Racism, and Xenophobia in Germany and the United States* (Cambridge: Cambridge University Press, 1998), 331–70. This list does not, of course, purport to be a complete bibliography of recent research on Weininger and reflects the Central European focus of my scholarly training. The Italian literature on Weininger, for instance, is omitted, as are also the Scandinavian readings.

# SELECTED BIBLIOGRAPHY

This bibliography includes only works cited in more than one chapter of this work. The notes record every source that I have examined.

## I. Works by Otto Weininger

Weininger, Otto. *Geschlecht und Charakter: Eine prinzipielle Untersuchung.* Reprint of 1st ed. (1903). Munich: Matthes & Seitz, 1980.

———. *Otto Weininger, Eros und Psyche: Studien und Briefe 1899–1902.* Edited by Hannelore Rodlauer. Vienna: Österreichischen Akademie der Wissenschaften, 1990.

———. *Taschenbuch und Briefe an einen Freund.* Edited by Artur Gerber. Leipzig: Tal, 1919.

———. *Über die letzten Dinge.* 2d ed. Edited by Moriz Rappaport. Vienna: Wilhelm Braumüller, 1907.

## II. Other Primary Material

Bachofen, J. J. *Das Mutterrecht: Eine Untersuchung über die Gynaikokratie der alten Welt nach ihrer religiösen und rechtlichen Natur.* Basel: Schwabe, 1897.

Biedl, Artur. *The Internal Secretory Organs: Their Physiology and Pathology.* Translated by Linda Forster. London: Bale, Sons & Danielsson, 1913.

Bloch, Iwan. *Das Sexualleben unserer Zeit in seinen Beziehungen zur modernen Kultur.* Berlin: Marcus, 1907.

Darwin, Charles. *The Descent of Man and Selection in Relation to Sex.* 2 vols. New York: Appleton, 1872.

———. *On the Origin of Species by means of Natural Selection.* 6th ed. New York: Appleton, 1876.

———. *The Variation of Animals and Plants under Domestication.* 2 vols. New York: Appleton, 1897.

Ellis, Havelock. *Man and Woman: A Study of Human Secondary Sexual Characters.* London: W. Scott, 1904.

———. *Studies in the Psychology of Sex.* 2 vols. New York: Random House, 1936.

Freud, Sigmund. *The Complete Letters of Sigmund Freud to Wilhelm Fliess, 1887–1904.* Translated and edited by Jeffrey Moussaieff Masson. Cambridge, Mass.: Harvard University Press, 1985.

———. *The Standard Edition of the Complete Psychological Works of Sigmund Freud.* Edited by James Strachey. 24 vols. London: Hogarth Press, 1953–74.

Goethe, Johann Wolfgang von. *Elective Affinities.* Translated by Judith Ryan. In vol. 11 of *Goethe's Collected Works.* 12 vols. New York: Suhrkamp, 1988.

Hertwig, Oscar. *Die Zelle und die Gewebe: Grundzüge der allgemeinen Anatomie und Physiologie.* 2 vols in 1. Jena: Gustav Fischer, 1893.

Hirschfeld, Magnus. "Die objektive Diagnose der Homosexualität." *Jahrbuch der sexuelle Zwischenstufen* 1 (1899): 4–35.

———. *Die Homosexualität des Mannes und des Weibes.* 2d ed. Berlin: Marcus, 1920.

Krafft-Ebing, Richard von. *Psychopathia Sexualis: A Medico-Forensic Study.* 12th ed. (1901). New York: Pioneer, 1939.

Lombroso, Cesare and Guglielmo Ferrero. *Das Weib als Verbrecherin und Prostituirte: Anthropologische Studien.* Translated from the Italian by Hans Kurella. Hamburg: Verlagsanstalt und Druckerei A-G, 1894.

Mach, Ernst. *Analyse der Empfindungen und das Verhältniss des Physischen zum Psychischen.* 4th ed. Jena: Gustav Fischer, 1903.

———. *The Analysis of Sensations and the Relation of the Physical to the Psychical.* Translated by C. M. Williams and Sydney Waterlow. New York: Dover, 1959.

Mayreder, Rosa. *Zur Kritik der Weiblichkeit: Essays.* Jena: Diederichs, 1910.

Moll, Albert. *Untersuchungen über die Libido sexualis.* Berlin: Fischer's medicinische Buchhandlung, 1897.

Nietzsche, Friedrich. *Basic Writings of Nietzsche.* Translated and edited by Walter Kaufmann. New York: Modern Library, 1968.

Schopenhauer, Arthur. *Arthur Schopenhauer: Sämtliche Werke.* Edited by Arthur Hübscher. 7 vols. Wiesbaden: Brockhaus, 1972.

———. *The World as Will and Representation.* Translated by E. F. J. Payne. 2 vols. New York: Dover, 1966.

Wagner, Richard. *Richard Wagner's Prose Works.* Translated by William Ashton Ellis. 6 vols. London: Kegan Paul, 1892–99.

Weismann, August. *The Germ-Plasm: A Theory of Heredity.* Translated by W. N. Parker and Harriet Rönnfeldt. New York: Scribner's, 1893.

Wittgenstein, Ludwig. *Tractatus Logico-Philosophicus.* Translated by C. K. Ogden. London: Routledge, 1922.

Zweig, Stefan. *The World of Yesterday.* New York: Viking, 1939.

## III. Secondary Sources

Abrahamsen, David. *The Mind and Death of a Genius.* New York: Columbia University Press, 1946.

Allen, Ann Taylor. *Feminism and Motherhood in Germany, 1800–1914.* New Brunswick: Rutgers University Press, 1991.

Anderson, Harriet. *Utopian Feminism: Women's Movements in Fin-de-Siècle Vienna.* New Haven: Yale University Press, 1992.

Beller, Steven. *Vienna and the Jews, 1867–1938: A Cultural History.* Cambridge: Cambridge University Press, 1989.

Blackmore, John T. *Ernst Mach: His Work, Life, and Influence.* Berkeley: University of California Press, 1972.

Buci-Glucksmann, Christine. *Baroque Reason: The Aesthetics of Modernity.* Translated by Patrick Camiller. London: Sage, 1994.

Danziger, Kurt. *Constructing the Subject: Historical Origins of Psychological Research.* Cambridge: Cambridge University Press, 1990.

———. "The Positivist Repudiation of Wundt." *Journal of the History of the Behavioral Sciences* 15 (1979): 205–30.

Ellenberger, Henri F. *The Discovery of the Unconscious: The History and Evolution of Dynamic Psychiatry*. New York: Basic Books, 1970.

Evans, Richard J. *The Feminist Movement in Germany, 1894–1933*. London: Sage Publications, 1976.

Field, Geoffrey G. *Evangelist of Race: The Germanic Vision of Houston Stewart Chamberlain*. New York: Columbia University Press, 1981.

Finney, Gail. *Women in Modern Drama: Freud, Feminism, and European Theater at the Turn of the Century*. Ithaca: Cornell University Press, 1989.

Foucault, Michel. *The Archaeology of Knowledge*. Translated by A. M. Sheridan Smith. New York: Harper, 1972.

———. *Discipline and Punish: The Birth of the Prison*. Translated by Alan Sheridan. New York: Vintage Books, 1979.

———. *The History of Sexuality*. Vol. 1: *An Introduction*. Translated by Robert Hurley. New York: Vintage Books, 1980.

Gilman, Sander L. *Jewish Self-Hatred: Anti-Semitism and the Hidden Language of the Jews*. Baltimore: Johns Hopkins University Press, 1986.

Gould, Stephen Jay. *Ontogeny and Phylogeny*. Cambridge, Mass.: Harvard University Press, 1977.

Haller, Rudolf. *Studien zur Österreichischen Philosophie: Variationen über ein Thema*. Amsterdam: Rodopi, 1979.

———. *Questions on Wittgenstein*. London: Routledge, 1988.

Harrowitz, Nancy A. *Anti-Semitism, Misogyny, and the Logic of Cultural Difference: Cesare Lombroso and Matilde Serao*. Lincoln: University of Nebraska Press, 1994.

Harrowitz, Nancy A., and Barbara Hyams, eds. *Jews and Gender: Responses to Otto Weininger*. Philadelphia: Temple University Press, 1995.

Herzer, Manfred. *Magnus Hirschfeld: Leben und Werk eines jüdischen, schwulen und sozialistischen Sexologen*. Frankfurt: Campus, 1992.

Janik, Allan. *Essays on Wittgenstein and Weininger*. Amsterdam: Rodopi, 1985.

———. *How Not to Interpret a Culture: Essays on the Problem of Method in the Geisteswissenschaften*. Bergen: Universitetet i Bergen, Filosofisk Institutt, 1986.

———. "Therapeutic Nihilism: How Not to Write about Otto Weininger." In *Structure and Gestalt: Philosophy and Literature in Austria-Hungary and Her Successor States*, edited by Barry Smith, 263–92. Amsterdam: Benjamins, 1981.

———. "Weininger and the Science of Sex: Prolegomena to Any Future Study." In *Decadence and Innovation: Austro-Hungarian Life and Art at the Turn of the Century*, edited by Robert B. Pynsent, 24–32. London: Weidenfeld and Nicolson, 1989.

Janik, Allan, and Stephen Toulmin. *Wittgenstein's Vienna*. New York: Simon & Schuster, 1973.

Jones, Ernest. *The Life and Work of Sigmund Freud*. 3 vols. New York: Basic Books, 1953.

Kiberd, Declan. *Men and Feminism in Modern Literature*. New York: St. Martin's Press, 1985.

Labanyi, Peter. "'Die Gefahr des Körpers': A Reading of Otto Weininger's *Geschlecht und Charakter*." In *Fin-de-Siècle Vienna: Proceedings of the Second Irish Symposium in Austrian Studies*, edited by G. J. Carr and Eda Sagarra, 161–86. Dublin: Trinity College, 1985.

Labisch, Alfons, and Reinhard Spree, eds. *Medizinische Deutungsmacht im sozialen Wandel des 19. und frühen 20. Jahrhunderts*. Bonn: Psychiatrie-Verlag, 1989.

Le Rider, Jacques. *Der Fall Otto Weininger: Wurzeln des Antifeminismus und Anti-semitismus.* Translated from the French by Dieter Hornig. Vienna: Löcker Verlag, 1985.

————. *Modernity and Crises of Identity: Culture and Society in Fin-de-Siècle Vienna.* Translated by Rosemary Morris. New York: Continuum, 1993.

Le Rider, Jacques, and Norbert Leser, eds. *Otto Weininger: Werk und Wirkung.* Vienna: Österreichischer Bundesverlag, 1984.

Lesky, Erna. *The Vienna Medical School of the 19th Century.* Translated by L. Williams and I. S. Levij. Baltimore: Johns Hopkins University Press, 1976.

Lucka, Emil. *Otto Weininger: Sein Werk und seine Persönlichkeit.* 3d ed. Vienna: Wilhelm Braumüller, 1921.

Luft, David S. "Science and Irrationalism in Freud's Vienna." *Modern Austrian Literature* 23, no. 2 (1990): 89–97.

Mayr, Ernst. *The Growth of Biological Thought: Diversity, Evolution, and Inheritance.* Cambridge, Mass.: Harvard University Press, 1982.

Medvei, Victor C. *The History of Clinical Endocrinology: A Comprehensive Account of Endocrinology from Earliest Times to the Present Day.* Lancaster: Parthenon, 1993.

Micale, Mark S. *Approaching Hysteria: Disease and Its Interpretations.* Princeton: Princeton University Press, 1995.

Otis, Laura. *Organic Memory: History and the Body in the Late Nineteenth and Early Twentieth Centuries.* Lincoln: University of Nebraska Press, 1994.

Oxaal, Ivar, Michael Pollak, and Gerhard Botz, eds. *Jews, Anti-Semitism, and Culture in Vienna.* London: Routledge, 1987.

Porter, Roy, and Mikuláš Teich, eds. *Sexual Knowledge, Sexual Science: The History of Attitudes to Sexuality.* Cambridge: Cambridge University Press, 1994.

Robinson, Gloria. *A Prelude to Genetics. Theories of a Material Substance of Heredity: Darwin to Weismann.* Lawrence: Coronado, 1979.

Rodlauer, Hannelore. "Von 'Eros und Psyche' zu 'Geschlecht und Charakter': Unbekannte Weininger-Manuskripte im Archiv der Österreichischen Akademie der Wissenschaften." *Österreichische Akademie der Wissenschaften, philosophisch-historische Klasse: Anzeiger* 124 (1987): 110–39.

Rose, Paul Lawrence. *Revolutionary Anti-Semitism in Germany from Kant to Wagner.* Princeton: Princeton University Press, 1990.

Russett, Cynthia Eagle. *Sexual Science: The Victorian Construction of Womanhood.* Cambridge, Mass.: Harvard University Press, 1989.

Schorske, Carl E. *Fin-de-Siècle Vienna: Politics and Culture.* New York: Vintage Books, 1981.

Steakley, James D. *The Homosexual Emancipation Movement in Germany.* New York: Arno Press, 1975.

Sullivan, Roger J. *Immanuel Kant's Moral Theory.* Cambridge: Cambridge University Press, 1989.

Sulloway, Frank J. *Freud, Biologist of the Mind: Beyond the Psychoanalytic Legend.* New York: Basic Books, 1979.

Swoboda, Hermann. *Otto Weiningers Tod.* Vienna: Deuticke, 1911.

Tuana, Nancy. *The Less Noble Sex: Scientific, Religious, and Philosophical Conceptions of Woman's Nature.* Bloomington: Indiana University Press, 1993.

Timms, Edward. *Karl Kraus, Apocalyptic Satirist: Culture and Catastrophe in Habsburg Vienna.* New Haven: Yale University Press, 1986.

Veith, Ilza. *Hysteria: The History of a Disease.* Chicago: University of Chicago Press, 1965.

Wagner, Nike. *Geist und Geschlecht: Karl Kraus und die Erotik der Wiener Moderne*. Frankfurt: Suhrkamp, 1981.

Wettley, Annemarie, and Werner Leibbrand. *Von der "Psychopathia sexualis" zur Sexualwissenschaft*. Stuttgart: Ferdinand Enke, 1959.

Willey, Thomas E. *Back to Kant: The Revival of Kantianism in German Social and Historical Thought, 1860–1914*. Detroit: Wayne State University Press, 1978.

Worbs, Michael. *Nervenkunst: Literatur und Psychoanalyse im Wien der Jahrhundertwende*. Frankfurt: Europäische Verlagsanstalt, 1983.

The Chicago Series on Sexuality, History, and Society
Edited by John C. Fout

*Improper Advances:*
*Rape and Heterosexual Conflict*
*in Ontario, 1880–1929*
by Karen Dubinsky

*A Prescription for Murder:*
*The Victorian Serial Killings*
*of Dr. Thomas Neill Cream*
by Angus McLaren

*The Language of Sex:*
*Five Voices from Northern France*
*around 1200*
by John W. Baldwin

*Crossing over the Line:*
*Legislating Morality*
*and the Mann Act*
by David J. Langum

*Sexual Nature/Sexual Culture*
edited by Paul R. Abramson
and Steven D. Pinkerton

*Love Between Women:*
*Early Christian Responses*
*to Female Homoeroticism*
by Bernadette J. Brooten

*Trials of Masculinity:*
*Policing Sexual*
*Boundaries, 1870–1930*
by Angus McLaren

*The Invention of Sodomy*
*in Christian Theology*
by Mark D. Jordan

*Sites of Desire/Economies of Pleasure:*
*Sexualities in Asia and the Pacific*
edited by Lenore Manderson
and Margaret Jolly

*Sex and the Gender*
*Revolution,* Volume 1
*Heterosexuality and*
*the Third Gender in*
*Enlightenment London*
by Randolph Trumbach

*Take the Young Stranger by the Hand:*
*Same-Sex Relations and the YMCA in*
*North America, 1868–1930*
by John Donald Gustav-Wrathall

*City of Sisterly and Brotherly Loves:*
*Lesbian and Gay Philadelphia,*
*1945–1972*
by Marc Stein

*The Politics of Gay Rights*
edited by Craig Rimmerman,
Kenneth Wald, and Clyde Wilcox